re-entered

DATE DUE

-4.OCT.19	Return		
20.OCT.19	Cowra		
14.MAR.1990	1-12-92		
28.APR.1990	Gilgandra.		
-6.AUG.1990	30.11.92		
	7 JUL 1993		
-6.DEC.1990	02 SEP 1993		
26.JUN.1991			
	24 JUN 1994		
18.JUL.	27292		
-5.SEP.	22 JUL		
-6.APR.199?	28 JUL		
16. .199			
as			
-7 AUG 1992			

RAECO

CAMPBELLTOWN

Australia
1788-1988

This publication has been funded by
The Australian Bicentennial Authority
to celebrate Australia's Bicentenary in 1988.

Allen & Unwin
Sydney   Wellington   London   Boston

CAMPBELLTOWN

The Bicentennial History

CAROL LISTON

First published in 1988
Allen & Unwin Australia Pty Ltd
An Unwin Hyman company
8 Napier Street, North Sydney, NSW 2060 Australia

Allen & Unwin New Zealand Limited
60 Cambridge Terrace, Wellington, New Zealand

Unwin Hyman Limited
15-17 Broadwick Street, London W1 England

Allen & Unwin Inc.
8 Winchester Place, Winchester, Mass 01890 USA

National Library of Australia
Cataloguing-in-Publication entry:

Liston, Carol.
Campbelltown, the bicentennial history.

Includes index.
ISBN 0 04 324015 1.

1. Campbelltown (N.S.W.) – History.   I. Title.

994.4'6

Printed in Australia by Macarthur Press

Contents

Illustrations *vi*

Preface *viii*

1 1788–1820 *1*

2 1820–1840 *28*

3 1840–1880 *68*

4 1880–1914 *115*

5 1914–1945 *163*

6 1945–1988 *197*

Appendix 1: Population *226*

Appendix 2: Mayors *227*

Notes *229*

Index *248*

Illustrations

Please note: because many of the photographs are very old, the quality varies throughout.

Details from 'Campbelltown from the tower of the Church of St Peter,' 16 February 1928. (Everingham, Mosman)   *Title page*
Map of the City of Campbelltown   *viii*
Bull Cave   *4*
Leumeah House   *15*
Dharawal and Gandangara at Camden Park   *27*
Glen Alpine c. 1880   *35*
St Peters Church of England School   *38*
Warby's barn, Leumeah   *43*
The windmill at Mount Gilead   *48*
John Hurley   *54*
Queen Street looking south c. 1909   *62*
Bocking's mill, bakery and store c. 1880   *74*
Doyle's Hotel and Fowler's store   *80*
Mrs Hickey's general store, Queen Street   *82*
James and Mary Bocking with their children c. 1890   *85*
Macquarie Fields House c. 1865   *96*
Bradbury Park estate   *105*
Eshcol Park   *107*
Looking south, c. 1885, to Cordeaux and Lithgow Streets   *116*
Campbelltown Council, 1892   *118*
Campbelltown town hall and fire station 1910   *120*
Thomas Jenner Winton   *122*
Upper Nepean Water Scheme   *125*
Campbelltown railway station c. 1900   *128*
Queen Street, near Allman Street, c. 1883   *131*
Drawing room, St Elmo c. 1920   *133*
Wilson's butcher shop, 249 Queen Street, c. 1880   *138*

Illustrations

Reeve's Emporium 1897   *138*
Campbelltown dressmakers c. 1910   *140*
Kate McGuanne in her classroom   *141*
The Kidd family, Blair Athol c. 1890   *144*
Minto, 1897   *147*
Ingleburn c. 1920–30   *149*
Ingleburn Baptist Church   *151*
Washday at Ferndale, Wedderburn   *156*
A. H. Etchells, Campbelltown Volunteers c. 1890   *157*
Rose (Babe) Payten   *161*
Packing Christmas parcels for the Front 1917   *165*
Campbelltown Soldier Settlement 1919   *168*
Looking west from St Peters tower c. 1925   *173*
Milton Park, Ingleburn c. 1912   *173*
Frederick Sheather   *177*
Campbelltown Fire Brigade c. 1910   *177*
Syd Percival's butcher shop, Ingleburn c. 1900   *180*
Milking time at St Andrews dairy, 1935   *184*
Canning fruit at Ferndale orchard, Wedderburn   *185*
Campbelltown Ladies Rifle Club c. 1930   *194*
Campbelltown, 1969   *198*
Inside Bursill's general store c. 1950   *207*
Harley Daley   *210*
The Campbelltown Cot   *216*

List of Colour Illustrations

Ager Cottage, 1828
Map of Campbelltown c. 1844
St Johns Catholic Church
St Peters Church of England
Glenlee
The Plough Inn and Holly Lea
Macquarie Fields House
Parkholme (Englorie Park)
St Elmo
St Helens Park
Campbelltown looking south-west
Broinowski's friar birds
Macarthur Square and the Macarthur Regional Centre
Old town hall
Civic Centre
Fisher's Ghost Parade, 1987

Colour photographs appear between pages 116 and 117

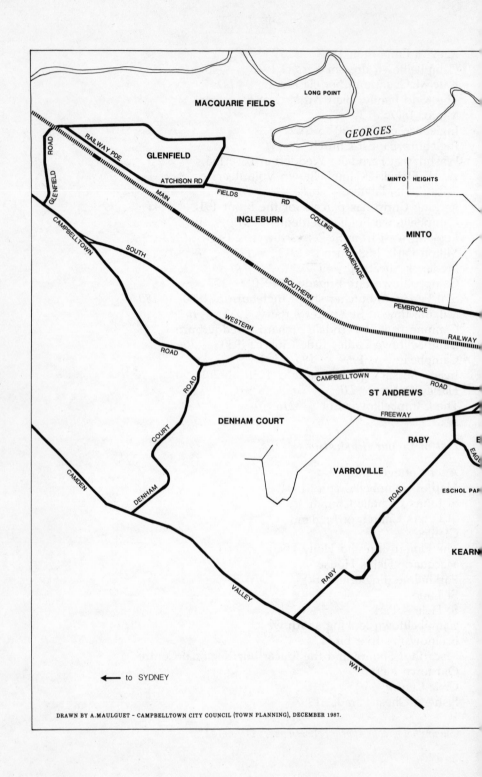

MACQUARIE FIELDS

LONG POINT

GEORGES

GLENFIELD

MINTO HEIGHTS

RAILWAY PDE

ROAD

GLENFIELD

ATCHISON RD

FIELDS

RD

MAIN

COLLINS

MINTO

INGLEBURN

CAMPBELLTOWN

SOUTH

PROMENADE

SOUTHERN

PEMBROKE

WESTERN

RAILWAY

ROAD

CAMPBELLTOWN

ROAD

ST ANDREWS

ROAD

FREEWAY

DENHAM COURT

RABY

E

COURT

CAMDEN

VARROVILLE

ESCHOL PAR

DENHAM

ROAD

KEARN

RABY

VALLEY

WAY

← to SYDNEY

DRAWN BY A.MAULGUET - CAMPBELLTOWN CITY COUNCIL (TOWN PLANNING), DECEMBER 1987.

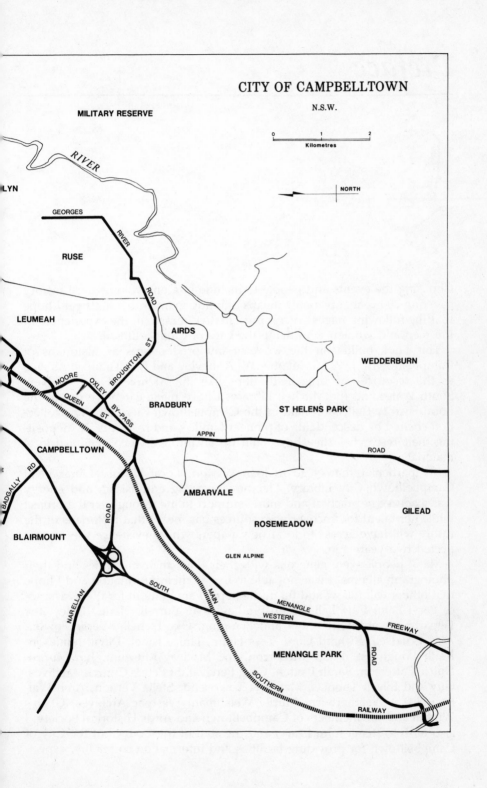

CITY OF CAMPBELLTOWN
N.S.W.

0   1   2
Kilometres

NORTH

MILITARY RESERVE

RIVER

LYN

GEORGES

RIVER

RUSE

ROAD

LEUMEAH

AIRDS

WEDDERBURN

BROUGHTON ST

MOORE

OXLEY

BY-PASS

QUEEN ST

BRADBURY

ST HELENS PARK

APPIN

ROAD

CAMPBELLTOWN

BADGALLY RD

AMBARVALE

GILEAD

ROAD

ROSEMEADOW

BLAIRMOUNT

GLEN ALPINE

NARELLAN

SOUTH

MAIN

MENANGLE

WESTERN

FREEWAY

MENANGLE PARK

ROAD

SOUTHERN

RAILWAY

Preface

Choosing the events and people to include in a one-volume local history covering 200 years invariably means omitting many individuals yet I hope that the following pages are a representative sample of the experiences of the men and women who made the City of Campbelltown.

This book builds on the work of my predecessors as historians of Campbelltown—J. P. McGuanne, W. A. Bayley and Ivor Thomas. As well as the resources of large institutions like the Archives Office of New South Wales and the Mitchell Library, I have made extensive use of the Local History Collection held in the Campbelltown City Library, a collection created by descendants of pioneer families and residents. By depositing their researches they have built up an impressive collection of local material.

My particular thanks go to Joan Warton, Local History Librarian at Campbelltown City Library. Her never-ceasing enthusiasm and energy was a source of practical and moral support to me throughout the project while her talent for uncovering resources has meant that historians of the future will have access to local newspapers whose existence was unsuspected two years ago.

Many people were generous with their time, their memories and their photograph albums. I was not able to use all their information and I hope that others will follow and fill in the gaps. I am grateful for the assistance of Beryl Bain, Edie Ball, Philip Bradley, Joan Burrell, Harley Daley, the Department of Environment and Planning, Oke Etchells, Verlie Fowler, Alex Goodsell, Richard Gore, Tess Holm, Janice Israel, David Jamieson, Keith Longhurst, Eddie McBarron, the Macleay Museum, Jim Munro, Dulcie Patterson, Sarah Payten, Greg Percival, St Peters Church Archives, Guy and Eileen Thomas, Margaret Townsend, Stella Vernon, Arch Walker, Hilary Weatherburn, Muriel Welshman, Westpac Archives, Gladys Winton and the members of Campbelltown and Airds Historical Society. I also wish to thank John Leary, and the staff of the Council of the City of Campbelltown for providing facilities and information so readily, especially the staff of Campbelltown City Library, Town Planning, Treasury and Public Relations. John Kooyman of Tahmoor spent many hours producing fine prints of the photographs identified during the project.

Heather Radi, Joan Warton and Alex Goodsell read the manuscript and offered useful comments to improve the text. The errors and omissions remain mine. Finally I would like to thank my family for their support and patience in living with Campbelltown's past for so many months.

Carol Liston
October 1987

One

1788–1820

FOR at least 40 000 years before Captain Cook sailed into Botany Bay in 1770, Aboriginal tribes peopled Australia. Possibly as many as one million Aborigines lived in Australia in 1788. Over the next 50 years their lives and traditional culture were subjected to unprecedented stress. By 1830 Aboriginal community life in Campbelltown had disintegrated.[1]

The Aborigines who lived in the Campbelltown region belonged to a group called the Cowpastures tribe by the European settlers. They spoke the Dharawal or Tharawal language and their territory covered a region from Botany Bay south to the Shoalhaven River and Nowra and inland to Camden. A dialect of Dharawal was spoken by their neighbours, the Gwiyagal, who lived on the sourthern shores of Botany Bay.[2]

North of the Dharawal lived the much larger Dharuk-speaking people who occupied the Sydney area from the Hawkesbury River in the north to the mountains in the west and as far south as Camden and Picton. The closest neighbours of the Dharawal were the Cobrakall clan who lived at Liverpool and Cabramatta. The Gandangara people lived west and south-west of the Dharawal in the mountains beyond the Burragorang River and south-west from Berrima to Goulburn, and had a reputation as fierce warriors. The Illawarra district was the home of the Wodi Wodi people.[3]

A nomadic clan of 30 to 50 people moved along routes determined by seasonal availability of food, meeting neighbouring clans for trade and social needs. The Dharawal travelled widely in the south-western regions of the counties of Cumberland and Camden, especially between the Picton area, along the George's River, which they called Tuggerah, and across the slopes of modern Campbelltown to Liverpool. Occasionally the Dharawal visited as far north as Prospect, Parramatta and even Broken Bay, west to the Hawkesbury and south-west to Lake Bathurst.[4]

Natural resources supplied all their material needs. The land of the George's River and its tributaries provided water, food and shelter. The streams and swamplands offered a variety of food—fish, eels, shellfish.

The forest lands sheltered possum and lizard, kangaroo and wallaby and there were roots, berries and seeds to gather. Birds provided meat and eggs. Other food sources were not easily identified by Europeans—insects, moths and the shipworm, 'cobra', found in water-soaked wood. Stones were carefully shaped for tools and weapons. Along the water-courses flat rocks were scored with many grooves, carved out by centuries of patient grinding. Stones were used to grind seeds into flour. Animal bones and shells were sharpened for fish-hooks, spear-tips and tools to make holes in animal skins. Bark provided a flexible material for shelters, canoes and water containers. Natural fibres and hair were twisted into string for belts, nets and bags. Possum furs were stitched together to make cloaks for winter. Wood and tree roots were fashioned into hunting tools, digging sticks and weapons. Each man and woman within the group had a function on which the whole depended. The men hunted the larger animals or speared fish while the women gathered food, water and firewood.[5]

Along the George's River, sandstone had eroded forming rock over-hangs which provided shelter. Especially favoured were the shelters that faced north, catching the sun and holding its warmth through the night. The walls of these shelters were decorated with hand stencils outlined in red ochre, white clay or charcoal. Animals were sketched—kangaroos and wallabies, lizards and snakes, emus and birds, sugar gliders, possums, fish and eels, with occasional human figures and weapons. On flat rocks near waterholes enormous mythological figures were chipped out in careful outline. Perhaps these figures represented the water monster, Gurungaty, which ate strangers who drank from his people's waterhole. Mumuga was another monster who lived in the mountain caves and overcame his victims with his foul smell.[6]

First Contact

The Gwiyagal, an associate clan of the Dharawal, lived along the south-ern shores of Botany Bay. They saw the ships of Captain Cook sail into the bay in 1770. Eighteen years later they saw another fleet.

British prisoners had been transported to the American colonies until the American War of Independence in 1776. There were not enough gaols to imprison them in Britain so the British government eventually decided on a new destination for its prisoners—Australia, a new land in a little-known part of the globe. Captain Arthur Phillip had sailed in May 1787 with a fleet of two military vessels, six chartered transports with convicts and his supply vessels. They reached Botany Bay on 20 January 1788. Three days later Captain Watkin Tench and a party which included a seven-year-old boy landed on the southern shore of the bay where they met a dozen 'Indians' with their children. An elderly, bearded Aborigine inspected the European child's white skin. Presents were exchanged—a looking-glass in return for a club—but the Aborigines took little interest in the toys offered to them.[7]

Phillip and the fleet moved north to the better harbour of Port Jackson. Word of the new arrivals would certainly have spread rapidly from the Gwiyagal to their kin, the Dharawal. For the Aboriginal clans living inland, the arrival of the Europeans was less traumatic than for their coastal brethren who saw the large ships firsthand. Life for the Dharawal and other clans changed even before face-to-face contact with the white people. European goods, especially iron and glass, rapidly spread as items of trade among the Aborigines, replacing the less convenient stone implements. Feral animals wandered into hunting grounds. Disease was an invisible conqueror. Smallpox decimated the Sydney tribes in April 1789. Knowledge of firearms spread long before most Aborigines experienced them.[8]

The founding of Campbelltown

The Europeans found their new home on the shores of Sydney Cove an inhospitable environment. It was the Antipodes, where the seasons were reversed and strange animals wandered a harsh landscape. Ill prepared for the work of pioneering, they learned by trial and error how to build huts and grow food, but in the first years of settlement starvation was a real possibility. Misfortune blighted their farming efforts. Animals had been purchased at the Cape of Good Hope, but the horses and poultry were difficult to graze and the sheep were killed by lightning and wild dogs.

Six months after their arrival, in July 1788, two bulls and four cows brought from the Cape of Good Hope were lost. The convict herdsman who tended the cattle drove them out daily to fresh pasture. He was meant to keep them always in sight, but often, as on this occasion, he went home at noon for his dinner. When he returned the cattle had strayed and he spent two days searching before reporting their loss to the governor. Several official search parties failed to find any trace of the cattle. In February 1790 a runaway West Indian convict, Black Caesar, claimed he had seen the cattle under the care of seven or eight Aborigines but no-one believed him.[9]

The cattle had wandered south, crossed the Cook and Nepean Rivers and found good grazing land about 90 kilometres south-west of the settlement in the Menangle–Camden area. The Dharawal saw these strange animals and sketched their characteristics on the walls of a sandstone shelter. The animals had no horns, having been polled to prevent injury during their long sea voyage, but the unknown artist clearly depicted their hooves, so different from the soft-pawed kangaroo. These drawings date to the first years of European settlement, as the colonial offspring of these animals had horns when rediscovered by the Euro-

Bull Cave, Campbelltown

peans in 1795. From accounts of other tribes the Aborigines' first encounter with cattle was a terrifying experience, and this fear is tangible in the size of the Campbelltown drawings where the bulls dominate the walls of the rock shelter. It is unlikely that they hunted the cattle. Governor King commented that the Aborigines climbed trees until the animals had passed, a wise precaution in view of their tendency to charge at intruders.[10]

The Dharawal saw the Europeans who came in search of the wild cattle in 1795. Lieutenant William Cummings exploring southwards from Botany Bay on foot met Aborigines, probably Gwiyagal or Dharawal, who indicated that they had seen large animals with horns, but they were unable to guide him to where they grazed. In the spring of 1795 Bass and Flinders sailed along the George's River but saw no evidence of the cattle.

The cattle were finally discovered by some prisoners shortly after Governor Hunter's arrival in September 1795. Henry Hacking was sent to investigate and he confirmed the reports. On 18 November 1795 Hunter, Captain Waterhouse, Dr George Bass, Judge Advocate Collins and some convict servants travelled south from Prospect, crossed the Nepean River and saw the herd. Hacking and two men attempted to capture a calf but were forced to shoot a charging bull. Examination of the carcass confirmed the wide-spread horns, moderate hump between the shoulders and short thin tail that was typical of the Cape breed of cattle. They counted 61 animals.

Concerned that the cattle might be killed for food, Hunter ordered that anyone interfering with the cattle would be punished to the utmost severity of the law. Collins reported the countryside where the cattle grazed was most attractive with thick grass, thinly scattered trees, large

4

ponds with ducks and black swans, and gentle hills. In June 1796 Hunter returned to inspect the cattle. He climbed what became known as Mount Hunter and was again impressed with the quality of the soil, the timber and the water. He fixed the latitude at 34'09" south, 9 miles (15 km) from Botany Bay. The area was called colloquially 'The Cow Pastures'.[11]

Floods in 1801 destroyed the Hawkesbury farms and food supplies were low. King turned to the wild cattle for emergency supplies and new breeding stock. Three convicts were promised a bonus of one animal for each ten cattle they caught, but the animals proved too ferocious. There were at least two herds of about 200 each. Some were killed and the meat salted for winter rations at a hut built at the Cowpastures. The challenge to domesticate the wild cattle attracted the Reverend Samuel Marsden in February 1803, but he also failed. The cattle tempted convicts wanting more food. On 6 July 1803 King prohibited travel into areas occupied by the wild cattle without the governor's signed permit. He sent John William Lewin, naturalist and artist, to count the cattle and chart their location, but he rejected Lewin's estimate of 800 animals for his own calculation of 3000. With visits to the Cowpastures forbidden, the cattle's sole predator was the dingo, 'the only Mischievous Animal in the Country'.[12]

Meanwhile Lieutenant John Macarthur was in England to face court-martial for duelling with his superior officer. Acquitted, he suggested to the British authorities a project to breed fine-woolled sheep in the colony and export wool to British factories. Britain was at war with France, isolated from its traditional sources of wool, but needing more woollen goods for the military. Macarthur was given a land grant of 5000 acres (2000 ha), to be increased to 10 000 acres (4000 ha) if he succeeded. Back in New South Wales in mid-1805, he asked for land at Mount Taurus (which is Latin for bull). Though King had hoped to keep the Cowpastures intact for the cattle, Macarthur claimed that he was unable to find 5000 acres elsewhere suitable for his sheep-breeding programme. King conceded only when the British government specifically approved the location. Thus Macarthur obtained exclusive access to the only known superior grazing land in the colony.[13]

In 1806 Governor Bligh reissued his predecessor's orders forbidding visits to the Cowpastures, and appointed John Warby and Thomas Harpur, employed to take calves from the herd, as constables at Birds Eye Corner, Menangle. In October 1806 Bligh visited the district with Marsden. The river was in flood and the Aborigines built a canoe so he could cross. By then the track to the Cowpastures from John Warby's farm at Prospect was well defined. The countryside was familiar enough by October 1809 for a party of ladies and gentlemen to go to the Cowpastures for a four-day pleasure excursion. The wilderness, if not the cattle, had been tamed.[14]

Exploration south and south-west of Sydney used the Cowpastures as a base. Ensign Francis Barrallier, a French-born engineer in the New South

Wales Corps, sought a route across the Blue Mountains from the Cowpastures in October 1802. In November he discovered the Nattai and Wollondilly Rivers and the Burragorang Valley. In December 1802 botanist George Caley crossed the Nepean River and then followed its course to Stonequarry Creek and Picton lagoon. In February 1804 Caley returned to the Cowpastures, which he called Vaccary Forest, and named Mount Hunter Rivulet. In December 1803 King charted the country between the Nepean and the mountains. The explorers made few comments about the quality of the country between Prospect and the Nepean River as their interest lay beyond the Cowpastures. Governor King noted that the land south from Prospect appeared suitable for pasture but was of uneven quality for cultivation. The banks of the Nepean were covered with thick brush. About 9 kilometres south from the ford was a pond which the Aborigines called 'Munangle'. In 1807 George Caley explored the George's River, Appin and the Cataract Falls, returning via Menangle.[15]

The Dharawal and the Europeans

Gogy was the best known of the Dharawal. He had been outlawed from his clan for a killing and had taken refuge with Goondel's family further south. After eight or nine months Gogy's own people allowed him to return home. Goondel's hospitality did not incur long-lasting gratitude. Gogy and three of his people later caught a woman from Goondel's clan near Nattai, tied her to a tree and killed her, removing some flesh to eat. Gogy was Barrallier's Aboriginal guide in 1802. Coming upon a group of Aborigines, including Goondel, Gogy was very pleased to have Barrallier and his party to protect him. Goondel and his family wore cloaks of animal skins. They were shorter than the Aborigines closer to Sydney but very strong and 'well-made'.[16]

Gogy was known at Parramatta. In March 1805 he faced Bennelong and Nanberry in a punishment ordeal for having killed another Aborigine. They threw spears at Gogy from about 4 metres. One barbed spear lodged above Gogy's hip and another in his back below the loins. The European bystanders were unable to remove the second spear but, to their surprise, Gogy survived with the spear protruding from his back for a week before it was removed. Gogy, despite his wound, proceeded with 'stoic composure' to the Hawkesbury to participate in a similar trial against another Aborigine charged by his tribe with murder.[17]

Young Bundle was another well-known member of the Dharawal. He appeared near Parramatta in September 1809 with Tedbury, the son of Pemulwoy, the Bidjigal warrior who led a guerilla campaign against the Europeans in the 1790s, ranging from the coast to Parramatta and George's River. Pemulwoy was shot by settlers in 1802 and his head sent to Sir Joseph Banks by Governor King. Tedbury continued his father's war in 1805 and again in 1809 when, with Young Bundle, he terrorised the settlers of the Cook and George's Rivers area, driving off their sheep and waylaying travellers to take their supplies.[18]

Permanent settlement at Campbelltown

In May 1809 and again in August of that year the disastrous Hawkesbury floods swept away most of the colony's wheat crops and many animals. It was a serious loss to a community that was still confused by the over-throw of Governor Bligh in January 1808 and the successive replacement of Major Johnston by Lieutenant-Colonel Foveaux and then Lieutenant-Governor William Paterson. Paterson, commandant of Norfolk Island from 1791 to 1793 and of Van Diemen's Land (Tasmania) from 1804, learnt of the coup against Bligh in February 1808, but, unwilling to intervene, remained in Van Diemen's Land for almost a year, finally arriving in January 1809 to take command of the colonial government.

Fatally ill and continually drunk, Paterson attempted to rule from Par-ramatta, but the real power remained with Lieutenant-Colonel Joseph Foveaux. Foveaux had returned to Sydney from Norfolk Island in July 1808 and taken control of the rebel government. Foveaux was no friend of deposed Governor Bligh nor of John Macarthur who had helped engineer the military coup against Bligh and had set himself up as colonial secret-ary in the rebel government. Foveaux dismissed Macarthur. When Pater-son arrived Foveaux stayed in Sydney as second in command, although in the face of Paterson's illness and incapacity much of the real admini-strative work was carried out by Foveaux.

In September 1808 Foveaux had considered settling the Cowpastures to discourage runaway convicts attracted there by the fresh beef. Foveaux may also have wished to restrict Macarthur's ambitions. The floods in the winter of 1809 provided additional incentive to look for new farming districts away from the river banks. Paterson decided to encourage cul-tivation of the forest lands south and south-west of Parramatta in the districts of Cabramatta, Bringelly and Minto. Here the Wianamatta shales had produced well-drained, open forest land intersected with small creeks. The forest lands had been avoided because of the labour needed to clear the land.[19]

Paterson was generous with land grants. He gave a number to people of 'good characters and habits of industry' and offered to exchange land in the new districts for land already held on the Hawkesbury. By July 1809 Deputy Surveyor James Meehan was at work along Bunbury Curran Creek. On 13 July 1809 he measured 110 acres (44 ha) for himself, 60 acres (24 ha) for Patrick Moore and 30 acres (12 ha) for Andrew Byrnes, both fellow Irish convicts. On 1 August 1809 Paterson made out the first six grants in the Campbelltown region. Richard Atkins received 500 acres (200 ha) (Denham Court); James Meehan 110 acres (44 ha) (Macquarie Fields); Patrick Moore 60 acres (24 ha); Peter Honory 60 acres (24 ha);

Thomas Reynolds 50 acres (20 ha), and James Chamberlaine 30 acres (12 ha). By the end of 1809, 34 settlers had received grants specifically located in the Minto district while several others had orders which they later took up in Minto.[20]

Minto, the name of the new district, was probably bestowed by Foveaux and Paterson to honour Lord Minto, the governor-general of India and closest high-ranking British official. The rebel government corresponded regularly with the Indian administration.

The largest grant in Minto was 1240 acres (496 ha) for Andrew Thompson. Transported at sixteen for burning a haystack, Thompson was appointed a constable by Governor King and showed great bravery in rescuing many people in the floods of 1806. Bligh made Thompson his personal agent and by the time he was 37 Thompson owned extensive land, animals, ships, a tannery and salt works. His bravery during the floods was rewarded with a grant which he called St Andrews. Dr Charles Throsby, whose resignation from the colonial medical service was accepted in October 1809, was granted 600 acres (240 ha) which formed the core of his Glenfield estate. At least eight soldiers received grants, most in late December 1809 when it was known that a new governor was on his way. Women who received grants included Charlotte Driver, 100 acres (40 ha) (measured for Charlotte Weir by Meehan in November 1809) and 200 acres (80 ha) for Ann Minchin, wife of Lieutenant William Minchin who carried the rebel government's first despatches back to England. Ann Minchin joined her husband in England and did not take up her land, though many years later she returned to the area as the wife of Eber Bunker of Collingwood, Liverpool.[21]

Measurement of land grants halted at the end of 1809 when the new governor, Lachlan Macquarie, arrived. Macquarie was a career soldier who brought to his appointment extensive experience of civil and military administration in India. Autocratic but paternal, Macquarie stamped a decade of Australian history with his personality. Most of the rebel administrators sailed to England to defend their actions at courtmartials. Paterson died on the voyage home.

Grants issued by the rebel government, including all land in the Minto district, were declared invalid and recalled for Macquarie to review them personally. In April 1810 he issued the 500-acre (200 ha) Denham Court grant to Deputy Judge Advocate Richard Atkins. Because of the recall of the New South Wales Corps, many soldiers' grants were not reinstated but by October 1811 most of Paterson's grants were confirmed, 38 of which were located in Minto or the new Airds district. In addition Macquarie gave seven new grants in the area.[22]

Governor and Mrs Macquarie made their first tour of inspection in November 1810. On 7 November they left Parramatta on horseback for a two-hour ride to the George's River. Accompanied by Captain Antill and James Meehan, deputy surveyor, they breakfasted at the new home of Thomas and Rachel Moore. Moore was a sailor and boatbuilder who had retired in 1809 to farm his estate, Moorebank. He was appointed magistrate for the George's River district in May 1810. Dr William Redfern met the governor's party at Moorebank and they took a boat upstream to a site that had been suggested for a town. Macquarie approved the location, named it Liverpool, after the Secretary of State for the colonies, and directed Meehan to survey it. The district was already settled and required only the town to formalise its identity.

The following day the governor's party inspected the Minto district. Already farms were well established with fields of wheat, numerous flocks of sheep and herds of cattle. Macquarie saw the farms of Guise (Casula), Throsby (Glenfield), Meehan (Macquarie Fields), Lewin (Mount Arden), Brooks (at Atkin's Denham Court), Dr Townson (Varroville) and Thompson (St Andrews), the latter under caretakers since Thompson's death a few months earlier. Thompson's and Townson's farms were on the best soils and bounded by 'a large creek of brackish water called Bunbury Curran'.

Macquarie returned to Parramatta but turned south again on 16 November, this time in carriages. At Prospect he was joined by John Warby as guide and Sergeant Whalan with three troopers. Travelling along the Cowpastures Road, through the open forests of Cabramatta, they reached the government hut on the Nepean River in three and a half hours. Over the river they travelled to Mount Hunter and Stonequarry Creek, seeing the wild cattle and visiting Mrs Macarthur, who was inspecting her farms, and the Menangle farm of Walter Davidson. They met and were accompanied by some Dharawal who told them the Aboriginal names of places.

Recrossing the Nepean at Camden, Macquarie visited the north bank opposite Menangle, known by the Aboriginal name Nowenong (now Menangle Park). The country was rough and barren with deep gullies, numerous swamps and lagoons, though Robert Campbell's cattle and sheep were grazing there. Between the Camden ford, which the Aborigines called Kirboowallie, and Nowendong was a high hill, called Bajelling, but later known by its European name, Mount Annan. On Tuesday 20 November the governor's party travelled to St Andrews where they spent a few days exploring the country between Bunbury Curran and George's River.

Macquarie had appointed Andrew Thompson a magistrate. Thompson died in October 1810 and bequeathed one-quarter of his estate, valued at £20 000–25 000, to Macquarie. The governor's visit to St Andrew's farm was therefore that of a new owner inspecting his assets. There was an excellent farmhouse, with offices, garden, stockyards, cleared timber, 10 acres (4 ha) of corn, 90 cattle and 1400 sheep. The farmhouse was under the care of Joseph Ward and his wife who supplied the governor's party with mutton, fowls, butter, milk, eggs and vegetables. South and west of St Andrews the soil was good and well watered, but of declining quality closer to the Nepean. Lack of water made this area unsuitable for small settlers. Macquarie visited 'the farms granted to several individuals by the late usurped Government'. At Bunbury Curran Hill he met Thompson's neighbour, Dr Robert Townson, who had selected a 'very ill chosen situation' for his new house, Varroville. They crossed the George's River, 'a very pretty stream of clear, well tasted running water', but found only barren, rocky country.

A week later Macquarie inspected the Nepean/Hawkesbury settlements. Dismayed at the homes, barns and clothing of most of the population, he urged them to economy and temperance and established the towns of Windsor, Richmond, Pitt Town, Wilberforce, Castlereagh and Liverpool. Throughout these tours Macquarie was judging the suitability of land for large and small settlers. After inspecting Bunbury Curran he wrote.

> *having rode between 14 and 15 miles through the best and finest country I have yet seen in the Colony and by far the most eligible centrical and fittest in every point of view for small settlers to have allotments of land assigned them in. I intend forming this tract of country into a new and separate district for the accommodation of small settlers, and to name it Airds in honor [sic] of my dear good Elizabeth's family estate.[23]*

Airds, between Bunbury Curran Creek and the George's River, offered excellent pasture, good soil and water. Free persons wanting land in this area were directed to supply details of their honesty, industry and sobriety. Two months later they were instructed to meet Surveyor Meehan on his farm at Bunbury Curran for grants to be measured.[24]

Farming Minto, Airds and Appin 1810–1820

Macquarie's grants at Minto, Airds and further south at Appin reinforced Paterson's and Foveaux's decisions to direct settlement away from the flood-prone river banks.

A turnpike road was built from Sydney to Parramatta, and in October 1811 Macquarie proposed a road from Sydney to Liverpool where he had recently made a 'very Considerable Number of Grants of Land to Small Settlers, who prove very industrious, and ... will be highly beneficial to the Country by the Clearing and Cultivating of Forest Lands'. The new road was opened in February 1814 and soon extended south to Appin, though it was little more than a dirt track cleared of timber and tree stumps when Macquarie travelled along it in 1815.[25]

There was a sizable farming community at Minto, Airds and Appin by July 1813 when over 80 settlers, free and ex-convict, subscribed £182 towards the fund to build a courthouse in Sydney. William Redfern of Campbellfield and Andrew Hume of Hume Mount contributed large sums, but many others gave £1 or £2 including John Warby, Thomas

Burke, Joseph Phelps, Thomas Rudd, Patrick Keighran, William Ray, Thomas Acres, William Tyson, James Mumford, James Bull of Liverpool and John Kennedy of Appin.[26]

In October 1815 Macquarie returned. In Airds he saw the Harrax farm near Bird's Eye Crossing, then visited Uther's farm, Mount Gilead, at Appin. He found the smaller farms 'tolerably well-improved' with crops planted. Uther had built a house high on a hill and his crops were superior to those of Andrew Hume on the adjoining farm. A rough track took them to Lachlan Vale where William Broughton was building a 'large one storey weather boarded house with two wings, on a very lofty eminence commanding a very extensive prospect'. Nearby the farm of his brother-in-law, John Kennedy, impressed Macquarie with its extensive wheat cultivation, house and garden and he promised to increase it from 200 to 300 acres (80 to 120 ha). Sykes' farm, 1 kilometre south, was the most southern in the colony. Here was another abundant crop of wheat and Macquarie again rewarded the settler's energy with an enlarged grant.[27]

Most of the small grants were concentrated along Bow Bowing and Bunbury Curran Creeks with the larger grants extending over the high ridges and slopes. The district of Airds, later absorbed in the parish of St Peters, was granted as small portions of about 100 acres (40 ha). Some had little interest in farming and sold their grants as soon as they received them, leaving little evidence of their existence aside from their names on a map. The columns of the *Sydney Gazette* between 1815 and 1818 list many land sales for Airds and Minto, mostly conducted by the sheriff with court orders to recover debts. Other grantees created working estates which were economically viable for their children. Sarah Byrne took up 70 acres (28 ha) in Minto in 1816 which she held until 1859. Warby increased his 1816 grant of 260 acres (104 ha) by purchasing the grants of Cable and Collet. These he consolidated into the Mossberry estate in northern Campbelltown which was held by the Warby family until 1900.[28]

William Ray and his father-in-law, Jonathan Brooker, occupied adjoining 60-acre (24 ha) grants on the northern outskirts of Campbelltown. Though the deeds for their farms were not issued until June 1816, their locations had been surveyed by James Meehan in November 1809 and Ray was living on his land in July 1813. By 1822 he had cleared half of his 60 acres and planted 18 acres (7.2 ha) with wheat and 2 acres (0.8 ha) each with barley and potatoes. He worked it with his family and one convict servant. Sarah Ray left William to live with their neighbour, Nathaniel Boon, and bore his child in September 1824. Three years later Ray sold half his farm to Boon. Portions of Ray's 1816 grant were retained by his descendants until 1884. Jonathan Brooker had less success and in 1817 sold his grant and leased a 20-acre (8 ha) farm nearby. By 1822 he had cleared 19 acres (7.6 ha) and planted 10 acres (4 ha) with wheat, a small orchard and garden. His home, crops and tools were destroyed in a bushfire in 1823 and, aged 60, he had to start afresh. Brooker moved his family to new country in the Illawarra district.[29]

Within two years of receiving his 100-acre (40 ha) grant in 1816, Thomas Clarkson had acquired five adjoining grants. He had arrived in 1806 under a fourteen-year sentence and was pardoned in 1811. He prospered as a publican and baker. By 1817 he controlled seventeen grants in the Airds district, houses in Sydney and farms at the Hawkesbury, owning some outright and others as mortgagee. His property was valued in excess of £12 000. By the time of his death about 1826 Clarkson's Eagle Vale estate covered almost 1400 acres (560 ha) and was the largest estate in the parish of St Peters.[30]

In Minto William Redfern had one of the largest estates. A man of abrupt, independent and forceful character, Redfern had arrived as a convict in 1801. He was surgeon on Norfolk Island until 1808 when he was appointed Assistant Colonial Surgeon. He attended Governor Macquarie's family and in 1811 was granted 800 acres (320 ha) at Minto which he named Campbellfield in honour of Mrs Macquarie. When not appointed principal surgeon in 1819, Redfern retired to Campbellfield and was appointed a magistrate in 1820. By 1820 he held by grant and lease about 2620 acres (1048 ha), having purchased James Oadham's adjoining 44-acre (17.6 ha) grant in 1816 and Richard Barnes 50 acres (20 ha) in 1821. The house at Campbellfield dates from this period. It is a simple brick farmhouse, single storey with a stone cellar. Though the land itself was not of good quality, Redfern had the trees felled and with 'intelligence and spirit' started farming by the best English methods.

Political opposition to the appointment of ex-convicts as magistrates involved Redfern in emancipist politics. He went to England to further their cause in 1821, returning in 1824 to Campbellfield, which he con-tinued to develop with sheep and vines imported from Europe. Redfern retired from his private medical practice in September 1826. Two years later he went to Edinburgh to take his son to school and died there in 1833. On his death Redfern owned 23 190 acres (9276 ha), of which 6296 (2518.4) were in Airds and Minto. He had married Sarah Wills, daughter of wealthy ex-convict merchant Edward Wills, in April 1811. They had two sons, William Lachlan Macquarie Redfern (b. 1819) and Joseph Foveaux Redfern (b. 1823). William remained in Edinburgh after his father's death and never returned to Australia. His mother remarried in 1834 and returned to Sydney with her second husband, James Alexander.[31]

Richard Atkins named his grant Denham Court after his family home in Middlesex. Deeply in debt, he transferred his grant almost immediately to Richard Brooks who also acquired four adjoining grants—Thomas Broadhurst's 50 acres (20 ha) and three grants of 200 acres (80 ha) to Simeon Lord. Brooks, a sea captain, had visited Sydney regularly from

1802. He acquired property and commercial interests but did not settle permanently until 1813 and was joined by his family in 1814. The Brooks family lived in Sydney until the mid-1820s though there was a small cottage at Denham Court by 1821.[32]

Dr Robert Townson received title to 1000 acres (400 ha) at Minto in 1810. A scholar, naturalist and friend of Sir Joseph Banks, he came to New South Wales in 1807 to join his brother, a captain in the New South Wales Corps. Townson named his Minto farm 'Varroville' after the Roman author Marcus Terentius Varro, who wrote about agriculture. His home was built of sandstock bricks on stone foundations, bonded with mortar containing cow's hair. His library, reflecting Townson's wide scientific, philosophic and social interests, was one of the most extensive in the colony. Dinner parties were intellectual gatherings at which the guests were expected to entertain their host with two hours of interesting conversation before the meal was served.

When Townson moved permanently to 'Bumburycurren' in early 1813, he wrote to the governor requesting additional land and a bridge over the creek. He had built one bridge but it had been washed away, and as the land on the other side had been allocated to someone else, he was unwilling to rebuild. Until his crops were harvested Townson had to send to Liverpool for supplies and had to unload the cart to cross the creek. Additional land on the opposite side of the creek would also add to the beauty of his estate. 'Nothing will so much induce a gentleman to live upon his Estate and improve it as having an agreeable situation suited to his Estate and I am the only Gentleman in this part of the colony ... residing upon his Estate.'

Macquarie refused. The two men had no liking for each other and Townson devoted his attention, almost obsessively, to his estate during the years that Macquarie was governor. After Macquarie's departure Townson returned to community life, taking an active role in the formation of an agricultural and a philosophical society. His years of work at Varroville were rewarded in the 1802s when his vineyard was acknowledged as one of the colony's best, and his sheep, his wool and his cattle were eagerly sought by purchasers. Robert Townson died, unmarried, at Varroville in June 1827.[33]

Charles Throsby was already farming his land when Macquarie visited in November 1810. Throsby, a naval surgeon who arrived in New South Wales in 1802, served on the medical staff at Norfolk Island, Castle Hill and Newcastle. Retiring in ill health in 1808, he received a grant of 500 acres (200 ha) from Paterson and two additional grants totalling 600 acres (240 ha) as compensation for flocks and herds left at Newcastle. Macquarie increased his grants to 1500 acres (600 ha). Glenfield House, named after Throsby's birthplace in Leicester, was built about 1817 when Throsby settled permanently on his farm. Glenfield was a single-storey brick farmhouse with a shingle roof, stuccoed walls, brick-lined cellars and a stone-flagged verandah. Behind the house a two-storey brick store was built in the late 1820s. The property overlooked the freshwater reaches of the George's River.[34]

In August 1816 William Howe, a newly arrived free settler, was informed that his capital and a letter of support from the Secretary of State entitled him to 3000 acres (1200 ha) at Upper Minto, eight assigned convicts fed by government for eighteen months and the loan of twelve cows for three years. His family would also receive rations for eighteen months. In contrast William Hilton Hovell, who had been some years in the colony, was informed that his family and convict servants would not receive rations until they were actually living on his grant at Narellan. Convict servants, provisions and stock, practical assistance that enabled a settler to conserve his own capital, were bait to entice grantees to live on their land and personally supervise its development.[35]

The most southern of the large estates was Lachlan Vale at Appin. William Broughton had come as a free servant to Surgeon White on the First Fleet. He became a government storekeeper, stationed at Norfolk Island for some years, and during the Rum Rebellion was appointed Acting Commissary which he remained under Macquarie. He served in Van Diemen's Land from 1816 to 1818, but returned to take charge in Sydney following repeated accusations of mismanagement against commissariat officers. Broughton received a grant of 1000 acres (400 ha) near Appin in 1811 and named it Lachlan Vale. Macquarie, impressed by his progress, granted him a further 700 acres (280 ha) in 1816. Broughton had five children by Elizabeth Heathorn (alias Ann Glossop) who was killed in a massacre following the shipwreck of the *Boyd* in New Zealand in 1809. Left with young children, Broughton married the widowed Elizabeth Simpson, née Kennedy, who had accompanied her first husband, Captain Simpson, to New South Wales. She was connected by marriage to the Kennedys and Humes who were her neighbours at Appin. Widowed a second time in 1821, she continued to live at and manage the isolated Lachlan Vale estate until her death in 1843. In 1828 her estate covered 2000 acres (800 ha) and she owned 1000 cattle and 2000 sheep. A stepdaughter married Charles Throsby Smith, a nephew of Charles Throsby of Glenfield, in 1822.[36]

Explorers

John Warby (1767?–1851)

The first European residents in the Campbelltown district were the constables stationed at Bird's Eye Crossing. Though his official appointment as constable at the Cowpastures dated from 1806, John Warby was probably living there from 1802 and was guide to the botanist George Caley in

1804. He enjoyed the support of Governor and Mrs King who recommended him to Governor Bligh as a trustworthy and well-informed man. Much of Warby's knowledge of the district came from his friendship with the Dharawal. As stockman in charge of the wild cattle, Warby explored the Cowpastures, west to the Oaks and Burragorang and south to Bargo.

John Warby had been transported for seven years in 1791. He married fellow convict Sarah Bentley in 1796 and farmed at Prospect. Following his appointment as herdsman and later constable at the Cowpastures, his Prospect farm became the starting point for most visits to the Cowpastures, a situation recognised in the surveyed line of the Old Cowpasture Road which went south from his farm to the Nepean River. His grant of 260 acres (104 ha) on the flats west of Bow Bowing Creek, along Badgally Road, was dated June 1816 though Meehan measured it in November 1809. Warby advertised for tenants for the Prospect farm in 1809, but did not move his family to Airds until his grant was formalised in 1816. His twelfth child, James, was born at Airds on 17 February 1817 and was the first child whose baptism was registered by the Reverend Thomas Reddall in May 1821.

From his farm which he named Leumeah, Warby looked to the grazing potential of more southerly districts. His squatting station at Gundagai was the furthest point of European settlement in 1829 when Sturt passed through on his exploration of the Murrumbidgee and Murray Rivers. John Warby died at Campbelltown in 1851, aged 84, and his wife Sarah died in 1869. Some of their fourteen children remained in Campbelltown, others joined the southward migration which their father had helped to pioneer.[37]

Leumeah House, home of the Warby family. Built around 1820, it was demolished in 1963. CAMPBELLTOWN AND AIRDS HISTORICAL SOCIETY

James Meehan (1774–1826)

Transported from Ireland for his part in the rebellion of 1798, James Meehan arrived in New South Wales in 1800 and was assigned to Acting Surveyor-General Charles Grimes. Pardoned in 1806, Meehan continued his work in the survey department, and on Grimes' departure in 1808 Meehan was Acting Surveyor-General until John Oxley's appointment in 1812, then was deputy surveyor from 1812 to 1821. As the only field surveyor for many years, Meehan claimed that he had personally surveyed every farm, road and town in the colony between 1803 and 1820. Meehan made his home on his grant, Macquarie Fields, from 1811. His brick house was known as Meehan's Castle.

As well as the routine duties of surveying, Meehan explored south towards Lake Bathurst in 1817, searched for an overland route to Jervis Bay in 1818 and discovered Lake Bathurst and the Goulburn Plains. In 1820 Meehan travelled west from Moss Vale, crossing the Lachlan and Macquarie Rivers. When ill health forced his retirement, Macquarie recommended him for a pension as a man of 'real worth and Probity'. Meehan determined the pattern of settlement in Minto and Airds. He was solely responsible for survey work during the rebel administration, the years when settlement in the south was initiated. He not only located his own estate there but directed other Irish to the district, thus shaping the Irish and Catholic characteristics of south-western New South Wales.

Meehan possibly left a wife and family in Ireland. In New South Wales he had children by Ruth Goodair of Campbelltown and Mary Meehan, who died at Campbelltown in 1842. James Meehan died at Macquarie Fields on 21 April 1826. Macquarie Fields estate had increased to 2400 acres (960 ha) by 1826 and was farmed by several tenants. His eighteen-year-old son, Thomas, inherited but the property was managed by his trustees and neighbours, Charles Throsby and William Redfern, until he turned 21. Unfortunately Throsby died and Redfern went overseas. Thomas Meehan inherited only debts and was forced to sell Macquarie Fields in 1831. The stress broke young Thomas's wife of two years, Mary Ann, née Tress, who was committed to Liverpool Asylum from 1831 until her death in 1876. Thomas Meehan served briefly as postmaster at Campbelltown and died in 1835, aged 27, leaving two infant daughters.[38]

Hamilton Hume (1797–1873)

Hamilton Hume was born at Toongabbie in 1797, the eldest of four sons of Andrew and Elizabeth Hume. His father, the son of an Irish Presbyterian clergyman, had joined the army and arrived in New South Wales in 1789 on the commissariat staff. Andrew Hume was stationed on Norfolk Island and transferred as superintendent of government livestock to Toongabbie in 1793. In 1796 he married Elizabeth Kennedy, a clergyman's daughter who had arrived in 1793 with her brother. Elizabeth Kennedy

Hume was briefly matron of the Girls' Orphanage at Parramatta. Andrew Hume was an unstable breadwinner for his wife and children, being several times dismissed for irregular management of the stores and stock under his control and once charged with rape. Andrew Hume received a 100-acre (40 ha) grant from Macquarie in November 1812 which he took up at Appin when his eldest son was fifteen years old. It was one of the most distant farms in the colony but his neighbours, Elizabeth Charlotte Broughton and John Kennedy, were relatives of his wife.

The Blue Mountains, barrier for westward expansion, had been broken by Blaxland, Lawson and Wentworth in 1813. Hamilton Hume made a less dramatic but equally valuable contribution to southward expansion, making at least thirteen journeys between 1814 and 1821. His expeditions uncovered the grazing lands of the counties of Argyle, Westmoreland, King, Murray and St Vincent. In 1814, a year of drought, Hamilton and his brother John made their first major trip with Duall, their Dharawal guide. Travelling south, beyond Bargo Brush to Berrima and Argyle, they found good grazing land and returned there in 1815 and again in 1816. In July and August 1817 Hume took Charles Throsby into Argyle. In March 1818 he travelled with Meehan and Throsby to Lake Bathurst and Goulburn Plains. In October 1819 he went to the south coast with Meehan and Oxley, travelling from Five Islands (Illawarra) to Jervis Bay. In the autumn of 1820 he journeyed south again with Throsby and William Macarthur to Taralga. The following year, in April 1821, Hamilton Hume led family and friends to Yass to select grazing land. In November 1821 Hume and Kennedy with Duall and Cow Pasture Jack went from Lake Bathurst across to the coast and the Shoalhaven River. Hume returned by boat in January 1822 with merchant Alexander Berry to select Berry's Coolangatta estate.

Hamilton Hume's most significant expedition was his journey in 1824 with William Hilton Hovell to Port Phillip. They were the first Europeans to travel overland to the southern ocean. An ill-matched pair, their partnership had been suggested by Berry because Hovell could navigate by the stars. Hovell, born in England in 1786 and a sea captain by his 22nd birthday, was married to Esther, a daughter of First Fleet surgeon Thomas Arndell. Hovell arrived in 1813 and was granted 600 acres (240 ha) in Upper Minto which he named Narelling. He did not settle to farming but went into business with Simeon Lord and Garnham Blaxcell, trading with New Zealand. Shipwrecked in Bass Strait for 10 weeks in 1816, Hovell ended his trading business with Lord in 1817 and settled permanently on his farm in 1819. He was in constant trouble with the local magistrates, fined for working on the Sabbath in 1820, found guilty of insulting and obstructing a magistrate in February 1824 and in June was charged with illegally taking stone from a quarry.[39]

Their expedition proved a journey of 'bitter success and mutual destruction', their joint achievement overshadowed by a life-long quarrel between them over who was leader of the expedition. Six convict servants who accompanied them settled in the south-west but retained links with Campbelltown. Thomas Boyd (1798?–1885) went to Tumut; Henry Angel (1790–1881) farmed at Wollongong and took up Uardry Station near Hay; Claude Bossawa settled at Goulburn; William Bollard managed Berry Jerry station, Coolamon, and died at Picton; Thomas Smith settled at Campbelltown; James Fitzpatrick (1796–1882), the most successful, bought Hovell's Narelling estate. Hovell went to Goulburn in 1830 and died there in 1875.[40]

Hume returned south again in 1825 and may have accompanied Surveyor-General Mitchell on surveys for the Great South Road in the late 1820s. He then turned to the western districts, exploring beyond Bathurst in 1827 and in 1828–29 accompanying Captain Charles Sturt on a four-month expedition which discovered the Darling River. Sturt paid tribute to Hume's bush skills and good relationships with the Aborigines. Hume was rewarded with a grant of 300 acres (120 ha), which he took at Appin in 1819, for his trip to Goulburn Plains with Meehan, and a further grant of 1920 acres (768 ha) in recognition of his journey with Sturt. He had established a grazing station at Lake George which he used as a base for his journey with Hovell in 1824. Sturt later settled in Campbelltown, purchasing Varroville in 1837.

In November 1825 Hamilton Hume married Elizabeth Dight of Richmond. They had no children. Sarah Mathew visited them at Appin in 1833 and thought Hamilton, though native-born, better informed than most and a young man of sense and amusing conversation. He purchased Cooma Cottage from the O'Briens in 1839 and settled permanently at Yass, though he retained strong links with Campbelltown and Appin. Hamilton Hume died in April 1873.[41]

Charles Throsby (1777–1828)

In the drought years Charles Throsby of Glenfield also turned his attention southward. By 1815 he had cattle grazing in the Illawarra and Moss Vale. Throsby's wife, Jane, was a relative of George Barber who married Hamilton Hume's sister in 1815. In July 1817 Throsby asked Hume to accompany him on an expedition in the Southern Highlands. In 1818 Throsby and Meehan journeyed from Moss Vale through Bundanoon to Jervis Bay. In 1819, accompanied by Thomas Rowley of Holdsworthy, Joseph Wild and John Wait, with Cookoogong of the Burrah Burrah and Duall of the Dharawal as guides, Throsby travelled from the Wingecarribee across the mountains to Bathurst. During this expedition he recorded the Aboriginal placenames 'Wallandilli' (Wollondilly) and 'Murrum-bid-gie', a river that the Aborigines told him about but which he failed to find. Macquarie was delighted with Throsby's report of fertile country and grazing land and rewarded him with a land grant of 1000 acres (400 ha) which Throsby took at Moss Vale. Macquarie named it Throsby Park on a visit in 1820.

Throsby, Hume and William Macarthur explored the Goulburn Plains in March 1820, and in August Throsby took his men, who were building a road to Argyle, in search of a lake known to the Aborigines which Joseph Wild discovered and named Lake George in August 1820. In March 1821 Throsby searched for the Murrumbidgee, travelling through the Canberra district. Throsby's last expedition, with colonial-born William Kearns of Minto, was a crossing from Argyle to Jervis Bay in November 1821.

Throsby repeatedly protested about the treatment of Aborigines in Minto and Airds and Macquarie in 1817 considered him a discontented troublemaker, though they later reconciled their differences. Appointed a magistrate in 1821, Throsby became a member of the first Legislative Council in 1824. His partnership with the merchant Garnham Blaxcell collapsed in 1817 and a decade of court battles left him financially ruined. He committed suicide at Glenfield on 2 April 1828 aged 51. His widow, Jane, died in 1838 and was buried at Liverpool. They had no children and Glenfield was inherited by his nephew, Charles Throsby junior.[42]

Conflict on the southern frontier

By 1810 the small groups of Dharawal had concentrated in the Cowpastures, though they travelled north of the river. One group included Gogy, his wives, Nantz and Mary, Budbury and his wife, Mary, a few young men—Young Bundle, Mandagerry, Jindle and Bill—and four or five children of various ages.[43]

Intensive European occupation of Airds and Minto did not take place until the Macquarie decade. Relations between the Europeans and Aborigines deteriorated in the autumn of 1814 with the first serious violence in the county of Cumberland since the raids by Tedbury and Young Bundle in 1809. There was a severe drought between 1814 and 1816. As the maize crops ripened on the new farms, Aborigines from the south coast and the southern mountains came to gather food. The first violence occurred in May 1814 on the farms of Milehouse and Bucher at Appin. Three members of the Veteran Company militia fired on a group of Aborigines gathering corn, killing a boy. His companions immediately attacked the Europeans with spears. Unable to reload their weapons quickly, the veterans fled, leaving Isaac Eustace behind fatally injured. They returned with reinforcements and found Eustace's body, minus one hand. Seeking vengeance they murdered Bitugally's wife and two children while they slept—the woman's arm was cut off and her head scalped, the skull of one child smashed with the butt of a musket and their bodies left unburied for their families to find. The next day the Aborigines retaliated and killed William Baker and Mary Sullivan, stock-keepers for Mrs Macarthur at Camden.[44]

By late May 1814 large numbers of Aborigines from Jervis Bay and the mountains had gathered in the Cowpastures. These tribes had an aggressive reputation, particularly the Jervis Bay people who had killed a number of shipwrecked Europeans. There were rumours that the Aborigines had declared that 'when the Moon shall become as large as the Sun', they would kill all white people. Full moon was on 3 June 1814. Settlers from Liverpool, Airds and Appin formed an armed guard at Andrew Hume's farm at Appin to keep watch. Their concern was intensified by reports that the Aborigines no longer feared their firearms. Two servants on Broughton's farm at Appin were speared to death during an afternoon attack in mid-June 1814. Macquarie blamed the settlers and their servants for the unrest of May and June 1814. The murder of Bitugally's wife and children had provoked much of the violence. The governor urged forbearance and suggested that they permit the Aborigines to take some of their crops as such losses were a small price for peace.[45]

The Dharawal seem to have tried to avoid conflict. Gogy decided to visit the Broken Bay people, though he added to the settlers' alarm by describing the mountain people as cannibals, a comment that may well have been a tactic to manipulate the Europeans against his traditional enemies. Other Dharawal sought refuge with friendly European settlers.[46]

In July 1814 the children of James Daley were murdered at Bringelly. Macquarie held five mountain Aborigines responsible—Goondel, who had met Barrallier in 1804, Bitugally (Bottagallie), Murrah, Yellooming and Wallah. John Warby and John (Bush) Jackson from Campbelltown were ordered to take an armed party, capture these Aborigines by force if necessary and bring them back for trial. Warby took two Dharawal guides, Budbury and Quayat (Quiet), with Mary Mary and Karryong (Harryong) and selected ten ticket-of-leave men and assigned convicts to accompany him. They returned after 21 days, reporting no trace of the outlawed Aborigines. The unrest receded in spring and summer, possibly because the other tribes had returned to the mountains. Daley abandoned his farm and took up land at Campbelltown.[47]

Two years later, in March 1816, the Gandangara again came from the mountains in search of food. Four of G. T. Palmer's men were killed at the Nepean, and when news came that three of Mrs Macarthur's men were dead, Samuel Hassall of Macquarie Grove and Bringelly magistrate Robert Lowe took action. With 40 farmers armed with muskets, pistols, pitchforks and pikes they approached the Aborigines assembled in Upper Camden with Budbury of the Dharawal as interpreter. Budbury told them the Gandangara would attack and when the Europeans approached there was a shower of spears. The settlers fired their weapons to little effect as the Aborigines had the advantage of high ground. Spears and stones rained down and the settlers retreated in panic. Some threw off their shoes to run faster; others rolled down the hill. Samuel Hassall fled on his horse. A few shots were fired during the retreat, but the Aborigines dropped to the ground whenever the muskets were raised and got up after the discharge. They did not pursue the fleeing settlers.[48]

Isolated shepherds, farmers and their families moved to the safety of more closely settled areas. Macquarie reported the deaths of five white men at the hands of the Aborigines in March 1816 and foreshadowed his intention to take severe measures against the mountain tribes. On 9 April 1816 Macquarie ordered the military to apprehend all Aborigines in the southern districts and the Hawkesbury because of their hostility in the previous two years and their recent attacks on settlers. If they resisted, they were to be shot and the bodies of the men hung from trees as an example to others. He was aware that women and children would also be killed and directed that their bodies be buried. Macquarie's orders made no distinction between friendly and aggressive Aborigines.[49]

Most Europeans could not distinguish individual Aborigines nor the different clans. Throsby was concerned that the 'fears and aversions of the ignorant part of white people' would lead to indiscriminate attacks against innocent Aborigines. This in turn would provoke retaliation killings of isolated stockmen. Budbury of the Dharawal had been named by a terrified settler and Throsby wrote to the *Sydney Gazette* in March 1816 to defend Budbury. He believed that Bitugally, Duall and Yellooming had not murdered Daley's children, though he acknowledged they had probably been involved in the murder of a stockman on Broughton's farm. Throsby argued that the Dharawal men were only taking vengeance 'for the barbarity practiced by our own countrymen'. Bitugally's wife and two children had been murdered in 1814 and Yellooming's child had also been killed by Europeans, but their retaliation was against specific Europeans. Gogy and Nighgingull with their families took refuge at Glenfield from February 1816 and they were joined by Budbury, Young Bundle and other Dharawal. Neither Throsby nor his guest, John Wentworth, feared personal danger from the Dharawal despite the recent violence, and John Wentworth had spent days fishing with Gogy at the height of the trouble.[50]

In April 1816 Macquarie ordered Lieutenant Charles Dawes and some soldiers to capture the Cowpastures Aborigines using John (Bush) Jackson and Tindal, a Dharawal, as guides. Dawes was led to a group of Aborigines not by Jackson or Tindal but by Mrs Macarthur's stockman, Cornelius Rourke. The Aborigines fled. The soldiers fired, resulting in an unspecified number of deaths and the capture of a fourteen-year-old boy. Despite his lack of active participation, Tindal was later awarded an order of merit by Macquarie.[51]

Captain James Wallis of the 46th Regiment was in command of the soldiers sent to Airds and Appin. His guides were John Warby with Budbury and Bundle from the Dharawal. For a month Wallis and his soldiers marched back and forth from Glenfield to Appin in pursuit of rumoured sightings. It was a frustrating expedition that was to have tragic consequences. Wallis later submitted a detailed report in which he recorded the considerable support, to the point of interference, that the European farmers of Airds and Appin had given the Dhara-

21

wal people who had become entangled in Macquarie's war on the Aborigines.

From the beginning Wallis found Warby an unwilling and uncooperative guide. Gogy, alarmed by the general hunt for Aborigines, had fled from Glenfield and taken refuge with the Botany Bay tribe. Wallis wanted to pursue him but Warby argued the Dharawal were friendly and should be left alone. Wallis reluctantly conceded that his priorities lay in the campaign further south. Warby then refused to take responsibility for the two Dharawal guides, Budbury and Bundle, and after a forced march through the rain, Warby allowed them to 'escape' with their blankets. William Cordeaux from Leppington and Hamilton Hume from Appin joined Wallis and the soldiers, possibly to keep an eye on the military.

Wallis went to the most southerly farms at Appin where he learnt that friendly Aborigines had taken refuge at Kennedy's farm. He promised not to harm them but then found that Kennedy had been sheltering two of the 'outlaws', Yellooming and Bitugally, the same men whose families had been brutally slain in earlier conflicts. Wallis's eagerness to take them prisoner alarmed Kennedy who argued that Yellooming and Bitugally had protected his and Broughton's farms and if they were arrested he would have to abandon his isolated farm for fear of reprisals. Rather than see them taken away by the soldiers, Kennedy offered his personal bond to escort them to the governor to explain their innocence. Hamilton Hume was able to convince Wallis that he had seen Macquarie remove the names of Yellooming and Bitugally from the list of outlawed Aborigines. This may have been a bluff since Yellooming's name was among the list of outlawed Aborigines published two months later, but within a few days confirmation arrived from Sydney that they were not to be arrested.

Wallis decided to follow up reported sightings of Aboriginal warriors near Redfern's farm in the more populated Minto area. Warby now disappeared, saying the Aborigines would suspect something if they saw him with the military. Wallis reached Redfern's farm after a forced march, only to find that the overseer, McAllister, who had sent the message, was absent. Wallis angrily reported he had been deceived by McAllister because of 'personal fears or a wish to succour the natives'. For a few days Wallis and his soldiers searched the rugged banks of the George's River at East Minto and Ingleburn, then word came from Tyson and Noble that seven outlawed Aborigines were camped at Broughton's farm at Appin. Wallis marched his soldiers through the night. They were met by Thomas Noble, a convict, who led them to the camp.

Fires were still burning but the camp was deserted. A child's cry was heard in the bush. Wallis formed his men into a line and pushed through the thick bush towards a deep rocky gorge. Dogs barked in alarm and the soldiers started to shoot. It was moonlight and the soldiers could see figures bounding from rock to rock. Some Aborigines were shot, some met their end by rushing in despair over the cliffs. Two women and three children were all who remained 'to whom death would not be a blessing'. Fourteen had died. Wallis identified Durelle and the well-known mountain chief Cannabayagal, whom Caley had meet at Stonequarry Creek in February 1804. Their bodies with difficulty were pulled up the cliff and hung from trees at Broughton's farm as a warning to others. Wallis regretted that the attack had led to the death of an old man, Balyin, and women and children. It was too difficult to recover the other bodies from the rocky gorge or to bury the women and children. Kennedy provided a cart so that the captured women and children could be taken to Liverpool.[52]

The Appin massacre is traditionally remembered as the annihilation of the Aboriginal people of Campbelltown. Durelle was Dharawal but Cannabayagal was a Burragorang man. Their association in death suggests that some Dharawal, who had previously attempted to manipulate the Europeans against their traditional rivals, had been pushed to join forces with a traditional enemy in the face of indiscriminate European attacks in 1816.

Leaving a corporal and three privates to protect Kennedy and Sykes who now feared reprisals, Wallis marched north to Airds. A detachment of soldiers was sent to lay in ambush for Budbury, their former Dharawal guide. Wallis patrolled the George's River looking for Gogy. He found a kangaroo dog, thought to be Gogy's, and fresh tracks, but the country was so rugged there was little chance of catching up with the Aborigines. On 21 April 1816 Wallis joined the other military contingents at Narellan and marched to the Wingecarribee district looking for Aborigines until their rations were finally exhausted. After a month on patrol the military returned to base. Meanwhile, Duall and Quayat had been captured at Kennedy's farm and sent to Liverpool.[53]

Macquarie explained the military action and deaths as a necessary deterrent in consequence of three years of hostility against the Europeans. His May 1816 proclamation forbade gatherings of armed Aborigines within 1 mile (1.6 km) of farms and villages. Aborigines who were friendly to the Europeans were offered land, food and work, and education for their children. Gogy gave up his arms in June 1816 and was later awarded a gorget medallion by Macquarie. A second proclamation on 20 July 1816 outlawed ten Aborigines and offered a reward for their capture or death, one of them being Yellooming. Settlers were forbidden to offer sanctuary or provisions to friendly Aborigines unless they gave information about the outlaws. In early August Dewal or Duall was arrested for encouraging his people to commit robbery. Because of his ignorance of law the death penalty was remitted and he was sentenced to seven years' transportation to Van Diemen's Land. The outlaw proclamation was withdrawn in November 1816 and amnesty offered to the survivors to allow them to attend the governor's meeting with the tribes in December.[54]

Disintegration of Aboriginal life

After the conflicts of 1816 the Dharawal stayed in the Cowpastures. North of the Nepean farming was well established but the Cowpastures remained grazing country. The Macarthur family had lost several employees in the violence, but maintained friendly contact with the Aborigines and did not try to remove them from the Camden estate.

Elizabeth Macarthur, John's eldest daughter, held the Aborigines in high regard, begging her friend to excuse 'the partiality of a native for native subjects'.

> *They are a singular race utterly ignorant of the arts [sic], living constantly in the open air, and without any other covering than occasionally, cloaks of the skin of wild animals, but even these are not universally worn, it is not uncommon to see them without any covering at all. They are nevertheless very intelligent and not obtrusive. They have great vivacity and a peculiar turn for mimicry—acquiring our language, tones and expressions with singular facility. Their carriage is very graceful, and perhaps they possess more native politeness than is found amongst any people. They deem a great want of good breeding to contradict. In all the European modes of salutation they make themselves perfect.[55]*

In March 1818 James Meehan marked out some land on the Macarthur estate for Aborigines who wanted to live there under the protection of the Macarthurs.[56] Tribal life continued in a limited way with corroborees at Camden Park and Denham Court when other Aborigines visited. John Macarthur and his wife also enjoyed the corroborees, commenting in the 1820s that:

> *it is not unusual for two or three hundred to collect, to paint and deck themselves with green boughs, and in sets perform various grotesque figure dances, in most excellent time, which is given by others who sit apart and chant a sort of wild cadence. These corroborees are always on bright moon light nights, some agreeable spot is always chosen for the exhibition amongst the woods. The number of small fires which are kindled causes just enough brilliancy to give affect to our beautiful woodland scenery; and throw sufficient light on the sable performers. This festivity is generally prolonged until past midnight, and always given to do honour to and entertain strangers, whom they call 'Myall'.[57]*
>
> *We had the grandest Corroboree here last night . . . There must have been at least a Hundred and Twenty men, with a Multitude of Women and children—they have been collected from all parts of the Coast—and to-day they rise and proceed to Bathurst to slay and eat—our Natives do not join the expedition, and look very suspiciously on this host—I fear they have made sad inroads on the poor Settlers' Corn over the water—ours of course is untouched—they observe a pretty general rule not to touch the resources near home, if supplies can be procured at a distance.[58]*

The Dharawal frequently guided the settlers to land in the south. In March 1818 Bundle from the Dharawal and Broughton from the Shoalhaven guided Meehan, Throsby and Hume on their search for an overland route to Jervis Bay. Bundle acted as interpreter at meetings with the Illawarra people, explaining, on Throsby's instructions, that

Aborigines were not permitted to carry their spears in the presence of white people. Bundle was familiar with European food and ate salt pork but the Illawarra men, Timelong and Munnaana, refused it. Duall and Biang, as interpreters and guides, in April 1819 accompanied Throsby from the Cowpastures to Bathurst. On this journey Throsby met a party of Aborigines near Bathurst and recognised several whom he had seen at the Cowpastures or who had visited him at Glenfield. Macquarie agreed to Throsby's suggestion that Duall and Biang receive inscribed medallions as rewards for their help. In November 1821 Duall and Cowpasture Jack accompanied Hume and Kennedy to Lake Bathurst and the Shoalhaven district.[59]

By 1821 Budbury was considered by the Europeans as leader of the Cowpasture people and he was a familiar visitor to the Macarthurs. John Macarthur, his mental health fast declining by 1828, compelled the Dharawal on the Camden estate to attend church dressed in European clothing and occasionally used them as a bodyguard, liveried in crimson, red and yellow and carrying spears.[60]

Dharawal numbers were depleted by disease. Catarrh or influenza struck with tragic impact in the winter of 1820. Throsby reported finding the bodies of whole families and a single surviving child in another family. T. V. Blomfield commented in 1821 that he had not seen any local Aborigines older than middle age. Throsby expressed the most frequent concern about the situation of Aborigines. As settlement moved south and south-west, strange Aborigines were often brought unwillingly to the Campbelltown district. Throsby wrote angrily in September 1824 of a sixteen-year-old Aboriginal girl who had been abducted at Lake George by the servants of Richard Brooks, assaulted and raped and brought back to Denham Court in a cart. As magistrate he intervened to have the convict servants punished. The girl's sister had been kidnapped by another of Brooks' men, but because he was a free man he had to be tried in court and Throsby was unable to punish him. Throsby arranged for Dr Reid to examine the girl, took statements from the overseer and took the men back to the scene of the crime at Lake George so that he could find Aboriginal witnesses.[61]

Official concern about Aborigines near Sydney from the 1820s was generally limited to an occasional report from the police magistrate who was responsible for the annual distribution of blankets. In reply to a circular about Aboriginal numbers in mid-1827, the Airds magistrates reported that there were 'no Natives residing in this district'. The Camden magistrates responded that there were 12 men, 9 women and 11 children of the Cowpastures tribe living in their district and 30 from the Burragorang tribe of whom only 5 were men. John Scarr, magistrate's clerk at Campbelltown, included two Aboriginal couples in a painting of his cottage and farm in 1828. One man wore a cast-off jacket and carried spears. His companion had stopped at Scarr's gate, raised his hat and, 'making one of his polite bows', had asked Scarr 'Got any Coppers master'. The women, one with a child, wore blankets tied over one shoulder.[62]

In 1833 the Dharawal at Campbelltown and in the Cowpastures received their blankets and a roll-call was taken: Budbury, aged 45; Duall, aged 40; Bundal, aged 30; Quayat, aged 20 with Wallah, 40, and Kurryong, 30, and their respective wives and children, and Jacky, Caro, Bonclai and Naredgin. Although the approximate ages and the practice of adopting the name of a dead relative makes positive identification difficult, it is likely that some were the people who had witnessed the traumatic events of 1816. By 1834 in Campbelltown itself only one Aborigine was considered a resident. Jacki Jacki or Jack Wollorong (Wallalang), aged about 30, a Burragorang man, lived with three wives, Kitty, Biddy and Hannah. As they also reported to the police magistrate at the Cowpastures, Wollorong claimed blankets from both settlements.[63]

Campbelltown magistrate James Chisholm reported to the Select Committee on the Condition of Aborigines in 1845 that over the last five to ten years the local Aborigines had gradually decreased from about 20 people to none. Deaths were due to natural causes. Blankets had been issued, but now there was no-one to receive them. Matthew McAlister, the neighbouring magistrate at Picton, reported that there were 67 full-blood Aborigines in his district—27 men, 23 women and 4 children. There were few mixed-blood people, only one family of a man, woman and nine children. One Aboriginal woman was cohabiting with a European. Numbers had fallen by about 5 per cent in the past five years due, he believed, to dissipation, lying on the damp earth and consumption. This was the first specific reference to alcohol and its effect among the Cowpasture people. McAlister said their food was inadequate, mainly possum and what they could beg from the whites, because their traditional foods had been decreased by European occupation of their hunting grounds. They had been regularly issued with blankets which they regarded as their right and were dissatisfied that it had ceased. They had not required European medical aid, having a 'carradgee' or doctor in their tribe, suggesting that as far as possible they had continued their traditional ways. The Aborigines made themselves useful to the police and local inhabitants, assisted with reaping and maize-husking, though the white farmers considered them lazy workers and only paid them in provisions, tobacco, old clothes and occasionally firearms. Mostly they were friendly with the whites and were quiet and friendly among themselves. McAlister asked that better-quality blankets be issued with woollen clothing in winter, conspicuously marked to prevent its sale to the Europeans.[64]

In 1855 a visitor to Camden Park photographed a small group of Aborigines on the estate. Six women, one with a young child, sat on the grass behind an older man while a European woman watched from the background. All were dressed in oddments of European clothing. In 1858 about 200 Aborigines were assembled at Campbelltown railway station to celebrate the completion of the railway line. Given the small number

Dharawal and Gandangara at Camden Park. (W.Hertzer, c.1850)
HISTORIC PHOTOGRAPH COLLECTION, MACLEAY MUSEUM, UNIVERSITY OF SYDNEY

of Dharawal and Gandangara by the 1840s, they had probably been gathered from a wide area. Some frequent visitors to Campbelltown and Menangle in mid-century came from quite distant tribes. Edrop at Menangle had a station at Coonamble and Aborigines from there occasionally worked on his farm at Menangle, crossing over the mountains and through the Burragorang Valley.[65]

The little that is known of the language and customs of the Dharawal was recorded by Europeans who met them in the mid- and late nineteenth century when their culture was already disappearing. John Rowley of Holsworthy had explored with Dharawal guides in 1817 and recorded some of their language in 1875. Surveyor Robert Hamilton Mathews (1841–1918) was born at Narellan and grew up in the land of the Dharawal and Gandangara. In the 1890s he recorded some Dharawal vocabulary and folklore remembered by the neighbouring Wodi Wodi of the Illawarra. Mathews copied the drawings of animals and mythological figures that he discovered in the rugged Eckersley plateau.[66]

Two

1820–1840

I N October and November 1820 Macquarie and Commissioner Bigge toured through the Cowpastures to Mittagong, Breadalbane Plains and Lake Bathurst. Neither the governor nor the commissioner commented on the need for a town in Airds or Minto, yet within a few weeks Governor Macquarie had laid the foundation for Campbelltown.[1]

Meehan had reserved a site for a township possibly as early as 1815, when the road was surveyed from Liverpool to Appin. The road formed the western boundary of the town and the neighbouring land grants were formalised in 1816, leaving about 175 acres (70 ha) unoccupied between the grants of Phelps, Kable, Neale, Ditchfield, Bayles and Bland. Macquarie had approved its location before December 1820. The settlers also were aware of the town site and by 1820 had erected a temporary bark hut for a school.[2]

The most likely reason for formally establishing Campbelltown was the appointment of the Reverend Thomas Reddall as resident clergyman for Airds, and Macquarie's decision to send his son to Reddall's school. Reddall had arrived in New South Wales two months earlier, in September 1820, with the dual appointment of colonial chaplain and schoolmaster to introduce a new system of education. He needed a church and a place to conduct his school. On 25 November 1820 Macquarie informed James Meehan that Macquarie Fields was a suitable location for an academy to educate 'upper class youths' and the government wished to rent his house for twelve to eighteen months. Meehan replied on 28 November 1820 agreeing, provided he could retain two rooms in the house for himself.[3]

Two days later Macquarie, his wife and six-year-old son set out for Liverpool. Details of the governor's visit were recorded in his private diary, but were not announced in the newspaper, suggesting that it was a private visit. The governor prefaced his diary entry for Thursday 30 November 1820 with his proposal 'to mark out a Township, and the sites of a Chapel and a School House, as well as a Burial Ground, in a convenient centrical part of the District of Airds'. The vice-regal party inspected Macquarie Fields with Reverend Robert Cartwright of Liverpool and Reddall, lunched with Dr Redfern at Campbellfield and then proceeded to the site of the new township.

About 2 pm on Friday 1 December 1820, before a handful of dignitaries and a crowd of 50–60 settlers, Macquarie formally marked the boundaries of the township, the sites for the church, school and burial ground and named it Campbell-Town, his wife's maiden name. Delighted by the hearty three cheers from the settlers, Macquarie and his party returned to Moorebank. Settlers applied for allotments in the new town but the colonial bureaucracy moved slowly. Over 50 applications were made to Reddall as magistrate in 1821, but, aside from the church lands, graveyard and school, no land was allocated until 1827.[4]

In March 1821 when Reddall was about to take up his duties, Meehan was directed to mark out 400 acres (160 ha) close to Campbelltown in consultation with Reddall for glebe land to support his church. This land had been set aside as a common for the district of Airds. It lay south of the town between the Menangle and Narellan Roads near Mount Annan.[5]

The Anglican church of St Peters was the first, and for many years the only, building within the township. By 1 September 1822 the church was roofed, but the interior unfinished when the Catholic congregation, who had been hearing mass in the open, took shelter from the rain, an action which infuriated the Reverend Reddall. The second building was a three-room school, 35 feet by 16 feet (11 m by 5 m), shared by the schoolchildren and the local magistrates, and probably the schoolteacher's family as well.[6]

On the eastern boundary of the town, on private land, foundations were laid for a Catholic chapel on 12 December 1824. Six months later Father Therry belatedly publicised the gift of 5 acres (2 ha) for chapel, school and burying ground from James Burke, colonial-born son of Thomas Burke, a Tipperary rebel transported in 1801. The graveyard had already been used in January 1824 to bury Thomas Acres, a First Fleeter. St Johns was the first Catholic church outside Sydney, where the foundations to St Marys had been laid in October 1821.[7]

By April 1826 there were three substantial buildings adjoining the official site of Campbelltown. Following the suggestion that troops be stationed in the town, the entrepreneurial Frederick Fisher offered to government a three-storey brick building which he had recently erected. William Dumaresq, civil engineer for roads and bridges and Governor Darling's brother-in-law, was sent to investigate and found that Fisher's building was poorly located opposite the government town site and was not well built. A better building was Hammond's public house, actually owned by Daniel Cooper of Sydney, but the best building belonged to William Bradbury. Built in early 1822, it had been named Bradbury Park by Macquarie. The two-storey brick house with wooden stables, granary and barn would be suitable for officers and troops or for a hospital, with the wards above and the surgery below.[8]

In June 1826 William Howe's application for land within the town stimulated the surveyor-general to provide an unsurveyed plan of town allotments, reserving land in the north-east for the church, rectory, schoolhouse, courthouse, gaol, burial ground and marketplace. A year later surveyor Robert Hoddle drew the first measured plan of Campbelltown. His five convict assistants worked barefoot and almost naked, their clothes and shoes destroyed from working in the thick bush of Irish Town (Bankstown) and along the George's River. Convicts were supplied with two suits of clothing per year, sufficient for convicts who lived in town, but not for those working in the bush. With his plan of Campbelltown, Hoddle transmitted a list of people who wanted to purchase allotments.[9]

Land was reserved for a courthouse and gaol but the government seemed unwilling to build. Instead, in November 1826 Thomas Hammond was awarded a contract to convert Cooper's public house into a courthouse and gaol at a cost of £152. Hammond, the licensee, was promised an allotment in the town. In late 1827 Hammond wrote that since the visit of the surveyors in June, he had hired mechanics to build a house worth £1000, but the government had not yet released the town allotments.[10]

Part of the delay in building approvals was because Surveyor-General Oxley had not added street names to Hoddle's plan. This was done by 4 December 1827, the choice of names showing little originality but certain to please the governor and his staff. The north-south streets were Oxley, Lindesay, Stewart and George. John Oxley was surveyor-general from 1812 until his premature death in 1828. His country estate from 1816 was Kirkham near Narellan and he was involved in commercial as well as farming activities. Colonel Patrick Lindesay (1778–1839) had arrived in Sydney in November 1827 to take control of the military garrison. Later, as the senior military officer, he was acting governor between the departure of Governor Darling and the arrival of Sir Richard Bourke. Colonel William Stewart (1769–1854) was commander of the Sydney garrison from 1825 to 1827 and acting governor between the administrations of Governors Brisbane and Darling. His regiment was transferred to India in 1827 but Stewart returned to settle at Bathurst in 1832. George Street commemorated the reigning king of England, George IV.

The east–west streets were Innes, Sturt, Cordeaux, Condamine, Lithgow and Dumaresq. Archibald Clunes Innes (1800–57) was, in 1827, brigade-major on the governor's staff. Later he settled at Port Macquarie. Charles Sturt (1795–1869) had arrived with his regiment in May 1827 and was soon appointed Governor Darling's military secretary and brigade-major to the garrison. In 1828 and 1829 he led expeditions into western

New South Wales, discovering and naming the Darling and Murray Rivers. William Cordeaux (1792–1839) had arrived in New South Wales in 1818 on the commissariat staff which was responsible for provisioning the convicts, government officials and the military. In 1825 Cordeaux was appointed one of three commissioners to divide the colony into parishes and counties, reserving one-seventh for the church and school purposes. His country estate was Leppington. Thomas De La Condamine (1797–1873) arrived in Sydney in 1826 as Governor Darling's aide-de-camp and in November 1827 was appointed private secretary to the governor. William Lithgow (1784–1864) was an officer in the commissariat. He arrived in 1824 and in mid-1827 was appointed auditor-general of the colony, the second most senior administrative position. Dumaresq was the maiden name of Governor Darling's wife, Eliza. Her three brothers, Henry (1792–1838), William (1793–1868) and Edward (1802–1906), were soldiers. Edward settled in Van Diemen's Land. Henry, Darling's private secretary, became clerk of the Executive Council in New South Wales, and William became civil engineer responsible for roads and bridges.[11]

Howe and Browne Streets, near St Peters Church, were the only streets named after local people. William Howe of Glenlee and William Browne of Appin were, with the Reverend Thomas Reddall, the first church wardens for St Peters.[12]

Although the survey department had completed its work in Campbelltown, land was not released for occupation until late 1831. In May 1828 Governor Darling decided that colonial town planning should be more systematic. William Dumaresq, William Cordeaux and John Busby, mineral surveyor, were appointed to enquire into town planning in general and into plans for Campbelltown in particular.

They reported a month later, classifying the towns of New South Wales according to their location. Sydney and sea ports had the highest classification. Parramatta, Liverpool, Maitland and towns which were at the head of river navigation were in the second class; while interior towns without such advantages fell in the third, or lowest, class. Campbelltown was in the latter category. They recommended standard town blocks of 10 chains square (0.4 ha), divided into twenty building allotments with frontages of 1 chain (20 m) and depths of 5 chains (100 m), streets 1 chain (20 m) wide with 9-foot (3 m) pavements on each side. Houses should be set back to allow for verandahs or shady gardens. To encourage purchasers to build, title should be conditional on buildings of a given value being erected. In Campbelltown the main road would be the most desirable location for shops. Purchasers should be limited to two allotments in the area bounded by the unnamed main road and Oxley Street and along Howe, Browne, Cordeaux, Lithgow and Dumaresq Streets.[13]

Campbelltown was separated by farm grants from the stream through the valley, Bow Bowing Creek. As early as 1823 government architect S. L. Harris had objected to the position of the town: '... this place ... is so ill supplied with water that it would not be advisable to recommend more buildings. There is, about 5 miles further East, a much more eligible scite [*sic*], commanding the Banks of the River Nepean'.[14]

Surveyor-General Sir Thomas Mitchell also protested, commenting in 1830:

> The road from Liverpool to Campbelltown is very hilly and ill laid out—that to the [Cowpastures] bridge is little better ... Some advantages ... for Campbelltown would result from the opening of the direct road ... [it is] well known that water is very scarce and of bad quality at that place; but there is abundance of good water at the head of the George's River, about one and a half miles east of Campbelltown. There is also vacant land where a new line [of road] would pass on which a Township may be laid out, and from whence a short branch road would lead along a connecting ridge to the Northern part of the Illawarra ... such a Township would also command the access to all that extensive portion of Cumberland, lying south of Botany Bay.[15]

One settler who argued strongly for the existing site was ex-convict Thomas Hammond of Clari Montes. Hammond was a London brickmaker who at the age of nineteen had been transported for seven years. He arrived in Sydney on the *General Hewitt* in February 1814. After his sentence expired he received a grant of 100 acres (40 ha) which he took up near Campbelltown. In 1824 he married colonial-born Ann Byrne, daughter of an Appin settler. By 1826 he claimed that he had spent about £800 on building, fences, clearing and cultivation on Clari Montes. However, the survey office was several years behind with its paperwork and Hammond had no formal papers for his land. His persistent questions about title deeds infuriated Oxley. By 1830 Hammond had cleared 80 acres (32 ha) and divided it into paddocks. He cultivated 50 acres (20 ha) and had planted grapevines, hops and fruit trees. His family lived in a 'commodious dwelling' with outhouses. Hammond's activities extended beyond farming. His trade as a brickmaker and knowledge of building were valuable assets in the expanding colony. Hammond also held a publican's licence.

In 1829 Hammond wrote to the government that since 1821 many wealthy landholders had been waiting for permission to build and there was 'great public desire ... in favour of the Township'. Hammond was granted allotment 96, the southern corner of Cordeaux and Queen Streets, and by 1831 he had built a house with twelve rooms, stables and kitchen, valued at £1000, which he used as an inn. He hoped to expand his business in Campbelltown by building a bakery and butcher's shop. Clearly Hammond considered that the town was well sited for his business interests. He sold his allotment in 1840 to John Farley for £1300.[16]

With the government's delay in releasing land within the town, the value of adjoining grants increased. The farms of Bland, Aston and Phelps, part of the Bradbury Park estate which adjoined the southern boundary of Campbelltown, were described in 1830 as 'comprising more than half the township'. Bradbury Park stood on the eastern portion of the Phelps grant. Opposite was the Royal Oak Inn, owned by William

Bradbury and 'most conveniently situated for business'. It was rented for £58 per year to Michael Byrne.[17]

In October 1831 the government finally gave permission for the settlers who had been allocated land in 1827 to take formal possession. Fifteen settlers had been promised land in 1827 but only six retained their original allotments by 1840. They were John Welsh (allotment 81), Charles Byrne (lot 88), Robert Bourke (lot 90), Michael Byrne (lot 91) and John Vardy (lot 93). The others—John Reddall, Thomas Cowper, Reverend Thomas Hassall, Richard Brooks, Peter Brennan, Daniel Brady, John Neil, James Kenny junior, John Patrick, John Franklin, William Byrne, Thomas Hammond and Charles Rennett had sold or mortgaged their allotments.[18]

The allotments promised in 1827 were free grants, but in 1831 the system of free land grants ended. In future all land would be put up for auction with a fixed minimum price. Settlers who wanted to purchase specific portions of land could request the surveyor-general to arrange an auction. Once the needs of the original settlers were met there was little demand for land sales in Campbelltown. There were about five sales in the 1830s and a similar number in the 1840s. Vacant Crown land was still available for purchase within the town as late as 1854.

Daniel Cooper was Campbelltown's first real estate developer. Cooper had arrived as a convict in 1816 but by 1818 was a storekeeper and publican. By the 1820s Daniel Cooper and his partners in the Waterloo Company had extensive investments and were even issuing their own banknotes. In 1826 Cooper held the mortgage on Fisher's farm and owned Hammond's inn. Cooper built the Forbes Hotel and celebrated its opening in 1830 with a public feast to announce the subdivision of some of his land in Campbelltown.

By 1832 Campbelltown was a small village in the midst of farming country. From the hill at Robin Hood farm, a variety of houses and cottages were visible, 'the whole country ... having a more animated and populous appearance, than any other part of the country'. In the village was the church, 'a small but neat structure; on the right is the Court House ... where the Court of Quarter Sessions and the Circuit Court have been held. There are only a few inferior houses in this town; the public houses are numerous.' From Campbelltown to the Nepean River at Bird's Eye Corner, the country was divided into small farms, well cultivated and prosperous-looking. Along the road to Appin the land between the road and the George's River or Tuggerah Creek was so rugged and inaccessible that surveyors did not map it until the early 1830s.[19]

Police magistrate Francis Allman was less impressed when he arrived in 1836. He complained that the town was overgrown with underwood and saplings, giving shelter for 'dissolute and dishonest characters'. Tree stumps had been left in the streets and trees remained where they had fallen causing danger and annoyance to the inhabitants. The street alignments were not defined nor were the town allotments properly identified.[20]

In November 1840 surveyor J. J. Galloway arrived to measure land and survey the township. He found Hoddle's original plan was virtually impossible to put into force. Buildings, fences and gardens had been built across street lines. Deeds to land had been issued without regard to the street pattern. All the allotments in Cordeaux and Lithgow Streets were too far to the north-east, thus requiring the portions between Condamine and Lithgow Streets to be made smaller and those between Lithgow and Dumaresq Streets larger so that Lithgow Street itself could be kept straight. Innes Street was completely closed by fences around land belonging to the Church of England and Thomas Hassall (allotment 68 on the corner of Innes and Lindesay Streets).

Galloway wanted to continue Innes Street through the Church of England land to the main road, thus separating the burial ground from the church, but Bishop Broughton objected. The town plan was redrawn and Innes Street stopped at Lindesay Street, with a remnant, Browne Street, joining the main road. In July 1841 Galloway returned to survey land for the Church of England and for the Presbyterian Kirk, manse and schoolhouse in Lithgow Street. At the Catholic cemetery several graves and tombs extended beyond the north-west boundary and he suggested that the church be given extra land to include the tombs.[21]

Galloway was frustrated that he was unable to put the town into a neat geometric pattern. Lithgow Street, though uniformly 1 chain (20 m) wide with parallel sides, had three different compass bearings, while the bearings of Dumaresq Street could only be described as 'peculiar'. Sydney Road (Queen Street) had originally been a straight, parallel street, but different building alignments had made it distinctly angular and Galloway wondered if it should be straightened. It was not. The north and south town boundaries were named. Broughton Street, near St Peter's churchyard, was named after Bishop William Broughton (1788–1853). Allman Street, the southern town boundary, was named after Campbelltown's police magistrate, Francis Allman (1780–1860).

There were buildings along the Sydney Road, in Cordeaux Street as far as Lindesay Street and in Lithgow Street, some in Dumaresq Street but few in Allman Street. Patrick Brennan had a substantial building on the corner of Lindesay and Lithgow Streets. Jonathan Webb had a smaller dwelling on the corner of Lithgow and Oxley Streets. Richmond Villa and Glenalvon, homes of the Byrne brothers in Lithgow Street, were among the earliest private residences within the government town. East of Lindesay Street, up the hill to the Catholic burial ground, land had been sold but there were no buildings of substance.[22]

Campbelltown was unusual in having its only official building, the courthouse, outside the government town. Another site in Oxley Street, between Lithgow and Dumaresq Streets, was never used for that purpose. Campbelltown lacked the symmetry found in other colonial towns in the 1830s. Possibly the main road passing at an angle on one boundary disturbed the pattern. The marketplace, a focus for community activity, was shown in different positions in the early plans. Its final location, opposite the courthouse, provided a visual, and implied moral, connection between the courthouse and the church across the green.

Churches and schools

Thomas Reddall (1780–1838), born in Staffordshire and educated at Oxford, studied Bell's Madras educational method, an Anglican system using pupil-monitors as teachers. Reddall was sent to New South Wales by the British government to introduce this system into colonial schools. At Macquarie Fields from mid-1821 he conducted an exclusive school for boys. His pupils included the sons of Governor Macquarie and Lieutenant Governor Sorrell of Van Diemen's Land. The school probably closed after Macquarie's departure in 1822, though Reddall continued to take some private students. He remained involved with education at the administrative level and from 1824 to 1826 was director-general of schools in the colony. At Campbelltown Reddall devoted his energies increasingly to his farm. He died on 30 November 1838, leaving his family almost destitute. His youngest child, fourteen-year-old Julia, followed him to the grave a week later.[23]

A church building was not necessary for his ministry and the parish records for St Peters open in May 1821 with the baptism of two sons of John and Sarah Warby. By January 1822 the exterior walls of St Peters Church were completed and by September it had been roofed, but progress then slowed. In November 1823, when William Howe of Glenlee

---

Glen Alpine c.1880. Built for the Reverend Thomas Reddall in 1830, his three unmarried daughters (right) lived here from their childhood until their deaths in the 1890s.

CAMPBELLTOWN AND AIRDS HISTORICAL SOCIETY

made arrangements for his household to attend services in the new church, he requested seats for his family of nine and for twelve servants and standing room for about 50 convicts who worked on his estate. The interior was complete by June 1824—a communion table and service vessels, a fine white linen cloth, a large Bible and prayer book, a clock, a bell, table and chairs, and locks for the front door and the vestry. Above the vestry door was a narrow gallery for the singers. St Peters held 200 people and during Reddall's ministry there was an average congregation of 150.[24]

Reddall lived at Macquarie Fields until 1822 when he leased Smeaton, a 30-acre (12 ha) farm owned by Charles Throsby west of Campbelltown, but much closer to the church than Macquarie Fields. There he remained until his private residence, Glen Alpine, was built in 1830. He wrote in 1822:

> *My residence among the people as their clergyman, and magistrate, is necessary as soon as possible, inasmuch as it might prevent many existing evils and be productive of some good. [The people have] interred [the dead] in their own grounds, a practice at once so shocking and revolting as will, I have no doubt, have a speedy remedy ... A portion of ground has been selected, but having been neither measured nor marked out, it cannot be consecrated.*[25]

Reddall's first entry in the burial register was the death of eight-year-old Sarah Smith in September 1823. In May 1824 he complained of the need for fencing as 'the Graves are much exposed and greatly disturbed by pigs and other animals'. While preferring a neat paling fence he recognised it would be more expensive than a post and rail fence—'a kind of fence highly objectionable in as much as it looks ill and is always out of order'.[26]

The school in the church grounds was built in 1823 with verandahs so that the children could be taught in the fresh air. The schoolmaster in the 1820s and 1830s was a convict, T. L. Robinson. Enrolments averaged 28 pupils. George Joll was schoolmaster at a similar school at Lower Minto with 26 pupils in 1828, but he had transferred to Appin by 1833.[27]

In July 1839, some months after Reddall's death, the Reverend Robert Forrest took up duty at St Peters. Forrest (1802–54) arrived in New South Wales in 1832 and was appointed the first headmaster of the King's School in Parramatta for pupils drawn from the upper ranks of colonial society. Forrest resigned because of poor health in June 1839. At St Peters he continued his interest in education, running a small private school for boys and supervising the local parish school. By 1841 the Church of England school, run by Mr and Mrs Robert Riley, had 23 boys and 20 girls enrolled. There was a slightly larger school at Narellan under Mr and Mrs John Armstrong with 27 boys and 20 girls, while James Moore ran a small Church of England school at Appin with 25 students.[28]

The role of the churches in providing education was fiercely debated. Governor Bourke wanted to introduce a national system in place of the schools run by the churches though funded by the government. He was opposed by the Protestant churches, especially the Church of England, and was forced to abandon the scheme. Bourke's *Church Act* in 1836 provided financial assistance to the four main Christian denominations in the colonial population—the Anglicans, Catholics, Presbyterians and Wesleyans. Funds collected by a congregation to build a church would be matched by government contributions and the government would also pay the clergyman's salary. The same principles applied to church schools.

Bourke's successor, Governor Gipps, also proposed government schools. Forrest and his parishioners defended the Church of England school at Campbelltown in a petition to Governor Gipps in August 1839, signed by 75 residents of Campbelltown, Minto and Menangle. The petitioners varied from large landowners like Jemima Jenkins of Eagle Vale, farmers like Benjamin Warby, John Farley and George Taber, to shopkeepers and tradesmen like Charles Beck and George Craft. They begged the governor not to consider 'an untried and dangerous system'.

Notwithstanding the difficulties and adverse circumstances as to education under which the Colony so long laboured, the rudiments of a useful and religious education have ever been communicated to the poorer classes to the great and lasting benefit of this neighbourhood ... no dispute or disagreement has ever arisen in consequence of this School being ... in intimate connexion with the Church of England, notwithstanding the diversities of religious sentiment which prevail in this District.[29]

The Anglican petition may not have been unrelated to the decision of the Catholic congregation at Campbelltown to build its own school.

Although the foundations for the Catholic church had been laid in 1824, construction was slow because of the lack of money. From January 1833 meetings were called to revive subscriptions for the building fund and to secure government money for the church, a resident priest and a school: 'by far the majority of the uneducated poor of this populous district profess the Roman Catholic faith'. A petition to the government in June 1833 was signed by 102 Catholics and Protestants, including W. R. Kenny, William Howe, William Byrne, Thomas Meehan, Daniel Brady, John Hurley and Thomas Rose. From 1833 government funds helped maintain Campbelltown's Catholic school and under P. Nihill it was the largest in the district with 40 boys and 20 girls. In March 1840 a new school, St Patrick's, was built at the southern end of town and there were 54 students in 1841, taught by Patrick Mulholland and his wife.[30]

Father John Joseph Therry was appointed resident priest and in July 1833 he engaged William McEnnally, stonemason, to increase the height of the walls. The simple church was replaced with a much grander building, to the dismay of many who wondered how the people of Campbelltown would ever afford to complete it. Dennis O'Brien carted lime from Liverpool and stone from a quarry near the church. In late 1833 George Fieldhouse, John Tasker and William Brooker submitted tenders

St Peters Church of England School with teacher's residence was built around
1838 and demolished in 1973. (W. Boag, c.1871)   DREDGE COLLECTION

to shingle the roof. The church on the hill overlooking the town was
subject to much comment, often unflattering, about its design and the
large number of windows that Therry had ordered, originally 80 but later
reduced to 37. From 1834 mass was said in the building and St John's was
formally consecrated in August 1841. There was a regular attendance of
about 350.[31]

Therry engaged James Cotter, an ex-convict stonemason, for a year to
work on the church and cemetery. Among work performed by Cotter in
1837 was a tomb for Darby Murray 'similar to and equal to that of Mr
Hugh Byrne's family'. Another gravestone erected in 1837 was that of
James Ruse whose homemade stone and epitaph drew attention almost
from the day it was erected. Therry was transferred to Van Diemen's
Land in 1838 and his place at Campbelltown was taken by Father James
Goold from March 1838.

Presbyterian minister the Reverend Hugh Gilchrist arrived in Campbelltown in December 1837. There was no church and the small congregation of 40 people met in the police office. Land for a Presbyterian church,
manse and school was surveyed in 1841 in Lithgow Street.[32]

Law, order and government administration

Campbelltown's most active magistrates were William Howe of Glenlee
and the Reverend Thomas Reddall. Others were Captain Brooks of Denham Court, Captain John Coghill, Robert Lowe and Dr William Redfern

of Campbellfield. Magistrates were not paid and sometimes not even their expenses were met. Howe complained in 1820 that he had no clerk and depended on the random assignment of a literate convict to complete his paperwork. Magistrates usually had a constable or two to support them in enforcing the law. In cases of major crime, such as bushranging, the magistrates took to the field with their sons, their neighbours and their servants to pursue the offenders.[33]

Law and order were largely directed to controlling the behaviour and work practices of convict labourers on the farms near the town. In July 1824 John Macarthur of Camden Park brought six of his men before the magistrates to be flogged for disobedience and mutinous conduct. The Reverend Thomas Reddall and Sarah Redfern also had difficulties in managing their convicts and turned to the magistrates to enforce their orders. Free men were not beyond the authority of the magistrates. W. H. Hovell was brought before the bench in 1820 for breaking the Sabbath by using his bullocks and cart to do farmwork on a Sunday.[34]

Major cases were heard briefly by the Campbelltown magistrates, then transferred to the superior courts in Sydney. Such were the proceedings for Campbelltown's cause célèbre in 1824, a civil case for damages following seduction. The parties in the civil case were ex-convict Joseph Ward, one-time constable and caretaker of the St Andrews estate, and his neighbour, colonial-born explorer William Kearns, a farmer of Epping Forest. In February 1823 Joseph Ward went to England, leaving at his farm in Minto his wife Ann, 'addicted to intoxicating habits', a 12-year-old son and two daughters, 14 and 10. Ward entrusted his business affairs to Mary Ann, his 14-year-old daughter, 'a fine, active, modest looking and proper well-instructed girl'. When he returned eighteen months later he found that Mary Ann had been seduced by William Kearns. She had 'yielded to the soft persuasions' of the young man, but two months before Mary Ann gave birth to a baby girl, Kearns married another woman.

In itself the story of Mary Ann Ward and William Kearns was neither unusual nor scandalous. It became both when her father decided to prosecute Kearns for the loss of his daughter's services as his business manager and to demand £1000 in damages. Yet the case took a strange twist which had little to do with the relationship between Mary Ann and William, and everything to do with the moral conduct of her father, Joseph Ward. Ward had returned to New South Wales in July 1824 with his English wife and daughter and had publicly disowned his colonial wife, Ann Euren commonly known as Ann Ward of Minto. Evidence was given that during their voyage out, Ward had sold his English-born daughter to an American ship's captain who had become infatuated with her at one of their ports of call. At her mother's hysterical pleading, Captain Lamb of the *Prince Regent* had called on the Portuguese authorities to retrieve the girl after a night aboard the American vessel. The chief witness to this affair was John Carter, Master of the Supreme Court of

New South Wales, who had travelled by the same ship. Chief Justice Forbes commented that the 'inhuman and unnatural behaviour' of Joseph Ward was 'unparalleled in this Colony'. He found in favour of Ward but awarded damages of only £17–10–0 and costs against Kearns. This was not Joseph Ward's last court appearance. Little more than a year later he informed the Campbelltown magistrates that his brother-in-law and nephew had attempted to murder him. Howe and Reddall found the accusation groundless and charged Ward with perjury.[35]

The Court of Requests sat at Campbelltown from 1827, permitting the recovery of small debts without the expense of travel to Sydney, and the Supreme Court sat on circuit from 1829 until 1839 when it moved to Berrima. The cemetery records of Campbelltown's churches record burials following executions in the 1830s. At least fourteen men faced the gallows in 1830 for murder, arson, bushranging and major theft. Few were local people as Campbelltown was then the most southern court and crimes from the Goulburn district were tried and punished in Campbelltown. Executions seem not always to have been the solemn occasions intended by the court. In August 1829 John Holmes was hanged at the scene of his crime, the farm of James Bean at Menangle where he had burnt down Bean's barn. His friends were ordered to bury the body immediately as the sheriff feared they had plans for a big wake that would have disturbed the town all night.[36]

William Howe was employed as police magistrate from 1828 to 1832 when Governor Bourke favoured a return to the system of honorary magistrates. When the people of Campbelltown complained that a full-time magistrate was necessary, the position was reinstated. For part of 1833 their police magistrate was George Kenyon Holden, but he soon left to become private secretary to the governor and later a leading Sydney solicitor. He was replaced by Robert Stewart from December 1833 to January 1835, when George Stewart took over until June 1836. Francis Allman, previously commandant at Port Macquarie and police magistrate at Goulburn, took charge in July 1836.

The police magistrate supervised the chief constable and eight ordinary constables in 1828, and a corporal and two troopers from the mounted police were stationed there. By 1835 the police establishment at Campbell-town was a salaried magistrate (£200 per annum), a clerk, a chief constable (£100 per annum), eleven constables and a scourger (£25–17–0 per annum). It was a larger establishment than that at either Penrith or Liverpool because of its position at the junction of the Great South Road and the Illawarra Road. Campbelltown residents appreciated the work of their police magistrate: in 1835 the honorary magistrates and free residents of Campbelltown and Illawarra petitioned for an increase in his salary so that he could 'support that rank and station in society which is so essential to ensure respect from all classes'.[37]

Campbelltown gaol held 38 prisoners. During 1833 there were 860 male and 101 female prisoners confined, mostly prisoners in transit. In October

1833 Holden drew attention to the unpleasant state of the gaol. The stench in the courtroom immediately above it was so offensive in warm weather that the Supreme Court was forced to move out. Quaker visitors to Campbelltown three years later, also in October, commented on the badly ventilated and foul-smelling cells. Backhouse reported that Campbelltown gaol was the most offensive prison he had seen in New South Wales. No improvements were made and the magistrates complained again in the summer of 1837. This time the authorities decided that a gaol in Campbelltown was unnecessary and a police office with cells would be sufficient.[38]

Crime was not a major problem in Campbelltown. More alarming were the intermittent appearance of bushrangers, runaway convicts from other districts. Tenant and his gang were tried at Campbelltown in August 1829 and Bold Jack Donahoe was killed in a shoot-out with police in the Bringelly scrub in 1830. The Reverend George Vidal was 'bailed up' near St Peters in 1841 by Jackey Jackey (William Westwood), who returned the money when he realised his victim was a clergyman.[39]

Secure confinement for those caught left much to be desired. Whilst Campbelltown gaol was a substantial structure, the constable's watch-house was not. It was a slab hut with three small rooms, two of which were occupied by the constable, his wife and family and the remaining room by the prisoners, both male and female. The lock could be opened from the inside without a key, simply by pushing back the bolt with a finger. There was no watchhouse at Appin. Prisoners were handcuffed to a chain and a block of wood until they could be transferred.[40]

In June 1835 the police districts were defined by the newly created parishes. The Liverpool Police District included eight parishes—St Luke, Cabramatta, Minto, Holsworthy, Sutherland, Wattamolla, St George and Bankstown. The Campbelltown Police District covered ten parishes—St Peters, Narellan, Cook, Menangle, Appin, 'Widderbourne', Southend, Eckersley, Heathcote and Bulgo, an area stretching from the ocean and Bulli almost to Penrith.[41]

Pioneer Farmers

Many of the small grants were soon consolidated into larger estates which dominated the perimeter of the town and the road between Campbelltown and Liverpool. Most of these estates remained intact throughout the nineteenth century, often with few changes of ownership.

The largest estates were worked by convict labour but several landowners leased portions to tenants, often former convict servants. Their rents required them to clear the forest land and cultivate it, the landowner then receiving a proportion of the crop. Smaller landowners farmed their own grants, sometimes enlarging their farms by buying out, or marrying into, a neighbouring family. Rural labourers were either assigned convicts or ex-convicts, some of whom were regularly employed, but many were casual labourers, hired according to seasonal needs.

When T. V. Blomfield visited Denham Court in November 1821 he was surprised to see so much cultivation in Airds and Appin. The wheat was almost ready for harvest and the maize would be harvested in March. The native grasses made tolerably good hay. Vegetables, except potatoes, grew well, though he saw no oats, peas or beans.[42]

By the 1820s cereal farming was well established in the Campbelltown district. Although the Hawkesbury settlements remained the largest farming area, the next most important area was the newly cleared lands of Lower and Upper Minto, Airds and Appin. By 1828, 18168 acres (7267 ha) had been cleared in Airds and Appin and 9172 acres (3669 ha) were under cultivation, but this level was not maintained. In 1831 there were 6384 acres (2554 ha) under crop in Airds and Appin of which 4011 acres (1604 ha) were wheat. In 1835 the district of Campbelltown covering the parishes of St Peter, Menangle, Narellan, Appin and Cook had 10 262 acres (4105 ha) under crop. Half the district total, 5354 acres (2142 ha), was grown on the small grants of the old Airds district, now described as the parishes of St Peter and Menangle. Here 2899 acres (1160 ha) were planted with wheat, 1603 acres (641 ha) under grasses for stock feed and 736 acres (294 ha) of maize. There was less farming in Minto, an area dominated by the large estates of Glenfield, Macquarie Fields, Denham Court, Leppington, Varroville, Gledswood and Campbellfield. Officially part of the Liverpool district where only 2222 acres (889 ha) were under crop in 1828, by 1835 only 219 acres (88 ha) of wheat were grown in Minto.[43]

Campbelltown's market for agricultural produce was Sydney. Wheat prices fluctuated widely, affected by competition from imported grain, ranging from 3s 6d to 7 shillings a bushel with fine-quality flour selling from 13s 6d to 19 shillings a bushel. Maize returned from 2s 6d to 4s 6d a bushel. In the growing city there was a steady demand for hay, and if the wheat was unlikely to ripen because of drought or a wet season it was cut green for hay.[44]

William Howe of Glenlee was respected throughout the colony for his knowledge of agriculture and in 1821 his views were sought by Commissioner J. T. Bigge who had been sent to investigate Macquarie's administration. Though discussing the general problems of colonial farming, Howe's views reflected his experience on Glenlee, and his knowledge of the small farmers of Campbelltown.

the present system of husbandry ... is very bad and if continued ... will lead to ruinous consequences. By the constant and close succession of grain crops put into the ground in the slovenly manner which is now customary, all lands (especially those not subject to floods) will in a few years become barren ... requiring more skill and capital to restore their lost fertility than would be necessary to bring land into cultivation from a state of nature. The mode generally pursued has been to clear the land and put in maize without manure, after that Wheat yielding a fair crop considering the management, third crop, wheat again very inferior, fourth worse, fifth foul, full of weeds and not yielding above Six or Eight Bushels an Acre—the land . . . no longer worth cultivating . . . The Forest Lands ought never to have more than two crops of Grain in succession, even if manured when newly broken up, but drilled-green crops, manured & horse & hand hoed, should always be introduced . . . For sowing these, such as Turnips, Rape etc there is generally time after harvest, during the Months of February, March & April, so that they may be fit for use in May, and during the Winter Months to August or even later . . . These green Crops have also another value to the Farmer which is daily increasing with the inclosing of lands, and which arises from the additional means they afford of rearing and fattening Cattle and Sheep.[45]

Howe was not impressed by the small farmers, many of whom he considered:

men of the most depraved life, without moral habits or religious principles; idle and drunken, ignorant of agriculture, and improvident in the highest degree; and from their proligacy and indolence, both unable and unwilling to buy stock & pursue a proper system of husbandry—Instead of living sparingly and laboring (sic) industriously, their practice is, when their Wheat or Maize has (almost spontaneously) come to perfection, to throw away on luxuries, very frequently on spirits, those proceeds which might have purchased stock or have inclosed a garden or field for their potatoes or Green crops. The consequence is that in a few months they are left with scarcely any food or clothing, and remain half-starved and half naked till another crop of Grain gives them the means of again running another round of the same excesses.[46]

Howe acknowledged the rigours of pioneering life. Even the most hard-working person found it difficult to turn forest into farmland.

Family assistance or other labour were essential for a farmer. In 1833 Henry McCudden applied for an assigned convict servant. He was an old man with a wife but no family and needed help to work his small 50-acre

Warby's stone barn at Leumeah, built around 1820–30.

(20 ha) farm at Airds. Transported for life in 1796, McCudden received a conditional pardon and was already farming at Airds in 1813 and was a police constable during Macquarie's administration. His nephew arrived as a convict in 1830 and McCudden wanted him as his assigned servant to assist on the farm and to protect him.[47]

In the area commonly known as Soldiers Flat, fertile alluvial land along the eastern bank of Bunbury Curran Creek, six small grants made in 1812 were intensively cultivated by four ex-convicts in the 1820s. Robert Miles and Ann Johnston had 25 acres (10 ha) of their 43-acre (17 ha) farm under cultivation. Abedmego Munn and his servant Philip Beats had crops on 30 acres (12 ha) of a 48-acre (19 ha) farm. Patrick Murphy and Mary Lawson had all their 12 acres (5 ha) under crop. Murphy's shipmates on the *Three Bees* in 1814 included David and Patrick Noonan, Limerick quarrymen transported for seven years. David Noonan (also called New- man and Newlan), the most successful farmer on Soldiers Flat, had purchased Neal's 80-acre (32 ha) grant from Richard and Christiana Brooks in 1826 for £150, and by 1828 he had 193 acres (77 ha) of which 54 acres (22 ha) were cultivated and he grazed 41 cattle.

Noonan may have benefited from advice from James Ruse, the first emancipist farmer. Mary Ruse was Noonan's housekeeper and possibly the mother of his daughter, Elizabeth. Her marriage had broken down when her husband, John Crook, was sentenced in 1822 for stealing from her father. By 1828 James Ruse, aged 68, no longer farmed his own land but worked as an overseer for Captain Brooks at Denham Court, across the creek from Soldiers Flat. Mary Ruse purchased the farm at Soldiers Flat from David Noonan for £300 in 1847 and retained it until her death in July 1871. Ingleburn House, Ingleburn railway station and Memorial Park were built on her farm.[48]

Drought in 1835 and 1836 caused much hardship for Campbelltown farmers. The maize and hay crops failed completely and the wheat fields yielded barely one-third their average. George Stewart, district magis- trate, reported in February 1836:

There are about 170 small settlers in the district—those having land from 100–30 acres and those having 30–10 acres. Many of the first class have stock in the interior and are in some degree independent of the farms they cultivate and some of the latter likewise consider their farms a secondary object, being mechanics, labourers, dealers, etc, their chief subsistence is derived by working at their trade. The number totally dependent on their farms are about 100. Of these, several have been careful and industrious and would scarcely require assistance while others though embarrassed would from honourable feelings try to struggle through without any. The number who would need assistance to save them from ruin would be about 70, of whom about 20 would be totally destitute before winter is over and from age, infirmity or other cause not able to earn a subsistence by labour.[49]

The Large Estates

Glenfield, Macquarie Fields, Campbellfield and Varroville estates had absentee owners from the late 1820s. Consequently there was little investment and the estates were leased out for grazing land.

Denham Court, 2000 acres (800 ha), was used by Brooks in conjunction with two other estates in the Illawarra to graze cattle. About 1828 Richard Brooks and his family took up permanent residence at Denham Court to be closer to his rural investments, though he maintained his mercantile and charitable interests in Sydney. In the 1828 census Brooks held 13 364 acres (5346 ha), of which 1110 acres (444 ha), mainly at Denham Court, were cleared, and he owned 48 horses, 2127 cattle and 3800 sheep. At Denham Court there were eighteen convict servants. Some laboured on the estate, others were skilled tradespeople, such as his blacksmith and carpenter, and house servants.

About 1832 Brooks engaged architect John Verge to enlarge the small farm cottage on the ridge overlooking Bunbury Curran Valley and dense forest to Port Hacking. Verge designed an elegant country house with a central two-storey block flanked by one-storey wings, drawing his inspiration from Brooks' description of Denham Court in Middlesex. Brooks died there the following year, gored by a bull, and his wife, Christiana, died two years later. Their children commissioned Verge to build a mausoleum and this became the church of St Mary the Virgin, Denham Court.[50]

Just south of Denham Court was Leppington, 'a small ... but very complete establishment', the home of William Cordeaux (1792–1839) and his wife, Ann (1800–77), the sister of Thomas Moore of Moorebank. Cordeaux took up his land at Leppington about 1816. At the census in 1828 William was at their southern property in Sutton Forest while Ann managed the Leppington estate and cared for their three young children. William owned 1500 acres (600 ha) while Ann held 2560 acres (1024 ha). They were the largest sheep and cattle owners in the district and major employers of convict labour, numbering 24 government servants among their 31 employees. William Cordeaux was the only person in the Campbelltown area who, in 1828, employed a large number of shepherds, convict and free. Though based at Leppington, most of the shepherds worked on their Wingecarribee estate.[51]

Colonial-born James Chisholm junior (1806–88) was the son of a Scottish private in the New South Wales Corps who became a successful merchant. James Chisholm senior (1772–1837) acquired land along Bunbury Curran Creek as early as 1814 when he purchased the 1812 grants of Loughlin and Alliott. These farms remained in the Chisholm family until 1880. Following the departure of Macquarie, who owned one-third of St Andrews, the estate was sold to Chisholm. James junior was living on the 4000-acre (1600 ha) estate in 1828 and had 100 acres (40 ha) cultivated, 100 cattle and nine government servants, including two brickmakers, three fencers, a carpenter and gardeners.[52]

William Howe, a Scot, had joined the 1st Royal Scots Regiment as an ensign at the rather late age of 36 in 1813. After the defeat of Napoleon in 1815 Howe and his family migrated to New South Wales. The Reverend Samuel Marsden praised Howe in 1821 as 'a gentleman of great practical knowledge in agriculture, a man of honor, experience, and sound judgement'. Howe increased his 3000-acre (1200 ha) grant by purchasing 500 acres (200 ha) of neighbouring land. He implemented his ideas on improved methods of agriculture and by the 1830s Glenlee estate was one of the best dairy farms in the colony, half a century before dairying was generally practised in the district. Dairying required improved pastures and Glenlee hay found a ready market. The estate was divided into fields with hedges of quince and lemon trees. Howe supported over 60 people, the majority being convict servants whom he described as his 'family'. Howe's paternalistic style extended over the district through his authority as magistrate. He and his wife Mary were referred to with affection as well as respect.[53]

The house on Glenlee was, like most of the gentry homes, built on a commanding hill with extensive views over Menangle and across the river. Howe commissioned architect Henry Kitchen in 1821, but when Kitchen died in April 1822 construction had not yet started. A year later Howe engaged Parramatta builders Robert Gooch and Nathaniel Payten, but twenty months later, the house still unfinished, Howe and his builders went to court over disputed accounts. The house was probably never completed, though only Sarah Mathew commented that it was 'an ugly ill-planned house'. The post office guide was more generous, describing Glenlee as a 'comfortable two-storey house; the staircase and steps are formed of a calcareous drab coloured stone, well suited for interior work'.[54]

Following the death of Thomas Clarkson, Eagle Vale was sold in 1828 to Jemima Jenkins, the wealthy twice-widowed cousin of Lord Nelson. About 400 acres (160 ha) of the 1500-acre (600 ha) estate had been cleared, enclosed by a fence and divided into paddocks. A substantial brick house, 70 feet by 30 feet (21 m by 9 m), commanded a view over the Bow Bowing Valley. Outbuildings included a detached kitchen, dairy, workmen's accommodation, sheds, piggery and an orchard and flower garden. Eagle Vale was one of several properties owned by Jemima Jenkins and, like Brooks at Denham Court, she found Campbelltown a convenient midway location between her grazing lands in the south and her business interests in Sydney. Jemima Jenkins lived at Eagle Vale with her two teenage sons from 1828 until her death in 1842. Criticised by Sarah Mathew as a 'disagreeable vulgar woman', Jemima Jenkins took a quiet interest in the affairs of Campbelltown, signing petitions favouring improved roads, schools and churches.[55]

South of Campbelltown the largest estate was Mount Gilead. Reuben

Uther sold his 400-acre 'Gelead Farm'in 1818, advertising that 50 acres (20 ha) had been cleared of timber and another 50 acres felled. It had been farmed for four years, its annual lease valued at £50. There was a good house and barn on the hill overlooking the Cowpastures. The purchaser in 1818 was Thomas Rose. Like Clarkson of Eagle Vale, Rose was an ex-convict, a publican and a baker in Sydney. In 1819 he was given 300 acres (120 ha) in exchange for land in Sydney on which Macquarie wanted to build a school. By 1821 Rose had consolidated the Mount Gilead estate, purchasing the grants of Early, Byrne, Haydon, Stafford, Wall, Appletree and Rushton before the deeds were formally issued by the government in 1823. Rose continued to live in Sydney until the death of his wife, Elizabeth, in 1826. The following year he moved permanently to Mount Gilead. Two years later he married Sarah Pye of Baulkham Hills.

In 1828 Rose owned 2460 acres (984 ha) of which 480 acres (192 ha) were cultivated, grazed 1020 cattle and 1100 sheep, and employed twelve convict servants at his Appin estate. Farming and grazing were severely limited by lack of water, leading Rose to experiment with water-storage schemes. The elevated position of the estate was ideal for the windmill of dressed sandstone and ironbark which Rose built in 1834. Thomas Rose died in March 1837.

Investment at Mount Gilead under Thomas Rose was impressive. In 1838 there was a large house with a hall, parlours, drawing-rooms and seven bedrooms, Rose having had six children by his first wife and five by his second. Domestic facilities included a detached kitchen, larder, bakehouse (for bread) and a washhouse. The farm buildings were a granary, a large storehouse, barn, cellars, piggeries, stockyard, milking sheds, a six-stall stable, coach house, horse mill, threshing machine and five-storey windmill.[56]

Water Supply

Though located near the Bow Bowing Creek and the George's River, water supply was a constant problem for both farmers and townspeople. Wells and tanks were unable to supply sufficient water to support a large population.

The first large-scale project to improve water supply was undertaken by Thomas Rose on Mount Gilead about 1823. Rose built an embankment of stone and rammed earth across a natural decline in his land and drained the run-off water into an artificial lake. This provided a constant source of water sufficient to withstand the extensive drought of 1829. Rose's efforts appear to be the first successful attempt at water conservation in New South Wales and attracted the attention of nearby settlers and the government. Governor Bourke visited Rose at Mount Gilead during 1833. The stone dam had been expensive but Rose constructed a cheaper dam

The windmill at Mount Gilead, built in 1834 by Thomas Rose. (C. Kerry, c.1886)

of rammed earth near the Campbelltown–Appin Road for the use of his neighbours and travellers.

In November 1832 the inhabitants of Campbelltown decided to build a water reservoir in the town at their own expense. The man behind the project was undoubtedly Thomas Rose, with the support of Campbelltown innkeepers John Hurley and John Patrick, Thomas Meehan and Clerk of Petty Sessions, John Scarr. By February 1833 surveyor Felton Mathew had declared the site suitable. The land chosen, on the hillside between Dumaresq and Allman Streets (allotments 34, 35, 56 and 57), formed a natural basin into which two small creeks flowed. The clay soil was suitable for constructing the embankment wall. The government granted the land, congratulating the people of Campbelltown for their initiative and their example to other communities.

The embankment was not constructed until the following summer. In September 1833 the Campbelltown Committee sought approval to build it further up the hill to avoid expensive earthworks. This resulted in the closure of Stewart Street, between Allman and Dumaresq Streets. The dam was funded by public subscriptions and built by contract in a 'comparatively unskilful and slovenly' manner. Nonetheless, it greatly improved the water supply for the local residents.[57]

This first reservoir had a rammed-earth embankment. In 1838 the colonial government decided, possibly at the suggestion of Campbelltown's police magistrate, Francis Allman, that the reservoir should be improved and constructed of stone. An adjoining reservoir was built by convict gangs from Liverpool, supervised by Major W. H. Christie, Assistant

Engineer. The first stone was laid in September 1838 and work was completed by mid-1839. Convict transportation ended the following year so Campbelltown's water reservoir was probably the last major project in the district built by convict labour. The reservoir was filled by the winter of 1840. Built at a cost of almost £400, it provided Campbelltown with its water supply until 1888. Permanent water increased the value of town land almost overnight.[58]

Campbelltown at work

Most of the local workforce were assigned convicts who laboured for the farmers and settlers. In 1825, 1003 of 1973 residents of Airds, Appin and Minto were assigned convict servants. Another 509 had been convicts but were now free. They became farmers, employing other convicts, or worked as labourers and tradesmen.

Under the assignment system settlers could apply to the local magistrate for a convict servant. Settlers housed, fed and clothed the convict for as long as they required the convict's labour. Unwanted convicts were returned to the government for reassignment. Most of the convicts were unskilled labourers, but some had knowledge of a trade and were called mechanics. These were the most valuable assigned servants.

An 1824 list noted 23 occupations among 216 people living at Campbelltown. About half were unskilled labourers. A further quarter worked on the land as settlers, stock-keepers and overseers. The remaining quarter were tradesmen with the largest group in building trades—ten carpenters, a painter, sawyers, two stonemasons, some quarrymen but no brickmakers. Clothing manufacture employed several people as the district was a long way from shops. There were eight bootmakers, three weavers and spinners and two tailors. Transport repairs were an essential service industry with four blacksmiths, two saddlers and harness-makers and a boatbuilder. Retailing was limited to a baker, two butchers, two publicans and a storekeeper, while professional services were represented by four schoolteachers, a clerk and an engraver.[59]

From the mid-1820s capital was invested in local industries, the most significant and enduring being flour-milling. By 1830 there were three windmills and a horse mill in the Campbelltown district. Two windmills were on the estates of Richard Brooks at Denham Court and John Coghill at Kirkham. The other windmill and a horse mill were operated by William Mannix.

William Mannix of Spring Hill Farm, near Molle's Mains, was Campbelltown's first industrialist. He had arrived free as a merchant's clerk in 1805. During the 'anarchial government' which followed the overthrow of Governor Bligh in 1808, Mannix had purchased promises for land grants totalling 350 acres (140 ha). These he consolidated with his own grant for 50 acres (20 ha) and took up 400 acres (160 ha) in Upper Minto. By the mid-1820s he held over 1000 acres (400 ha) but this was not sufficient to carry his stock, over 500 head of cattle, and he received further land grants. In 1824 he built the Minto Flour Mill, a horse-driven mill at Spring Hill Farm, 5 kilometres from Campbelltown. Settlers brought their wheat to the mill and paid Mannix 1s 6d per bushel to grind it to flour. Mannix cultivated only 83 acres (33 ha) himself. By 1828, as well as three assigned convicts, one a blacksmith, he employed two free carpenters, another blacksmith, a miller and a clerk. His windmill, probably built in 1829, operated until 1836.[60]

By 1833 there were four windmills and two horse mills, the largest concentration outside Sydney with its nine windmills and increasing number of steam mills. Dr John Dight, father-in-law of Hamilton Hume, had built his windmill in Airds by 1833, and in 1834 Thomas Rose built the best known of the Campbelltown windmills at Mount Gilead. Within an impressive stone tower, the machinery of ironbark timber survived relatively intact for almost a century. Rose died in 1837 but the mill continued under lessees. By the late 1830s the Denham Court and Mannix windmills had ceased, but there were others to take their place—George Muckle at Minto; colonial-born William Rixon on the Appin Road from 1838; Captain G. B. Christmas at Mount Gilead, and John Tooth at Narellan, possibly in the old Kirkham mill. Tooth and Newnham of the Kent Brewery were operating a windmill as well as a horse mill in 1841, probably connected with their malt brewery that operated briefly at Narellan from 1845. They appear to have diversified from their city site for some operations from the late 1830s.

Milling required support trades—blacksmiths, wheelwrights and carpenters. All were in demand in Campbelltown. George Graham, colonial-born, ran a blacksmithing business at Minto in 1828, employing no convicts but a carpenter, a blacksmith, two wheelwrights and an apprentice wheelwright.[61]

Tanning and the associated trades of shoemaking and saddlery required access to water. Self-employed bootmakers in 1828 included Samuel Lovely with a three-man business, Richard Woollock and colonial-born George Fieldhouse[62], a cordwainer or shoemaker, who had a small business employing another cordwainer. In 1831 there were three tan pits in Minto and Airds. Thomas Avery of Minto, a ticket-of-leave saddler in 1828, by 1831 operated his own tan pits as did Edward Taylor, a ticket-of-leave shoemaker in 1828, and Charles Hollingshead. Avery was replaced by William Bursill and then by David Hennessy, a Sydney shoemaker who by 1835 owned tan pits at Campbelltown. Taylor, Hennessy and Hollingshead were the major tanners of the district into the 1840s.

Few colonists could afford wax candles. Robert Lack and Paul Huon had candle factories in 1831 in Airds, using animal fats or tallow to make their candles. On the George's River Sydney merchants Cooper and Levey operated two watermills at Holsworthy and Woronora, and

Mathew Kirby, a weaver, had a coarse woollen mill at Lower Minto in the 1830s.

By 1841 the substantial buildings of the district were built from stone. Common building stone was easily found but permanent quarries did not appear until the 1840s. Isaac Dowse, who died in 1853, was a brickmaker in the 1820s, probably using the clay on his Campbelltown allotment in Oxley Street to make bricks. This site was used for brickmaking as late as the 1850s. Lime was needed for building mortar. There was little natural limestone in the Sydney region so the alternative was to burn shells. In the Campbelltown area George Weavers, an ex-convict, had the largest lime-burning operation based at the George's River near Holsworthy. Here in 1828 he employed two convict lime-burners and five ticket-of-leave men who gathered oyster shells from the river and from Aboriginal middens.[63]

General labourers were always in demand in the Campbelltown district, the Police Magistrate, Allman, reporting in 1837 that 100 could find work at wages from £15 to £28 a year with rations, or about 3 shillings a day. House servants, for whom there was less demand, earned about the same. The best-paid jobs were in the building industry. Carpenters, bricklayers and stonemasons could earn £56 a year or 7 shillings a day. Most jobs provided food and accommodation. Those who had to purchase food paid about 5 pence per pound for beef and 19 shillings for 100 pounds (45 kg) of flour. Christiana Blomfield of Denham Court preferred convict servants, rogues though they were, because they knew colonial ways and she thought them more useful than the lazy free immigrants. Farming labourers at Denham Court were paid 10 shillings a week with rations of 10 pounds (4.5 kg) of flour and of meat, 1.5 pounds (680 g) of sugar and 3 ounces (85 g) of tea. Female domestic servants were paid £12–£15 per year.[64]

Farmers also relied on their children's labour to weed crops and feed stock. Some settlers and publicans employed girls as young as eight as domestic servants. Some of these children were orphans in the care of guardians and worked no harder than the children of the household. For others, their parents had been unable to support them and had found them employment. Most were unskilled labourers or servants rather than apprentices. In 1828 there were about 40 children in the Campbelltown district who were not living with their parents. Georgiana Sweetman, aged thirteen, worked as a servant for William Cordeaux. Eight-year-old James Masterman described himself as a servant working for Thomas Burn at Airds.[65]

Neil Campbell and William Byrne were the only storekeepers in Campbelltown in 1828. Public houses partly filled this void in commercial life. The roadside inns of colonial Australia catered for many needs— refreshments for travellers, who were usually walking, basic accommodation, a staging post for coaches and the Royal Mail and a meeting place for local residents where games were played and business conducted. In

1830 new licensing laws required publicans to provide better accommodation for travellers. Under this system eight licences were issued for Campbelltown, about the same number as Maitland, and slightly over half the number in Liverpool. One of the Campbelltown inns received a free licence, valued at £25 per year, to encourage the construction of better quality inns. This was possibly the licence for the new eighteen-room Forbes Hotel, built by Daniel Cooper to replace his building that was converted to the courthouse. By 1833 fourteen licences were issued for Campbelltown, so contemporary comment about the prevalence of inns was not exaggerated. Innkeeping provided the opportunity for several Campbelltown businesspeople to launch their careers.[66]

Along the Campbelltown Road one of the best-known inns was about halfway between the Cross Roads and Campbelltown. At the bridge over Bunbury Creek near Varroville was the Robin Hood Inn which opened in late 1830. Mine host was Thomas Humphries until 1837. In Campbelltown were numerous public houses. In the view of one visitor in 1841 if it were not for the 'numerous grog shops' there would be no town at all. On the northern approaches to the town was ex-convict John Eggleston at the St Patrick's Inn from the late 1820s through the 1840s; the Graham family at the Wheelwright's Arms, and Nathaniel Boon at the Three Brothers Inn. On the corner of Cordeaux and Queen Streets Thomas Hammond's house opened in 1830 under the sign of the King's Arms. From 1832 the licence was held by John Hurley.

Opposite was the Forbes Hotel built in 1830 with Lewis Solomon as the first licensee. J. W. Bridges was the licensee in 1836 when the Forbes Hotel was the venue for a subscription ball and supper for the local races. Aside from a selection of wines, spirits and ales, Bridges offered well-aired beds and excellent stabling. At the southern end of town was the Royal Oak, licensee Michael Byrne, and the Brewer's Arms of William Byrne from 1833 to 1837. Other inns in the 1830s included the Traveller's Rest (Thomas Avery) and the Crown (Joseph Scott) at Upper Minto; the Harrow (John and Catherine Patrick) and the Crown and Anchor (Sarah and Ann Andrews).

Most of the inns were very small but their number did little to encourage sobriety in the population. William Bradbury confessed that he was more frequently drunk than not, his favourite tipple being a cask of rum. The magistrates refused to prosecute when Bradbury's watch was stolen because it was a regular town sport to bet on how long it would take Bradbury to sober up and discover his watch was missing.[67]

One of the most successful of Campbelltown's publicans was John Hurley. An Irishman who arrived with a seven-year sentence in 1824 on the *Prince Regent*, Hurley completed his sentence as a labourer in the service of Captain Terence Murray, who had arrived in 1827 and taken land at Lake Bathurst. When Hurley's sentence expired he became licensee of the King's Arms Inn, Campbelltown, from 1831. This gave him a base to establish a coaching contract. In the mid-1830s with fellow publican Patrick Fennell as partner, Hurley bought and sold hay and cattle from the southern districts, planned the local horseraces, sponsored the Catholic church and attended Governor Bourke's farewell levee. Hurley dissolved his partnership with Fennell in January 1837 at the time of his marriage of Mary Byrne, daughter of the Irish rebel Hugh Byrne.

There were no banks in Campbelltown during these years. Indeed, there was very little cash in circulation, most business being conducted by the exchange of promissory notes. By the late 1830s John Hurley was virtually Campbelltown's private banker, partly because of his extensive business interests but also because of his friendship with fellow Catholic John O'Sullivan, the bank manager for the Commercial Banking Company in Goulburn. Hurley was Irish and Catholic but above all literate. He was trusted in Campbelltown and by Father Therry who used him as his agent.[68]

Transport

The road through Campbelltown to Appin had been built in 1815 and in the 1820s was maintained by convict road gangs. Primitive construction, usually only cutting down trees, removing the stumps and filling the holes, meant that the roads quickly broke up in bad weather. The road from Liverpool to Campbelltown was very hilly and badly designed. The alternative southern road was the old Cowpastures Road further to the west. In 1821 a route through Appin to the Illawara district was discovered and a road was built the following year. With an overland crossing to Bass Strait confirmed by Hume and Hovell in 1824, Campbelltown became the gateway to the southern inland districts and to the south coast.[69]

From 1826 until the opening of the railway in 1858 the most important road for the people of Campbelltown was not the road to Sydney but the road to the southern districts. Cleared by a convict gang in April 1826, the road crossed the Nepean River at the Menangle Ford or Bird's Eye Corner, skirted the eastern side of the Razorback Range to Picton, then went south to Goulburn. A bridge was planned at the Menangle Ford in 1826 but the timber was swept away in a flood before work started.[70]

In 1827 the Cowpasture Bridge was built at Camden 10 kilometres from the Menangle Ford. A new road across Hovell's estate linked Campbelltown with the Cowpastures Road and the bridge. However, the route south from the Cowpasture Bridge led over the treacherous Razorback Ridge and the people of Campbelltown preferred the old route. In August 1830, 72 landowners in Airds, Appin, Upper and Lower Minto requested a convict gang to improve the road from Campbelltown to the Menangle Ford. A year and a half later another numerously signed petition urged repairs as the bad state of the road damaged vehicles and teams.

Surveyor-General Mitchell preferred a third route further east. He argued for two decades that it was the better route, a choice verified by later railway and road engineers, but the colonial government would not approve expenditure on bridges at Pheasant's Nest or Broughton's Pass. Mitchell believed that a straight, flat road would stop bushrangers who attacked on the hills and river crossings where the roads were in worse condition.

Despite eleven voluminous petitions from the residents of Campbelltown and district between 1829 and 1834 urging work on the Menangle Ford road, little was done because the Surveyor-General's office opposed the route. In July 1832 Governor Bourke approved the route through Campbelltown and the Menangle Ford for the Great South Road, but still the survey department hesitated. Proposals for a stone bridge across the river at Menangle were considered in 1834 but flooding posed technical problems. In 1835 a stone causeway was laid to improve the crossing. Deputy Surveyor-General Perry wrote in 1839 that the road from Campbelltown to Menangle and southward should never have been built. It was a 'subject of perpetual erroneous or partial representation', its selection a 'gesture of perverseness' due solely to the weight of local representations.[71]

The road north from Campbelltown to Liverpool was just as bad. In 1831, 163 inhabitants of Airds and the surrounding district complained that it was so broken up that two wagons could not pass without risk of overturning and no-one ventured to travel at night because of the deep holes and ruts. At least 100 bullock teams loaded with produce for Sydney from the southern districts used the road each week.[72]

John Hurley, Campbelltown publican and member of parliament

AUSTRALIAN MEN OF MARK

With the introduction of a colonial postal service in 1828, mail contractors provided coach services to Campbelltown and further south. Following a serious coach accident at Liverpool in 1834, several residents of Campbelltown complained of the furious driving of drunken coachmen incited by 'blackguards and profligate women'. They decided to form a non-profit-making company to run coaches between Campbelltown and Liverpool, but the company failed to raise the capital needed to start its service.[73]

Coach services in the 1830s were expensive and inconvenient. John Ireland, a mail contractor in partnership with Campbelltown publican Charles Morris, offered two services between Sydney and Liverpool, Goulburn and Yass via Campbelltown. The journey between Sydney and Campbelltown took five to six hours and cost 10 shillings, more than a skilled tradesman's daily wage. One coach left Sydney at 7 am, reaching Campbelltown after lunch and returning almost immediately to Sydney. The Royal Mail left Sydney each evening at 5 pm, arrived at Campbelltown at 10 pm, departing for the return journey to Sydney at 3 am. A new road from Appin to the Illawarra over the once impassable Bulli Mountain opened in 1838, increasing traffic via Appin and Campbelltown, and Watkins and Titterton proposed to run a mail coach on this route.[74]

Life in Campbelltown 1820–1840

Two travellers through Campbelltown in about 1830 left colourful descriptions of their impressions of the district, its people and their way of life. One traveller, Alexander Harris, was a free immigrant tradesman; the other was a convict, James Tucker, who wrote about his experiences in his autobiographical novel, *Ralph Rashleigh*. Despite their different social standing, their impressions of home-life in Campbelltown were very similar.

Alexander Harris's first Australian job was as a carpenter in the Illawarra district. To get there he had to walk from Sydney. His mate was a convict, still under sentence. Walking was thirsty work and, as there was rarely drinkable water along the way, they called at roadside inns. Harris was surprised that the colonists preferred to drink Bengal rum and water rather than beer and everyone smoked a short pipe. Liverpool was a straggling, pretty little country town beside the river. The road to Campbelltown passed through a forest which was ablaze from a bushfire. Terrified possums, goannas, snakes and bandicoots ran from the fire and blazing trees fell across the road.

About midnight Harris and his convict companion stopped on the outskirts of Campbelltown at the home of an ex-convict who was splitting timber and making fences for a local settler. It was one room, 6 by 9 feet

(1.8 by 2.7 m), made from sheets of bark with a bark roof. The hut had been built with green wood which had twisted in every direction as it dried. Along one wall was the chimney and on the facing one a bark bunk. Blocks of wood, about 18 inches (45 cm) long, substituted for chairs. Supper was a generous helping of hot fried beefsteaks, damper bread and quart pots of tea. When it was time 'to pig down', their host cleared the floor, with his guests standing in the chimney, put the wood blocks under the table and made a bed on the floor with layers of clothing, spread over with half a dozen sheep fleeces. The wooden blocks became pillows. Mosquitoes were repelled by the 'dull peculiar scented smoke' of dried cow dung smouldering on the fire. Breakfast was boiled salted beef, cake baked on the hot hearth and tea.[75]

James Tucker arrived as a convict in 1827 and was assigned in the Airds district. He drew on this experience for his fictional character Ralph Rashleigh. Like Harris, Rashleigh travelled the colony on foot with his worldly goods tied in a handkerchief. He wore a stout pair of boots, trousers, shirt, a blue jacket, a black silk handkerchief around his neck and a straw hat. He thought Liverpool one of the dullest villages in Australia, despite its grand government buildings. Rashleigh spent a night with an Irish family near Liverpool. Supper was fried pork, damper bread and tea, lots of eggs but little butter and no potatoes. Plates, knives, forks and tablecloth were superfluous as the family cut their meat from a dish in the centre of the table with a pocket knife and ate the pork on bread. Light came from cups filled with grease with rag wicks. The family shared their cottage with three pet pigs, a sick calf, a favourite mare recently delivered of a foal and some fowls which roosted in the rafters. After the meal the table was cleared for a rum cask and tobacco, and the neighbours came in to dance to the beat of a tin dish tambourine until the party disintegrated into a fight.

It took Rashleigh and his companion a morning to walk from Liverpool to 'the few scattered huts then dignified by the name of Campbelltown' where Rashleigh visited the home of an ex-convict farmer. The outer walls were split timber coated with mud daub and whitewash, the roof of bark and a verandah held up with rough wooden pillars around which some flowers grew. The floor was cow dung and ashes trod solid. The interior walls were whitewashed and decorated with bunches of scented native shrubs. Stools and tables were made of rough timber scoured white. Their midday meal was salt pork, pumpkins, bread cooked under an inverted iron pot and tea. The evening meal was the main meal of the day with short cakes, light bread, fresh butter, cream for the tea, young fowls broiled and plenty of eggs.

Bob, the farmer, had served his whole sentence with a master in Campbelltown, including four years as overseer while he held a ticket-of-leave. When free, he found some undeveloped land owned by a military officer who had left the colony. He arranged with the officer's agent to occupy 1280 acres (512 ha) on condition of clearing 50 acres (20 ha) over seven years. Later he extended this to a fourteen-year-lease to clear another 50 acres. It was hard work felling, stumping and burning off timber. Bob was able to borrow an oxen from his former master to yoke to the plough and this was easier than breaking up the land with a hoe. He had a herd of eight milking cows, costing £20 each. He hoped that at the end of his fourteen-year lease he would have saved enough to buy his own farm.

Bob relied on the labour of his wife and children. His wife helped him on the cross-cut saw, put up fences and drove the bullocks behind the plough, working harder than any convict servant as she and her children would reap the benefit. The children weeded the tobacco crop. Bob wore a striped shirt, sleeved waistcoat, duck trousers, all well mended, and patched boots. His wife wore a dimity jacket buttoned to the throat, hip length with short sleeves, a blue dungaree petticoat, checked apron and homemade slippers. The children were dressed in smocks of coarse fabric which covered them from neck to ankle, with straw hats and no shoes.[76]

The families that Harris and Rashleigh visited were probably typical of the labouring families and small farmers in the district. The census of 1841 revealed that 54 per cent of houses outside Campbelltown itself were built of wood. More prosperous farmers, such as the Kearns family at Epping Forest or John Farley at Denfield, lived in brick single-storey cottages with stone-flagged verandahs. Campbellfield and Glenfield were also built in this simple style. Compared to English houses there was little furniture and the floor was more usually covered with Indian matting than carpet. Kitchens were detached so that the heat of the kitchen fires did not make the house uncomfortable. Few utensils were needed—an iron pot for boiling meat, or turned upside down for an oven, a frying pan, some saucepans and a tomahawk for a meat cleaver.[77]

Within the town of Campbelltown brick and stone buildings predominated because of covenants which required buildings of specified values to be erected within a few years of occupation. By 1841 there were 77 buildings within the town, most of stone or brick. Contemporary descriptions of Campbelltown, concentrating on the inns, ignored this evidence of considerable investment. The houses of the Byrne brothers typified the extremes of style—the grand two-storey Glenalvon and the neighbouring single-storey cottage, Richmond Villa.[78]

Horseracing was the most organised sport in the 1820s and 1830s. As early as June 1827 a race meeting was held by Colonel Henry Dumaresq for the Sydney Turf Club in the bush near Campbelltown. In June 1836 a meeting was called at John Hurley's King's Arms Inn to form a committee for a subscription race meeting. John Dight, Charles Byrne, Hugh Watt and Joseph Ward were stewards, John Hurley, judge, Patrick Fennell, secretary and John Chippendall, clerk of the course. A two-day race meeting was planned for September. All imported horses and locally bred champions from imported thoroughbred sires were barred so that local horses would be more evenly matched. A crowd from a radius of 30 kilometres attended the races, a native dog hunt, in which the women took as much enjoyment as the men, and cock-fighting for a purse of £50, a larger sum than the prizes for the horseraces. The final event of the programme was a women's race in which six local 'lasses', 'exhibiting uncommon good judgement and skill', raced their horses around the track to win a saddle.[79]

The inns were the only community meeting place apart from the churches or the courthouse. Informal competitions of strength and endurance from foot races to prize fights, always with bets on the side, were commonplace. The large number of public houses in small towns like Campbelltown was seen by visitors such as James Backhouse as evidence that 'drunkenness, profligacy, and dishonesty' were prevalent in the district. Some were surprised by colonial preference for overproof Bengal rum instead of beer and believed that this was a major factor in premature death.[80]

In 1827 Nathaniel Fowler found himself before the magistrates. His offence against law and order was 'throwing in a fit of passion a teapot of hot tea at his fellow servant Mary Niver and continually abusing her for being an Irishwoman'. Anti-Irish prejudice was strong in colonial Australia. For some observers the most obvious feature of Campbelltown in the 1820s and 1830s was its Irishness, though it was not as Irish as Bankstown which was known as Irishtown. The settlement of Campbelltown had coincided with the end of the sentences of many Irishmen transported for their involvement in the troubles of 1798–1803 and James Meehan encouraged them to take grants in the new district. The pattern was strengthened in the 1820s and 1830s by intermarriage among their children and more recent Irish convict arrivals. This sense of identity was further reinforced by support for Father J. J. Therry, before and after his term as their parish priest. John Vardy of Campbelltown was one of Therry's executors. Maryfields, Therry's farm near Campbelltown, passed to the Rudd family of Campbelltown and Wagga Wagga.[81]

In 1820 Minto, Airds and Appin were the frontier, but as the frontier moved south, following in the tracks of Campbelltown explorers like Hume and Throsby, so did the population. In the early 1820s convicts under sentence formed the largest part of the district's population. The 1828 census recorded 1691 people living in Airds and Appin. Eight years later that figure had dropped slightly to 1546 in the districts now defined as the parishes of St Peters, Menangle and Appin. The most populated district was the parish of St Peters, of which Campbelltown formed the centre and where 50 per cent of the district lived. Convict transportation to New South Wales ended in 1840. By then Campbelltown had already lost much of its convict identity. Over one-third of the population of the

Campbelltown Police District in 1841 were Australian-born. Free immigrants formed just under 30 per cent of the population.[82]

Frederick Fisher and his ghost

In the history of Campbelltown one incident has captured the imagination of generations—the murder of Frederick Fisher and the appearance of his ghost. Five men were arrested. One was hanged. All, including Fisher himself, had arrived as convicts.

Frederick George James Fisher was born in London on 28 August 1792, a son of James (d. 1830) and Ann Fisher, London bookbinders and booksellers of Cripplegate and Greenwich. Of average height with a fair complexion and brown hair, by his early twenties Frederick Fisher was a shopkeeper, unmarried though possibly the father of two children. Fisher obtained possession of forged banknotes, either innocently through his work or deliberately to pass through his shop. He was arrested, tried at the Surrey Gaol Delivery on 26 July 1815 and sentenced to fourteen years' transportation to Australia.

Fisher arrived in Sydney a year later, one of 187 convicts aboard the *Atlas*, a schooner of 501 tons (511 tonnes), and was sent to Liverpool. He was probably assigned to John Wylde or his brother-in-law, J. J. Moore, both of whom had land at Cabramatta and were senior legal officials. Frederick Fisher could read and write and Wylde's father, the crown solicitor, recommended Fisher to the colonial administrator, J. T. Campbell, who attached Fisher to his staff. Literate men were rare and it was not unusual to have convict clerks. Campbell's office was an ideal situation to learn about the colony. Within two years Fisher was assigned as superintendent to the Waterloo Flour Company. This company, under William Hutchinson, Samuel Terry and Daniel Cooper, was owned and managed by ex-convicts. Through its manufacturing activities, its commercial ventures and its mortgaging power, the Waterloo Company was the most influential and dynamic enterprise in colonial New South Wales. It provided Frederick Fisher with valuable contacts.[83]

In 1818, within two years of his arrival, Fisher and two partners, George Duncan and John Walker, launched a public company to manufacture paper. Duncan had the technical knowledge, Walker would provide the raw materials and Fisher would be manager and salesman. To raise capital for machinery they sold shares to fifteen merchants, including Campbelltown residents Robert Jenkins, Richard Brooks and Thomas Rose. By June 1818 they were established with a waterwheel operating the millstones on John Hutchinson's land. Hutchinson, the colony's 'mad scientist', was always ready with a scheme for scientific experiment and fantastic machines. With Simeon Lord, he had already tried unsuccessfully to make glass and cloth and was experimenting with paint, paper and dyes. Macquarie considered the genius of Hutchinson to be 'unsteady'.

Hutchinson was a troublesome landlord and Fisher appealed to Macquarie to stop Hutchinson from diverting water from his mill. In July 1818 four Sydney magistrates, all shareholders in Fisher's company, ordered Hutchinson to give Fisher use of the premises for six months rent free as recompense for his interference. The paper-making venture did not prosper and Thomas Clarkson of Eagle Vale, Campbelltown and Sydney probably bought the mill in 1820.[84]

Fisher returned to work for J. T. Campbell, this time as managing clerk in the Provost-Marshal's office to which Campbell had been appointed in 1819. The Provost-Marshal was the chief sheriff of the court, responsible for prisoners before trial, executions, sale of goods for debts and bail applications. It was probably here that Fisher acquired the forged pardon later found among his possessions. Fisher's next position, on the recommendation of solicitor James Norton, was as quit rent clerk in the surveyor-general's department. Meehan had been put in charge of quit rent collections in 1814, but had been too busy with his exploration and survey work to collect them. His application to retire was delayed until the backlog of paperwork was cleared. Meehan needed an extra clerk—Frederick Fisher.[85]

In 1822 Fisher had served half his sentence and applied for a ticket-of-leave and permission to rent or purchase a small farm at Newcastle as he had £300 to invest. He received a ticket-of-leave but turned south, to Campbelltown. By 1825, when he applied unsuccessfully for a conditional pardon, Fisher owned four farms—50 acres (20 ha) at Cabramatta; 30 acres (12 ha) at Appin; 53 acres (21 ha) on the Nepean River at Upper Minto, all under cultivation, and 32 acres (13 ha) adjoining Campbelltown, with stone and brick buildings worth £800. The land at Campbelltown lay between the main road and Bow Bowing Creek and was part of Joseph Phelps 140-acre (56 ha) grant, issued in 1816 but occupied by Phelps as early as 1813. Phelps sold 30 acres (12 ha) to Thomas Clarkson of Eagle Vale who mortgaged it to Daniel Cooper. Cooper foreclosed and sold the farm to his former employee, Frederick Fisher, retaining an £80 mortgage over the farm. Fisher prospered at Campbelltown. In December 1824 he tendered to supply wheat to the government at Liverpool, the only person from the Campbelltown area to do so.[86]

Fisher turned his attention to speculative building in Campbelltown. His first venture was the Horse and Jockey Inn, built in mid-1825 for Fisher by local carpenter William Brooker. Brooker disputed payment and took his claim to the magistrates who found in his favour. When Brooker, not quite sober, called at the inn in late 1825 to demand his money, Fisher pulled a knife. Brooker was not badly hurt but all assumed that Fisher would face a lengthy gaol term. Fisher was concerned less about himself than his property—his land, houses, horses, pigs and wheat—and gave a power of attorney to his neighbour to manage his affairs during his imprisonment.

Fisher's neighbour was William George Worrall who had arrived on the *Marquis of Wellington* with a life sentence in 1815. He was a shoemaker by trade and, like Fisher, a Londoner by birth. Obtaining his ticket-of-leave in February 1823, Worrall rented a small farm at Campbelltown from William Bradbury. Worrall was considered an honest and industrious man and the most appropriate person to act as Fisher's agent.

Fisher stood trial for assault but Brooker's evidence was so abusive that the court considered the assault had been provoked and Fisher received a light sentence and a £50 fine. Fisher soon returned to his speculative building in Campbelltown. By April 1826 he had a large, three-storey brick building which he offered to sell to the government as a barracks for troops. Nearby he had started another building which he offered to the government as a gaol and courthouse. Both buildings lay 'mouldering to decay' a decade after the murder of their owner. Later the site was acquired for an hotel and still later became a branch of the Bank of New South Wales.[87]

Fisher's farm had no residence so he, his employees and convict servants lodged with his neighbour, George Worrall. Worrall's house was about 16.5 metres long, with three large rooms and skillion verandahs, and was located on the western side of Queen Street, south from Allman Street. In the winter of 1826 Worrall had a full house. Aside from himself and Fisher, there were two bricklayers and two drainers employed by Fisher and two convict servants employed by Worrall.

On the evening of 17 June 1826 Frederick Fisher disappeared. Worrall announced that his neighbour had sailed for England because he was concerned about a charge of forgery made against him by Nathaniel Boon. Three weeks after Fisher's disappearance Worrall sold Fisher's horses and personal belongings, claiming that Fisher had sold them to him before sailing. Worrall offered Fisher's horses to James Coddington. Coddington knew Fisher's handwriting and was sure that the papers were forgeries, probably written by John Vaughan, a ticket-of-leave man who lived in Worrall's house and kept his accounts.

Coddington was agent for Daniel Cooper who held the mortgage on Fisher's farm. He alerted Cooper and when Worrall approached Cooper for title to Fisher's farm, Cooper reported Fisher's disappearance to his solicitor, James Norton. Norton knew Fisher—he had recommended Fisher for the job with Meehan—and instituted the first official enquiries in a letter to the attorney-general on 11 September 1826. In this letter Norton claimed that either Worrall knew of Fisher's accidental death and had concealed it or that Worrall was involved in his murder.[88]

Fisher's sentence did not expire until 1829 so it was unlikely that he would return to England and risk imprisonment as a convict at large. Fisher was prospering in the colony and, despite recent conflicts, had

Queen Street looking south, around 1909. Fieldhouse's Jolly Miller Hotel (later the Commonwealth Hotel), built in 1858 and the Fieldhouse Brothers' store (later Tayor's store), built 1878, face Kendall's mill on Fisher's Ghost Creek.

much property and few debts. The residents of Campbelltown knew him as 'an artful and covetous' man who would not have left without trying to make some profit from his possessions. His brother, Henry, also a convict, had not known of his brother's intention to leave for England.

Worrall was arrested on suspicion of Fisher's murder on 17 September 1826 and Campbelltown magistrate, the Reverend Thomas Reddall, began an investigation into the movements of Worrall and the other inhabitants of his house. After repeated questioning, Worrall alleged that Fisher had indeed been murdered, not by himself but by four of the men in his house who had beaten Fisher to death on a dunghill in the backyard. Worrall had kept silent because of threats to his safety. The four men were arrested. All were confined in Liverpool gaol but no action could be taken because there was no body. The *Sydney Gazette* on 23 September 1826 announced a £20 reward (equal to a year's wages) for information leading to the recovery of Fisher's body or proof of his departure from the colony.

A month later, on 20 October 1826, the Campbelltown police were instructed to intensify the search for Fisher's body. On 25 October 1826 two boys, Rixon and Burrows, were returning home across Fisher's farm and noticed bloodstains on a fence. Closer investigation found a lock of hair the same colour as Fisher's hair and a tooth. Constable Luland searched the wheat paddock, prodding the ground with an iron bar, but found nothing. Old John Warby suggested Aboriginal trackers be called in. The ground was marshy, and Gilbert, the tracker from Liverpool, tasted the water in the puddles and announced 'white fellow's fat there'! They followed the puddles, prodding the ground, and found Fisher's remains in a shallow grave on Worrall's land.

The body was partially decomposed, 'a soddened death-like sickly white', and the flesh fell from the hands and feet when touched. The face and head had been shockingly disfigured but the clothes, a plum-coloured jacket, a full-bloused shirt and buckles on the braces were easily recognisable as Fisher's. The coroner, Mr Horsley, was sent for; the body was removed from the ground and a coronial enquiry held the following day. Formal identification was impossible due to decomposition and inse-cure storage of the remains: 'since he had been out of the hole those who had the care of the body had let the dogs eat the putrid flesh of the legs'.[89]

Following the coronial investigation, the remains of Frederick George James Fisher were buried in St Peters graveyard on 27 October 1826. Despite his wealth, no-one provided him with a headstone. His brother Henry commented 'I myself buried him as decent as I could. I was seven weekes looking for the boddy witch gave me a grate cutting up.'[90]

Three days after the discovery of Fisher's body Worrall was committed for trial in Sydney for the murder of Fisher and the theft of his property. The Criminal Court sat before Chief Justice Francis Forbes in Sydney on 2 February 1827. The evidence against Worrall was largely circumstantial but Worrall was the only one who benefited in any material way from Fisher's death. The jury took fifteen minutes to find him guilty. He was sentenced to death and executed three days later on Monday 5 February 1827. On the scaffold he confessed that he had killed Fisher by accident, thinking him a horse in the wheat crop, and was then too frightened to confess. Worrall's confession was never accepted in Campbelltown by those who had seen the injuries to Fisher's head. Worrall had assumed when he was appointed Fisher's agent that all Fisher's property would belong to him. Disappointed by Fisher's release from prison, he had murdered Fisher to obtain the property.[91]

After Fisher's death

Fisher died without leaving a will. His considerable property—cash, anim-als, two or three farms and some buildings—was entrusted to the Curator of Intestate Estates. On 17 March 1827 a mare, foal and clothing were auctioned by the Registrar of the Supreme Court as was the lease of the farm at Campbelltown. In December 1827 Cooper and Levey, who held the mortgage on Fisher's inn, took action against Jackson, Fisher's partner and the licensee.[92]

Fisher's brother, Henry, lodged a claim as heir. Robert Henry William Fisher had been transported, aged 21, for seven years in 1818 and had arrived in Sydney on the *Baring* in June 1819. His claim was not accepted by the Registrar of the Supreme Court, G. G. Mills. Mills wrote to Fisher's mother in August 1827, more than a year after Frederick Fisher's dis-appearance, informing her that her 'very unfortunate son Frederick' had been murdered. Papers among Fisher's possessions suggested that he had a wife and daughter in England. Proof of his daughter's legitimacy was required to settle the estate in her favour. Whether Fisher had a child in England is uncertain. No claim was made on her behalf.[93]

Ann Fisher of Shoreditch made a statutory declaration in January 1832 that her son Samuel Fisher, bookseller of the parish of Bethnal Green, Middlesex, was the brother and next of kin to Frederick Fisher. Henry Fisher had believed that his elder brother, Samuel, was dead, but Samuel was alive and wanted Frederick's estate. The family in England entrusted settlement of the estate to an agent rather than to Henry who was already in the colony. Their agent did nothing. By July 1831 Mrs Fisher and Samuel were willing to sell the estate to Henry Fisher of Windsor but Henry could not afford to buy it.

In April 1835 Henry Fisher married Elizabeth Owen at Parramatta, the ceremony performed by the Reverend Robert Forrest. Frederick Fisher had been a well-lettered man but his brother Henry was barely literate. In September 1835 Henry wrote home deploring the mismanagement of his brother's affairs. Nine years had passed since Frederick's murder and his property had dwindled to nothing because Henry had no authority to act. Property worth £300 and £107 in cash had been held by the court trustee in 1831, but by 1835 claims against the estate had exhausted the funds. Aside from the farm at 'Cambleton', Henry knew of other property but he required power of attorney to act.[94]

No further action was taken by the Fisher family until the 1840s. By this time the ghost story was in circulation. About 1842 Frederick Fisher's nephew, Samuel, son of his brother Samuel, migrated to Australia to find out about the estate. The family was concerned by reports of the fraudulent activities of J. E. Manning, guardian of intestate estates. Manning was declared bankrupt in the depression of 1841 and most of the funds of which he was trustee were lost. Samuel Fisher junior met his uncle Henry at Parramatta and wrote home, urging that a power of attorney be sent as there was still a farm worth many hundreds of pounds and Henry knew of other property. Henry died in July 1844. Young Samuel remained in Sydney, married in 1849 and, still without any letter of authority from his father, tried intermittently over the next fifteen years to get Frederick Fisher's estate settled, though he never went out to the farm at Campbelltown.

The legend of Fisher's ghost

The legend of Fisher's ghost is the earliest and best-known Australian ghost story. 'The Spirit of the Creek', an anonymous poem of 29 verses, was published in *Hill's Life in New South Wales*, a Sydney literary paper, in September 1832, six years after the discovery of Fisher's body. The poem was prefaced with a note that it was based on the murder of poor F***** at Campbelltown and the details in the poem correspond with contemporary accounts. However, a new factor is the ghost who arouses suspicion of murder, leading to the discovery of the body. 'Fredro', a wealthy ex-convict, is murdered by his friend, 'Wurlow'. A pale, blood-covered spectre appears to 'Falvonis' on his way home from the inn and a search in daylight near the bridge where the ghost appeared leads Gilbert, a black tracker, to the mangled corpse in its unhallowed and lonely grave. The ghost is appeased by the execution of 'Wurlow' and never seen again.

Four years later 'Fisher's Ghost: A Legend of Campbelltown' was published anonymously in the first issue of *Tegg's Monthly Magazine* in March 1836. It claimed that most of those involved were still alive and could verify the truth about the appearance of Fisher's ghost. In this account a drunken and dissolute Fisher is imprisoned for debt and, at Worrall's suggestion, makes over his property to Worrall to defraud his creditors. A week after his release from prison, Fisher disappears. Six weeks later at 10 pm on a cloudy moonlit night, Hurley sees Fisher's ghost sitting on a fence. Hurley faints, strikes his head and during a week of delirium raves about the ghost. The magistrates suspect foul play, Gilbert is called in and the body uncovered. The author of this version may have been journalist William Kerr. The magazine was published by the Tegg brothers, sons of a London bookseller and publisher who had arrived in New South Wales in 1834. The Teggs may have known the Fisher family who were also London booksellers.[95]

The earliest known reference to the ghost by someone who was involved in the search for Fisher was written by Thomas Leathwick Robinson about 1838. Robinson had arrived as a convict in 1823 with a fourteen-year sentence. As he was a literate man he was sent to Campbelltown to teach in the Church of England school. Robinson identified Fisher's clothing at the coronial hearing and at the Supreme Court, and drew a plan of the scene of the crime. Robinson's account was written more than ten years after the event when he was free. He gave it to the Reverend Richard Taylor, assistant chaplain at Liverpool and relieving minister at Campbelltown between the death of Reddall in November 1838 and the arrival of Forrest in July 1839.

Robinson described 'a strange circumstance' which occurred after the discovery of the bloodstains on the fence but before the Aboriginal trackers were called in. Farley, a wealthy and respectable farmer, had been drinking heavily at Patrick's Inn. He and a companion were returning home past Worrall's house, argued and separated. At this point Farley claimed he saw Fisher's ghost—'it sat upon the rail at the bridge [over the creek in Queen Street], looked like dried leather, it beconed [*sic*] to him and pointed backwards'. Robinson was sceptical, writing that it was

strange that an injured spirit should appear only to a half tipsy man, and that at a time his temper was in a state of great excitement and perhaps the leather-like figure might be some sun-burnt labouring man who sat there enjoying the folly of two sincere friends calling each other ugly names.[96]

Though John Hurley saw the ghost in the Tegg version, in most accounts John Farley of Denfield (1787?–1841) was named as the man who saw Fisher's ghost in October 1826. A native of Surrey, England, Farley was transported for life and arrived on the *Guildford* in 1812. He obtained a conditional pardon and by 1828 was a prosperous farmer living with his wife Margaret on their 325-acre (130 ha) farm on the Appin Road, south from Campbelltown. In 1826 John Hurley was still under sentence and did not become a prosperous man until the mid-1830s.[97]

The ghost story quickly gained credence in the late 1830s as the reason for Norton reporting Fisher's disappearance or for indicating the spot where the body was buried. Farley maintained until his death in 1841 that he had seen a ghost. Later his wife claimed that he had invented the ghost because he had been drinking with Fisher and Worrall the night Fisher disappeared. He had seen them walk home together and suspected that Worrall had something to do with Fisher's disappearance. The ghost story was put about to ease his conscience yet provoke some action. If so, Farley waited almost four months before taking any action. Norton was solicitor for both Fisher and Farley so it is possible that Farley told Norton of his fears, prompting Norton to make official enquiries.[98]

In 1840, while Farley was still alive, two young men attended classes at Campbelltown with the Reverend Robert Forrest. One was the son of the solicitor Norton, who told his school friends that his father had instituted enquiries into Fisher's disappearance because Farley saw the ghost. Young Norton, later senior partner in the Sydney law firm Messrs Norton and Smith, published his memories of his father's involvement in the case in 1892. The other schoolboy, the Reverend James Hassall, remembered the ghost story in his memoirs of Old Australia in 1902.

Fisher's ghost proved endlessly fascinating for publishers. R. M. Martin referred to Gilbert, the tracker, in his *History of the British Colonies* (1836). Charles Dickens' *Household Words* (1855) included a version of the ghost story by John Lang, as did the French magazine *L'Ami de la Maison* the following year. Marcus Clarke, author of *For the Term of His Natural Life*, referred to it in 1875. The *Australian Town and Country Journal* sent a correspondent to Campbelltown in 1880 to interview old residents about the ghost. W. H. Rusden included it in his *History of Australia* in 1883 as did W. H. Suttor in *Australasian Stories Retold* (1887). James Norton told his reminiscences to the *Daily Telegraph* in 1892 and Hassall's account appeared in 1902. In that year B. R. Wise KC, attorney-general and minister of justice for New South Wales, defended the ghost story before a sceptical English audience at Oxford. Andrew Lang the following year read Justice Forbes' original case notes to write his *Truth about Fisher's Ghost* (1903). Generations later in 1960 Douglas Stewart, poet and playwright, wrote an historical comedy, *Fisher's Ghost*.[99]

Perhaps the strangest testimony to the impact of the story of Fisher's ghost is the completeness of the legal records surrounding Fisher's disappearance and Worrall's trial. The case remains the best-documented colonial legal drama. Aside from the newspaper accounts, other surviving records include verbatim notes of the trial by the chief clerk of the Supreme Court, John Gurner; documents written by Fisher to prove Worrall's forgery; the proceedings of the preliminary investigation at Campbelltown Police Court; the original statement by the police on the discovery of Fisher's body; a hand-coloured plan of the scene of the crime, and Robinson's eyewitness account. Even the original list of convicts on the *Atlas* in 1815 carried a marginal note against Fisher's name— 'murdered'! Only Robinson mentioned the ghost.[100]

Three

1840–1880

BETWEEN 1840 and 1880 New South Wales was transformed from a convict settlement to a self-governing colony. Transportation of convicts to New South Wales ended in 1840, and the dramatic growth of population and wealth in the gold rush era of the 1850s effectively disguised the convict past. In 1860 Isabella Tyson was proudly introduced to the visiting Duke of Edinburgh as the mother of the richest man in the colony. No-one commented, in public, that she had arrived as a convict in 1809.

The population of Campbelltown from the 1840s to the 1870s was small with never more than 1000 people in the town, and often fewer because of fluctuations in casual work on the railway and farms. In 1856 children under fourteen formed 44 per cent of the population with adults over the age of 60 only 3 per cent. A little over half the residents (52 per cent) were Australian-born. The largest group of migrants were English (25 per cent) and Irish (16 per cent). There were more Germans (182 individuals) than Scots (179) and nine Chinese. Most lived in weatherboard or slab cottages with a bark or shingled roof. Only six cottages had corrugated-iron roofs.[1]

Campbelltown suffered a continuing drain of people, funds and resources to the southern districts. The drift south was most noticeable among the Irish Catholic families who had formed such a large proportion of the original grantees. Their land in Minto, Airds and Appin was not as fertile as land further south and the 'perennial Irish obsession with land and livestock' drove them into the frontier.[2]

Hume and Hovell first blazed the trail to the south in 1824 and they were soon followed by relatives, friends and neighbours. From the late 1830s the route to the south led also to new settlements at Port Phillip and South Australia where there were markets for livestock and meat. Prospects in the southern districts became more attractive when free land grants were abolished. From 1831 land around Campbelltown had to be purchased, but further south land was held on squatting licences from 1836 and leases from 1847. Those who already had land in Campbelltown rarely owned more than a few hundred acres. In the south they counted their land in tens of thousands of acres. Aside from the outlay for stock, little capital was needed. Campbelltown's squatters were not rich free settlers but ex-convicts and their colonial-born offspring. The exodus of the younger generation was accelerated by lack of land around Campbelltown where most of the large estates remained intact until the 1880s.

Squatting provided opportunities not available in Campbelltown, but most squatting families retained an almost sentimental attachment to their earlier home, rarely selling their Campbelltown farms and houses. Many retired back to Campbelltown. Whilst the families prospered, the town did not. Family capital and enterprise was directed to the squatting stations and little was invested in Campbelltown.

Darby Murray received a 56-acre (22 ha) grant at Airds in 1816. He purchased more land in the Campbelltown area and on the Lachlan he held 16000 acres (6400 ha) on a squatting licence. In 1839 he married Martha Dwyer of Campbelltown and settled his Campbelltown lands on her and her daughters while his sons had the southern lands at Yass. William Bridle was in 1828 an assigned convict at Macquarie Fields, married to a colonial-born woman. He went with his family south and by 1850 was a squatter at Tumut occupying 12000 acres (4800 ha). They remained in the south yet a connection lingered with Campbelltown where Bob Bridle kept the toll gate on the road at Denham Court in the 1860s.[3]

A brief inspection of the leaseholders in the squatting districts reveals extensive occupation of the Lachlan, Murrumbidgee and Maneroo by Campbelltown families (see Table 3.1). Others went south looking for work or occupied land without paying for a squatting licence. Some purchased stations from the original occupiers. John Warby was at Gundagai, the furthest station in the south-west, in 1829. William Ray teamed up with Harry Angel, one of the convicts with Hume and Hovell, to establish Uardry station at Hay by 1839. Luke Reddall, son of Reverend Reddall, had a station on the Murrumbidgee in 1840. E. L. Moore, later of Badgally, Campbelltown, squatted on the Lachlan, and the Ashcroft family had stations at Tumut.

The railway

The drift to the south was reinforced by construction of the Great Southern Railway. In May 1846 a meeting was called by Sydney merchant F. W. Unwin to form the Great Southern and Western Railway Company to build a railway from Sydney to Goulburn and Windsor. The colony was

Table 3.1 Squatting licences held by Campbelltown families, 1847–1850[4]

Name	Run	Acres[a]
Lachlan pastoral district		
George Barber	Nimby	31 360
Thomas Bray	Narraba	24 000
William Broughton	Burroowa	13 400
James Fitzpatrick	Cucumla	56 320
Edward & William junior Howe	Wedgagallong	11 500
William Hovell	Bellingeranoil	48 000
John Hurley	Cootamondra	50 000
John Hurley	Houlahan's Creek	40 000
John Jenkins	Tooyal	25 600
Darby Murray	Dunderalligo	16 000
William Mulholland	Stony Creek	13 000
Isaac Rudd	Houlong	19 200
John Scarr	Marengo	40 000
James & William Tyson	Geramy	22 400
Murrumbidgee pastoral district		
John Bray	Berry Jerry	86 400
Thomas Chippindall	Naas	15 360
John Dight	Bungowannah	64 000
A. A. Huon	Gerogery	38 000
Edward & William junior Howe	Long Point	3500
Robert Pitt Jenkins	Bangus	25 000
Robert Pitt Jenkins	Brewarrena	45 000
John Keighran	Brundell	13 000
Thomas & John Keighran	Dudal Comer	60 000
Redfern and Alexander	Moroca	64 000
James Rudd	Wogangobiramby	40 320
Charles Throsby	Warcoal Creek	30 000
Rev. J. J. Therry	Billabong	50 000
John Vardy	Eughranna	15 000
James Warby	Walbundery	40 000
James Warby	Burrangong	50 000
E. Woodhouse	Yathong	19 200
Maneroo pastoral district		
Thomas Valentine Blomfield	Coollamatong	35 000
William Bridle	Island Lake	12 000
Amos Crisp	Jimen Buen	30 720
John Eccleston	Doodle	10 240
John Hosking	Glenbog	32 000
John Pendergrass	Homeo	25 000
John Pendergrass	Cottage Creek	15 000
John Pendergrass	Moonbar	24 000
Charles Throsby	Maharatta	22 000
Charles Throsby	Kybean	20 000
Ellen Woodhouse	Inchbyra	16 000

Notes: [a] One acre equals 0.4 hectare.

just recovering from a depression and investors were nervous, but investigation of routes went ahead, financed largely by James Macarthur of Camden. A company was again proposed in 1848 with Charles Cowper of Wivenhoe, Narellan, as one of the leading advocates. The Legislative Council agreed in June 1848 to assist with grants of Crown land along the track, £30 000 in capital and a guarantee of interest on company funds.[5]

In November 1849 a meeting of gentlemen living on the southern outskirts of the county of Cumberland formed the Liverpool Provisional Tram and Railway Committee to support the Sydney Railway Committee. The Liverpool committee favoured a western line from Parramatta to Windsor and Bathurst and a southern line to Liverpool, Campbelltown and Camden, thus providing transport for all the major settlements in the Sydney region. Several members of the Liverpool committee owned estates along the proposed route, including Thomas Holt of Sophiaberg south of Liverpool, Richard Sadlier at Casula and John Hosking of Macquarie Fields.[6]

The Sydney Railway Company started construction of the initial stage from Sydney to Parramatta in 1850. The gold rush in 1851 led to escalating costs, labour shortages and management crises. After years of difficulties, the Sydney Railway Company and a similar company in the Hunter Valley were taken over by the colonial government in 1854. The first 16 miles (27 km) of railway from Redfern to Parramatta were completed by September 1855, but extensions were slow despite the high cost of road transport. In 1855 road freight from Sydney to Goulburn, 216 kilometres, took eighteen days and cost £12.5.0 per ton. By September 1856 the southern branch from Parramatta had reached Liverpool. Construction paused for a year until, in August 1857 the contract for the extension to Campbelltown was given to William Randle. The 12 miles (20 km) of track to Campbelltown crossed many small creeks and was laid at a cost of over £7000 per mile.

The railway to Campbelltown was opened on Tuesday 4 May 1858 when a distinguished group of visitors, including the governor, Sir William Denison, and many members of parliament travelled out on the first train, leaving Sydney at 1.15 pm and reaching Campbelltown at 3 pm. Campbelltown's official representatives were John Keighran, Charles Morris and Joseph Leary who spoke of the benefits conferred on 'this old and extensive agricultural district' by the new railway. The new goods shed was temporarily transformed into a banquet hall with decorative banners, corn cobs, waratahs and stuffed wallabies. Nearly 200 sat down for a banquet until recalled to the train at 5.30 pm. With the departure of the officials, the locals settled down to enjoy the occasion and danced until dawn.[7]

The scenery along the railway was attractive with the George's River on one side and fine farmland with 'elegant cottages and substantial homesteads' on the other, adding a touch of English-style beauty to the countryside. The single track from Liverpool to Campbelltown carried four trains per day. Journeys were often delayed by flooding across the line in the 1860s. The railway reached Picton in 1863, Mittagong and Moss Vale in 1867, and Goulburn in 1869, but for the first decade of railway service Campbelltown was the effective terminus. Even though services were progressively extended southward, there was no substantial town on the line until Goulburn.

A platform called Riversford was opened on the northern bank of the Nepean River in August 1862 and operated for barely a year while the railway bridge was built. Farmers at Menangle Park were encouraged to use it, as were farmers as far south as Picton. It was useful for the construction gangs and their families, an itinerant community of about 500 people. The bush at Menangle Park was covered with tents and small huts surrounded by cranes and forges and there was always the clank of hammers on rivets. Men cut stone from a nearby quarry for the enormous foundations needed for the bridge to withstand the Nepean floods.[8]

Initially there were no intermediate stations between Liverpool and Campbelltown because there were no villages. As the rural estates were subdivided in the 1870s and 1880s, platforms were added and by the 1870s the traveller could stop at Glenfield, Ingleburn and Minto. Glenfield platform was opened in September 1869. So too was the first station on the Macquarie Fields estate, originally called after that estate but later renamed Ingleburn. Closer to Campbelltown the Campbellfield estate was subdivided and a railway platform, Campbellfields, was opened in May 1874. This became Minto station. The earliest morning train, leaving Campbelltown at 7.55 am and arriving at Redfern at 9.20 am, was not suitable for working people to commute. In the evening the return train left Redfern at 5 pm and arrived at Campbelltown at 6.30 pm.[9]

Farming in Campbelltown

The southern districts were grazing lands. Those who remained at Campbelltown earned their living as farmers. In the four decades from 1840 to 1880 agriculture in Campbelltown bloomed then faded. By 1880 rust had ravaged the wheat crop, the flour millers had left town or changed professions and farmers were trying new products.

Transport difficulties kept wheat farmers close to the Sydney markets during the 1840s and 1850s. Most wheat was still grown in the areas pioneered in the 1790s and 1800s along the banks of the Hawkesbury–Nepean River system, either west at Windsor or south around Camden and Campbelltown. Large quantities of wheat were imported from other colonies. Loss of labour during the gold rushes caused difficulties, but demand for wheat always exceeded supply so farmers were able to cover their costs. Wheat was considered a crop for the lower classes, its production constrained by the physical labour a person could do in a day using hand tools.

A combination of circumstances from 1860 led to the destruction of wheat farming in the county of Cumberland. The railway was moving south and west, opening up new country and providing transport for more distant wheat farmers. The railway did not cause the decline of coastal wheat farming but it provided incentive for change. Access to new districts coincided with land reforms to favour small farmers. Disease attacked the traditional wheat areas at this crucial time. Fungoid stem rust (*Puccinia graminis tritici*) had been a minor problem from the earliest years. Increased virulence in coastal areas from 1860 cut wheat production by up to 75 per cent within five years. The worst-affected areas were Camden–Campbelltown and by the mid–1870s wheat was no longer a viable crop for Campbelltown farmers. The financial impact of the failure of the wheat crops spread throughout the community, from owners of large estates whose income came from rents to agricultural labourers who had no work and shopkeepers whose accounts remained unpaid.

Wheat was grown by the smaller landowners or by tenants on the larger estates. Most tenants occupied 20- to 75-acre (8 to 30 ha) farms, cultivating about half with cash crops and using the remnant as grazing pasture for working animals. Clearing leases for five to seven years were common, suiting both landowners who wanted their land cleared of scrub and trees and tenants who usually had little capital to develop land and little cash to pay rents.

Draught animals were an expensive investment and bullocks and equipment were borrowed by farmers who did not have their own. Grain was sown by hand, broadcast. James Payten, owner of Woodbine, in 1875 walked his fields casting grain left and right. Robert Brooksbank, a tenant farmer on Denfield, borrowed a spiked roller, pulled by a bullock team, to break up his paddock then used his bullock team to drag a 'big bushy limb' across the field to cover the grain with soil. The Macarthurs at nearby Camden had a 'marvellous implement' that did this with ease. The crop was harvested by hand, providing casual work for many families. Mary Ann Brooksbank reaped 2 acres (0.8 ha) of seed oats at Campbelltown in the 1850s for three sovereigns. Rust on the wheat made the reapers look 'like red foxes'. Steam threshing machines were at work in Camden in 1859 but most farmers relied on hand or horse-drawn reapers and threshers.[10]

Dominating the landscape, the windmills of Campbelltown were symbols of prosperity and gradual decay. Their power as visual images overstated the economic importance of the flour-milling industry to the town. By 1842 there were three windmills in Campbelltown—one at Mount Gilead and two others operated by Edward Larkin, a Sussex miller who migrated to Australia with his wife, Jane, in 1837 and by 1840 had started a mill at Campbelltown. In 1856 there were two windmills working; one a post-mill leased by Thomas Rixon on John Wild's grant along the Campbelltown/Appin Road and the other owned by Edward Larkin at Windmill Hill, 1.5 kilometres south of Appin. Larkin erected his windmill, also a post-mill, about 1845 and operated it for almost 25 years.[11]

In 1843 Laurence Kendall, a miller of Liverpool, and William Orr, engineer, purchased lot 33 of the Bradbury Park subdivision at the southern end of Campbelltown to build a mill on the creek that ran through the estate. The creek was already dammed at Queen Street and was used by Hugh Murphy's tannery. By January 1845 construction had started on the first steam mill in Campbelltown and it was in operation by winter. Three storeys high and made of brick, the steam flour mill was the largest building in town and for ten years its only steam mill. Kendall operated the mill until the mid-1850s when he returned to the Illawarra. The mill was then leased to Samuel Sims, Frank Barker and James Bocking who in 1878 purchased it from Laurence and Mary Kendall and opened a store.[12]

In March 1844 John and Sarah Warby sold 9 acres (3.6 ha) to John Keighran, publican of West Bargo, for £180. The main road from Liverpool to Campbelltown passed through the land and Keighran probably intended to build an inn. Ten years later he erected a steam flour mill. A third steam mill may have been built at Mount Gilead but never operated and its fine windmill was rarely used from the 1850s.[13]

James Bocking acquired the grinding rights to Larkin's windmill in 1870 but, in view of declining wheat production, probably never operated it and in 1873 it stood silent. John Keighran died in 1858 and, though his

Bocking's mill, bakery and store, around 1880. Built by Kendall and Orr in 1844, this was the first steam flour mill in Campbelltown and dominated the southern end of Queen Street for many decades. CAMPBELLTOWN LOCAL HISTORY COLLECTION

mill may have continued under lessees, by 1875 it had ceased operations. James Payten, who owned the land, nailed up the windows and doors after it had been abandoned for some years. By 1878 the only flour mill in working order was the old Kendall mill, now owned by Bocking, but local wheat crops no longer produced enough grain to support flour milling. Bocking had closed his mill by 1884.[14]

A more valuable but less recognised component of local agriculture was the annual hay crop, an unpredictable quantity depending on the season and whether farmers cut their crop green for hay or left it for the grain to ripen. In 1847 Campbelltown crops of wheat and maize would have brought between £7700 and £10800. Hay at the lowest price that season returned £10510, almost as much as the best-possible prices for the wheat and maize harvest. Hay in the 1850s, when labour was scarce due to the gold rushes, brought as much as £50 a ton.[15]

Five to six thousand acres (2000 to 2400 ha) were cultivated annually in Campbelltown in the 1840s and 1850s, peaking at 8845 acres (3538 ha) in April 1851 on the eve of the gold rushes, declining to 6858 acres (2743 ha) in 1853 and remaining below this level for the rest of the 1850s when travellers commented that farms seemed abandoned. At least half was planted with oats for hay but wheat cultivation varied markedly from year to year, as did cultivated grasses for fodder. In 1861, 1940 acres (776 ha) were planted with wheat, producing 15901 bushels. In 1870 only 1093 acres (437 ha) were planted with wheat, yielding a mere 30 bushels. In 1861 there were three reaping and threshing machines, probably operated by horsepower, in the Campbelltown area. Nine years later agricultural equipment was more varied, despite the continued decline in wheat with five threshing machines, six winnowing machines, a hay press, nineteen chaff-cutters, one corn-crusher and seven corn-shellers. Nevertheless, John Norton Oxley of Kirkham considered that few farmers in the district had either the capital or knowledge to adopt improved farming methods, such as fertilising their land with manure. Though a comparatively wealthy man, he claimed he could not afford the new steam ploughs. Horses, not machinery, were the pride of the land. Edward Larkin of Windmill Hill owned the prize-winning imported Lincoln draughthorse Honest Tom and his mare Lady Lincoln.[16]

The early 1860s brought great distress to Campbelltown's farmers. Hailstorms in one year, two years of drought and then rust devastated the crops. In the autumn and winter of 1863 the government advanced seed wheat to the Campbelltown farmers, but the next harvest was destroyed by rust. At a public meeting in February 1864, Reverend Smith of St Peters and Father Roche of St Johns both said that they had not seen such widespread poverty and hunger in 30 years. A deputation of local magistrates and clergymen requested the government not to press for payment of debts contracted for seed wheat. Despite these years of agricultural distress, there was little change in the number of farmers occupying the land—189 in 1861, 194 in 1870—with the area cultivated falling slightly from 3728 to 3419 acres (1491 to 1368 ha) with 55 per cent of cultivation on land worked by freeholders, the balance on leasehold.[17]

Many small leasehold farmers sought waged jobs to maintain their families. Robert Brooksbank was probably typical of the small settlers of the 1850s and 1860s. A tenant on Denfield, he worked as a casual farm labourer for the Howes at Glenlee, and between planting and harvest took contracts for carting and road-, bridge- or fence-making. His daughter earned money by reaping wheat or stripping wattle bark for tanning. The family income was supplemented by intermittent visits to the goldfields.[18]

Difficult years stimulated experimentation. Alexander Munro and his sons planted 2 acres (0.8 ha) of sugarcane near Denham Court. They harvested 1 acre (0.4 ha) in 1871, crushed it in primitive machinery and extracted a ton of syrup, but Munro was not able to granulate it. The Throsbys also experimented with sugarcane in the 1850s.[19]

James Payten kept a diary of his farm routine. He married Sarah Elizabeth Jane Rose, youngest daughter of Thomas Rose of Mount Gilead in 1866. The Paytens farmed the 700-acre (280 ha) Leppington estate near Denham Court until 1873, when James acquired Woodbine, a 76-acre (30 ha) estate at Campbelltown, from his brother-in-law, Alfred Rose. Woodbine remained the home of the Payten family for the next century. James Payten died there in December 1890, aged 56, and Sarah in 1929, aged 93.

At Leppington the Paytens grazed dairy cattle, sheep and horses, and grew hay and vegetables. James's diary for 1869 recorded the routine of his farm. From January to March Payten and his man planted peas, French beans, broad beans, parsnips, carrots, pumpkins, three varieties of turnips, cabbages and cauliflowers. February to May saw them ploughing and sowing oats and barley as green feed for the stock. As well as his own stock, Payten agisted 10 bullocks and 228 sheep. In June the ewes lambed and the vegetables were cut and sent to market. From July to September another crop of vegetables was planted. In September the lambs were tailed and in October the sheep were shorn. November was the season to mow the barley and make hay. Each year the cycle was repeated.

Birth, illness, accident and death were part of the pattern—the illness of the children with whooping cough, a man gored by a bull, the near-drowning of the butcher in the flooded creek, a child falling out of the train, the death of Mrs Rose at Woodbine in June 1869 and the sale of her furniture in September. Civic responsibilities were not ignored, whether it be attendance at the Quarter Sessions or polling day for the elections.

Another diary, for 1875, records the Payten family two years after it had settled at Woodbine. This was a much smaller farm and James Payten had more leisure to enjoy his fishing, his dogs, cricket, the races and visits to his relatives. Nonetheless the remorseless cycle of the seasons dictated life on the farm. In February and March Payten and his man sowed barley, mangolds, wurtzel and turnips for animal fodder. The lucerne was cut in May and the corn in July. In August the asparagus was manured, peach trees were grafted, 100 cabbages were planted and oranges were sent to market in Sydney. Potatoes, pumpkins, cucumbers, watermelon and rockmelon were planted in September. The lucerne paddock was ploughed up in October and sown broadcast with corn. November was shearing time and in December Payten sent 20 lambs and 13 pigs to market. Every month there were frequent trips in the cart to get manure for the crops and firewood.[20]

A visitor about 1880 queried: 'What will become of Campbelltown and its district since hay-making will not pay, wheat will not grow and the seasons are too dry for maize?' Campbelltown was cleared, settled country now. Oaten hay grew well without manure and with indifferent attention. The well-drained hilly country seemed suitable for fruit and vines. Agricultural commentators in the late 1870s were surprised by the lack of interest among Campbelltown farmers in diversifying to these crops. Surely Campbelltown could challenge the prominence of Parramatta in orange production, especially when the proposed Nepean water supply could provide reliable irrigation. With water, suitable soil and railway access to the ever-growing urban market in Sydney, opportunities were being ignored in Campbelltown.[21]

Vinegrowing had been attempted with some success, especially on the Macarthurs' Camden Park estate. Most German families in the district had migrated because of interest among the large estate owners in winemaking. In 1847 James Chisholm of Gledswood was given permission to import vine dressers from Europe. Frederick and Anna Maria Worner from Wittenburg, Germany, arrived in December 1852 with six of their children and went to work for Chisholm. Frederick Worner was still a vigneron on Gledswood in 1881. Children and adults worked on the vines. Ten-year-old Leah Worner picked the caterpillars from the grapevines. Joseph and Marie Sherack came from Germany to work for the Macarthur family in 1852 and later settled at Minto. Peter and Elizabeth Kershler arrived from Germany in 1853 to work for Sir Thomas Mitchell at Park Hall, Douglas Park. Their children stayed in the Campbelltown area. Eagle Vale estate was renamed 'Eshcol' (misspelt as 'Eschol' after 1975), a reference to vineyards in the Old Testament, and William Fowler employed Mr Zorno as vigneron to develop the estate from 1858. Vineyards for winemaking increased only from 3 to 4 acres (1.2 to 1.6 ha) between 1860 and 1871, but planting for table grapes had added nearly 3 acres of new vines.[22]

Industry and commerce

Many people became indebted speculating in land and stock in the late 1830s. Falling wool prices were offset by markets for livestock in the new settlements in the Port Phillip district and South Australia, but when

British investors lost confidence and withdrew funds from 1840, credit became tight. Mortgage payments could not be maintained and many properties changed hands. Livestock and grain prices collapsed. Unemployment increased, especially in the building trades. Legislation in 1842 enabled people seeking voluntary insolvency to retain the use of their property if there was a chance their debts would be repaid when the economy improved. Of almost 2000 insolvencies between 1842 and 1849, 1830 were voluntary, and some regarded voluntary insolvency as a ploy to cheat creditors.[23]

The biggest company failure was the merchant partnership of Hughes and Hosking. Their firm was in debt to the Bank of Australia for about £150000, a debt which led to the collapse of the bank in 1843. The shareholders of the bank were not protected by limited liability and were forced into deeper financial difficulties, spreading the crisis. John Hosking (1806–82), partner in Hughes and Hosking, had just been elected as the first mayor of Sydney when his business failed. His wife, Martha Foxlowe, daughter of Samuel Terry, had inherited Macquarie Fields estate and her marriage settlement enabled them to retain Macquarie Fields from Hosking's creditors. The estate remained the property of Mrs Hosking until her death in 1875.[24]

Among Campbelltown residents, sixteen people from a population of about 500 sought the Insolvency Court to resolve their financial difficulties in 1842 and 1843. They came from a broad social spectrum. Three were farmers; two were storekeepers; there was a publican, a dentist, two schoolteachers, a butcher, a builder, a bricklayer and several labourers. Others felt the strain. John Hurley commented to his banker friend, John O'Sullivan of Goulburn, in November 1840 that there was a great 'scarcity of money' and asked O'Sullivan to help him with £600, 'being completely blocked up at present'.[25]

Michael Byrne was the licensee of the Joiner's Arms and a stock owner in the Argyle and Burragorang districts. He had built an elegant two-storey sandstone house, later known as Glenalvon, in Lithgow Street where he lived with his wife, Jane, née Warby, and their six children. His brother-in-law, John Keighran, foreclosed on the mortgage over Glenalvon, obtaining possession of the house in 1844. In October 1844 when Michael Byrne sought voluntary insolvency his debts amounted to £1886 and his assets to less than £100. Byrne's largest creditor was his mother, to whom he owed £1140 from the sale of cattle three years earlier. His farming equipment was sold to pay his servants' wages but his other creditors received little. Michael's brother, Charles Byrne, with his wife, Elizabeth, had built a single-storey stone cottage, later called Richmond Villa, in Lithgow Street, Campbelltown. In 1840 Charles Byrne mortgaged this cottage to John Vardy for £1000. Unable to repay the loan, he forfeited the house to Vardy who in turn sold it for £520 to John Keighran in 1847.

Michael Byrne continued to run the Joiner's Arms. An 1840 map marked

Byrne's inn on the western side of Queen Street at the southern end of town. Another map drawn about 1842 showed the Joiner's Arms on the corner of the Old Menangle Road and the Narellan Road. Emily Cottage may have been one of the outbuildings on the 10 acres (4 ha) around the inn. The Joiner's Arms had four bedrooms, two parlours, detached laundry and kitchen and a taproom with four tables, eight chairs, a bench and a bird's cage.[26]

Other publicans felt the financial pressures of the 1840s. The owners of the Forbes Hotel, near the courthouse, advertised for a new licensee in mid-1844, offering a rental of only £50, one-third of the previous lease because of the difficult times. The Forbes Hotel had nine bedrooms, two parlours, a taproom, bar and cellar. At the back was a detached kitchen, gardens, a yard, well, twelve-stall stable and grazing paddock. Charles Morris, licensee of the Coach and Horses Inn, was also· selling out, offering his furniture at valuation. The Coach and Horses Inn opposite Bradbury Park had eight bedrooms, four sitting-rooms, a large ballroom and hall, cellars, a detached kitchen and laundry with stabling for sixteen horses, a coach house and ample paddocks.[27]

With the arrival of the railway in 1858 old coaching houses like the Robin Hood Inn on the road from Liverpool to Campbelltown faded away. Within six months of the railway's arrival, the licensee of the Railway Hotel was in financial difficulties. The publican, Sylvester Byrne, who rented the premises from John Doyle, was new to the trade and blamed this and neglect of business for his difficulties. Mrs Byrne's father, John Vardy, helped to support her and the children. Still standing in Queen Street, the Railway Hotel had a bar, two parlours, a dining-room, three bedrooms and another small room with a bed. In the kitchen was a meat safe, a water fountain, saucepan, frying pan and a boiler. Byrne rarely had many customers. His bar room with one table and two benches had only seven tumblers and four decanters and his drinking stock in September 1858 consisted of four kegs and 23 bottles of ale. After Byrne's failure John Doyle took up the licence and later Thomas James ran the hotel, converting the wooden coach house into a music hall for dancing.[28]

Despite its small population, there were many storekeepers, most of whom were related to local publicans, butchers or farmers. William Graham senior came to Campbelltown in 1832 as a child with his Irish immigrant parents who farmed at Spring Creek near Campbelltown. He became licensee of the Forbes Hotel and diversified into a general store, which was carried on by his sons, William, James and John. George Fieldhouse (d. 1880) followed his convict father to New South Wales in 1828. In the late 1840s he opened the Jolly Miller Inn opposite Kendall's mill. His sons, William and Edwin Hallet Fieldhouse, opened a general store nearby in 1853. Colonial-born Daniel Fowler (1822–1900) trained as a cooper. Fowler came to Campbelltown in the 1840s, married Mary Bursill and became a butcher and storekeeper. He retired in the early

Doyle's Railway Hotel (288–290 Queen Street) and Fowler's grocery and drapery store (292–294 Queen Street). (W.Boag, c.1871)

1870s, selling the butchery to his Scottish-born partner of sixteen years, James Wilson. His sons continued the family's commercial activities. Charles Beck was a draper and auctioneer in the 1840s.

A cabinetmaker by trade, William Fowler was Campbelltown's longest-serving early postmaster. From 1846 to 1863 he ran the post office from his general store, a substantial stone two-storey building in the main street near Allman Street. On the ground floor was the shop and four rooms with another six rooms upstairs, a separate kitchen, pantry and storeroom in brick and stone, and a timber stable and coach house. The store was taken over by his sons, George and William, about 1879. William Bursill, convict settler and farmer in Airds and Dapto in 1820s and 1830s, had opened a store and a tannery in Campbelltown by 1846. He went to Gulgong and Home Rule during the gold rush, but returned to Campbelltown in the late 1850s as a publican and storekeeper in partnership with his sons.[29]

Tanneries were cottage industries, using local resources—hides, bark, water, animal dung and nightsoil. It was a foul-smelling trade, banned from the Sydney area in 1848. As well as making leather for boots, there was a steady demand for leather for harness, saddlery and belts for machinery. From the 1840s to the 1870s there were usually three tanneries at work in the Campbelltown area, using the stream through the Bradbury Park estate. One tannery with two small pits was operated here by Hugh Murphy in the early 1840s. William Bursill had a tannery in conjunction with his boot shop on part of the Bradbury estate. Charles

80

Huckstepp, arriving as a convict in 1833, settled in Campbelltown in the 1840s. He also had a tannery and worked as a shoemaker. Huckstepp was verger at St Peters Church where he was buried in 1887.[30]

Another unpleasant industry was 'boiling down', introduced in the 1840s when sheep prices were very low. Slaughtering the animals and rendering down the carcasses for fats became more profitable than selling wool or meat. The tallow, used in soap and candle manufacture, was shipped to Britain in wooden casks. The first boiling-down works at Campbelltown opened in 1850 under J. Pendergrast. In 1851 it processed 379 sheep and 582 cattle to extract 430 hundredweight (21 844 kg) of tallow. When stock values rose during the gold rushes, boiling down became less attractive, and by 1856 it was operating as a slaughter yard, processing 1800 sheep, 700 cattle and 140 pigs during the year. Because of the smell it was located away from the town on a creek between Campbelltown Road and the railway, near Raby Road.[31]

Common building stone was quarried by George Onslow on the George's River in 1843 and by George Muckle at Narrawa, Minto. Better-quality stone, 'Cowpasture marble', was available from George McLeay's estate at Brownlow Hill. Limestone, needed for mortar and fertiliser, came from a quarry and lime kiln at Picton. Brickmaking was a minor occupation. Simple clamp kilns were erected near building sites and the bricks made as needed in hand moulds. In 1859 John Dowse made the bricks for the Congregational church on the corner of Oxley and Dumaresq Street. Each brick was imprinted with crosses on the frog. There were two brickmakers at work in the district in 1861.[32]

Construction of the railway to Campbelltown in 1857 and 1858 attracted new residents but the 1860s were hard years. As the railway moved south one resident observed in 1863: 'Our town presents rather a quiet appearance and I regret to see so many houses to let ... there are no buildings or public works going on in the town, consequently the labouring class have to seek some other spot where work can be obtained.'[33]

One storekeeper who came to Campbelltown as a result of railway construction was John Kidd who arrived from Scotland in 1857, aged 21, and set up a bakery in Sydney. Recognising the financial prospects in feeding railway navvies, he moved to Campbelltown where he prospered, expanding his bakery into a general store. In the 1870s he became interested in bulk milk supply to Sydney. Another Scot who settled in Campbelltown in these years was William Blythe Caldwell who was farming in the district in 1861. He married Mary Percival and established a butchering business. Railway contractors James Cobb and James Bocking used Campbelltown as a base and, in the case of Bocking, diversified into commercial activities.[34]

William Gilchrist ran a general store in Campbelltown which he rented from John Hurley for £35 per annum. His store was stocked with cannisters of rice and barley, bottles of pickles and oil, starch, soap powder, boot blacking, gloves, flannel shirts, stockings, socks, some fabric and 48

Mrs Hickey's general store in Queen Street. (W.Boag, c.1871)

packets of hooks and eyes. By 1866 he faced financial disaster after extending credit to the local people 'whom I know to be honest'.[35]

The largest storekeepers in the 1870s were Fowler Brothers, E. & W. Fieldhouse, James Bocking, John Kidd, Samuel Clarke and E. McSullea. Several small shopkeepers were women. Mary Bray had been deserted by her sailor husband in 1869. Five years later she was able to get some assistance under the *Deserted Wives' and Children's Act*. She ran a small grocery shop in a building rented from John Hurley for 8 shillings a week, selling pipes and purses, pickles and polish, golden syrup, marbles and eau de cologne. For Empire Day in 1876 she stocked fireworks, Chinese crackers, rockets and roman candles. Mrs Hickey conducted a general store in Queen Street in a small weatherboard building with a shingle roof, where she sold an assortment of manufactured goods—pots, pans, lamps, cutlery and fabric in the 1870s.[36]

The railway had a mixed impact on Campbelltown's economy. For Doyle, Henty and Company, with stockyards at Campbelltown station in the 1870s, the railway provided rapid transport to city markets and encouraged city buyers to come to the town and purchase stock. For the farmers, their once extensive local market for hay was substantially reduced. Thomas and Mary Milgate arrived in Sydney in 1840 with their nine children, all under fourteen. Thomas established a hay and corn business in Newtown and by the 1870s had four produce stores managed by his sons at Newtown, Camperdown, Parramatta and Campbelltown. He died at Newtown in 1874 and his sons continued the business. The Campbelltown hay and corn store was managed by Spencer Samuel Milgate near Milgate Lane, now Milgate Arcade.

Spencer Milgate had married in 1855 and planned to live permanently at Campbelltown with his wife, their seven children and his widowed mother. He rented, then purchased Eshcol Park from William Fowler in 1878 but tragedy struck. His mother died at Eshcol Park in March 1877 and a year later two of his daughters died of diptheria, followed by a third daughter in January 1879. The one happy event was the marriage of the Milgates' eldest daughter, Elizabeth, to Thomas H. Reeve of Campbelltown in 1878. Spencer Milgate sold Eshcol Park and moved back to Sydney, turning his attention to real estate development at Leura. He died at Wentworthville in 1891, aged 57.[37]

From the mid-1860s post offices accepted deposits for the government savings bank and by the 1870s banks recognised the need for branches in the larger towns. The Commercial Banking Company of Sydney, formed in 1834, established the first bank in Campbelltown when it opened a branch in 1875 with George Jones as temporary manager. The following year A. J. Gore came to Campbelltown as manager, staying until he retired in 1904. The Bank of New South Wales, established in 1817, opened its Campbelltown branch in February 1878. Its first manager was William Hurley, a son of the local member of parliament and former publican, John Hurley, who had for many years acted as a private banker.[38]

There were attempts to improve the town in 1878 to induce farmers to spend their money in Campbelltown. Mr R. Campion, a painter and decorator, converted a 'very ugly building' into the most ornamental business premises in town. In 1875 he had redecorated Glenlee House, painting the stair hall to resemble marble, a fashionable touch which he also added to Glenalvon. Campion Road was the original name of Badgally Road and part of Broughton Street near the railway where Campion lived.[39]

> In former days, Campbelltown was a place of considerable importance . . . it long enjoyed a considerable amount of commercial prosperity . . . [as] one of our principal wheat districts. It may almost be said it was the granary of New South Wales. The establishment of the township of Camden, on private lands, between thirty and forty years ago, gave the town its first check. The line of the main road having also been changed so as to pass through that township and over Razorback, missing Campbelltown, it lost a large proportion of its business both with the farmers and the travellers. Next came the change from coach and bullock teams to railway traffic, by which a large source of gain was removed from the locality. But still worse, was the advent of the rust disease in wheat.[40]

Such were the causes of economic decline in Campbelltown. Part of the problem, in the opinion of outsiders, was the slowness of Campbelltown residents to take up new opportunities. By the 1870s abundant reserves of coal were known to exist near the town and there were plans for improved water supplies. With coal, water and railway transport, Campbelltown could have a manufacturing future. Water also offered the key to more varied agriculture. There seemed no reason why orchards, vineyards, market gardens and farms should not flourish and Campbelltown, in the words of the *Australian Town and Country Journal*, become a centre

> *where gigantic wine cellars, and fruit drying establishments, meat preserving, ham and bacon curing and numerous other flourishing manufacturing businesses are carried on. Then will Campbelltown rise from her long continued stunted-seedling state and take her place as the most important inland town not only of Cumberland but of the colony.*[41]

Roads and bridges

Before the railway reached Campbelltown in 1858, public transport was limited to the mail coaches. The government contract in the 1840s specified a daily coach (except on Sundays) to and from Campbelltown, Liverpool and Sydney, with daily connections to Appin, Wollongong and Dapto and to Camden, Picton, Berrima, Marulan and Goulburn. Charles Morris of the Coach and Horses Inn was one of the mail contractors. His inn was the meeting point for the Illawarra and south-western routes. Coaches from Appin and Camden left his inn at 4 am for Parramatta where passengers caught the steam boat along the river, arriving in Sydney at 8.30 am. Return coaches met the Sydney steamer at Parramatta at 6.30 pm.[42]

The lack of a bridge over the Nepean River at Menangle continued to anger the people of Campbelltown. A bridge would give Campbelltown's squatters more direct access to Goulburn and Gundagai, with a flat route between Campbelltown and Picton, sparing them the Razorback. In October 1845 public meetings were held at Hurley's Hotel and the Campbelltown courthouse. James Macarthur of Camden attended by invitation and was the main speaker. The Macarthurs had let the Menangle part of their estate as small farms in the mid-1840s. The meeting accepted his proposal for improvements on the existing road from Menangle Ford to Picton and to dam rather than bridge the river. A fund-raising committee was formed and, at William Fowler's suggestion, the members were William Hume, James Macarthur, William Macarthur, Edward Hume, Mathew McAlister, John Keighran, John Warby, John Vardy, Sheahan, Sabar and Bursill with Hurley as treasurer.[43]

Little had been achieved by 1848 when further meetings were held at Rudd's inn and the Jolly Miller Inn. A petition signed by residents of the southern districts of Argyle, St Vincent and Murray as well as the counties of Cumberland and Camden argued that sales of Crown land in Campbelltown would be stimulated by a bridge over the Nepean at Menangle, thereby improving government revenue. Another petition from the landowners, carriers and mail contractors on the southern route urged Governor Fitzroy not to develop the road across the Cowpastures Bridge and over the Razorback. Investment in high-level bridges over the

Cataract River would provide a more convenient route for the Illawarra district and would

restore the towns of Campbelltown and Appin, now almost ruined, to their originally flourishing condition; whilst the village of Camden, although the main part of the traffic would be diverted from it, would not suffer in consequence of its being the heart of a fine agricultural district.[44]

In August 1850 James Graham, George Taber, Laurence Kendall, Charles Morris and William Fowler wrote to the Reverend John Dunmore Lang, a member of the Legislative Council, appealing for his assistance to improve the road through Campbelltown. In 1852 a private company, headed by W. H. Hovell, was formed to build toll bridges across the Nepean at Pheasant's Nest and across the Cataract. However, the prospect of the railway deterred prospective shareholders and the project never started.[45]

Construction of a bridge at Menangle finally started in November 1855, about 1 kilometre from the traditional ford at Bird's Eye Corner. A low timber truss bridge, 26 feet (8 m) wide on four piers with three spans of 57 feet (17 m), opened in 1856, was destroyed in the floods of 1875 and was subsequently rebuilt. Employment on the bridge brought new people to the district. One who was to have a significant impact on Campbell-

---

James and Mary Bocking with their children, around 1890. *Left to right* Edie, George, Campbell, James, Mary Charlotte (nee Robinson), May and Norman.

town was the foreman, James Bocking. A young man of about 25, his work on the bridge was greatly appreciated by the people of Campbelltown, Menangle and Appin, and in July 1856 they presented him with a watch. Bocking settled in Campbelltown, initially in a stone cottage in Queen Street where he continued his contracting business. Bocking was a Congregationalist and was responsible for building the Congregational church (1859), the temperance hall (1862) and the Congregational manse (1870). As well as construction projects with his partner, James Cobb, Bocking owned a flour mill and a general store. An original member of the Campbelltown Council and mayor in 1890, Bocking lived to see Campbelltown change from pioneer township to twentieth-century rural town. He died in 1927 aged 96, Campbelltown's oldest resident.[46]

The coaching services did not cease when the railway reached Campbelltown. Camden required coach links to the new railway until its own branch track was opened in 1882. Appin and the Illawarra still required road transport because the railway from Sutherland to Wollongong was not completed until 1887. Thomas Kelly operated a coach service between Campbelltown and Wollongong competing against the coaches of James Waterworth. Running expenses included harness and saddlery, horseshoes and feed. Liberal credit, over £100, was extended to Kelly by Fowler Brothers' store in Campbelltown, but misfortune overtook him when his new coach, the security for his loans, was destroyed in an accident on the Bulli Pass.[47]

Legislation in 1849 created local trustees to maintain district roads. The Campbelltown Road Trust, appointed in December 1849, had five members—William junior and Edward Howe of Glenlee, John Norton Oxley of Kirkham, George Beresford Christmas of Mount Gilead and John Hurley of Campbelltown. Funds were voted by parliament and the road trustees received the rents from toll gates on the major roads through their district. Usually the contractors were local farmers and labourers who hired out their carts and shovels to patch the roads with gravel.[48]

From 1848 toll gates were established on the road to Liverpool at Landsdowne Bridge, on the Campbelltown Road at Denham Court and at Carnes Hill on the intersection of the Cowpasture and Bringelly Roads. The toll houses at Denham Court and Carnes Hill were linked across country by Cordeaux's Lane, now Denham Court Road, and were built in December 1849 by Alexander and William Munro of Liverpool. They were brick with cedar woodwork, built to a standard design for about £165 each, and were handed over to lessees of the road trust in January 1850. There is no evidence that Emily Cottage on the old Menangle road at Campbelltown was a toll house.[49]

The first Campbelltown Road Trust served for nine years. The next trustees, appointed in 1858, included William Fowler, John Bray, Laurence Kendall and Henry Rose. After the latter two left the district, John Hurley, John Doyle, publican, and Edward Guthrie, farmer, were appointed in December 1865 but were unable to work together, mainly because Hurley and Fowler had quarrelled over business and political matters. In 1866 a group of Campbelltown labourers complained that their road trust was not using its funds to provide work. Unemployed agricultural labourers had hoped to get casual work, but the trustees were not making decisions because of internal squabbles. John Hurley alleged that William Fowler delayed cash payments, paying the men in orders on his store so that they owed him their wages. Hurley also alleged Fowler had favoured his relative, Joseph Warby, with road contracts. The government reacted in February 1866 by dismissing the trustees and appointing Thomas Chippendall, Thomas Byrnes, John Vardy, John Grant and Joseph Warby as new trustees.[50]

Campbelltown roads were the subject of constant complaint.

> Let the unwary traveller but leave the high road, being the direct track through town and he becomes at once alive to the many ills and difficulties of this healthy neighbourhood. Nothing but deep and dangerous ruts are to be met with, and even our main road is not free from very dangerous spots.[51]

Governing Campbelltown

Country towns in New South Wales were managed by government departments in Sydney and local magistrates appointed by the governor. Superficially, this changed in 1842. Representative government was introduced with an elected Legislative Council to advise the governor and his officers in the making of laws and the administration of the colony. Local matters would be controlled by district councils.

The British government forwarded new legislation to Governor Gipps in September 1842 with provision for 'local boards chosen from among the inhabitants', elected by the landowners and residents and presided over by a warden appointed by the Governor. Local communities would be taxed to pay for their roads and police costs.[52]

Gipps created 28 district councils in 1843. His initial plan for a southern district council was conveyed to William Macarthur in early June 1843. Gipps proposed that the new council cover the police districts of Liverpool, Campbelltown, Camden and Narellan so that much of the Great Southern Road would fall under one council. Macarthur thought this plan impracticable and suggested that if Liverpool were removed he would be willing to act as warden of the smaller council. Gipps agreed to remove Liverpool but added Picton, with its length of the southern road.

One of the practical difficulties was that members of the district councils had to own land valued at £2000. At Liverpool Dr Hill reported that Pritchard, a respectable man who kept the post office and shop, would be suitable, as would George Muckle, a local farmer, 'a very decent man but I don't think he is very bright'. Another possibility was Mr Jamieson, 'rather an eccentric man' living on the Bringelly Road. The recommended councillors for Liverpool were Captain T. V. Blomfield of Denham Court,

Samuel Moore of Moore Bank, David Johnstone of Georges Hall, Joshua John Moore of Horningsea, William Thomas Jamieson, Richard Sadlier, George Muckle, John Hosking of Liverpool and William Pritchard. Blomfield declined to act, claiming he was not accustomed to public business. Samuel Moore accepted but J. J. Moore declined as his estate had just been sequestrated for insolvency proceedings.

Warden of the council covering Camden, Campbelltown and Picton was William Macarthur. Approached to recommend possible councillors, he sent in July 1843 a list of 21 names. For Picton he suggested Major Antill, Richard Blackwell, L. MacAlister, Jonathan Wild; for Camden, George Macleay, Henry Shadforth, Alexander Martin and James Macarthur; for Narellan, Thomas Moore, Charles Forbes, James Chisholm, J. S. Howell, James Hassall, Robert Lowe and Jonathan Buckland; for Campbelltown, he suggested William junior and Thomas Howe and Robert Pitt Jenkins; for Appin, Donald McLean, Rawdon Hume and Mr Garland.[53]

A week later William Macarthur wrote to remedy an omission from his list—John Hurley of Campbelltown:

He is an Innkeeper and mail contractor but possesses some landed property in the Airds and Appin Districts and is a man of considerable substance. He is a man of great respectability of character, active, intelligent and likely to make a busy bustling member of a District Council. He is an emancipist and a Roman Catholic and I may here remark that amongst the twenty names on the list I forwarded there is not one belonging to either of these classes. This circumstance, together with Mr Hurley's popularity and well known eligibility for the office makes me peculiarly desirous that he should form one of the Council.[54]

In September 1843 Governor Gipps announced the district council for Campbelltown, Camden, Narellan and Picton under the wardenship of William Macarthur. The councillors were H. C. Antill, George Macleay, James Macarthur, John Wild, William Howe, Thomas Moore, James Chisholm, Richard Blackwell and John Hurley.[55]

There was immediate opposition in Campbelltown to the new district council. Outside the town opposition to the councils was widespread, led by the Legislative Council which objected, as part of a larger constitutional battle with the British government, to the councils' taxation powers for police expenses. No such issues of principle concerned the people of Campbelltown. Their opposition was specific, local and bitter, based entirely on jealousy between Campbelltown and Camden. On 28 September 1843 William Howe called a public meeting to protest that 'our rights and privileges are to be invaded and conferred on the recently erected and comparatively small village of Camden, almost entirely surrounded as it is by the private property of two individuals'. Of the ten councillors, seven were interested in Camden and Picton. What benefits would Campbelltown get when its three members had to fight the 'formidable self interest' of the majority? 'The Council as presently constituted is the height of injustice and will end in the annihilation of Campbelltown,

Appin and the whole of this beautiful and fertile district.' The public meeting supported the concept of district councils but argued that no council could act 'for the mutual benefit of Campbelltown and Camden, their interests being quite irreconcilable'.

Campbelltown in 1843 had over 90 houses, three churches, a gaol, a courthouse, four schools, many large buildings and a respectable population. It deserved its own district council. By implication, neither Camden, Narellan or Picton had such assets. Even Appin had two churches, two schools, other valuable buildings and extensive cultivated land. Camden had a few large estates, a thin population and comparatively little cultivated land. The meeting endorsed a separate council for Campbelltown, covering the police district defined in 1840. Those who attended the Campbelltown meeting and spoke in favour of these changes were: John Buckland, Dr R. C. Hope, Donald McLean JP, Paul Huon, John Scarr, James Graham, Dr W. R. Kenny, John Hurley, William Bursill, Messrs Brown and Warby.[56]

Among the many heated political arguments aroused by the introduction of district councils, only the complaints from Campbelltown were accepted as valid criticism by Governor Gipps. He agreed to divide the district and legislation was passed to separate Campbelltown, with Appin, from Camden and Picton. A Select Committee on the boundaries suggested that the matter be resolved by a roads and bridges approach. Those who usually travelled by the Cowpasture Road would be in the Camden District Council; those who travelled by the Campbelltown road and the Menangle Ford would come under Campbelltown District Council. The two smallest district councils were Liverpool with only 103 908 acres (41 563 ha) and Campbelltown/Appin with only 133 964 (53 586); while Camden, Narellan and Picton covered 469 386 acres (187 754 ha).[57]

In June and July 1844 Gipps presented three Bills relating to the district councils to the New South Wales Legislative Council. Clauses included lowering of property qualifications for members; defining the authority of the councils; the manner of raising local revenue for police expenses, and a Bill to correct technical problems in the election of councillors for Campbelltown and Appin. All three Bills were rejected by the Legislative Council.[58]

So, despite its efforts to obtain a district council that reflected its needs, Campbelltown found itself defeated by larger political issues. Its district council never met. Lacking legislative authority to raise revenue and faced with local residents who objected to paying rates for roads through Crown land, by 1845 most district councils became inoperative. The British government was still anxious to introduce local government and the *Australian Colonies' Government Act* of 1850, which separated Victoria from New South Wales, also provided for local government in any district at the wish of the inhabitants. Campbelltown did not take voluntary action to form a local council until nearly 40 years after this first unsuccessful attempt.[59]

Government under the Police Act

Failure of the district councils meant that Campbelltown was administered until 1882 under the provisions of the *Police Act* of 1833, which had been extended to Campbelltown in 1840. Under the *Police Act* the governor appointed a bench of magistrates who, in addition to supervising the local police and administering the law, carried out the most essential tasks of local government. The magistrates were responsible for maintaining roads and footpaths; regulating buildings; controlling commercial and noxious activities, such as the weight of a loaf of bread and the condition of the butcher's slaughter yards; and enforcing basic public health such as disposal of nightsoil and prevention of water pollution. Government grants paid for roads and public buildings and fines raised in the local court from civil offences funded the rest.[60]

The magistrates administered law, order and government policy, as they understood it, in a personal and autocratic way. William Howe of Glenlee was 'a strict disciplinarian of the old school', but his decisions were respected and generally satisfactory. In 1844, after the failure of the district councils, Howe decided to withdraw from public life and resigned as magistrate and warden of the defunct council. The position of magistrate was not hereditary, but in families of recognised wealth and respectability it was not unusual for sons to follow their fathers on to the bench. Howe's son Thomas, 'a person of peculiarly retired habits', was frequently absent at his properties in the interior. William Howe junior was considered by his father to be better suited as a magistrate, even though he did not own any land. Edward Howe would be 'a more efficient magistrate' despite his absences in the interior, sheep shearing. In April 1845 William Howe junior was appointed warden and magistrate.[61]

Paid police magistrates were sometimes appointed, but the government believed the local gentry should fulfil their community responsibilities as unpaid magistrates. Campbelltown was one of six towns to lose salaried magistrates in 1843 as an economy measure. A public meeting at Hurley's Hotel in August 1842 protested at the news that their police magistrate, Captain Allman, would be withdrawn. Delays in appointing a magistrate after William Howe senior retired in 1844 and Allman was transferred caused much inconvenience, not only in Campbelltown but also for Appin and Narellan. Two magistrates were required to hear disputes between employers and their employees over wages and working conditions, so the appointment of another magistrate was a matter of some urgency. James Chisholm of Gledswood was appointed to the Campbelltown bench in 1847. Extension of the jurisdiction of the Court of Requests after 1844 created more work for the local magistrate. This court dealt summarily with debts under £10 once a month and heard cases for debts between £10 and £30 four times a year.[62]

The Campbelltown bench of magistrates was aware that its revenue and importance depended on the area that it served. In January 1878 magistrates William Fowler, John Kidd, E. H. Fieldhouse, James Bocking and Thomas Chippendall, all but Chippendall being local storekeepers, suggested that the boundaries of their district be extended. In the north, Liverpool Police District extended to within 2 miles (3 km) of Campbelltown so for many police matters, especially small debts (a matter of some interest to storekeepers), people had to go to Liverpool. The Campbelltown magistrates suggested that their district be extended north to Denham Court and the municipal boundary with Liverpool. The change was a fair proposal and was supported by the Liverpool magistrates, R. H. Blomfield, G. R. Johnstone and C. A. Scrivener. Next the magistrates suggested that their boundary be extended westward to the Nepean River and along the river for the full boundary between the counties of Cumberland and Camden. This was an attempt by Campbelltown to extend its authority over Narellan in the west and to redefine its boundary with Wollongong, in particular to bring the coalmines at Coalcliff within its jurisdiction.

Narellan was in the Camden Police District and its magistrates were affronted that Campbelltown dared to claim control over the Nepean River within sight of Camden. Narellan was little more than lines on a map and was owned by one person who used it as grazing land. There was no reason to change its administration. The Campbelltown magistrates had tried to include the coalminers of Coalcliff to alter the size of their electorate, Narellan, which was under threat of amalgamation. The Wollongong magistrates argued convincingly that Coalcliff was 28 miles (45 km) from Campbelltown and would cost its residents 7 shillings in coach fares each time they needed a magistrate. Wollongong was only 8 miles (13 km) away with nominal transport expenses. Campbelltown's efforts were resoundly defeated.[63]

The senior government official in Campbelltown for most of the nineteenth century was the Clerk of Petty Sessions. From 1856 to 1869 George White was Clerk of Petty Sessions for Campbelltown, Appin and Liverpool. An English solicitor who migrated with his family in 1854, he enjoyed the right of a small private legal practice and was the first resident attorney in Campbelltown. With a declining population in Campbelltown, White moved his home and his law practice to Liverpool in 1871. Clerk of Petty Sessions during the 1870s was Henry Arkell Smith. By choice or necessity he undertook many community and semi-official activities including secretary of the Public School Board, commissioner for the local water reserve, trustee of the recreation reserve, secretary of the Road Trust and church warden at St Peters.[64]

The gaols at Campbelltown, Liverpool and Windsor were closed at the end of 1843, following the refusal of the Legislative Council to provide colonial funds for a prison system that was largely a result of the convict system. Campbelltown Gaol continued to serve as the local police lock-up. The gaol in the basement of the courthouse had a day room, a constable's waiting room, nine small cells measuring 10 by 4 feet (3 by

1.2 m) with 9-foot (2.7 m) ceilings. The yard was enclosed by a 12-foot (3.6 m) wall and contained a cookhouse and privies. The gaoler lived in the upper storey of the courthouse.[65]

The major problems of law and order were highway robbery and stock theft. Appearances in the courthouse in Campbelltown were usually for minor complaints such as wandering livestock, shooting rabbits on Sundays, drunk, disorderly and obscene language and civil prosecutions for debts. One of the more severe sentences was three months' hard labour in Darlinghurst Gaol for stealing a swag with blankets. More serious offences were remanded for the Quarter Sessions and District Court. Punishments by the magistrates included confinement in the cells, fines or the stocks. In 1878 the old stocks were uncovered during work on the recreation reserve (Mawson Park) and townsfolk reminisced about the last occupant, an old woman who spent four hours in the stocks in the rain for using obscene language.[66]

The courthouse was substantially renovated in the 1860s resulting, in the opinion of Judge Dowling, in a better courthouse than many in Sydney. In 1857 magistrates John Bray and William Howe junior had complained of the bad state of the courthouse and the old gaol. They proposed a building, similar to that at Camden, financed by the sale of the old building and the surrounding 15 acres (6 ha). However, it was more economical to repair the old building. Major repairs were carried out in 1859 by Richard Basden of Camden with Edward Lusted and Thomas Hobbs, storekeepers of Camden, standing guarantors for work costing over £400. In the 1860s Cobb and Bocking had several contracts to repair the courtroom, the chimneys, the jury box, the gaoler's room, and drainage as well as improve security.

The military were despatched twice in 1861 to restore order during anti-Chinese riots on the Lambing Flat goldfield. On the second occasion the troops came to Campbelltown by train, camped overnight in the courthouse and started their march to Lambing Flat the next day. The magistrates were less concerned by the anti-Chinese riots than by the damage done to their courthouse where doors and windows were broken by the soldiers and the fences broken by their horses.[67]

With the spread of settlement in the 1840s the Supreme Court circuit moved further south. Major crimes were no longer tried at Campbelltown and the scaffold fell into disuse; however, one execution made an impact on the small town. In March 1863 the train from Sydney brought to Campbelltown the body of Henry Manns. Tradition holds that while his grave was prepared at St Johns cemetery, Manns' body was laid out in one of the hotels as an awesome deterrent to the young men of the town of the fate of bushrangers.

Henry Manns was baptised at St Peters, Campbelltown, in 1839, the son of William Manns, a ticket-of-leave man, and his wife, Mary. The family went to the Adelong goldfields where Henry Manns worked as a carrier. He became involved with bushrangers Frank Gardiner, John Gilbert, John Bow and Alexander Fordyce. Manns was arrested for a gold escort robbery in 1862, confessed, was found guilty and sentenced to death. Despite petitions from members of parliament and 15 000 citizens, the sentence was carried out at Darlinghurst Gaol on 26 March 1863. Controversy continued at the scaffold. The hangman did not adjust the noose properly and Manns convulsed violently on the gallows for ten minutes until the noose was readjusted and the drop completed. Further indignities followed. The gaoler was caught trying to steal the boots from the corpse. Manns' body was taken by train to his birthplace, Campbelltown, where he was buried at St Johns cemetery by Father Roche on 27 March 1863. The grave was not marked.[68]

Bushrangers still roamed the countryside near Campbelltown as late as 1866 when Waterworth, the mail contractor, was 'bailed up' 6 kilometres outside Campbelltown on the Appin Road by three armed men. The passengers were robbed and the mailbags opened. The bushrangers escaped in the coach, leaving passengers and driver to walk back to Campbelltown. The abandoned coach was found in the scrub near town. It was the second hold-up of the Wollongong mail coach within a fortnight. Waterworth built a concealed compartment under his seat for a revolver.[69]

William Fowler was appointed postmaster in January 1846 on a salary of £60 per annum, and he remained postmaster until 1863. Fowler used his store in the main street, near Allman Street, as the post office. Another building on the corner of Cordeaux and Queen Streets was rented from John Bray and was probably used as the post office in the early 1840s and again in the 1860s and 1870s. Originally an inn, it was a brick building, roofed with shingles with a separate brick kitchen. Mackel, postmaster from 1875, complained that he worked out of a 12-foot (3.6 m) room, divided into his office and the area where people came to collect their mail. From 1854 there was a delivery by horse three times a week along the road from Campbelltown to Picton via the Menangle Ford. John Ray had the contract in 1854 for £180 per year. His mailbag was not heavy, carrying about 30 letters per week each way and some newspapers. Only two people in Picton regularly received newspapers. At the Menangle Ford (Riversford) the Church of England schoolteacher acted as postmaster.[70]

Householders collected rainwater from their roofs in tanks, carried water from streams or used the Hurley Park reservoir. Steps led down into the reservoir and water was carried up in buckets. Hurley Park reservoir, which 'it will not do to disparage ... if you wish to remain friendly with the Campbelltonian', provided sufficient water in normal circumstances for the townspeople. Water carters were employed by those requiring large quantities, such as publicans. During the drought of 1862 farmers watered their cattle at the reservoir, causing anxiety that the reservoir might dry up. In November 1854 legislation created the Campbelltown Water Trust. The Trust was given authority to lay pipes, levy fees for the use of water and to prosecute polluters. Water cost 1 penny for a 63-gallon (287 L) cask, £5 for piped water to hotels and butcher shops, and £2.10.0 for private residents and other users. The trustees in 1855 were John Bray, Dr Arthur Scouler, John Hurley, Michael Byrne and Laurence Kendall. The Campbelltown Water Trust was responsible for water supply until the 1880s when local government took over.[71]

Parliamentary representation

In 1842 the first elections for representative government were held in colonial New South Wales. Little more than a decade later, in 1855, the colony was granted self-government and held its first elections for a two-house parliament. Not everyone could vote in early elections. In 1842 only men over 21 who owned land worth £200 or rented a house worth £20 per year could vote. Campbelltown residents were divided between two electorates. From 1842 to 1859 Campbelltown was part of the electorate of Cumberland Boroughs, a seat which represented the four larger towns of the county of Cumberland—Windsor, Richmond, Liverpool and Campbelltown—while the rural areas of the county of Cumberland formed another seat. From 1859 Campbelltown and the southern part of the district became the electorate of Narellan. The northern area became part of the Central Cumberland seat.[72]

Campbelltown experienced its first election campaign in 1843 when the two candidates for Cumberland Boroughs, both Hawkesbury men, came to town. Richard Fitzgerald, colonial-born son of one of Macquarie's most successful Irish emancipists, advocated civil and religious freedom, education for all and an immigration policy that made no 'invidious distinction or preference for emigrants from either of the three Kingdoms of Great Britain'. His opponent was William Bowman of Richmond, also colonial-born, whose local supporters included Benjamin Warby, James Graham, Dr Scouler and Charles Beck. Bowman promised to promote agriculture and grazing, build silos to store wheat and improve roads. Questions about religion and race turned the meeting violent and Bowman was accused of being anti-Catholic, anti-convict and anti-Irish by Fitzgerald supporters. William Howe was unable to retain order and dissolved the meeting. Politics had come to Campbelltown.[73]

Each electorate voted on a different day. There was no secret ballot and votes were cast verbally and in public. In Campbelltown the 1843 results were 23 votes for Bowman and 24 for Fitzgerald. However, Robert Burke had mortgaged his land so his vote for Fitzgerald was disallowed, resulting in a tied vote in Campbelltown. On the evening after the election, riot broke out in Campbelltown. Bowman's supporters were attacked on the streets and in their homes. Robert Woolbridge, a Bowman supporter, had his door broken down and windows smashed. Bowman won by a small majority and was re-elected until 1857. Campbelltown was also a polling place for the neighbouring seat of Camden where sectarian controversy dominated the first election. Roger Therry, a Catholic lawyer, was supported by James Macarthur and defeated Protestant Charles Cowper, who had attacked the low Irish and Catholic character of the district, yet whose supporters included the Ryans and Keighrans.[74]

The creation in 1858 of a new electorate, Narellan, which included Campbelltown township and its rural hinterland, reinforced an emerging sense of local identity and ensured a strong preference for members of parliament with Irish Catholic backgrounds, until 1880 when the seat disappeared in an electoral redistribution. Throughtout these two decades the local member alternated between John Hurley and Joseph Leary. The major political issues debated in these years were land policy, State aid to education and religion.

John Hurley, ex-convict, Catholic, publican, banker, horseracing patron, coaching proprietor and squatter, had since the 1830s been the leading community voice outside the magistracy in Campbelltown. He had been active on committees for schools, churches, roads, water supply and Irish emigration, and was a known advocate of any project that would advance Campbelltown. This identification with local matters was his strongest political asset. Hurley was looked up to as 'a man of strong sound sense, of unflinching integrity and of truly liberal political principles'. His supporters included all the well-known families of Campbelltown, whether Catholic or Protestant—the Roses, the Fowlers, the Byrnes. Hurley's first opponent was a sitting member, John Norton Oxley of Kirkham, whose supporters included Chisholm of Gledswood and Chippendall of Bradbury Park. The nomination meeting was stacked with shouting Hurley supporters and Oxley had little chance to speak. Narellan supported Oxley but the Irish, Catholic and Campbelltown gentry vote, together with support from Appin, produced a convincing win for Hurley.[75]

Members of parliament were not paid. By standing for election Hurley implied that his personal affairs had flourished and he had both the financial resources and the time to pursue a political career. Over the next twenty years his political statements favoured squatting, State aid to religion and education, free trade and local government. No-one, in public, mentioned that the member for Narellan had arrived as a convict.[76]

Joseph Leary (1831–81) was Hurley's regular opponent for the seat of Narellan. Campbelltown-born, of Irish descent and Catholic, Leary married local girl Catherine Keighran in 1854. Leary was well educated, with two years at the University of Sydney before he took up law. He was admitted as a solicitor in 1866 and returned to practise in his home town as Campbelltown's first locally born lawyer. He was appointed to the Campbelltown bench of magistrates. Leary assisted W. B. Dalley in his defence of the bushranging Clarke brothers who were executed in 1867. Later Leary actively opposed capital punishment. In politics he frequently

Reverend G. F. Macarthur (left) with pupils, Macquarie Fields House, around 1865. JAMIESON COLLECTION

offended his Catholic friends by opposing State aid to religion and supporting public education and civil divorce. Leary served briefly as Minister of Justice and Public Instruction in Farnell's Cabinet of 1878. He died from heart disease, aged 49, in 1881.[77]

Town and country life 1840–1880

Education

In 1856 two-thirds of the adult population in the Campbelltown area could read and write. There were several small primary schools run by the local churches and a handful of private boarding and day academies for boys and girls. Thomas Hammond ran a boarding school, the Campbelltown Academy, during the 1830s and 1840s. Fees were £40 per annum for boarders and £8 for day pupils who were given a 'Mathematical and Classical Education, with the accomplishments of Music and Drawing if required'. One of his more successful students was Thomas Colls, MLA for Liverpool and Yass. Private academies run by clergymen such as the Reverends David Boyd, Henry Gordon and Mr Beecham offered finishing classes for boys in classical studies.[78]

The Reverend Robert Forrest, foundation headmaster of the King's School at Parramatta and rector at St Peters, Campbelltown, from 1839, taught six private boarding pupils, at £100 per year each, to pay his house rent, there being no parsonage. The boys were 16–17-year-olds and stayed with Forrest for two years. When Forrest returned to the King's School in 1848 several Campbelltown families sent their sons there, including Henry and Alfred Rose, Reuben Rose and James Payten.[79]

96

One of Forrest's pupils at Campbelltown was George Fairfowl Macarthur (1825–1890), third son of Hannibal Macarthur, a grandson of Governor King and great-nephew of John Macarthur. Entering the clergy in 1849, G. F. Macarthur was rector from 1851 of St Marks, Darling Point, where he conducted a small school. In 1858 he left his parish to concentrate on teaching and moved his family and pupils to Macquarie Fields House, the site of Reddall's 1821 school and close to the new railway. Borrowing money from family and friends, Macarthur leased the house and 1500 acres (600 ha). There were two resident tutors and visiting teachers from Liverpool, such as Elizabeth Nutt who taught music. Despite the temporary embarrassment of bankruptcy in 1859, G. F. Macarthur was able to continue the school and over the next decade it prospered. By the mid-1860s he had about 80 boys enrolled as boarders at fees of £70 per year and had established the first student cadet corps. Meanwhile the King's School at Parramatta had closed. The bishop of Sydney approached Macarthur to revive it and he accepted in 1868. Initially, the new King's School operated at Macquarie Fields, but after a year Macarthur moved the school back to its traditional and more central premises in Parramatta.[80]

Some private classes were offered for girls. Reverend Thomas Reddall's widow and three unmarried daughters ran a school for girls intermittently at their home, Glen Alpine. Wives and sisters of Congregational ministers held classes in the church and Miss Gordon conducted a girls' school at Denham Court.[81]

From 1849 church schools were supervised by the Denominational Board of Commissioners which distributed government funds to them. A second board, the National Board of Commissioners, established government schools in areas not served by church schools. Three schools in Campbelltown and one at Denham Court received assistance from the Denominational Board. This system changed in 1866 with the *Public Schools Act*. No longer would government funds be provided for church and government schools to compete for pupils, and church schools which accepted government aid had to provide secular education for half of each day and accept children of any religious denomination.

Enrolments in denominational schools in Campbelltown in 1863 totalled 247, divided among the Church of England (105 students), Catholic (99 pupils) and Presbyterian (43). By 1874 school enrolments were 225, reflecting the decline in the town's population. The Church of England school fell to 47 pupils. The main beneficiary was the Presbyterian school where almost half the pupils were Anglican. The largest was the Catholic primary school with an enrolment of 118, almost one-quarter of whom were Anglicans.

St Peters Church of England School was the oldest in the district. It was a certified denominational school and George Rupert Evans was the teacher in the 1860s. Evans had trained at St James during the 1850s but had no formal teaching qualifications. An inspector described him as 'respectable in appearance, of good address and quiet manner in addressing the pupils' and tolerably competent. Evans was also the Campbelltown district registrar of births, marriages and deaths and secretary of the Campbelltown Road Trust. In 1867 there were 92 enrolments at St Peters School, with an average attendance of 72.[82]

Evans resigned in 1873 to join the Bank of New South Wales because the church could not provide suitable accommodation in Campbelltown for his large family. It was difficult to find a suitable married man as his replacement. Henry Mills was transferred from the public school at Menangle. There he had been paid only £16 per year in school fees from 48 pupils, but his income was supplemented by presents. He never had to buy firewood, water or hay for his horse, and parents, unable to pay fees in cash, made it up in fresh meat and vegetables. Mills was not married and this was a source of constant prejudice against him at Campbelltown. He was unable to control the children at the Church of England school. The boys sang during lessons and threw their books across the classroom. The girls threw each other into the mud at the school gate, and both boys and girls refused to submit to corporal punishment. Student numbers fell as parents withdrew their children.[83]

At the Denham Court Church of England School 47 boys and 51 girls were enrolled between 1859 and 1871 with an average class of 12–16 children each year. Their ages varied from 3 to 14 and only half were Anglicans. With the exception of the Reverend Woodd's own children, all were children of tenants on Denham Court, Leppington and Macquarie Fields estates or of farmers at Soldiers Flat and Lower Minto. There was a small Church of England school at Riversford, Menangle Ford, in 1855 while the bridge was being built. The teacher, and acting postmaster, was Edward Lomas. In 1874 the Church of England school at Sugarloaf Hill, Menangle Bridge, was reopened for children of men rebuilding the bridge. Esther Aitken taught eighteen children and the rector of St Peters, Campbelltown, hoped that it would become a public school but there was no permanent community.[84]

The Catholic primary school at Campbelltown opened in 1840 on the Old Menangle Road. A. D. Carolan was replaced by Patrick Newman in 1864. This was Newman's first teaching position and he was assisted by his wife, Eliza, whose time was divided between teaching and caring for their large family. By 1873 Eliza Newman had ten year's experience in the infants' department and received favourable reports from the inspectors. She could not advance her teaching career because she had no leisure to prepare for examinations. Her husband found it difficult to extract school fees from parents, but received no support from the magistrates when he took legal action.[85]

The third church school in Campbelltown was run by the Presbyterians and it was they who initiated moves for a public school as early as 1869. In a letter to the Council of Education in January 1869, James Grant and John Kidd offered to give the Presbyterian land and buildings to the government for a public school. Built on half an acre (0.2 ha), part of the Presbyterian grant in 1843, the brick schoolroom was 26 feet by 16 feet (8 m by 5 m) with two adjoining rooms for the teacher's residence. Under an excellent teacher, A. Gilchrist, the school had outgrown its classroom. There were 42 children enrolled in 1869, but only 12 were Presbyterians, with 17 Church of England, 11 Catholic and 2 Congregationalists. There were few Presbyterians in Campbelltown so the number of Presbyterian children was unlikely to increase, therefore the local committee would not finance repairs. The parents of the non-Presbyterian children were not interested in paying for the upkeep of the church's property.

There was no resident Presbyterian clergyman in Campbelltown but the Reverend Holland was appointed as soon as the Moderator was informed of this scheme. Holland and the Moderator agreed to offer the school and land to the government on a 21-year lease at a nominal rent. A local public school board, tactfully composed of a representative of the four major Christian denominations in Campbelltown—Congregational, Church of England, Presbyterian and Catholic—was formed, but the project came to a sudden end when the school inspector pointed out that funds for repairs were only available for government-owned buildings.[86]

In 1871 local parliamentarian Joseph Leary, a supporter of government schools, arranged for 3 acres (1.2 ha) to be reserved for a public school between the Church of England and the Sydney Road, opposite the courthouse. By the mid-1870s both Protestant schools in Campbelltown had assessed their financial realities and decided to support one large public school rather than continue their small schools.

Under the *Public Schools Act* a local community had to provide one-third the cost of a new school. A public meeting in July 1874 started the fund-raising and within a month had promises of sufficient funds. The Council of Education was assured by 38 parents that a minimum of 107 children would attend a public school. Only two Catholic families supported it. Further assurances were given that the two Protestant schools would close when the public school opened. The fund-raising committee which guaranteed the finance consisted of E. H. Woodhouse of Mount Gilead; William Fowler, landowner and magistrate; Edwin Hallett Fieldhouse and John Kidd, both storekeepers and magistrates; H. Arkell Smith, Clerk of Petty Sessions; James Bocking, storekeeper and miller; Daniel Fowler, grazier, and George Brown, storekeeper. Their numbers were increased to include Arthur Barant James Chauvel, magistrate and squatter; Thomas Chippendall, landowner, and Patrick Dwyer, station master and the only Catholic member of the school committee.

The sitting member of parliament in 1874 was John Hurley who, with other residents, objected to the site reserved for the school because it was the market reserve. The Presbyterian committee was still willing to give its land for a public school, but the Campbelltown committee proposed the police paddock, a site reserved in 1827 for a courthouse but never built on. As Campbelltown was a permanently settled community with a number of affluent residents and few poor ones, the government approved a public school. In a population of about 900 there were 250 children of school age within 3 kilometres, and as a number of the children at the Catholic school were Protestant, it could be anticipated that some would transfer to the public school. With the likelihood of compulsory secular education in the near future, plans were made for a projected enrolment of 100 boys and 100 girls.

G. A. Mansfield designed the buildings which were constructed during 1875. The local board had wanted two buildings to separate boys and girls, a school kitchen and a water supply, but was unable, or unwilling, to pay for these additional facilities. The local committee provided £400 of a total cost of £1400. The new school, opened by the Secretary of the Council of Education in January 1876, was a brick building with shingle roof and an attached residence for the teacher on a 5- acre (2 ha) site. The first headmaster was John Humphries, formerly a teacher at the Wollongong Church of England School, assisted by two pupil teachers. From an initial enrolment of 89 children, the year closed with 126 pupils, slightly more than the combined enrolment of the now closed Protestant schools. The pupils were 'clean, orderly and attentive'. The older boys were taught algebra, geometry, Latin and squad drill, though apparently not book-keeping or French, subjects requested by the local committee. Except for sewing, it is unclear what the girls were taught.[87]

Children at Minto received intermittent education from a small school on the Campbelltown Road south of the track leading down to Campbellfields (Minto) station. The land had been given to the Catholic Church by J. Pendergast for a school prior to 1866. Pendergast provided timber and his neighbours erected a slab building. Known as Saggar's or Saggart Field, the small school was run by Nanno Clark, a widowed Irishwoman, under the general supervision of Father J. P. Roche, parish priest at Campbelltown. The local residents were very poor and, despite general Catholic opposition to government schools, Roche arranged to transfer Saggart Field School to the government. It became a provisional public school in 1867, thus ensuring a small, regular salary for Mrs Clark, and was the first government school in the Campbelltown district. When Mrs Clark died two years later, Father Roche reported that she was destitute, and requested an advance on her salary to cover her funeral expenses.[88]

Saggart Field School continued under several women teachers for the next decade, but by 1878 the building was so unsatisfactory that the school was closed. Draughts whistled between the slabs and there were no secure fastenings to close windows or doors. From September 1878 to August 1879 the children were provided with free train tickets to attend the public school at Campbelltown. Following a petition from twelve families—Lyons, Meredith, Bolger, Keating, Scanlon, Blain, Sherack, Allison, Thompson, Knock, Piggott and Wilson—Saggart Field Provisional School was reopened in September 1879. The parents could not afford to furnish it and old desks and benches were borrowed from Camden Public

School. The new teacher was James Funnell, assisted by his wife. The school was promoted to full public school status in 1880.[89]

In 1880 the New South Wales *Public Instruction Act* foreshadowed the end of government assistance to denominational schools in 1882. In Campbelltown the Protestant schools had already closed but the new legislation put great pressure on the Catholic primary school. The situation became critical when the teacher at the public school accepted a transfer. Rather than recruit a new teacher from outside the district, the Campbelltown School Board approached Patrick Newman, the teacher at the Catholic school. Newman was respected by Protestants as well as Catholics in the town where he had taught for eighteen years.

Newman formally applied for the post in August 1880, pointing out that in his school of 147 children about one-third were not Catholics. Monsignor J. T. Lynch of Campbelltown protested that the Department of Education had poached his teacher and, while supporting Newman's attempts to further his career, considered it very bad taste to appoint Newman to the public school in the same town. In September 1880, 100 parents and residents of Campbelltown signed a petition supporting Newman's transfer to the public school.[90]

Churches

In 1841 about half of the population in Campbelltown and the surrounding district gave their religion as Church of England. About 39 per cent in the town and 34 per cent in the district were Catholics. Though these proportions altered slightly over time, affiliation to the Church of England and the Catholic Church remained higher than the colonial average, while Campbelltown had significantly fewer Presbyterians or Wesleyans than the rest of New South Wales.[91]

Apart from a few isolated incidents, there was little sectarian conflict between Catholic and Protestant in Campbelltown. The Reverend William Stack, rector of St Peters in 1846, had previously served in Maitland where he had clashed with the local Catholic schoolteacher, William Duncan, in heated theological argument. Shortly after, Duncan established the *Australasian Chronicle*, the first Catholic newspaper. Stack's ministry at Campbelltown was remembered as a troubled decade for sectarianism and there was general relief when he moved to Balmain in 1855. From the 1860s religious differences rarely attracted attention in Campbelltown.

The Reverend Thomas Verrier Alkin was rector of St Peters for 28 years. Born in Kent, England, and educated at Cambridge, Alkin had arrived in Australia in the late 1860s and gained his colonial experience at Toowoomba, Queensland, before becoming rector of St Peters in 1876. Alkin was interested in botany and his scientific acquaintances, both secular and clerical, broadened intellectual life in the town. Alkin started the Campbelltown Botanical Collecting Society in 1878 to encourage young people to collect, examine and preserve Australian plants. In his view, wandering the bush, observing, collecting, noting details in a systematic way and displaying a neat collection was as valuable as a classroom lesson. Membership was open to adults and children, but the annual competition and temporary natural history display of borrowed microscopes, minerals, fossils and electromagnets was specifically arranged for the local schoolchildren. The Campbelltown Botanical Collecting Society was supported by the Catholic and Congregational clergy, not least because it provided an occasion for 'people of differing ways of thinking to meet on common ground'. The Campbelltown botanical group faded away in the 1880s. Alkin's extensive herbarium of Campbelltown plants was sold to Zurich University, Switzerland, about 1904.[92]

In November 1844 T. V. Blomfield, Christiana Blomfield and their second son, Richard, who inherited Denham Court under his grandfather's will, gave the Brooks family chapel at Denham Court to the Church of England for a church, parsonage and burial ground. St Mary the Virgin, Denham Court, became part of the parish of Minto and Cabramatta under the Reverend G. N. Woodd in 1858. It had a regular congregation of 70, mostly from Minto and Ingleburn.[93]

James Goold (1812–86) trained for the priesthood in Ireland and arrived in Australia in 1838. He was appointed successor to Father Therry at St Johns, Campbelltown, where he served for five years, overseeing the completion of St Johns Church and the building of St Patricks School. He was appointed the first bishop of Melbourne in 1847. His successor, Father John Paul Roche, was Campbelltown's parish priest for the next quarter century, retiring in 1877. As well as his congregation at Campbelltown, Roche served the Camden and Menangle churches.

Sectarian conflict increased in the 1840s and 1850s with debates about State aid to the clergy and public education. During one period of heated debate in October 1856, St Johns was desecrated and the crucifix thrown into the reservoir. Continued tension resulted, in 1863, in a fund to build a watchman's cottage overlooking the church and graveyard. Subscriptions were made by Catholics in Wagga Wagga, Gundagai, Yass and Albury as well as by local families.[94]

The Campbelltown congregation followed church affairs closely. Archbishop Polding's sudden departure for Rome in March 1854 caused rumours of his resignation. The congregation of St Johns, Campbelltown, met in April 1854 to express their concern. Hurley, Doyle, Keighran, Guthrie, Ryan, Burke, Pendergast and Vardy spoke of their support for Polding's work and confidence in his administration. Father Roche, a Benedictine like Polding, chaired the meeting. Polding remained archbishop until his death in 1877.[95]

The Presbyterian congregation in Campbelltown was very small, composed largely of families who had migrated from Scotland and Northern Ireland. St Davids Presbyterian Church was built over eighteen months from 1840 to 1842 with government assistance under the 1836 *Church Act*.

The architect was James Hume, who also designed St Andrews Cathedral in Sydney in 1837 and St Saviours at Goulburn, and the builder was Mr Leslie of Campbelltown assisted by Samuel Bursill. Lacking tower and vestry, St Davids was opened in July 1842 by the Reverend John Tait of Parramatta. Land for a burial ground was given by Alexander McDonald who died in 1847. The church had a capacity for 200 but the congregation rarely exceeded 60. The first minister was the Reverend Hugh Robert Gilchrist who came to Campbelltown in 1837 and served until his death in 1852. His successor was the Reverend William McKee, from 1853 to 1867. During his ill health the congregation was without a clergyman. The Reverend Edward Holland served for three years, but the small congregation could not ensure a stipend after State funding of salaries ended in 1862 and for most of the 1870s there was no regular clergyman.[96]

The corner of Oxley and Allman Streets was selected for a Wesleyan school and minister's residence in 1845. The Methodist Wesleyan stone chapel was opened in October 1846 with a sermon by the Reverend W. B. Boyce before an audience of 150. The first clergyman was the Reverend M. Kenny. John Vidler, a lay Wesleyan preacher who migrated to New South Wales in 1838, came to Campbelltown from Dapto about 1840. For seven years he rented part of Bradbury Park and preached. He left when the Wesleyan chapel opened and settled in Jamberoo, where he was still an active preacher in 1885. His home, Vidlers Hill, was later acquired by James Bocking who called it Austin Park.[97]

It was probably not by accident that Campbelltown's Congregational church was built diagonally opposite the Wesleyan chapel. The Congregational movement was brought to Campbelltown by James Bocking and his business partner, John Cobb. In Campbelltown, as in Sydney, the most active members of the Congregational Church were businessmen such as miller Laurence Kendall, son of New Zealand missionary Thomas Kendall, and building contractors Cobb and Bocking. Initially they worshipped with the Wesleyan congregation, but doctrinal differences caused them to invite Congregational pastors, the Reverends William Slayter and Edward Robinson, to preach in Campbelltown. Bocking married Robinson's daughter.

In 1857 land in Allman Street was purchased and Cobb and Bocking designed and built a chapel. Funds for the building, opened in December 1859, came from Congregationalists in Sydney. It was the third regional church outside Sydney and the first along the southern road. A Congregational cemetery was opened on land donated by Benjamin Warby on the corner of the Wedderburn Road and Smith Road.[98]

The town

The most significant subdivision affecting the physical shape of Campbelltown was the sale of the Bradbury estate in 1844. Bradbury's land, originally Joseph Phelp's grant, lay south of Allman Street. The southern road passed through it and branched to Appin, Menangle and the Cow-pastures at its southern boundary. William Bradbury died in 1836 and his estate was inherited by his daughter, Mary Sheil (later Mary Cannon).

Bradbury Park estate was subdivided in 1843 and offered for sale the following year. Surveyor Goodall created small allotments along Queen and Allman Streets with larger farming sections at the eastern end of Allman Street and along the Appin Road. There were already a few buildings on the corner of Allman Street and on the western side of Queen Street. The Georgian buildings on the eastern side of Queen Street and the flour mill were built on the Bradbury subdivision. Bradbury Park House, a two-storey brick building with verandahs, was retained in 16 acres (6.4 ha) of parkland. Behind the house was a quadrangle of kitchen, servants' quarters and farm buildings. Elaborate flower and kitchen gardens lay south of the house. In 1856 Thomas Dyer Edwards and Henry Burton Bradley sold the house and remaining land to Thomas Chippendall. Though churches, schools and water supply were within the bounds of the official town north of Allman Street, the focus of commercial and residential life in Campbelltown became the Queen Street frontage of the Bradbury estate.[99]

At the census of 1861 Campbelltown had a population, within the town, of 938 people, about the same as Liverpool (953) and Albury (981), considerably larger than its neighbour, Camden (685), but much smaller than the queen city of the south, Goulburn (3241 people).[100]

A visitor in 1878 commented that the town had few new buildings and looked the same as it had 40 years earlier. House and churches showed signs of wear. The only new buildings were the railway station and goods sheds, the Cumberland Hotel near the railway and two new cottages in Railway Street. With the coming of the railway in 1858, land near the station had been subdivided. John Hurley owned most of the land in the vicinity, including the site of the present civic centre, and subdivided between 1858 and 1860 and again in 1878, creating L-shaped Patrick Hurley Street (later divided into two streets) and Railway Street. At the southern end of the town, opposite Bocking's mill, a new store was under construction for the Fieldhouse brothers.[101]

By 1879 Campbelltown was one long street, still unnamed, with several smaller cross streets, all badly drained. The clock in St Peters tower was stuck permanently at 10 to 2 and access to the Catholic church on the hill in the dark was difficult. The town served an agricultural district, offering a post and money order office, a government savings bank, telegraph office, courthouse, gaol, temperance hall, four churches, four hotels, a bank and insurance agency, several stores, butchers and bakers. The population was falling and the best that could be said was that Campbelltown was 'noted for the salubrity of its climate and the consequent longevity of its inhabitants'.[102]

Bradbury Park estate (R. H. Goodall, surveyor, c.1844)

Country estates

Campbelltown, apart from the straggle of buildings along the main road, was a rural district whose fortunes fluctuated with the seasons and the colonial economy. Following the discovery of gold in 1851 many able-bodied men and women had left for the goldfields. Those who remained to work their farms found that labour was scarce and they could not afford the high wages. By 1853 overgrown and abandoned farms were common and Campbelltown itself had a 'poverty-stricken aspect'.[103]

Most farmers developed their land but there were several absentee landowners with little interest in estate improvement. Redfern's Campbellfield estate was one of the latter. In January 1843 Campbellfield was offered at auction. Consisting of 6000 acres (2400 ha) of parkland, wheat fields, pasture and grazing land, well situated between the main road to Campbelltown from Liverpool and the George's River, it was subdivided into 122 portions ranging from 700 to 2-acre (280 to 0.8 ha) allotments. The allotments suitable for small farmers were along the main road and Bow Bowing and Bunbury Curran Creeks and the forest lands were kept in larger acreages. The sale, held during the economic depression, was a failure. The trustees leased out most of Campbellfield as rough grazing land for the next 40 years.[104]

Macquarie Fields was owned by Martha Foxlow Hosking (1822–77) and her husband, John. About 1840 they built a country house, probably designed by John's brother, William, who was an architect in England. Martha, her husband and three young daughters sometimes lived at Macquarie Fields House and the estate was divided into tenant farms. From 1858 Martha Hosking preferred to live at her Mount Pleasant estate near Penrith and Macquarie Fields House was leased to G. F. Macarthur for a school until 1869. In 1877 Martha Hosking died and her executors sold Macquarie Fields in 1881.[105]

Nearby Denham Court remained the home of the Blomfield family. Richard Brooks had left the estate to his daughter for her lifetime and then to her second son, Richard Henry Blomfield. Christiana Blomfield died there in 1852, followed by her husband in 1857. Their son lived in Goulburn and the farms were probably tenanted.

Varroville was the home of the Raymond family. James Raymond was Postmaster-general of New South Wales from 1835 until his death in 1851, and he introduced the first prepaid stamped covers in the world in 1838. Varroville was inherited by his son but his four daughters could also live there as long as they wished. James Raymond junior died in 1855 and his sisters, Honoria Australia, wife of Robert Lethbridge King, Aphrasia Margaret Day, Anna Maria Bolden and Elizabeth Sydney Raymond, sold the estate in 1858 to Alfred Cheeke, a judge of the District and later Supreme Court of New South Wales. Cheeke was an ardent follower of horserac-ing, owning racing stables at Mount Druitt. The old Campbelltown race-course was on the flats below Varroville, which became a successful horse stud. Cheeke's brown filly Clove won the first Australian Derby in 1865. The Varroville stables were managed by John Chaffe from 1872. Vice-president of the Australian Jockey Club, Cheeke was a well-dressed, portly figure who visited Varroville by train each weekend to inspect his horses. Unmarried, he died at his Darling Point home in 1876.[106]

Adjoining Varroville was the Inch grant. Joseph Inch, a Sydney storekeeper, had died in 1836 and his wife Elizabeth died two years later. Their only child, Jane Ann Inch, inherited the 200-acre (80 ha) grant at Minto and considerable land in Sydney, including part of the site of the Sydney General Post Office. Jane Inch was declared a lunatic in 1843 and confined to an asylum at Cook's River for the rest of her life. Periodically the court sold her land to pay debts incurred on her behalf. Her Minto land was kept until the end of the century and was leased for rough grazing. The lessee in the 1870s was Rachel Rush of Sydney.[107]

Eagle Vale estate was inherited by Robert Pitt Jenkins (1814–1859), a member of the Legislative Council, on his mother's death in 1842. Jenkins and his wife Louisa née Plunkett, decided to take their family to England in the late 1850s and sold their various estates, including Eagle Vale. Their ship, the *Royal Charter*, was wrecked off the coast of Wales on 25 October 1859. Robert Jenkins, his wife and all their children except one daughter drowned. Jenkins' trustees continued the arrangements for the sale of his estates. Eagle Vale in 1858 covered 608 acres (243 ha). Apart from the house, there was a coachman's house, stables, gardens, pigstyes and a gatekeeper's lodge at the entrance from the Narellan road (Raby Road). Only one paddock was fenced for wheat.

Eagle Vale was purchased in 1858 by William Fowler of Campbelltown.

Eshcol Park, built in 1860 for William Fowler is here shown at the time of his residence. The name of the adjoining suburb is misspelt as Eschol Park.

Fowler had married Eliza Warby in 1840, opened a store and operated the post office from 1846. Fowler renamed Eagle Vale 'Eshcol Park'—after a vineyard in the Old Testament—planted vines and built a two-storey winery where, within ten years, he was producing 2000–3000 gallons (9100–13 650 L) of wine annually. Fowler sold Eshcol Park to S. S. Milgate in 1876, but two years later it was purchased by John Tangelder Gorus, a Dutch photographer, who lived there until the end of the century.[108]

William Howe retired from public life in 1845 and died at Glenlee ten years later. His widow Mary moved to Dapto to live with one of her eight sons. Glenlee in the 1840s and 1850s was famous for its 'Sun and Thistle' butter. Most of its 3000 acres (1200 ha) was farmed by tenants. In 1839 William Howe and his son Ephraim had purchased a large number of cattle and horses from the estate of William Redfern. They mortgaged Glenlee for £20 350 to cover their purchase, but the 1840s were depression years and they never recovered their outlay on the stock. Glenlee was transferred to the mortgagees, H. G. Antill and Thomas Wills, in 1850, but the Howe family remained lessees until the death of William Howe junior in 1858. The following year Glenlee was sold to James Fitzpatrick for £14 500.[109]

James Fitzpatrick was one of the convict servants who accompanied Hume and Hovell in 1824. Born in Limerick about 1800, in 1822 he was one of 43 Irish protesters transported to New South Wales aboard the *Mangles*. The Limerick men were victims of the 1822 *Insurrection Act* under which persons away from home at night, as well as those found with weapons, could be transported for seven years. Fitzpatrick was assigned to Hamilton Hume and held a ticket-of-leave from July 1825 in the Appin district where he acquired some land. His sentence expired in 1829 and the following year he married Mary Ann Atkins, aged 23, who had arrived with a seven-year sentence on the *Elizabeth* in 1828. From his base in Appin, Fitzpatrick returned to the southern districts that he had helped discover. By 1833 his squatting run, Cucumla, covered 56 000 acres (22 400 ha) between Cootamundra and Gundagai. He acquired interests in several other runs in the Cootamundra–Yass district, from where he overlanded sheep and cattle to Victoria.

From the late 1840s, and particularly during the 1850s, Fitzpatrick purchased many farms south and west of Campbelltown. Why did Fitzpatrick move back to the county of Cumberland and invest capital in farms at Campbelltown rather than develop the leaseholds he already held? Many of his friends in the south-western districts had their colonial roots in Campbelltown. His neighbours at Cootamundra included John Hurley who had divided his interests between Campbelltown and the south since the 1830s. The answer may also lie in the quarrel between Hamilton Hume and William Hilton Hovell over leadership of their 1824 expedition. In 1855 Hume published his account of their journey, including a statement of support from Fitzpatrick. W. H. Hovell had sold his 700-acre (280 ha) Narellan estate to William Mowatt in 1830 to cover his expenses for the southern expedition. In 1849 Fitzpatrick purchased the estate from Mowatt, now living in England, for £700. In 1851 Fitzpatrick purchased the adjoining Grimes grant of 335 acres (134 ha) for £300 and acquired Smeaton, Throsby's 550-acre (220 ha) grant, for £600. Finally in 1859 James Fitzpatrick purchased Glenlee.

By the 1860s James Fitzpatrick owned most of the farms west from Campbelltown towards Narellan and many lying south towards Menangle. He had no children by his first wife and following her death in 1866 he married eighteen-year-old Elizabeth Cummins, daughter of a tenant farmer on Glenlee. They had three children—Mary Ann (b. 1870), Elizabeth Susan (b. 1873) and James Glenlee Fitzpatrick (b. 1876). Elizabeth Fitzpatrick died in April 1882, aged 32. Three months later James Fitzpatrick died at Glenlee, leaving three children under twelve and vast estates.[110]

Charles Throsby junior of Glenfield died in 1854. Glenfield was leased in 1859 as a working dairy farm with a comfortable country residence of fourteen rooms, kitchen, pantry and cellar. The 1000 acres (400 ha) of grazing land had a mile (1.6 km) frontage to the George's River and included large areas of rye, field peas, corn and sugarcane as well as 200 fruit trees and vegetable gardens. An underground dairy produced quality butter. Outbuildings included piggeries, cow yards, two large farm sheds, four new farm huts and a substantial brick four-stall stable and coach house with a granary above.[111]

Extensive clearing along the Appin Road gave the traveller a view of Mount Gilead with the old windmill on the hill and the house below reflected in the lake. Thomas Rose had died in 1837, leaving his second wife to rear an infant family. The estate was managed by trustees until 1858 and leased to Captain G. Christmas. In 1858 Rose's eldest son, Charles Henry Jacob Rose, took control. Henry Rose was a magistrate in Campbelltown and regularly attended the bench. Drought, flood and rust in the early 1860s ruined many farmers and in 1864 the mortgagee foreclosed. Henry Rose worked as postmaster in Campbelltown for a few years then left the district. Mount Gilead was owned briefly by Walter Friend and in 1867 was purchased by Edmund Hume Woodhouse (1824–1875) who was born on a neighbouring property, a grant to his father G. M. Woodhouse. A bank manager by occupation, E. H. Woodhouse married Gertrude Aitken, née Bingham in 1853. She bore seven children. At 44 years of age, Woodhouse turned to farming.

Over the next six years, until his premature death aged 51, Woodhouse was a remarkably innovative farmer, introducing to the Campbelltown district a bewildering variety of livestock and agricultural techniques. In the late 1860s, with its traditional wheat industry badly ravaged by rust, Campbelltown farmers needed new activities. Woodhouse was generally credited with recognising the prospects for large-scale dairying. He invested in cattle, both dairy and beef breeds, sheep for wool and meat, varieties of poultry and Berkshire pigs, as well as experimental farming of exotic animals like deer and llama under his overseer A. J. Chauvel.

E. H. Woodhouse died in 1875 and Mount Gilead was inherited by his eldest son, Edmund Bingham Woodhouse, who continued his father's interest in breeding cattle. Mount Gilead's most famous animals were the champion shorthorn bulls, but the prize herd was dispersed in 1878 and E. B. Woodhouse changed to Devon cattle. New piggeries costing £200 were built for imported Poland-China pigs, the first of their breed in the colony. The estate was regularly visited by agricultural journalists who were impressed by the artificial grasses, stock-feeding techniques and machinery.[112]

Also on the road to Appin was Glen Lorne, the country house of architect G. A. Mansfield. Glen Lorne was part of a grant to G. M. Woodhouse in 1823. Mansfield purchased the estate in 1876. Around the original small timber cottage, Mansfield built a home which he named after his wife, Lorne. By 1878 it was an attractive cottage with garden where Mansfield lived until his death.[113]

On the Menangle Road was Glen Alpine, the 400-acre (160 ha) estate of the Reddall family. When the Reverend Thomas Reddall died in 1838 the estate was heavily mortgaged, but by selling other land, their cattle and running a school with her daughters, Isabella Reddall was able to clear the debts by 1844. Her sons were unable to help her—Thomas was in Cambridge studying for the clergy; Luke drowned in the Murray River in 1840. Her eldest son, John, was declared bankrupt in 1840, suffered a nervous breakdown and by 1844 was confined in the Tarban Creek Lunatic Asylum with his children in his mother's care. John and his mother both died in August 1855 and were buried at St Peters. The Reverend Thomas Reddall junior became rector of St Peters in 1855, retired in ill health in 1857 and died unmarried in 1860, leaving Glen Alpine to his three unmarried sisters. Eliza, Clara and Amelia lived in the house until their deaths and the farm was worked by tenants.[114]

Further south the Edrop estate was the largest in North Menangle, comprising a 200-acre (80 ha) grant to James Harrax at Bird's Eye Corner and a 200-acre grant to J. W. Lewin as well as smaller grants to Armstrong, Woodham, Marsden, Doyle, Dogherty and Taber, totalling 640 acres (256 ha). James Edrop, a butcher of Parramatta, married Adah Harrax who inherited the estate from her father. Edrop by 1848 had a 12 000-acre (4800 ha) squatting run in the north-west and his principle grazing interests were at Coonamble. At Menangle Edrop planted apple orchards, cultivated imported English grasses, and grew wheat, oats and maize. He had a small dairy herd and he tried running sheep, but found the land too wet. On his death in 1873 Edrop divided his property between the sons of his first and second marriages. Edward John Edrop, Adah's son born in 1843 at Parramatta, inherited the Menangle estate.[115]

Daily life

Campbelltown had a strong sense of identity with Ireland. Many of the convict settlers were Irish and the free immigrants who came after 1840 were attracted to areas settled by their fellow countrypeople. Dr Kenny of Campbelltown returned to Ireland in 1841, employed by the government to select Irish immigrants. Before leaving he consulted John Hurley who had many friends who wanted to bring out their families from Ireland. In 1842 a public meeting in Campbelltown discussed ways to help Caroline Chisholm settle Irish immigrants in the southern districts and Hurley provided a building for a staging centre. In September 1846 Father Goold chaired a public meeting at which Protestants as well as Catholics heard of the failure of the potato crop and the widespread distress in Ireland. A year later another meeting to relieve Irish and Scottish poverty raised £60. By the 1860s this Irishness had been dissipated by the exodus to the southern districts.[116]

English migrants formed the largest proportion of settlers in the nineteenth century. Mary Ann Simons arrived in Sydney in October 1853 with her husband Thomas, a flour miller. She imagined that the faces of Australians were indelibly stamped with their convict origins and the women were all 'drunken, loose reprobate characters'. Thomas Simons was offered a job in Yass. They travelled south by coach, an open box with ten passengers, leaving Sydney at 5.45 am and arriving at Campbelltown at 11 am, shaken by the bad roads but fascinated by the laughing jackasses (Kookaburras) and cockatoos along the way. Dinner at the inn at Campbelltown, her first Sunday on land since she left England so many months earlier, included a joint of roast beef, boiled beef, a leg of boiled mutton, a dish of mutton chops and a boiled duck, with peas, other green vegetables, baked potatoes and tea. In the evening Mary Ann and Thomas wandered up to St Peters Church. Roses had run wild over the graves but the interior of the church was neat and comfortable, with stained-glass windows and marble tablets on the walls. At 9 pm they left for Goulburn. Many years later Mary Ann returned with her second husband, John Percival of Northampton Dale.[117]

Homes in Campbelltown varied greatly between gentry, storekeeper and labourer. Patrick McMahon was a wheelwright and a lessee of 298 Queen Street until 1858, when he moved to his own land on which he had a house and his workshop, valued at £400. His home was a four-roomed cottage comprising a dining-room with nine chairs, a bedroom with two beds, a washstand, dressing-table and mirror and the children's room with two stretchers. In the kitchen was a boiler, two saucepans, a few knives, forks and crockery and a pair of candlesticks. The yard was littered with old carts, wheels and ploughs, while in the workshop were many bars of iron, bellows, anvil and tools, valued at £10.[118]

William Ray junior (1814–1885) was born in Campbelltown. His mother, Sarah Wade, father, William Ray, and stepfather, Nathanial Boon, farmed and operated the Three Brothers Inn. William junior retained the inn but also took up squatting runs near Wagga Wagga, and in 1855 purchased Mount Pleasant near Campbelltown from his brother-in-law, John Jenkins of Gundagai. Mismanagement led to insolvency in 1869. William Ray and his wife, Eliza, née Jackson, had ten children by

1869. Their two-storey home at Campbelltown was richly furnished. On the ground floor was a formal room with cedar tables, chairs, sofas and sideboard. There were six pictures on the wall, workboxes and books, china vases and candlesticks, a birdcage and a clock. The parlour was fashionably cluttered with a loo-table, whatnot, chiffonier, cottage pianoforte, chairs and sofa with carpet on the floor, curtains on the windows and pictures on the walls. The back dining-room was furnished with cedar chairs and leaf-table and boasted an ornamental clock, glass decanters, cruet-stand and knife-box. There was one bedroom downstairs with a cedar bed and child's cot, washstands and commode chair. Two bedrooms upstairs slept at least seven people, with one double cedar bed and a single bed in the first bedroom and two double beds in the second bedroom. In an adjoining cottage was another furnished bedroom and a spare room with bedstead. There was accommodation for at least two servants, one sleeping in the dairy and another in the detached kitchen. In the yard were carts and drays, harness, ploughs, tools, shingles and tubs and wash boilers for the outdoor laundry.[119]

Campbelltown had several resident doctors, some practising, others retired on farms. In the 1840s were Dr W. R. Kenny, Dr Palmer, Dr R. C. Hope and Dr Isadore Blake; in the 1850s and 1860s Dr William Bell and Dr Arthur Scouler set broken bones, pulled teeth and prescribed powders and medicines. Little Mary Brooksbank was treated by Dr Scouler after an horrific accident when she was caught under a spiked roller. Without chloroform, using a silver needle and silk thread he took all morning to stitch her wounds. The child, after two years in bed, was able to lead a normal life.[120]

Campbelltown was, unfortunately for Dr William Bell, a healthy neighbourhood and his business fell by £400 from 1858 to 1859. Surgeon, apothecary, magistrate and coroner, Bell charged £1.1.0 for a visit and about 10 shillings for medicines. James Kennedy, a small farmer at Denham Court, and Archibald Casey, a coachman in Campbelltown, both found that medical costs were critical items in their family finances. Casey, with a wife and five children, saw illness lead his family to poverty while he was unemployed in 1859. The constant ill health of Kennedy's wife and daughter caused him great expense. Bad costing on a timber carting contract, the loss of a valuable horse and medical bills sent Kennedy from a tolerable life to destitution in 1880.[121]

The sick and elderly relied on family support or charitable institutions such as the asylum for the destitute at Liverpool. Friendly societies were an alternative, mutual support group. For a small annual subscription they offered a medical service for members and their families, sickness and funeral benefits. Membership of the Sons of Temperance Friendly Society had reached almost 6000 throughout the colony by 1879. In Campbelltown the Congregational church formed the Band of Hope, a temperance friendly society, and built the temperance hall in 1862 to provide an alternative public meeting venue to the hotels. The Campbelltown temperance hall was owned by the Crystal Spring No. 35 Division of the Sons of Temperance Society, with John Kidd, James Bocking, George Brown, tailor, James Wilson, butcher, and Alexander Munro, contractor, as trustees.[122]

Sport and leisure

Campbelltown came alive each September with the annual races, held in the 1840s on the Campbellfield estate along Bow Bowing Creek (now Memphis, Nelson and Francis Streets, Minto). In 1851 the Campbelltown Turf Club, represented by John Bray of Denfield, William Fowler, postmaster, James Graham, wheelwright, John Vardy of Menangle and Michael Byrne, farmer, leased 60 acres (24 ha) from John Keighran for a racecourse. Visitors and horse owners, riders and grooms thronged Campbelltown on the days before the races, with 'mysterious looking animals, supposed to be horses, under a mountain of blanket clothing'. Two days became three days of racing, with the major races on the first and third days and hurdle races and sweepstakes on the second day. Each night the town echoed with the music and frivolity. Champion jockey Charles Stanley rode for Judge Cheeke of Varroville. Stanley rode the winners of the AJC Derby in 1866 and 1867, the Victorian St Leger in 1868 and won the Melbourne Cup on Glencoe in 1868. He married Emma Fieldhouse and ran the Sportsman's Arms Hotel in Campbelltown.[123]

Sunday sport was frowned upon, as was carrying firearms on Sundays. Game was plentiful, especially wallabies along the George's River. On one occasion in 1878 a party went wallaby hunting with a dozen dogs over Peter's Meadow, bagging teal, pigeons, hares, rabbits and seven wallabies in two hours. Hares had been brought for sport to Mount Gilead and Orielton Park in the early 1870s. Coursing with live hares was held in Hurley's Paddocks adjacent to the Campbelltown courthouse, at Orielton and Harrington Park. Sportsmen took the train to Campbelltown where there were two boarding houses and horses and vehicles for hire. Foxes were appearing though the Eastwood and Cumberland Hunt still chased the dingo across the Campbelltown fields with as many as 30 gentlemen and packs of hounds in pursuit—and the dingo often got away.[124]

Cricket was popular, especially on holidays at Christmas and Easter. On Boxing Day 1843 a Campbelltown eleven defeated a team from Camden. Fencing the town recreation reserve (Mawson Park) in 1878 enabled cricket to be played without the nuisance of straying stock and gave impetus to the formation of an athletic club. An athletic meeting was held in July 1878, with a crowd of 150 attending to see distance, speed and age races.[125]

Bazaars and concerts raised funds for local churches and charities. In the first half of 1878 bazaars aided the brass band, St Peters Church, the Catholic church and the Sons of Temperance. At a literary evening in the Church of England schoolroom the audience was entertained by readings of comic and serious verse. Two hundred attended the tea meeting at the Congregational church to hear a religious lecture. Families went fishing and picnicking at the George's River, visited the circus or, most exciting of all, went to Sydney, perhaps to see the Great Exhibition of 1875.[126]

Four

1880–1914

I N 1881, 688 people lived in the Campbelltown Police District. Municipal incorporation in the following year and a decade of public works stimulated the municipality, which increased to 2381 people by 1891. Depression in the 1890s led to gradual but persistent decline (1825 in 1911) and the population was not to reach its 1891 size again until 1921. The new Ingleburn municipality north of Campbelltown suffered less dramatic growth and reversals. From a population of 217 in 1891 prior to incorporation, the district had grown to 379 in 1911, largely due to an increase of women, as farmers and their families replaced timber-cutters.

A new nation, Australia, emerged from the federation of the six colonies in 1901. In that year the majority of residents in Campbelltown and Ingleburn were Australian-born. Of those born outside Australia, most were English (16 per cent in Ingleburn and 7.8 per cent in Campbelltown, where the Irish influence was still apparent). A handful of individuals in both municipalities were non-British, mostly German or French immigrants.

By 1911 there were five distinct localities—Campbelltown, Ingleburn, Glenfield, Minto and Menangle (on both sides of the river). Macquarie Fields and Leumeah were not large enough to be registered as local communities. Most of the people of Campbelltown and Ingleburn municipalities were already urban dwellers by 1911, living in the towns rather than in the outlying districts. The town of Campbelltown had 1429 residents, 78 per cent of the population of the municipality while the village of Ingleburn had a population of 317, 83.6 per cent of the population of Ingleburn municipality. Minto, divided between both municipalities, had a larger population than Ingleburn in 1911—481 people living in 114 houses. Glenfield was a small village with 36 homes and 170 people. At Menangle, divided by the river and partly in Campbelltown and Camden, there were 258 people and 54 houses.[1]

View from St Peters tower looking south, around 1885, with Cordeaux Street in the foreground and the rear of Glenalvon (Lithgow Street) in the centre.

Municipal government 1880–1914

With the defeat of the district councils in the 1840s, interest in local government throughout the colony declined. Many districts included vast areas of Crown land and no ratepayers wanted the expense of maintaining well-used roads through these areas. Ultimately, demand for facilities outgrew reluctance to pay for them and moves were started to bring local government to Campbelltown. A Campbelltown Progress Committee appeared in 1879 and a meeting was called in the temperance hall on 14 March 1879. The list of those attending was headed by the local magistrates on whose shoulders, in the absence of local government, the daily problems of road repairs, public health and civic improvement had fallen. About 70 citizens attended the meeting.

One newspaper commented:

> At length the inhabitants of this town have been awakened from the lethargy that has been their distinguishing feature for many years, and are alive to their interests . . . this step has been initiated by the infusion of new blood in our midst, and by the conversion of several of the landed proprietors who for years have opposed all action.

Charles Bull and Patrick B. Hurley moved the formal resolution for the creation of a municipal district and a committee was formed to prepare a petition to the governor. It was an interesting mixture of landowners and townspeople, newcomers and old families—P. B. Hurley, E. H. Fieldhouse and C. Bull were colonial-born members of old local families; J. Payten, born in Parramatta of a family with links to the district; E. McSullea, a landowner in the town from the 1830s; J. Bocking and J. Kidd, who had established businesses in the 1850s; and more recent

Above John Scarr's farm and home, Ager Cottage (later called Rose Cottage and Woodbine), in 1828. Scarr is at his fence talking to some Aborigines. His servant's small hut is on the right and on top of the hill is the hut of a tenant farmer. Behind the barn on the hillside four stacks of wheat have been harvested. (Watercolour by John Scarr) *Campbelltown and Airds Historical Society*

Left Map of Campbelltown c.1844. *Campbelltown and Airds Historical Society*

Above St Johns Catholic Church. The foundation stone was laid in 1824 but most of the church was built in the early 1830s and was roofed in 1838. *C.Liston*

Below St Peters Church of England, built 1823. The town clock, purchased by public subscription, was installed in the tower in 1839. *C.Liston*

Above   Glenlee, built for William and Mary Howe in 1823–24. *C.Liston*

Below   William Ray's Plough Inn (c.1818–21) beside Nathaniel Boon's Three Brothers Inn (c.1830–32), now called Holly Lea. *C.Liston*

Above Macquarie Fields House, built c.1840 for John and Martha Hosking. *Jamieson Collection*

Below Parkholme (later called Euglorie and Englorie Park), built in 1880 for A. L. Park. *C.Liston*

Above St Elmo (built c.1890) against a background of the Central Hills.
C.Liston

Below Designed by G. A. Mansfield, St Helen's Park was built in 1887 for
George Westgarth. *C.Liston*

Above   Campbelltown, looking south-west to the Macarthur Institute of Higher Education. *C.Liston*

Left   The friar birds of eastern Australia were among several hundred illustrations of birds painted by Polish-born G. J. Broinowski while he was living at Wedderburn in the late 1880s. *Campbelltown and Airds Historical Society*

Above Macarthur Square and the Macarthur Regional Centre. *C.Liston*

Below The Temperance Hall, built by the Congregationalists in 1862, became Campbelltown's town hall in 1884. When the neighbouring fire station, built in 1891, was converted to council offices in 1892 a matching facade was added to the town hall. *C.Liston*

Above   The eight storey council administration centre, opened in 1964, was Campbelltown's first high-rise building. It continues to dominate the northern entrance to the city. *C.Liston*

Below   Floats from community groups are a feature of the annual Fisher's Ghost Festival. The Campbelltown City Library entry was one of the more colourful in the 1987 parade. *Campbelltown Local History Collection*

businessmen R. Campion (painter), W. T. Airey (publican) and G. Brown (tailor).[2]

One hundred and ten signatures were collected in favour of local government and presented to the governor on 28 March 1879 by Charles Bull, John Kidd, James Payten and John Hurley. The petition stated in standard phrases that those who signed it would be liable to pay rates; that the area proposed for the municipal district covered about 14 square miles (36 km^2) and the population exceeded 500. The 14 square miles stretched from Mount Annan in the west to the George's River in the east, with Raby Road as the northern boundary and a line from Mount Sugarloaf to St Helens Park as the southern limit.[3]

Three months later an opposing petition with 160 signatures was presented to the governor. It stated that many of those who signed the first petition would not be liable for rates so their signatures were invalid. Others had signed without understanding the implications of rate assessment. Their particular objections concerned the state of roads which they wanted the government to repair before incorporation: 'if incorporation takes place before such work is done, the expense of repairing the roads would be ruinous to the inhabitants, oppressive to those liable to taxation beyond the town, and would plunge the Municipality into debt from the time of incorporation'.

The signatories included Daniel Fowler, John Bray of Denfield, James Fitzpatrick of Glenlee and Smeaton Grange and Edwin Fieldhouse, for himself and the estates of the late R. Stewart, the late John Eccleston, the late Edward Guthrie and Agnes Lennox. The three Misses Reddall of Glen Alpine, Edward Moore of Badgally, John Vardy of Menangle and Campbelltown, Bursill, Lack and Rixon had signed. Names appearing on both petitions included various members of the Huckstepp, Bamfield, Chinnocks, Tripp, Larkin, Brooksbank, Hinde and Ray families.[4]

Controversy about the petitions split Campbelltown. Daniel Fowler, William Graham and the Fieldhouse brothers were named as the main opponents to incorporation. These three families reputedly owned a large proportion of houses and land within the town so they would bear the greatest liability for rates.[5]

Supporters of local government calculated that annual rate income would be about £400 which would be matched by a government grant, giving £800 a year for the upkeep of streets, as well as an extra allowance for repairs to the Great Southern Road which formed the main street of Campbelltown. For this sum surely the streets would be passable in wet weather instead of the present 'treacherous bogs and quagmires', and properties would increase in value.

Most of the complaints about both petitions centred on the validity of the signatures. It was alleged that the counter petition had duplicated names, with Edwin Fieldhouse signing six times on behalf of each of his properties. Fowler, Graham and Fieldhouse were accused of getting wood-carters, railway porters, single men, lodgers and 'other birds of passage' to sign, and intimidating those who had earlier favoured incorporation with exaggerated claims about the rates everyone would have to pay.[6]

Those who favoured incorporation were not prepared to accept defeat. John Kidd, James Bocking, George Brown and W. T. Airey wrote to the Premier, Sir Henry Parkes, on 15 August 1879 requesting an enquiry into the counter petition and alleging that many who had signed were not liable for rates, others lived outside the proposed boundaries and some signatures were forgeries, being the names of men who could not write, including a person who had been dead for seven years. The government appointed James K. Chisholm of Gledswood to hold an enquiry which lasted for three days and called 94 witnesses. Solicitor Charles Bull appeared for the original petition and Joseph Leary represented the counter petition. Both deplored the widespread illiteracy that was evident from the number who had signed with their mark. Chisholm resolved the authenticity of the signatures by calling everyone named on the petitions to appear at the courthouse and identify their marks and signatures. Signatures were declared invalid if improperly witnessed.

Many women had signed the petitions, either as property owners or

Campbelltown Council 1892. *Top row, left to right* Nicholas Doyle (publican and undertaker), Alexander Munro (town clerk), William Cummins (farmer), William Graham (storekeeper). *Front row left to right* D. H. Barker (saddler), H. E. Vaughan (estate agent), W. B. Caldwell, mayor (butcher), J. Scanlon (farmer), Sculdham Woodhouse (gentleman).

CAMPBELLTOWN LOCAL HISTORY COLLECTION

leaseholders. Originally women property owners had been, by default, entitled to a vote in local government affairs, but amendments to the law in 1867 had restricted the franchise to male property owners. The Campbelltown women who joined in the controversy about local government came from all social groups—single women of property, married women, women supporting themselves, and the wives and daughters of labourers and farmers. Chisholm disallowed the signatures of women whose husbands were alive unless legally separated. Women whose votes were thus discounted included Margaret Donnelly, Margaret Pendergast; Susan Maria Merritt; Sophia Kennedy; Mary Larkin; Mrs E. Etchells and E. Lusted. Emma Monk and Mrs E. Bamford were married women who supported themselves and their families so they were permitted to sign the petition. Other women who signed the petitions included the three Misses Reddall, Mary H. Hinde, Catherine Greenhill, Ann Brooksbank, Mary Giddy, Ann Lynch, Eliza O'Neil, Johanna Sweeny, Elsie Reach, Ann North, C. Helm, Ann Francis, Elizabeth Blackburn, Elizabeth Ferguson, Margaret Wilkinson and Hannah Bursill.

Chisholm disallowed several signatures on both petitions, though he did not try to resolve the conflicting views of those who had signed both petitions. The final result, in September 1879, was 98 in favour and 134 against incorporation.

A little over a year later the pro-incorporation forces regrouped under Kidd, Bocking and Bull and presented another petition signed by 131 residents. Particular care was taken, with most people signing their name and those who made their mark being witnessed by as many as three others. Again there was a counter petition, published in the *Government Gazette* of 2 July 1881. Its 186 signatures were headed by John Hurley, signing both as freeholder and leaseholder, the Misses Reddall, John Bray, John T. Gorus, E. H. and William Fieldhouse, signing as freeholders, leaseholders and trustees, and Daniel Fowler.

It was almost a repeat of 1879, except that this time the opponents of incorporation offered a compromise. They would support incorporation if everyone who regularly used the roads of the district paid rates. They proposed an enlarged area of 45 square miles (116 km^2) instead of 14 square miles (36 km^2), including all of the parishes of St Peter and Minto and parts of Narellan, Menangle and Appin. Supporting signatures for the enlarged area totalled 193, including Hurley, the Fieldhouses, the Grahams and Daniel Fowler. People living on the Campbellfield estate, such as John Spence, Jeremiah Lyons, James Funnell (teacher at the public school), E. Knock and C. Meredith gave their support as did Gorus at Eshcol Park. Families living near Menangle, such as the Tabers and Vardys, supported it as did the Woodhouses at Mount Gilead.[7]

By October 1881 differences had been reconciled and the proclamation of the municipality of Campbelltown, incorporating about 45 square miles, was signed by the Governor of New South Wales, Lord Loftus, on 21 January 1882. A returning officer was appointed for the election of

A crowd outside the Campbelltown Town Hall, celebrating the coronation of George V in 1910. (P. C. Marlow, 1910)

councillors. John Tangelder Gorus of Eshcol Park was the unanimous choice, having served as alderman and mayor in the municipality of St Peters in the 1870s.

Elections were held in February 1882. The nine aldermen of the first council were Charles Bull of Cordeaux Street, solicitor; William Graham and James Bocking, storekeepers; Joseph Atkinson and Walter Thomas Airey, publicans; Charles Edward Matthews, auctioneer; Alexander Munro and John Knight, both contractors and builders; and John Ahearn of the waterworks at Ousdale near Appin and probably also a contractor. Four—Bull, Graham, Bocking and Munro—came from families established for two or three decades in the town. The others had been attracted more recently by opportunities on public works. The choice of newcomer Ahearn as the first mayor meant that no established factions within the town took leadership in the first council. Ahearn and Airey were related and suffered a common bereavement in late 1882 and soon left the district. Bull became the second mayor in March 1883. The Graham family, having initially opposed local government, became active participants.

At the first council meeting on 7 March 1882 three standing committees were formed—finance, works and by-laws. Council met on alternate Thursdays. The casting vote of the mayor was needed to choose between the Bank of New South Wales or the Commercial Banking Company as bankers. The Commercial was chosen and council immediately applied for a £200 cash advance. A council clerk (T. J. Winton), a pound-keeper (George Brown) and an inspector of nuisances responsible for public health and safety (Sydney Marsden) were appointed.

R. F. Stack, engineer for the water scheme, offered temporary premises. William Gee and John Spence tendered successfully to undertake the first valuation of properties so that rates could be determined. Rates were pegged at 1 shilling per £1 of improved capital value and most ratepayers responded promptly when the first rate notices went out in May 1882. Council called on the government to advance road-maintenance funds. The Water Reserve Trust, several local road trusts and the Recreation Reserve Trust were revoked, their powers vested in the council and the trustees instructed to hand over their funds. By 1885 income from rates was estimated at £650 per annum.

In April 1884 Campbelltown Council purchased for £800 the temperance hall for a town hall. Three of the five trustees for the owners, the Sons of Temperance Society, were municipal councillors (Bocking, Wilson and Munro) and a fourth trustee (John Kidd) was the local member of parliament. The town hall, 65 by 35 feet (20 by 11 m) with a 25 by 18-foot (7.6 by 5.5 m) stage, could seat 400 people and was lit by kerosene lamps. A fire station, designed by Alfred Rose Payten, was built by George Lusted next to the town hall in 1891. Almost immediately it was taken over by the council for the clerk's office and the following year a matching facade, also designed by Payten, was added to the town hall. The Board of Fire Commissioners threatened court action to retrieve the fire station, but in 1909 it accepted £75 from the council for the premises.[8]

Two major concerns dominated council's deliberations in its early years—an efficient water supply and the state of roads. Council debated a proposal to pump water from the George's River to Campbelltown for use in locomotives and to provide a town water supply. Within the town, preparations were made for the streets to be surveyed and aligned, though the main street remained unnamed. Lithgow Street, leading to the school, was the other important street. Most roads were gravel and crushed stone. Difficult, boggy sections, such as the bottom of Maddens Hill on the Menangle Road, were corduroy roads, stabilised by timber logs laid lengthwise across the surface. Priority was given to culverts and drainage to prevent further break-up of the road surface.

Campbelltown Council's by-laws permitted it to prosecute citizens for careless driving and driving without lights (as dangerous in horsedrawn as in motorised vehicles); impound straying animals, a common offence when most people had horses and cows; prohibit the keeping of pigs within 40 yards (37 m) of the street, a health hazard, although in the absence of garbage collection household pigs were a practical alternative. Council was empowered to license vehicles for hire and regulate the water carts which carried water from the reservoir to shops and residences.[9]

Campbelltown's first town clerk was Thomas Jenner Winton. His parents, William Winton and Mary Anna, née Larkin, migrated from England in February 1840. Thomas Jenner Winton was born at Sugarloaf, North Menangle, in 1846. For several years Thomas Winton was bailiff at the Campbelltown District Court where he had a reputation as a kind-hearted man who frequently paid the small debts of locals rather than see their homes repossessed. Winton was town clerk of Campbelltown from 1882 until his premature death on 6 October 1887, aged 41. His advice and opinions, offered in a friendly way, and his ability to perform unpleasant duties in a kindly manner assisted the town through its transition to modern government.

News of Winton's death in 1887 sped rapidly around the small town and work was 'almost entirely suspended'. His funeral was one of the largest ever known; the procession to the Congregational cemetery was headed by members of the Oddfellows Lodge, followed by the mayor and aldermen, council labourers, family members, then local members of parliament, justices of the peace, both bank managers and the rest of the town. Bocking commented that although it might seem a small matter that council had lost its clerk, 'in a small community like theirs it was a great matter ... A prince in Campbelltown has fallen today.' A marble memorial was erected by public subscription over his grave.[10]

Alexander Munro junior (b. 1847), a contractor, was town clerk from 1887 to 1900, when he was replaced by J. Long junior, formerly manager of a local store. Frederick Sheather became council clerk in 1901. Born at Mittagong, the son of a butcher and grandson of an English migrant who

---

Thomas Jenner Winton (1846–1887),
Campbelltown's first town clerk.

had worked at Camden Park in the 1840s, Sheather took his first job with his uncle, James McGlynn, proprietor of the *Campbelltown Herald*. Sheather had some knowledge of local government, his father having been an alderman at Mittagong. He worked as town clerk on Tuesdays and Fridays from 10 am to 12 noon and Thursdays from 3 to 5 pm. For the rest of the week he ran an agency business.[11]

Public health responsibilities were the most onerous for small councils like Campbelltown. In 1898, on receiving new directions about infectious diseases from the Board of Health, Campbelltown Council replied that it felt the Board was 'unfairly' taxing their resources with expenditure on 'sanitary supervision'. Alderman Gorus favoured abolishing cesspits and installing a pan service, but failed to convince fellow councillor Thomas Gamble who, in his 1897 campaign for mayor, had opposed this expenditure. When inspectors from the Board of Health condemned Campbelltown sanitation in 1901, council responded that it was 'all a tissue of falsehoods'. At the next meeting Dr John Wilson reported an outbreak of typhoid at the Federal Hotel. In 1902 the Board of Health threatened to declare the municipality a health risk if pail closets did not replace cesspits, and in 1903 council introduced stricter controls over sanitation. In 1909 the duplicate pan system was introduced.[12]

Street lighting was an issue that affected all residents. Most streetlamps were kerosene. In 1901 council bought its first incandescent vapour lamp, an impressive novelty, attracting interest from neighbouring Camden Council, and in 1902 Edward Bamford became lamp-lighter, a position he held for over twenty years. By 1904 there were half a dozen vapour gas lights in the main street and several kerosene lamps at 'other useful places'. A gasworks was discussed in the 1890s but was never built.[13]

By 1906 the municipality had 64 miles (103 km) of road, of which only 8 miles (13 km) were metalled, 23 miles (37 km) ballasted and the rest only 'formed'. Alderman Reeve, a draper and captain of the fire brigade, complained that too much was spent on country roads yet the townsfolk paid the larger portion of rates. 'Something should be done to modernise the place, to make it more attractive for visitors.' A footpath was built on the western side of Queen Street, after lengthy debate over whether stone flagging, concrete paving or ashphalt was the most appropriate surface.[14]

At the celebrations for the opening of the Campbelltown courthouse in January 1889, James Bocking and E. B. Woodhouse (himself Australian-born) hoped that colonial-born young men would participate in the official life of their country. But with few exceptions public life continued to be dominated by men born outside Australia. The most notable exception was William Graham junior who became Campbelltown's youngest mayor in 1889, having stood for election to council as soon as he turned 21. With his brother he ran a general store and was described by the *Sydney Mail* as 'a young man of public spirit and private wealth'. Fred Moore of Badgally, colonial-born, educated at the King's School and Sydney University, was mayor from 1901 to 1909.[15]

Work started on a new courthouse in 1887 on the old site, the corner of Queen and Railway Streets. The architect was James Barnett, the contractor Peter Graham, with A. P. Graham as contractor's foreman and A. T. Telf as foreman of works. Built of brick on a sandstone base, the main courtroom was 54 feet (16.5 m) long, 32 feet (10 m) wide and 30 feet (9 m) high. The impact of its bold facade was spoiled, in the eyes of the *Sydney Morning Herald*, by the high brick wall surrounding it on three sides. Unlike the old court, it was well ventilated with excellent acoustics. '1888' was prominent on the facade but the new courthouse was not opened until January 1889.[16]

A new police residence had been built in 1880 near the old courthouse. In the early years of the twentieth century Senior Sergeant W. Saunders was the senior officer, assisted by five constables. Their district extended from Campbelltown to Appin and Cataract Dam and north to Ingleburn. When Saunders was transferred to Gundagai in 1911 there was general regret. Stationed at Campbelltown for 20 years and an active member of the School of Arts committee, his success in the eyes of the townsfolk was less apprehension of criminals than crime prevention. He was presented with a gold watch, two suites of furniture and a fitted travelling bag.[17]

Earning a living

Public works brought prosperity to the district. In 1867 the Upper Nepean with its tributaries, the Cataract, Cordeaux and Avon Rivers, were identified as the most suitable source of water for Sydney. A vast catchment area of 347 square miles (900 km^2) south of Appin was in sandstone country considered too barren for any other useful purpose. Weirs near Wilton on the Nepean River at Pheasant's Nest and on the Cataract at Broughton's Pass would divert water into a series of tunnels and canals leading to a storage reservoir from which water would be distributed to Sydney. Prospect was selected as the most suitable and economic site for the storage reservoir, well away from the flood-prone rivers, though some consideration was given to a site at Kenny Hill near Campbelltown.

In 1879 £1 million was allocated to the project, and in February 1880 officials, press and a crowd of 150 workmen and spectators gathered at Broughton's Pass. The river was in flood. Two workmen swam across with detonation equipment to start the excavations. Construction of the Upper Nepean Scheme took six years. Twelve feet (3.7 m) wide and about 8 feet (2.5 m) deep, the canal ran west of Campbelltown, relying on natural sandstone bedding, lined where necessary with sandstone rubble or cement, and with brick in the shale country nearer Campbelltown. Intervening creeks, gullies and the railway between Menangle and Campbelltown were crossed with wrought-iron pipes, up to 8 feet (2.5 m) in diameter, balanced on aqueducts high above known flood levels. The canal relied on gravity to convey the water. Sugarloaf tunnel, between

Building the Upper Nepean Water Scheme. (C. Bayliss c.1880–83)

Mount Gilead and Glen Alpine, was the longest at 3907 feet (1192 m). The two tunnels at Mount Annan were 2248 and 366 feet (686 and 112 m) respectively; Badgally tunnel, 3783 feet (1154 m) and Mollesmain tunnel, 703 feet (214 m). Construction was supervised by Edward Orpen Moriarty, engineer-in-chief for harbours and rivers, with district engineers R. F. Stack and H. M. Kenny based in Campbelltown. The contractor was W. J. Edwards.[18]

Campbelltown benefited from the water-supply project in two significant ways. Construction works provided employment for local men and income for shopkeepers, carriers and tradespeople. New people were attracted to the area, increasing the population for almost a decade. The second major benefit for Campbelltown was the acqustion of its own water supply. It was the first country town to receive water from the Nepean system. By 1889, 893 yards (817 m) of pipe had been laid along Queen, Railway and Hurley (now Patrick) Streets. By 1892, 748 people in Campbelltown had been supplied with water at a cost of £4433, and by 1901 most of the town had been connected. Neighbouring farms were connected to town water by 1905. In Camden there were complaints that the Nepean River was being drained and the George's River should have supplied Campbelltown.[19]

In the 1901–02 drought the level of Prospect reservoir was dangerously low and stringent water restrictions were imposed. Following a royal commission in 1902, legislation authorised construction of a large storage dam on the Cataract River for an estimated cost of £126000. Clearing began immediately and, as Campbelltown was the closest large town and

125

the only one with a railway siding, carting materials and supplies provided work for local people. Unemployed men from Sydney as well as locals worked as day labourers, cutting timber from the site for railway sleepers or firewood. Life was strictly monitored because the camp was within the water catchment area. Single men lived in two-man cubicles in barracks with corrugated-iron roofs and canvas walls. Waste water from the communal bathrooms and laundry was purified through sand filters and nightsoil was carted out of the area daily. Married men were allowed to have their families in the camp and there were 60 children, though no school. A post office, four grocers and general stores, two barbers, a butcher, newsagent and stationer catered for their daily needs. Six boarding houses provided meals rather than lodging in the tent city. There were two soft-drink shops, a licence having been refused for an hotel. About 320 workmen and 80 tradesmen (many of them local people) were working on the site in early 1903.[20]

Excavation for the wall foundations started in late 1903. Sandstone at the site was quarried into massive blocks which were put in place by pulleys powered by 500-horsepower (373 kW) boilers. Generators provided electric light so three shifts could be worked. Cataract Dam was completed in 1907 but did not fill until January 1911. During construction it became a popular tourist spot and remained so. The picnic grounds were landscaped by the Botanic Gardens nursery at Campbelltown.[21]

The *Tramway Extension Act* of April 1880 approved light railways and tramways in fourteen areas not served by the railway system. These tramlines were intended for Sydney's growing suburbs, but a country project, Campbelltown to Camden, was included to test the system's broader possibilities. It would pass through well-populated farming land likely to provide passengers and freight. Perhaps more importantly, the Cowpasture Bridge was strong enough to take a tram and the expense of a new bridge was avoided. Contractors were W. H. Topham and James Angus from New Zealand, better known as the owner and manufacturer of Minchinbury champagne. Except at Kenny Hill, heavy earthworks were not required and all the work was done by men using picks and shovels. The line opened in March 1882. The journey took 45 minutes with eight stops between Camden and Campbelltown.

Technically a tramway, it used standard railway carriages and became part of the railway network. From Campbelltown railway station the tram used the main southern track to the level crossing at the Camden Road, and then travelled on its own track parallel to the northern side of Camden Road, past Maryfields (or Rudd's Gate), up Kenny Hill, over Curran's Hill, through the western side of Narellan village, then parallel to the Cowpasture Road through Kirkham and Elderslie, across the river and into Camden. Vandalism caused the first accident in May 1882 when the Saturday night tram struck large logs placed across the line.[22]

The Great Southern Railway passed through Campbelltown with new stations opened at Glenlee in August 1884, Menangle in August 1885 (renamed North Menangle in 1889), Leumeah in 1886 and Macquarie Fields in October 1888 (the original Macquarie Fields station having been renamed Ingleburn in August 1883). The Illawarra line reached Wollongong in 1887, reducing patronage on the coach route from Campbelltown station via Appin. Track duplication on the main southern railway started in 1891. By Easter there were 48 men living in tents at Minto, and at Campbelltown there were 63 tents, 8 housing families. Three of the tents were barracks with 10–13 men each.[23]

Travellers from Campbelltown changed trains at Liverpool to travel via Parramatta and the main western line to Redfern. Parramatta to the city in the 1880s took nearly an hour. Alternative routes from St Peters to Bankstown and Liverpool or through East Hills were proposed to relieve congestion on the main track to Parramatta. Work on a second route started in 1890 and had reached Bankstown by 1909. Its promise, more than its reality, attracted settlement south of Liverpool.[24]

Campbelltown station was the furthest point south in the suburban railway network. The earliest regular weekday train did not leave Campbelltown until 7.32 am and reached Sydney at 8.46 am. Returning from Sydney there was no train between 1.30 pm and 5.15 pm, the latter arriving back at Campbelltown at 6.04 pm. Both services were too late for working people and, despite agitation from the 1890s for an earlier train, the timetable remained unchanged until 1909 when a 6.20 am service from Campbelltown picked up at Minto, Ingleburn and Glenfield, arriving at Granville at 7.11 am and Sydney at 7.43 am. The journey home was still difficult, especially for Ingleburn residents, as the first afternoon train which set down there was the 5.17 pm from Sydney. Ingleburn Council feared it was losing population because people could not travel to work.[25]

James Waterworth, Campbelltown's mail contractor, operated a large horsedrawn omnibus called the *Sovereign*. Appin, the waterworks at Broughtons Pass and Cataract Dam were only accessible by road. In 1902 Byrne's coach left Campbelltown from Hogan's Royal Hotel twice daily at 11 am and 7 pm for Appin and Cataract.[26]

Most people lived close to their workplace and walked. From the 1880s the bicycle became common in the tangle of horses and carts that waited outside shops and hotels.

Earning a living on the land

By the 1890s dairying was the major rural industry in the Campbelltown district. Without refrigeration butter and cheese travelled better than milk and cream. Traditionally, each dairy made its own cream, butter and cheese. Milk was poured into wide, shallow pans and left for a day or more for the cream to rise and be skimmed off by hand. It was a time-consuming process. Milk was easily contaminated with dirt and insects and on hot days quickly turned sour. Cream was churned by hand by the farmer's wife and daughters to make butter.

127

In 1875 Thomas Sutcliffe Mort established the New South Wales Fresh Food and Ice Company. Mort was experimenting with refrigeration for meat exports. Though the technology was not sufficiently developed for long journeys, it overcame the problem of transporting milk from country dairies to the city along the rail network. John Kidd recognised the potential for dairying and acquired extensive grazing pasture, including St Andrews and the lease of much of the Campbellfield estate. By the turn of the century Kidd was one of the largest ratepayers in Campbelltown municipality.

In 1878 a Swedish engineer, Gustav de Laval, patented a centrifugal cream separator. Milk no longer had to be left for the cream to rise, with all the risks of contamination. Factory separators powered by horses or steam engines were in use on the New South Wales south coast by the early 1880s. Small separators were not available until the late 1880s so dairy farmers had to combine their milk in the large separators. The first cooperative factory opened at Kiama in 1884. In 1890 an American, S. M. Babcock, developed a quick method to test the fat content of milk. Dairy factories could now purchase milk by its fat content rather than quantity alone, removing the risk of buying watered-down milk.[27]

Dairies were supervised by the Board of Health from 1888. Milk was easily polluted from a dirty environment, impure water or sick cows, and could carry disease such typhoid and tuberculosis. The first inspections in 1890 revealed inadequate sanitation on many farms. On one in three there were no privies and raw sewage flowed into creeks from which the dairies drew their water. Of the eleven licensed dairies in Campbelltown inspected by the Board of Health, several were dirty and some cattle were diseased. The local council was directed to enforce cleanliness and by the

---

Dairy farmers wait for the train at Campbelltown railway station, around 1900.

CAMPBELLTOWN AND AIRDS HISTORICAL SOCIETY

next inspection, in December 1891, the 24 dairies registered in that year were found to be satisfactory. By 1901 there were 2816 dairy cattle in the Campbelltown district and, while this represented only 13 per cent of dairy cattle within the county of Cumberland, Campbelltown dairy farmers had the greatest investment (25 per cent) in dairying equipment. They sent 833 998 gallons (3.8 million L) of milk to Sydney, 47 per cent of milk processed in the county of Cumberland. In 1906 there were 73 registered dairies in Campbelltown municipality and 7 in Ingleburn municipality.[28]

Campbelltown dairymen were slow to agree to a local dairy factory. One operated at Camden from 1893 to 1895 and then at Menangle. The Campbelltown Co-Operative Creamery Company opened in 1899, close to the railway, behind Queen Street where it shared premises with the cordial factory. J. P. Seddon was manager of the creamery and cordial factory for 20 years. The railway platform at Campbelltown was improved in 1906 and in 1908 to provide better milk-loading facilities. Dairy farmers were concerned about the price paid for their milk and agitated through their local branch of the United Milk Suppliers' Association.[29]

Several of the larger estates were leased for dairy pasture by 1914. Charles Axam leased 2000 acres (800 ha) of Mount Gilead. Varroville was leased by its owner, Sydney solicitor Thomas Salter, to H. R. Pockley for dairying. Towards Menangle, the Edrop estate (2000 acres [800 ha]) was leased to several dairy farmers. W. H. Fieldhouse owned ten dairies, including Denfield (315 acres [126 ha]), Glen Lora and Sugarloaf farms between the Appin and Menangle Roads.[30]

By 1901 over half the area of the Campbelltown Police District was privately owned and fenced and 2270 of its 97 920 acres (908 of 39 168 ha) were cultivated. There were 373 farms, about two-thirds occupied by their owners, the rest held by lesses. Wheat and grain crops had virtually disappeared. Oats was the most usual crop. Sorgham and maize were also grown. Hay was needed for winter feed for the cows. Haymaking remained labour-intensive. The grasses were cut, scattered to dry, gathered in overnight, and scattered again the next day until dry enough to put into a hayrick.[31]

Grapevines and other fruits by 1901 covered about 28 per cent of cultivated land. At Eaglemount, Minto, the Genty family planted a vineyard in the late 1880s. They were immigrants from France and made ports, sherries, hock and claret. In 1891 they lived on Eshcol Park. After phylloxera caused havoc in the vineyards in the 1890s, Eugene Genty became a wine and spirit merchant in Sydney.[32]

During the 1890s greater interest was shown in orchards and vineyards as land prices increased in the fruit areas north and north-west of Sydney. Across the George's River in Holsworthy and Eckersley, selectors cleared land on the ridges along the road from Liverpool. The slope, soil, good drainage and easterly aspect made it suitable for vine-growing. Among those who planted orchards and vineyards were J. Kidd and J. Hurst at

Holsworthy and Isaac Himmelhoch at Grodno. Himmelhoch had emi-grated from Russia about 1870 and had prospered as a money lender. He developed his Eckersley vineyard as a hobby, employing J. F. Ryan as a full-time manager. He cleared a 640-acre (256 ha) selection, terraced the land with stone walls, and built a large winery and cellars. In 1901, 17 acres (6.8 ha) were under hermitage and malbec vines and 15 acres (6 ha) were in preparation for new vines. Ten acres (4 ha) of fodder crops provided feed for the draughthorses. The land was resumed by the military just before World War I.[33]

Despite phylloxera in the 1890s, Campbelltown produced almost 24 000 gallons (109 200 L) of wine and 150 gallons (682 L) of brandy in 1901 from 126 acres (50 ha), and had 94 acres (38 ha) under table grapes. There were 300 acres (120 ha) of other fruits. Beehives were common. Campbelltown was second only to Liverpool with the largest number of beehives in the county of Cumberland, yielding 49 355 pounds (22 407 kg) of honey a year.[34]

Farming relied on unpaid family labour. One-third of those working in Campbelltown dairies in 1901 were women. Teachers were urged to ensure that children returned home quickly after school to assist on the farm. In 1898 about 70 parents from Campbelltown Public School peti-tioned the minister for public instruction to reduce the lunchbreak from one and a half hours to one hour and end classes at 3.30 instead of 4 pm. Parents at Ingleburn signed a similar petition in 1900. When classes did not finish till 4 pm, in winter it was dark by the time the children walked 2 miles (3 km) home and they were unable to help in the dairy or around the house.[35]

In 1881 the Botanical Gardens established the State Nursery at Camp-belltown on 22 acres (9 ha), west of Campbelltown railway station in Badgally Road between Bow Bowing Creek and Johnson Road. The first superintendent, Alexander Moore, died in March 1884. His successor was John McEwen who remained at the Campbelltown State Nursery until his death in January 1913, aged 70. The nursery propagated evergreen shrubs and plants from overseas, testing their adaptability to Australian condi-tions. Campbelltown's dry, hot summers and frosty cold winters were a good testing environment. Experiments were carried out with cotton in 1897 and phylloxera-resistant grapevines in 1899. It was a training ground for botanical staff. W. Weston left Campbelltown State Nursery to estab-lish gardens in the new federal capital and William Hardie and John Nichol became superintendents at Centennial Park, Sydney. The State Nursery supplied plants to official residences, government departments and for landscaping public works.[36]

Town life in Campbelltown

Age and a picturesque setting attracted visitors to Campbelltown. One tourist described it as a pleasant place for a holiday, the town set in a valley with residences on the surrounding hills. It was great country for riding and walking. Visitors could take a brisk morning walk to the George's River, swim in the clear, cold water and walk back to town for a hearty breakfast. Though too far for commuters, Campbelltown was close enough for a weekend country home.

Unfavourable comparisons were made between Campbelltown and newer Camden, which displayed more energy and prosperity with its woollen mill and dairy factory. 'Why should Campbelltown, with its age, situation, and evident advantages over Camden, be so much behind it in many respects? ... The solid and conservative inhabitants of Campbelltown ... should bestir themselves or lose the advantages which may be assuredly theirs.'[37]

To those accustomed to the rapidly changing scene in Sydney and its ever-expanding suburbs, Campbelltown looked part of another world with its colonial buildings, a few two-storey Georgian houses, some low shingle-roofed buildings with wide verandahs and plenty of open space. The modern Victorian buildings were isolated at each end of the town. The Commercial Bank, built by Langley and Thompson in 1880 for £3500, the adjoining post and telegraph office built by W. Burton and Company in 1881 at a cost of £1999, the fire station and the town hall were at one

Queen Street, near Allman Street, looking south, around 1883. On the right are the post office (1881) and Commercial Bank (1880), with Alpha House on the crest of the hill facing the Railway Hotel and Fowler's store.

end, and the new courthouse at the other. In 1895 a *Sydney Mail* correspondent wrote

Here we are brought face to face with the colony as it was in the crudeness of its youth, and while still innocent of art. From the primitive looking 'Saint Patrick's Inn' . . . to the yet quainter 'Jolly Miller' . . . is plainly writ the time when every man was his own architect, and built as seemed right in his own eyes.[38]

Residences, prominently located on the hills around Campbelltown in the 1880s, included Blair Athol, the home of the Honourable John Kidd, Postmaster-General; the Honourable John Davies' Holly Lea; Mrs E. L. Moore at Badgally and Hillcrest, home of Marshall D. Woodhouse of the New South Wales Fresh Food and Ice Company.[39]

The newest mansion to grace the hills in 1880 was Parkholme. One of many farms owned by Samuel Terry, it was tenanted until 1875 when, following the death in 1873 of Terry's daughter Esther Hughes, it was sold to William Nunn Patrick. He sold it in 1879 to Alfred Leath Park, well known in sporting circles as a coursing enthusiast. Park built on a hill with a view across the town and Glen Alpine, Blair Athol and Claremont visible on the neighbouring hills. Parkholme was a seven-room villa of brick and stone with a slate roof, designed by Fitzpatrick of Sydney and built by J. & H. Vernon of Redfern. The outbuildings included a four-stall brick stable, with coach house and harness room, a pigeon loft for 700 birds and kennels for his 40 pedigree greyhounds under the care of their trainer, McDonald. Other pedigree stock included Ayrshire cows and the winning Ayrshire bull from the Melbourne Exhibition, some hunters and prize-winning poultry. The farm around the house was manured with 'deodorised blood and bone-dust' and 70 acres (28 ha) were planted with oats. Nearer the house Park planted fruit trees and ornamental trees.

About 1892 Parkholme became the country residence of Henry Edward Vaughan (1842–1901), mayor of Campbelltown in 1893–94. He added a billiard room and built dams on the farming land. Henry Vaughan, his father, was an 1840s immigrant hatter who established a successful employment bureau and diversified as an auctioneer and house agent. His son continued the business until he retired to Campbelltown. H. E. Vaughan was a director of the Equitable Building Society and a leading mason. A member of Campbelltown Council in the mid-1890s, he had previously been an alderman on Glebe Council and in the late 1890s was an alderman at Katoomba. Vaughan's business interests took him from Campbelltown and he leased Parkholme to Frederick Clissold and Thomas Cunningham for dairying.

Following Vaughan's death in 1901 the estate was sold to Frederick Lockyer Mitchell Merewether. Merewether was a descendant of the well-known Hunter Valley pioneering families of Merewether, Scott and Mitchell and a cousin of David Scott Mitchell who gave New South Wales his library. Merewether sold Parkholme to Charles Burcher of Euglo

Drawing room of St Elmo in Broughton Street around 1920 during the residence of the Allen family.

Station, Condobolin, who renamed the house 'Euglorie Park', though it was usually mistakenly called 'Englorie'. The Burcher family were connected by marriage to several local families—the Bulls, the Chippendalls of Bradbury Park and the Moore family of Badgally. Charles Burcher died at Euglorie Park in 1916.[40]

The most imposing new home in town was built on the Warby estate by John and Sarah Moore. John and Benjamin Moore had migrated from England in the mid-1850s, set up as publicans in Sydney and in the 1860s both had married daughters of Joseph and Elizabeth Warby. John and Sarah Moore built St Elmo, a two-storey house in Broughton Street overlooking Campbelltown. In its grounds were stables, a coach house, cowbails, a fowl-run and an orchard. On John Moore's death in 1911 St Elmo passed to his brother-in-law, Ephraim Warby.[41]

Along the Menangle Road Glenlee was leased until just before World War I. The lessees included the Cummins family, Michael J. Vardy, the Tabers, Conroy and Doyle. In 1910 John Glenlee Fitzpatrick took up residence. The adjoining estate of Smeaton Grange was occupied by Elizabeth Sedgwick (1873–1957), James Fitzpatrick's daughter, while his other daughter, Mary Ann, lived with her husband, James Francis O'Donnell, at Kilbride.[42]

On the Appin Road the Mount Gilead estate fell into decay. Edmund Bingham Woodhouse had inherited as a young man in 1875 and for the next fifteen years he invested heavily in pedigree stock. In 1879 he married Agnes Neill in one of the most lavish weddings of the year. By 1890 it was over. Bankrupt and legally separated, unable to meet maintenance payments of £2 per week, E. B. Woodhouse died of pleurisy in July 1891, not yet 40 years old. His mother, Gertrude Woodhouse, had moved to Marleford in Campbelltown where she died in 1915. Mount Gilead was leased from the mortgage company by Charles Axam.[43]

In 1887 George Charles Westgarth (1845–1908) and his family moved into their new country home, St Helens Park, on the Appin Road. It was an ornate gabled house designed by George Mansfield, architect for the Department of Education and Westgarth's father-in-law, and erected by Campbelltown builder George Lusted. St Helens Park covered 600 acres (240 ha) and included Samuel Larkin's Ambarvale grant and John Wild's Egypt Farm. Westgarth was a solicitor. Left a widower with two young children, in 1879 he married Lucy Mansfield and they had seven children. His father-in-law had purchased a nearby estate of 400 acres (160 ha), Glen Lorne, in the 1870s. Westgarth died at Campbelltown in October 1908.[44]

Another member of the Merewether family, H. J. M. Merewether, built a home on the Appin Road for his bride, Wilhelmina Gore, daughter of Campbelltown bank manager, A. J. Gore. Raith, a sixteen-room Indian bungalow-style house, was designed by Wardell and Denning in 1903 and built by D. McIntyre and Sons of Sydney at a cost of £3000.[45]

By the 1880s one of the largest landowners in the Cowpastures district was Edward Lumas Moore (1822–87), the son of a convict on the Macquarie Fields estate. As a squatter on the Lachlan in the 1840s, he prospered. He lived with his second wife and family on Oran Park estate in the 1870s. Moore purchased land at Campbelltown where, shortly before his death, he built Badgally.[46]

On the Sydney Road, north of Campbelltown, was Eshcol Park, the estate of John Tangelder Gorus. Born in Gelderland, Holland, about 1830, Gorus arrived in Australia in 1854 and went to the goldfields. By 1864 he had a photographic studio in King Street, Sydney, and lived at St Peters. Gorus purchased Eshcol Park in 1878 but retained his Sydney studio until 1891. He was an active member of his community, serving as an alderman and as chairman of the school boards for Minto and Ingleburn. Elizabeth Gorus died at Eshcol Park in October 1893. Gorus sold the estate in 1902 and moved to Parramatta where he died in June 1916.[47]

Before municipal incorporation, most land within the town was owned by the Fieldhouse family, the Grahams and the Fowlers. In 1884 E. & W. H. Fieldhouse, Mrs Fieldhouse, J. Bocking, Miss and Mrs Hurley, P. B. Hurley, the Hurley trustees and W. Graham were the largest property owners in the town, and the trustees of James Fitzpatrick were the largest outside the town. The Hurley family owned Alpha House, the Bank of New South Wales building, the Royal Hotel, Hurley farm between Appin and Old Menangle Road, extensive property in Allman and Dumaresq

Streets and the Campbelltown Flats, paddocks near the railway. Most of the land remained in the family until the death of Sarah Hurley in 1922.

George Fieldhouse, storekeeper and publican of the Jolly Miller, died at Campbelltown in 1880. His sons, Edwin Hallet Fieldhouse (b. 1832) and William Fieldhouse (b. 1834), were storekeepers in Campbelltown. They purchased much land in the 1870s and 1880s and inherited more from their father. By 1884 the Fieldhouse family owned 44 properties within the town including 10 commercial premises, Glenalvon and Richmond Villa and 18 farms in the neighbourhood.[48]

When Edwin and William Fieldhouse dissolved their partnership in 1904 they owned about 90 properties in Campbelltown. William Fieldhouse died in April 1910. Most of his 22 dairy farms were bought by the tenants who put up 25 per cent as deposit and borrowed the balance from the Fieldhouse estate at 6 per cent interest. The local manager of the Bank of New South Wales was sceptical about their long-term prospects as most were paying out more than they had in rents. Edwin Fieldhouse had married Ann Bray of Denfield. She inherited property within Campbelltown from her father, including the hotel on the corner of Cordeaux and Queen Streets, known as the Sportsman's Arms and leased to Charles Stanley, husband of Emma Fieldhouse. Edwin and Ann Fieldhouse moved to Turramurra and later to Randwick where he died in January 1922 and she in 1933.[49]

One man who had not lived in the district since childhood was James Tyson, yet his success brought substantial benefits to Campbelltown. His father, William Tyson (d. 1827), had followed his convict wife Isabella, née Coulson (d. 1874), to New South Wales following her conviction for theft. They arrived in 1809 and Isabella was assigned to her husband for the duration of her seven-year sentence. They farmed at Narellan and Appin. William Tyson was not very successful, losing his position as constable in 1816, forced off his farm by debts and moving further south to East Bargo. James was one of eleven children, many of whom married locally and lived in Campbelltown. Families connected by marriage included the Sheil, Doneley, Hewitt, Moore, Herring, Macdonald and Henry families.

James and his brothers took up squatting runs along the Lachlan and Murrumbidgee in the 1840s with only moderate success. In 1852 James and William Tyson drove their first mob of cattle to the gold diggings at Bendigo, Victoria, and set up a butcher's shop. Within three years they sold out, having made about £80000, and invested in more grazing stations near Deniliquin. From this base, a week's droving from Melbourne and its rapidly growing population, James Tyson expanded his pastoral interests across the eastern colonies, overlanding cattle from Queensland, fattening them on his Riverina stations and then droving or railing them to Melbourne. A member of the Legislative Council of Queensland from 1893, when he died in 1898 Tyson held about 9.6 million acres (3.8 million ha).

A reticent man of frugal personal habits, nicknamed 'Hungry' by the press and 'the Billycan Millionaire' by the public, Tyson did not drink, smoke, swear—or marry. James Tyson, millionaire, died without leaving a will. His estate was eventualy divided among about 30 nephews and nieces, several of whom lived in Campbelltown. His personal estate of over £2.3 million provoked extensive legal battles between the Victorian, New South Wales and Queensland governments over the right to probate duties, with the Queensland government being the victor. James Tyson was buried in Toowoomba in 1898, but after settlement of his estate his remains were moved to St Peters Church of England at Campbelltown and reinterred on 4 December 1901. Among the local beneficiaries was Stephen Hewitt, the son of Tyson's sister Elizabeth (1817–1888). Stephen Hewitt used his inheritance to purchase Eshcol Park in 1902.[50]

Commerce and industry

The water canal, the Camden tramway, duplication of the railway track and construction of Cataract Dam brought many labourers to the district. The railway station at Campbelltown was the gateway for most of these projects, and local farmers found work for their horse teams carting building materials and supplies. There were opportunities for new businesses such as boarding houses, fruit and vegetable shops and general stores. There was little specialisation among the storekeepers—all carried some clothing, china and grocery lines.

A visitor walking through Campbelltown from the south in 1896 would pass on the western side of Queen Street Fieldhouse's store; the Jolly Miller Hotel (run by Elizabeth Cooper in 1891, Meyer in 1894 and Stanley in 1896); two small fruit shops (one run by Mrs A. L. Coles); some houses; a saddler (Michael Croghan); the fire station; town hall and council chambers; a chemist and dispensary (run by Arthur Power, formerly a doctor for a Newcastle coal company); a house; a blacksmith; the Commercial Bank; the post office; another fruit shop; Hickey Brothers' butchery; a tailor (Brown); W. Oswald Lees, tinsmithy and bootmaker; the jubilee hall concealed behind the shops; another butcher; then Lees' Glasgow House general store (approximately where Dumaresq Street now continues across Queen Street). William Lees was the only licensed plumber in town and was also the local tinsmith. From their store in Bursill's Buildings, Mr and Mrs Lees operated a bakery and general store selling drapery, boots and shoes, fancy goods, china, glass, earthernware, groceries, ironmongery and patent medicines, hay, corn, chaff and pollard. Plumbing and tinsmithing work included water connections and mending leaking roofs. Behind the shops along the railway line Shu Gut had leased land for a market garden.

Continuing north was the Bank of New South Wales; Patrick Clifton's drapery; a boarding house (run by W. W. Berry); Graham Brothers' general store; Graham's boot shop, with the military volunteers' drill shed behind, and Caldwell's butchery in a two-storey building. North of Milgate Lane there was very little development, with a large vacant block to Patrick Street and three buildings between Patrick and Railway Streets—a boot shop and refreshment rooms soon to be replaced in 1897 by Reeve's Emporium, behind which the fire brigade was based, and the Forbes Hotel. The courthouse and police station on the corner of Queen and Railway Streets were isolated on the northern entrance to the town.

Returning south toward Appin on the eastern side of Queen Street, the traveller passed the two-storey Club Hotel (previously the Sportsman's Arms and rebuilt in 1893); the old newspaper printing office (formerly the post office and used by Barker the saddler in 1896); a grocery store opposite Patrick Street, then a large vacant allotment next to Lithgow Street. Between Lithgow and Dumaresq Streets there were only a draper's shop and a few empty stores, then from Dumaresq Street to Allman Street, a blacksmith; a photographer; a barber; a fruit shop; Michael O'Shanessy's store, and a large house. South of Allman Street were the well-known Georgian buildings occupied by McGuanne's boot shop; Doyle's Railway Hotel (John Doyle's home in 1891); with a coach builder behind; Thomas Gamble's store and home; a small cottage; a private home in the two-storey building with the archway, and three small houses, one formerly a saddlery and a butcher.

Beyond the creek was the old mill, by the 1890s Commerce House, the premises of James Bocking and Sons, grocers, drapers, bakers and general storekeepers. Bocking's sold general ironmongery, galvanised iron, ridge capping and spouting, crockery, furniture, bedding, boots and shoes. They were also produce and timber merchants and agents for the *Bulletin*, the *Evening News* and *Town and Country Journal* and the New Zealand Fire Insurance Company. Dressmaking, millinery services and mourning clothes were available at the shortest notice.[51]

In 1880 Newling and Walker operated cordial factories at Campbelltown and Parramatta. The technology for making cordials, ginger beers and soda was fairly simple. Carbon dioxide was made by the reaction of sulphuric acid on baking soda then compressed into distilled and filtered water to produce soda water. In the 1880s Gilbert Bray and Company operated a cordial factory, Gilbert being the proprietor of the Forbes Hotel. Later cordial manufacturers were Samuel M. Jenner and Joseph Pickles Seddon (1845–1937) whose cordial factory was also used as the Campbelltown Co-operative Creamery.[52]

The Railway Hotel and St Patricks Hotel had closed by 1912 and were private homes. The Jolly Miller Hotel became the Commonwealth, recognising the end of the old era and the start of a new. The Cumberland Hotel became the Royal under T. F. Hogan; Mrs Honora McCarthy was at the Club Hotel, remodelled premises on the site of Hammond's 1830 inn, and Joseph Sherack was the licensee of the Forbes Hotel.

Above Wilson's butcher shop, 249 Queen Street, around 1880, with G. Mabbott's blacksmithy on the southern side and Newling and Walker's cordial factory on the north. The sign of Tripp Brothers, coach and buggy builders, on the opposite side of Queen Street is reflected in the butcher's window. *On the verandah* Mr and Mrs Wilson and Nell. *In the street* D. Crammond (on white horse), J. Cook, G. Chinnocks and J. Hickey (butchers).

Below Reeve's Emporium (1897) still stands on the northern corner of Queen and Patrick Streets.

Charles Nicol operated the sawmill near the railway in 1911. Building tradesmen were few, and found routine work repairing schools and public buildings. Government contracts varied from small projects to construction worth about £1300. Sureties for the completion of their work were usually provided by local shopkeepers. The most active contractors were William Gee, a builder in partnership with George Bullock or Fowler; William Craft, carpenter, and George R. Lusted. Their sureties were usually one of the butchers—William Blythe Caldwell, George Chinnocks or James Wilson. Other regular guarantors included Henry John Craft and George Lusted, both builders; Thomas Henry Reeve, ironmonger, of 748 George Street and of Campbelltown; William Graham and James Bocking, storekeepers; George Brown, tailor, and George Kershler, farmer.[53]

There were four bootmakers and two saddlers. Locally crafted implements and repairs supported several trades. Blacksmiths were Doyle Brothers, J. Jones junior (also the wheelwright), James Lynch, Charles North, J. Swann and Charles Tripp. Charles and Thomas Tripp, coach builders, had horses and sulkies for hire, advertising with the slogan 'If you want a good Turn-Out go and C. Tripp'.[54]

In the 1890s there were two undertakers, Doyle Brothers and Gee and Fowler. Professional men were rare and the turn-over was rapid. Solicitors in 1880, Joseph Leary and Charles Bull both had parliamentary ambitions. Bull could be consulted at home every evening after 7 pm and at any hour on Saturdays. They were replaced by S. Moore and Charles J. Passmore in the 1890s. There was one auctioneer, Thomas Gamble. Most businesses met purely local needs, the exceptions being the Campbelltown Co-Operative Creamery and the Campbelltown State Nursery.

As the new century advanced, there were changes in individual businesses but few new services. The list of bakers was increased with a pastry cook. Dressmakers had a higher profile by 1908 with Miss Ellen Chinnocks, Miss Annie Kershler (later Mrs P. C. Marlow) and Miss Emma Whitehead advertising their services. Among the professional classes by 1908 were a doctor (Wilfred B. Dight), a chemist (Ian W. Tyerman), a dentist (Norman Gilbert), an architect (Alfred Payten) and an engineer (Thomas Houghton). Real estate agents appeared. By 1911 C. J. Marlow and T. H. Reeve, both from local storekeeping families, were land and real estate agents.[55]

There was little commercial development in the outlying villages. There were no shops at Wedderburn. Most people living north of Campbelltown shopped in Liverpool. William J. Collins and Alex B. Kavanagh ran general stores at Ingleburn railway station and W. R. Simpson ran one at Minto. At Glenfield there were two stores, Mrs Magee and Mrs Thompson, and a greengrocer, William Kilduff. Mail-order catalogues from the city retailers provided access to a wider range of goods. Marcus Clarke regularly advertised in Campbelltown in these years.[56]

Annie Kershler and her dressmakers, Queen Street. (P. C. Marlow, c.1910). *Left to right* Misses Kershler, Hyman, Wilkinson, Davies, Willis, Wiggins.

Campbelltown schools

The *Education Act* of 1881 had little impact in Campbelltown where the Protestant churches had closed their schools in the mid-1870s. Throughout the colony Catholic parishes continued their schools without public aid.

Patrick Newman was headmaster of Campbelltown Public School from 1880 until he retired in 1901. He died in Campbelltown in October 1909. Saggart Field was renamed Minto Public School in 1882, but did not move to the more populated eastern side of the railway until the new century. Glenfield parents had a similar problem. The public school opened in a tent in 1882 on the western side of the railway near Canterbury Road. Parents argued that the school should be moved to the eastern side of the railway where the children lived. In 1911 land was purchased near Glenfield station on the eastern side for a new weatherboard school which was opened in 1913. Public schools were opened at Ingleburn in 1887, Wedderburn in 1896 and East Minto in 1898, each serving children within a 3-mile (5 km) radius.

Teaching provided careers for local children. Among the pupil teachers at Campbelltown Public School were Sarah Lusted, daughter of a local builder, and Alice McEwen, daughter of the Superintendent of the State Nursery. Kate McGuanne, daughter of a Campbelltown shoemaker, was appointed to the school in 1894 and remained until her retirement in 1922. Amy Steel, daughter of the Presbyterian minister, was sewing teacher from the 1890s to 1901. Patrick Newman listed among his achievements 30 former students who became teachers, including Patrick McGuanne, Newman's son Gerald and James McEwen.[57]

By 1901 a majority of children in Campbelltown and Ingleburn attended public schools. In the Ingleburn municipality, where there was no real alternative, 66 of 74 children of school age attended the public school. At Campbelltown parents had a choice between the public school, three Catholic schools and a few small private academies. Less than half of the children attended the public school.

Catholic education in Campbelltown stagnated until the arrival of the Good Samaritan Sisters. In 1882 the Good Samaritan Sisters purchased Westview estate, close to St Johns Church, from George Scarr. The weatherboard home became a school for boys, later known as St Johns School, with fifteen pupils by 1891. A new St Johns Church, more conveniently located in Cordeaux Street, was opened in 1887 and the old church on the hill became St Patricks Convent for the Good Samaritans and a boarding school for girls. Emily Vardy was the first boarder in 1888 and by 1891 there were about eighteen boarders. St Patricks Primary School was at the southern end of Campbelltown on the Old Menangle Road. Enrolments had declined when Newman left and in 1889 the school was taken over by the Sisters of the Good Samaritan. The school continued in its 1840 building until 1914 when it moved to new premises

Kate McGuanne in her classroom. She taught at Campbelltown Public School from 1894 to 1922. (P. C. Marlow, c.1910)

CAMPBELLTOWN AND AIRDS HISTORICAL SOCIETY

and the old building was old. The new owner, Keihone Bourke, renamed it 'Quondong'.[58]

On Appin Road the Campbelltown Grammar School and Commercial College was opened under headmaster Mr H. Oliver. A special coach ran to the school daily at 9 am and 11 am, returning to town in the afternoon. By 1902 the grammar school had moved to Studley Park at Narellan and the children caught the Camden tram. There were several small schools run by daughters of local families. In the 1880s Miss Rutherford had a school in the Congregational church and Miss Spellman and Miss Clarke took pupils in their homes. May Bocking held classes at the Retreat in Allman Street in 1903 and Miss Moore had a girls' school at Leumeah. At Wyangar, Minto, Miss Kate Ohlfsen-Bagge taught violin and her sister gave painting and drawing lessons.[59]

Campbelltown newspapers

One of the more significant changes was the appearance of a weekly newspaper. No record survives of the first newspaper which was probably printed in 1879. William Webb, proprietor of the *Campbelltown Herald*, referred to an earlier newspaper, but did not name either the paper or its publishers. The first issue of the *Campbelltown Herald and Camden, Liverpool, Appin, Picton and Menangle Advertiser* appeared on 14 February 1880, price 3 pence. William Webb, proprietor and editor, was born near Penrith in 1848, educated at Mudgee and apprenticed to the *Western Post*. He started a newspaper in Bourke about 1870 and in the next 30 years established a dozen other country newspapers, concentrating in the 1880s in the Southern Highlands. They included the *Wilcannia Times* (1874), *Burrawang Herald* (Berrima, 1880, sold 1884), Kiama *Odd Fellow* (sold 1880), *Campbelltown Herald* (1880), *Camden News* (1880), *Bowral Free Press* (1883, sold 1884), *Campbelltown Liberal* (1885), *Picton Argus* (1885), *Liverpool Herald* (1887) and the *Nepean Argus*.[60]

Webb moved to Campbelltown from Kiama in 1879 and set up his printing press in a building owned by James Bocking. He had selected Campbelltown because of its central location between Liverpool, Camden and Picton. Webb announced that he would promote the moral, social and political interests of the neighbourhood. 'Sectarianism, personalities, slang and black-guardism ... will be eschewed ... Toleration in its widest sense, irrespective of creed, country or colour, will be the principal feature.'[61]

In colonial Australia, a newspaper developed a town's sense of identity and was the loudest advocate for 'progress'. A country newspaper (according to Thomas Garrett, newspaper proprietor and MLA for the Campbelltown district 1872–91) could be established with £200 if the proprietor were reporter, editor, typesetter and printer. Financial difficulties were common and Webb was no exception. In March 1883 he was threatened with insolvency over a debt of £275 to his paper suppliers in Sydney. The sale of his Berrima papers in 1884 may have been to rationalise his financial commitments.[62]

In July 1885 he left the *Campbelltown Herald* to start the *Campbelltown Liberal*. No known copies survive. The surviving 1886 issues of the *Campbelltown Herald* were published and printed by Edward H. Myerson of Campbelltown. The owner in 1886 was P. R. Holdsworth but John Kidd acquired the *Campbelltown Herald* in 1887. The Campbelltown papers may have ceased publication during the 1890s depression. By 1898 the *Campbelltown Herald, incorporating the Campbelltown Liberal,* was printed and published by Joseph McGlynn, who remained the publisher until 1914. Webb continued as a district correspondent for various newspapers. He lived at Wedderburn from 1898 and, between mining ventures on the Yerranderie silver field, was an auctioneer, general agent, bottle-and-bone man, and publican. At Wedderburn he encouraged the formation of a fruitgrowers' association. William Webb died in November 1910 and was buried in the Campbelltown Congregational cemetery.[63]

Webb's sale of the *Campbelltown Herald* in 1885 may have been a consequence of an action for criminal libel brought against him by Sir Henry Parkes in 1884. The *Campbelltown Herald* had alleged that Parkes had evaded his creditors by leaving the colony, that he had been involved in a fraudulent project to construct a bridge across Sydney Harbour and that he had sold ministerial appointments for personal gain. Webb's barrister argued that these comments were in the public interest. He read the offending paragraphs to the court, including

> *Sir Henry is a man who never in his life paid anyone if he could help it. If he made a man's acquaintance it was solely for the purpose of borrowing money from him or getting him to endorse a promissory note, which the unfortunate invariably had to pay. He always deserted his old friends, no matter how good, for new ones, and has altogether been a man unworthy of confidence.*

Parkes appeared in court to deny the allegations. The jury was locked up overnight, but was unable to come to a verdict and the case against Webb was dismissed.[64]

The *Campbelltown Herald* routinely published the minutes of council meetings, sporting and social activities, public meetings, obituaries and weddings (the latter two both rare in a small population). Sometimes the editor was sufficiently stirred by events outside Campbelltown to include an editorial on political or social matters, and occasionally he risked offence by reporting the bench of magistrates' hearings.

Parliamentary representatives

In the 1880 redistribution, Campbelltown became part of the three-member Camden electorate. Ingleburn municipality was part of the large-

The Kidd family in the garden of Blair Athol, around 1890. *Left to right* Jessie Loney (nee Kidd), Fred Kidd, Mary Brown (nee Kidd), Sophia Kidd (nee Collier) and the Honourable John Kidd, MLA. CAMPBELLTOWN AND AIRDS HISTORICAL SOCIETY

ly metropolitan electorate of Central Cumberland until 1894 when it became part of the Camden electorate.

Thomas Garrett (1830–1891) held Camden from February 1872 until his death in 1891. Trained as a printer, he worked on newspapers in Goulburn, Sydney and the goldfields before establishing the *Illawarra Mercury* with W. F. Cahill in 1855. In the 1860s Garrett established newspapers in the Monaro and purchased a share with G. F. Pickering in a sporting newspaper, *Bell's Life in Sydney*, in 1867. In 1871 *Bell's Life* was incorporated into the *Sydney Mail*. Garrett entered parliament in 1860 for the southern seat of Monaro and later held the seat of Shoalhaven. In 1872 he became the member for Camden. He was a roads and bridges member and an advocate of land reform. Garrett held office as Secretary for Lands in 1875–77 and 1887–88. His judgment was increasingly undermined by his alcoholism while his moral standing was badly injured by scandals about his mining speculations and corruption. Garrett ended up on the backbench and died of 'softening of the brain' in November 1891.[65]

John Kidd (1838–1919) was also MLA for Camden from 1880 to 1882, 1885 to 1887, 1889 to 1895 and 1898 to 1904, when he retired from politics. From 1860 Kidd had been a successful baker and storekeeper in Campbelltown. On his return from a visit to Scotland in 1877, Kidd turned to dairying and was an early breeder of Ayrshire cattle. He was a director of

144

the Farmers' and Dairymen's Milk Company Ltd and of the Australian Mutual Fire Insurance Society. A supporter of the temperance movement, of Federation and of free trade, Kidd was Postmaster-General (1891–94) and Secretary for Mines and Minister for Agriculture (1901–04). In Campbelltown he was an active member of the Presbyterian School committee and later of the Public School Board and the school of arts. Kidd lobbied successfully for bridges, roads and public buildings: the post office (1881) and the courthouse (1887–89) were approved while Kidd was the local member.[66]

William McCourt (1851–1913) successfully opposed Kidd in 1882 and again in 1887. He had served his apprenticeship under Garrett at the *Illawarra Mercury* before going out on his own to establish the *Moss Vale Scrutineer* in 1874 when he was 23 years old. McCourt speculated in land and was chairman of the Intercolonial Land and Investment Company from 1887 till his death. Generally successful in his land dealings, he suffered reverses in the mid-1890s and sought relief in the bankruptcy court. He had a long parliamentary career as the member for Camden 1882–85, 1887–94 and later for Bowral (1894–1904) and Wollondilly (1904–13). He was Speaker of the Legislative Assembly from 1900 to 1910.[67]

In the 1890s the major ideological difference between politicans was the economic issue of free trade or protection. From 1894, when the electorate had one member, the voters of Camden and Campbelltown tended to vote for the protectionist candidate, John Kidd. In 1895 local solicitor Charles Bull defeated Kidd by only 21 votes. Bull (1846–1906), the son of wheelwright William Bull and his wife Catherine Rowley of Holsworthy, started his practice as a solicitor in 1873. Twice married, his first wife was Mary Morris of Campbelltown and his second Fanny Australia Chippendall of Bradbury Park. Bull became the second mayor of Campbelltown in 1884 and was later mayor of Liverpool and Hurstville. He died at Bexley in 1906.[68]

Frederick William Arthur Downes (1855–1917) represented the seat of Camden from August 1904 to November 1913 as a Liberal. His home was Brownlow Hill and he had been educated at Macarthur's Macquarie Fields School. John Charles Hunt (1857–1930) was the member for Camden from 1913 to 1920. Hunt was an unusual choice, being an alderman on Hornsby Council and active in the fruitgrowers' associations of Dural and Castle Hill.[69]

Though not a local member, John Davies (1839–1896) lived at Campbelltown and took an interest in its affairs. Davies was a Sydney ironmonger who entered parliament in 1874 as the member for East Sydney. In 1887 he was appointed to the Legislative Council. Davies' career was propelled by the passions of the temperance lobby and anti-Catholicism. His appointment to the licensing bench in 1882 created near hysteria among the brewing interests. In 1884 Davies purchased a Campbelltown inn, the Three Brothers, and converted it to a home for his wife, Elizabeth, their son and five daughters. A ballroom and tennis court were built, elaborate cast-iron lacework altered the facade and it was renamed Holly Lea. Davies commuted to parliament, flagging passing trains from the bottom of his garden. In 1886 Holly Lea platform was added to the railway network. Offended by this new name, local residents successfully lobbied for the station to be renamed Leumeah after John Warby's pioneer grant. In Campbelltown Davies took the lead in establishing Lodge Federation in 1890 but the organisation collapsed when Davies retired due to ill health in 1895. He died the following year.[70]

Growth in the north

Minto

Minto was often called Campbellfield after the Redfern estate which covered much of the area. In the early 1880s it had a small population of farmers. Development had been at a standstill since the death of Dr William Redfern in 1833. By 1883 Campbellfield homestead was virtually uninhabitable and for many years the estate had been leased for grazing for an annual rental of only £315. John Kidd leased 1050 acres (420 ha) for £75 per year; Patrick Scanlon had 3700 acres (1480 ha) for £220, and Patrick Cleary 163 acres (65 ha) for £20 per annum. Much of the land had never been cleared of timber and by the 1880s this was a valuable resource. The railway added greatly to its potential. Campbellfield platform had been built in 1874 but no trains stopped there until 1877. It was renamed Minto station in 1882 and was used by small farmers who lived mostly on the western side of the railway.[71]

Subdivision of Campbellfield was arranged through Richardson and Wrench in 1883. The first subdivision was the southern part near Minto railway station. The second subdivision created the Ingleburn township near the old Macquarie Fields station, renamed Ingleburn station in August 1883. The third subdivision of the northern half was completed in February 1885. Covering all of Ingleburn, southern Macquarie Fields and northern Minto, this subdivision of 20-acre (8 ha) farms created a street pattern that still survives. The main streets through the subdivision from north to south were Bensley Road and Fields Road.[72]

The purchasers were mostly real estate investors and speculators. Charles A. Scrivener and his sons from Liverpool, publicans and aldermen, purchased extensively as did Inglis and Thornwaite. Elizabeth Chaperon bought three portions in Ben Lomond Road for £700 in 1886 and built a small stone cottage, later known as The Jug. Other purchasers included Uh Chong and Ah John Sue who paid £166 for 13 acres (5.2 ha) in 1883.[73]

A weatherboard school with shingle roof was built at Saggart Field on a new site, the northern corner of Campbelltown Road and Redfern Road, in 1882 and renamed Minto Public School. Though over 50 were enrolled, only an average of 35 children attended regularly throughout the 1880s and 1890s. Several of the children walked over 3 kilometres to school across the paddocks. Others came from as far as East Minto (Minto Heights).[74]

There were signs of growth at Minto by 1886 with a brickmaker at work and small farms established. Braill had started a butchery and P. R. Holdsworth had offered land for a church, but the onset of the 1890s depression, coinciding with the end of the railway works, halted development. New stimulus came from release of land on the Campbelltown Common, about 2000 acres (800 ha) between Smiths Creek and the George's River, south of Peter Meadows Creek (now Kentlyn). The common had been declared in March 1879 under the *Crown Lands Occupation Act* of 1861 to provide temporary rough grazing land and firewood for householders. It became available for homestead selections in 1894.

By 1896 there were twenty children among the families living on the common and at East Minto. As they lived more than 3 miles (5 km) from the closest school, they did not go to school. East Minto Public School was opened in Hansens Road in September 1898 with Cecil George Browning Sutton as teacher until he retired in 1921. He remained in the district, an active member of community groups, until his death in 1951. The altar at St James Church of England, Minto, was dedicated to the memory of Cecil Sutton.[75]

Minto village by 1908 had a mixed population of orchardists, dairy farmers, vignerons, tradespeople and a few city commuters such as C. H. O. Bagge, a civil engineer, and John C. Rider, a glass engraver and etcher. The Minto School of Arts Committee purchased land in 1910 to build a hall. There were two builders, H. Hodkin and Robert Porter, the

The home of the Whitehouse family in Eagleview Road, Minto, 1897.

CAMPBELLTOWN AND AIRDS HISTORICAL SOCIETY

latter also a brickmaker. Robert Porter had operated a brickyard at Marrickville from 1871 to 1876 when he turned to orcharding at Kenthurst. Later he moved to Minto, possibly to continue orcharding. There were no brickmakers so he started a small brickworks which operated until the 1920s. Bricks were made by hand, employing only one or two men and a horse to turn the pug mill.[76]

Ingleburn

Old Macquarie Fields railway station was renamed Ingleburn in August 1883. The station was built in 1869 on Neale's 80-acre (32 ha) grant, a farm owned by Mary Kennedy, née Ruse, until her death in 1874. Elias P. Laycock purchased her farm in 1881 and his home was called Ingleburn House. Unoccupied land from Cumberland Road to Bunbury Curran Creek, covering most of Ingleburn township and valued at £3500, was purchased in February 1885 by Sydney auctioneer R. FitzStubbs, who resold in small portions. Purchasers by 1886 included David Warby, publican; A. Laycock and A. L. Jamison, gentlemen; Collins the storekeeper; G. W. Burgess, a brickmaker, and William Sharp, a servant at Macquarie Fields House. Settlement concentrated in two areas—near the railway station and near Chester Road and Gertrude Street.[77]

In August 1886 Warby, Collins, Laycock and John Ward, a sawmill proprietor, applied for a school for the 16 boys and 26 girls in the area. Ingleburn school, on the corner of Oxford and Cumberland Roads, opened in 1887 in a building relocated from Brooks Point near Appin, where the water construction camp was being dismantled. It was replaced with a new building in 1892.

By 1891, 21 families were listed as residents of Ingleburn. Most had large families. Charles Linklater had ten in his household, as did William J. Collins, while John McLeod had nine. Sarah Ann Johnston may have run a boarding house as she had 19 living in her house. Ingleburn's most impressive home was Milton Park built in 1882 for David Warby, a son of Joseph Warby of Campbelltown and licensee of the Liverpool Arms Hotel in Sydney. He was a generous supporter of the local school and well respected by his neighbours.[78]

Ingleburn in the mid-1890s was a community of fruitgrowers and woodcutters. It already had a Progress Association, under Arthur Lubeck and William Pidcock, which had moved the old school across the road to become the Ingleburn School of Arts in 1892. The Progress Association arranged the first local government election.[79]

On 22 October 1895 the *Government Gazette* published the petition of 61 Ingleburn residents requesting municipal government for their district. The proposed area lay between the boundaries of Liverpool Council in the north and Campbelltown in the south, with the George's River as

Ingleburn around 1920–30. To the left of the railway is McIlveen's general store and Ingleburn House and on the right, Harper's real estate agency.

the eastern boundary and including Denham Court on the west—in all, about 9 square miles (23 km²). The signatures for incorporation were collected by Thomas Brown, William Harris, Alexander Bede Kavanagh and William Pidcock. No objections were received and the municipality of Ingleburn was proclaimed in April 1896.[80]

Ingleburn municipality in 1896 covered the southern half of the modern suburb of Ingleburn and parts of Minto. The municipality's northern boundary was Oxford Street and the villages of Macquarie Fields and Glenfield were in Liverpool municipality. In June 1896 Samuel George Barff, William John Collins (storekeeper), James Livingstone (orchardist), Malcolm McInnes (orchardist), Sydney Percival (butcher) and Joseph Whitehouse were elected to the council. S. G. Barff was the first mayor (1896–97) and J. Williamson was the first town clerk. Later mayors included Joseph Whitehouse (1898–99) and Thomas P. Latter, a builder, in 1900.[81]

Ingleburn Council purchased the former Church of England mission hall on the corner of Gertrude and Chester Streets for its council chambers. By 1903 Ingleburn Council's total expenditure was £220 compared with a rate income of £95 supplemented by a £150 grant from the government. Apart from the town clerk, who also acted as treasurer, there were no regular employees. Road maintenance was funded by special grants and men were employed as casuals when needed. Ingleburn Council tried unsuccessfully to have the major road from Campbelltown through Minto, Ingleburn, Macquarie Fields and Glenfield to the Crossroads declared a main road so that the government would maintain it. The clerk in 1906, J. P. Walsh of 'Woodville', Minto, was also treasurer, overseer of works and a valuer for rate assessments for which he was paid £25 per annum. His office was open one night a week, from 4 to 6 pm. Because there were no streetlights, Ingleburn Council met at 8 pm on the Tuesday night preceding the full moon so that councillors could find their way home by moonlight.

At least one resident had extensive previous experience in local government. Percy Charles Lucas was a son of John Lucas (1818–1902), building contractor and member of parliament. Percy Lucas and his brother were wine merchants specialising in colonial wines. He lived in Glebe before moving to 'Bertswood', Ingleburn, and had been simultaneously an alderman on Glebe and Camperdown Councils, as well as being mayor of Camperdown for four years and mayor of Glebe in 1888–89. At Ingleburn he signed the petition requesting local government in 1895 and was mayor in 1906 and from 1908 to 1911. Lucas and Frederick A. Suttor, grazier of Varroville, were involved in real estate speculation in the 1890s at Ingleburn and were associated with the Glenwood subdivision of Macquarie Fields.[82]

In 1907 Ingleburn municipality, covering 6592 acres (2637 ha), had a population of 375 people living in 106 buildings. There were no street-lighting, no public parks or recreation areas, no water, gas or electricity, no sealed roads and less than 3 kilometres of properly formed roads. Commercial activities had concentrated near the railway station. In 1901 the two butchers were John Bruton and Syd Percival; the stores were run by William Collins, also the first postmaster and brickmaker, and A. B. Kavanagh who sold out to McIlveen. There was a draper, Thomas Hill, and a hairdresser/tobacconist, George Craft, who was also the blacksmith and harness-maker. Good building timber, especially ironbark, provided work for the sawmill, initially operated by Bosci and later by Charles Thorn. Bullock teams pulled the logs to the mill, and the timber, for building or firewood, was sent by train to Sydney.[83]

The Reverend Thomas Alkin came from Campbelltown once a fortnight to hold Anglican services in the St Barnabas mission room, built on the corner of Gertrude Street and Chester Road in 1892. A new church, St James, on the corner of Cumberland and Minto Roads was completed in 1898. Designed by Wilshire and built by Thomas Latter, it served parishioners in both Ingleburn and Minto until it was moved to Redfern Road, Minto, in 1918. The Reverend P. Presswell was appointed rector to St James in 1901. The Wesleyans held Sunday school and services in the Ingleburn School of Arts until 1911 when the Wesleyans and Baptists both opened churches.[84]

By 1911 Ingleburn was 'fast becoming a township' with a public school, a building used as a church, a school of arts and two stores. Train journeys to the city took only an hour on a fast service. The district had ample good land for dairy farms, orchards and grazing.[85]

150

Ingleburn Baptist Church, built in 1911. (T. Swann c.1920)

Macquarie Fields and Glenfield

Meehan's Macquarie Fields estate was subdivided, creating the suburbs of Macquarie Fields and Glenfield. Mrs Hosking's executors, Richard Rouse Terry and George Rattray, sold Macquarie Fields House and the western portion of the estate in 1877, and arranged with Hardie and Gorman for the subdivision of land east of the railway into suburban allotments and small acreage farms in 1881.

Macquarie Fields House with 1660 acres (664 ha) was purchased by James Ashcroft, a grazier from Canonbar, near Nyngan. Ashcroft was born in Campbelltown in 1823, the son of John Ashcroft and Elizabeth Tebbutt. He joined the exodus to the south and settled at Tumut where he married. Later he sought new grazing land in the west. A man of independent means, Ashcroft and his wife, Amelia, lived at Macquarie Fields until their deaths—James in June 1893 and Amelia in 1902. In the 1891 census only five families gave their address as Macquarie Fields— James Ashcroft at Macquarie Fields House (one male, four females); John Ahearn and family (five males, three females); William and Thomas Sharp with their families, and Patrick McMahon and his family. Amelia Ashcroft's brother, Edward Rea, and his family came to live at Macquarie Fields after the death of James Ashcroft. Macquarie Fields was inherited by her nephew, Thaddeus Bourke Rea, shortly before his death in June 1904.[86]

151

In 1908 the estate was sold by the executors to the Ross brothers, graziers from Germanton (renamed Holbrook during World War I). Alexander, John, James, William and Robert Ross were the sons of Scottish immigrants. The Ross family farmed in South Australia, moved to Albury in 1867 and acquired many grazing properties in south-western New South Wales. Macquarie Fields became part of their network of stations, but may also have been a Sydney base for Alexander Ross (1843–1912) who was appointed to the Legislative Council in 1900.[87]

East of the railway Thomas Saywell purchased 1558 acres (623 ha) from the Hosking trustees in 1881. Saywell (1837–1928) was a well-known Sydney merchant and real estate developer. From modest beginnings as a tobacconist, Saywell had invested in coalmining at Bulli, Clifton and Lithgow, and anticipated the boom in real estate and coal from the Illawarra railway. Saywell was attracted by proposals for a railway from St Peters to Liverpool. In purchasing at Macquarie Fields he hoped to profit from subdivisions at both ends of the railway. Apart from Saywell Road, little remains of his Macquarie Fields subdivision and the unsold portions were transferred to his company, Saywell's Tramway and Estates Limited, in 1906.[88]

In September 1883 William Edgar Harold Phillips purchased about half of Saywell's land, 700 acres (280 ha), from Saywell Road north to Harrow Road and from Atchison Road east to the George's River, covering most of modern Macquarie Fields. In March 1886 Phillips purchased another large area. A draftsman by profession, William Phillips was a speculator. The bushland of Macquarie Fields was an unlikely location for grand boulevards; nevertheless, Phillips produced a creative marketing brochure for his Glenwood estate at Macquarie Fields. The elegant township of Glenwood featured broad esplanades leading to a grand hotel. Prospective purchasers were beguiled with the elegant homes and thriving vineyards of neighbouring estates and encouraged to purchase a few acres where they could enjoy boating, bathing and fishing on the George's River. Much emphasis was given to the convenience of the railway which permitted Sydney businessmen to work regular city hours yet still enjoy a country residence. In fact, Phillips assured his customers, the railway brought Macquarie Fields and Glenwood as close to the city as Randwick![89]

Average price per half-acre (0.2 ha) allotment at Glenwood was £15–£17. From May 1886 to December 1888 about 150 people purchased small sections, and by 1891, 10 families, 55 people, gave their address as the Glenwood estate. The 'heads of households' at Glenwood were Alfred J. Young, Nicholas Olsen, N. Duncan, Hugh Wallace, William Wallace, Paradine Hodgkins, William Burgess, W. Baldwin, William Stubbs and Henry Quelch. Macquarie Fields railway station, the second of that name, opened at its present location in October 1888, stimulating land sales.[90]

The real estate market collapsed in the early 1890s. Subdivisions had proceeded far beyond realistic commuting distances. The Macquarie

Fields land was transferred to the Burwood Land Building and Investment Company, of which Phillips was a partner, but in 1892 he was bankrupt and imprisoned for fraud. By 1906 part of Macquarie Fields had been acquired by another speculator, Sir Arthur Rickard.[91]

The northern portion of the Hosking estate became the suburb of Glenfield. The railway platform at Glenfield, opened in 1869, was one of the earliest on the southern line. Though named after the Throsby estate, Glenfield is substantially built on the Macquarie Fields estate, part of 1600 acres (640 ha) subdivided and sold in August 1880 by Hardie and Gorman as Point Farm. Most of the estate was purchased by speculators, but some people took advantage of the cheap prices to buy land to live on.

North of Harrow Road was subdivided by Thomas Saywell in the early 1880s. Among the purchasers were the Connelly family from Surry Hills. At their home on the corner of Harrow Road, Newton Avenue and Fawcett Street, the Misses Connelly ran a small school. As this was a more central location than Glenfield Public School, it was well supported by parents during the 1890s. In 1907 the Misses Connelly taught about 10–20 pupils. Neither was a trained teacher; nor was Edwin Moore, the teacher at Glenfield Public School from 1882 to 1909. Church meetings and Sunday school were organised at Glenfield from 1886 by the Hinsch family of River View. Its first church, a Presbyterian one, was designed by J. Shaw and built by M. Christiansen, both of Liverpool. It opened in July 1901 without a resident clergyman.[92]

Glenfield Farm, covering about 1200 acres (480 ha), lay between Glenfield and Casula railway stations. The Throsby estate had been inherited in the mid-1860s by Archer Broughton Throsby (1843–1925), but it was occupied by lessees. From 1891 to 1896 it was leased to the New South Wales government for a convalescent farm attached to the Liverpool Asylum for the Destitute. An average of 85 patients with two staff lived at Glenfield Farm where they worked the estate and supplied the Liverpool Asylum with fresh vegetables and milk.[93]

Denham Court

Denham Court estate covered 1368 acres (547 ha) extending west from the southern railway line, across Bunbury Curran Creek, Campbelltown Road, the water supply canal to the Cowpastures Road. In October 1884 Mills and Pile of Sydney and Finlay of Goulburn subdivided and auctioned the estate in allotments from half an acre (0.2 ha) to 100 acres (40 ha). Sixty-six acres (26 ha) were reserved around the house, a substantial brick building of two storeys with large entrance hall, drawing-room, dining-room, seventeen rooms on the ground floor and four on the upper level. The subdivision was designed by Atchison and Schleicher, the same team who surveyed the Campbellfield estate. Terms were 15 per cent deposit and the balance over three years at 5 per cent interest. Road names were associated with the Brooks and Blomfield families—Zouch

Road, after Henry Zouch (1811–83), the husband of Maria Brooks; Gibson Road after Susan Gibson, wife of Richard Blomfield; Dagworth Road, the Blomfield property in the Hunter Valley. Few of these roads were constructed.

Denham Court House was not sold at the 1884 auction. In 1889 the unfurnished house with 200 acres (80 ha) was leased, and a year later purchased, by John Colburn Mayne of Greendale, Bringelly. J. C. Mayne (1834–1924) was born in Dublin, the son of William Colburn Mayne (1808–1902), who migrated with his family in 1847 and became inspector-general of the New South Wales police in the 1850s, auditor-general of New South Wales from 1856 to 1864 and the first agent-general for New South Wales in London from 1864 to 1871. The Mayne family had extensive pastoral interests in western New South Wales where John Mayne lived with his first wife and their three children. In 1901 John C. Mayne married Alice Maude Macdonald whose family had leased part of Denham Court in 1898. John and Maude Mayne lived at Denham Court until their deaths in 1924 and 1957 respectively.[94]

Settlement in the east and south

Eckersley

Settlement concentrated on the shale lands west of the George's River. East of the river were rugged sandstone gorges covered with thick scrub; on the plateau were small pockets of farming land. The parish of Eckersley was named in 1835 by Surveyor-General Mitchell after Nathaniel Eckersley, a Quartermaster-general during the Peninsula War. There was no permanent European settlement in Eckersley until it was opened for selection under the *Crown Lands Act* of 1884. The boundaries of Campbelltown municipality were extended east to Williams Creek to include the new district.

A dozen families took up land for orchards and vineyards in the 1890s. Road access was easiest from Liverpool, along an extension of Greenhills Avenue and the Old Illawarra Road to Darkes Forest. Fords across the George's River at the Woolwash near O'Hares Creek and further north at Frere's Crossing provided cross-country routes to Campbelltown and the school at East Minto. Downstream at the junction of Peter Meadows Creek and the George's River was a third ford called the National Park crossing. George's River Road was to be extended across the river to join the Old Illawarra Road and the National Park on the coast. The road was surveyed in 1886 and built as an unemployment project between 1889 and 1891, costing over £1200. The Old Coach Road, popularly mistaken for a convict or a coach road, was neither. It was opened in 1897 and linked Harry Etchells' selection to Frere's Crossing.[95]

Frank Etchells from Appin was the first permanent settler at Eckersley, taking up a 200-acre (80 ha) selection in 1889, followed by his younger brother, Harry (1862–1951) and his sixteen-year-old wife, Ellen (d. 1894). They grew fruit and vegetables and raised poultry and bees but found distilling rum more profitable. The stills were concealed under rock ledges near waterfalls. Molasses was mixed with water and boiled in a cauldron for a day or two. The steam was condensed and run off into 4-gallon (18 L) kerosene tins. Four tins were hauled up the gully, loaded on a pack-horse and overlanded to Bulli. Etchells' moonshine was well known locally as '3P Rum'—pure, profitable and private. Sold to distributers for £1 a gallon (4.5 L), each trip grossed £16, two months' wages for a labourer.[96]

Nathaniel George Bull (1842–1911), son of a Liverpool storekeeper, was apprenticed to Anthony Horden at his Haymarket store. He married his employer's daughter, Harriet Horden, in 1861 and in 1872 Nat Bull and his family moved back to Liverpool where he opened a store and built his home, Cabramatta Park. Nat Bull was an alderman, several times mayor of Liverpool and a member of the Legislative Assembly from 1885 to 1887. Bull and his brothers took up selections in Eckersley. He built a substantial stone house, now known as Nat Bull's Tanks because of tanks cut in the sandstone to conserve water. In 1891 it was called Gettysburgh and was occupied by Nat Bull and a household of seven people.[97]

Several of the pioneers of Eckersley were European migrants. French-born Charles Leonce Frere and his brother Gustav took up 1600 acres (640 ha) which they called Monville in 1889. They planted a 40-acre (16 ha) vineyard, built houses, sheds and wine vats using kanaka servants whom they had brought from Noumea. A labourer, Black Sam, was buried at Campbelltown. The Freres abandoned their selection at the turn of the century. Jules Gandid, J. P. Rochaix and Alexander Reverce took up land towards Darkes Forest. Reverce had the largest household, ten people, in 1891. Charles and J. Wroblewski selected land at Carrant Tree Forest where they were living in 1891, but sold out to Issac Himmelhock who renamed it Grodno. Paul Victor Ladislas de Schedlin Czarlinski and Casimir Lebinski selected land along Williams Creek. Czarlinski was a civil engineer who migrated from Prussia in 1883, aged 34.

Wyndham Albert Trott and his wife lived on a small block. Mrs Trott often made mysterious trips across the river at night and it was assumed that she was avoiding excise duty on her brandy. James Heffernan supplemented his income by crushing the trunks of tree ferns to extract shellac which he sold to a gunpowder merchant. Others made charcoal. Edmond G. Kelso and Charles G. L. Kelso took up land in 1889 for orchards.[98]

The Eckersley selections were gradually abandoned after 1906 when the area was proposed for a military reserve. Eckersley post office closed in 1912 and the plateau east of the George's River was formally acquired for the army in March 1913.

Washday at Ferndale, Wedderburn. *Left to right* Mrs Joseph Swann, Agnes Swann (nee Scobie) and baby Tom. (T. Swann c.1915)

Wedderburn

Wedderburn was taken up by selectors in the 1880s and 40-acre (16 ha) blocks were laboriously cleared and planted with orchards. It was isolated and offered few of the comforts available in Campbelltown. The 10-kilometre track to town wound precariously around the gullies and forded the upper reaches of the George's River where a bridge was built in 1892.

Among the earliest residents was the Broinowski family. By 1891 Felix Broinowski lived in a household of five people and Leopold Broinowski lived with three. Gracius Joseph Broinowski (1837–1913) lived at Morning Glory, Wedderburn. G. J. Broinowski had fled his native Poland to avoid conscription and arrived in Victoria in 1857. He taught painting in private schools and was commissioned to draw Australian birds and animals for classroom displays. From the late 1880s Broinowski, his wife Jane and their children lived at Wedderburn. Here Broinowski completed 300 illustrations of Australian birds for a popular edition similar to Gould's well-known books. Mary Ann Percival moved from Appin and lived with the Broinowski family, teaching English to their neighbours, the Matthei family.

A provisional public school was opened at Wedderburn in September 1896. Church services were held in the home of Elizabeth Greenwood, the honorary postmistress, until the Wedderburn Union Church, built on land given by her, opened in October 1898. Robert Steel, the Presbyterian minister from Campbelltown, was president of the Wedderburn Mutual Improvement Association, an adult education group.

Joseph Swann, a blacksmith, settled at Wedderburn in the 1890s and, with his son, Thomas, grew plums, peaches, apples, grapes and vegetables. Their fruit was carted to Campbelltown station and railed to market in Sydney. In 1912 Tom Swann married Agnes Scobie, daughter of a neighbouring orchardist. Tom Swann's hobby was photography and his photographs were displayed in New South Wales railway carriages. Some Wedderburn residents, such as builders J. Knight and Charles Oatway and journalist William Webb, worked in Campbelltown.[99]

The Campbelltown volunteers

In 1885, the year of the Sudan campaign, the Campbelltown Infantry Reserve Corp of Volunteers was formed. By October 40 men practised drill twice a week on the reserve (Mawson Park) under the command of William Lyttlemore Moore, a local solicitor and son of the Presbyterian clergyman. The volunteers included the bank manager, storekeepers, farmers, tradesmen and labourers. Their equipment was stored in the town hall until a drill hall was built. In September 1886 volunteers from Picton, Camden, Albury, Hay, Narrandera, Young, Braidwood and Mittagong came to Campbelltown for field exercises. Though it was the first review for the Campbelltown men, military exercises were not an unusual sight. The annual Easter review of colonial volunteers had been held on the Campbellfield estate since the 1870s and attracted many visitors. In 1898 the annual camp was moved to Rookwood, to the disappointment of Campbelltown shopkeepers and the local girls.

Arthur Herbert Etchells (1870–1899), Campbelltown Mounted Infantry Volunteers around 1890.

By 1892 the Campbelltown Volunteers had become a Mounted Infantry Regiment or Light Horse under Captain Arthur Fisher Lloyd and Lieutenants Newman and Broinowski. The horsemen wore cord riding trousers and khaki jackets trimmed with red and green and emu feathers on their slouch hats. The men practised on the hillsides of Leumeah.[100]

Campbelltown Volunteers sailed with the New South Wales contingent to the Boer War in 1899. Throughout 1901 welcome banquets were held in Campbelltown and Ingleburn for men returning from the Boer campaigns. Among those who served were R. Holman, F. Axam, A. Spooner, G. Huckstepp, M. Bourke and Joseph Vardy, who remained in South Africa.[101]

Rifle clubs were part of the military reserve, receiving government funds for ammunition. The Campbelltown Rifle Club was formed in 1907 by L. W. Smith, A. R. Payten and P. C. Marlow, and an indoor rifle range was built at the showground.[102]

Daily life

The Camden Cottage Hospital on Menangle Road was opened in 1902. For 70 years it was the closest general hospital to Campbelltown and the town supported one of its fourteen beds. The annual cost, £30 in 1905, was raised by public balls and fetes. Campbelltown also supported a cot at the Ashfield Infants' Home.[103]

A provisional committee was formed in 1907 to establish a hospital in Campbelltown. In its first year the Campbelltown Cottage Hospital Auxiliary raised £300. The government architect drew up plans but, at a cost of £3450 for a seven-bed hospital, they were too expensive. The committee wanted a locally designed and built hospital but nothing eventuated.[104]

Healthy climate and comparative isolation were among the attractions of Campbelltown to the Parliamentary Standing Committee on Public Works in 1896 when it proposed building a new hospital for the chronically ill at Campbelltown, rather than extending the Rookwood Asylum for Infirm and Destitute Persons. The number of destitute persons had increased from 2448 in 1890 to 3540 by February 1896. Health authorities wanted a new hospital for consumptives, cancer and ophthalmic patients, those suffering from scabies (an infectious skin disease) and from senile decay. It had to be in a healthy location, away from the sea but close to good water; isolated, though convenient to transport; with sufficient land for a separate building for each medical problem; on porous land which would not contaminate adjoining water supplies but able to run its own sewerage system; and the site had to be large enough to house about 1400 people.

Charles R. Scrivener, a Liverpool surveyor, recommended 700 acres (280 ha) of Crown land east of Campbelltown as the most suitable location. Isolated and unoccupied, it was 2.5 kilometres from Leumeah and

Campbelltown stations, 53 kilometres from Sydney, and part of the Campbelltown Common which had recently been opened for selection. The Campbelltown site was supported by Liverpool Council, which wanted to close the Liverpool Asylum because the townsfolk found it offensive to see people on the streets of their town with advanced cancer and venereal disease. The Public Works Committee approved the Campbelltown site, but the estimated project cost was £52 000 and it was never built.[105]

Attitudes to public and private morality were demonstrated most clearly in reactions to the local schoolteachers. Teachers were not allowed to express political opinions. In 1880 when Patrick Newman of Campbelltown Public School drove John Kidd to a political meeting at Narellan because Kidd's horse was lame, Newman was accused of political bias. Another teacher was removed after temperance advocates complained. Parents defended the teacher, but he confessed to having a little too much to drink occasionally and was immediately transferred. One teacher was transferred because he had created a great scandal in another country town when he and his wife lived in separate hotels. A teacher scandalised the small community when he forbade the butcher, baker and storekeeper to extend any credit to his wife and child. The village women fed and clothed them and reported his conduct to the Department of Education. The school inspector described him 'as hard and as cold as road metal' and he was dismissed for his failure to set an example in citizenship.[106]

In 1880 Freeman ran a private circulating library from his store. For 5 shillings a quarter, residents could borrow history, biography, romances and novels. In August 1882 Alderman Matthews proposed that Campbelltown Council take advantage of the *Municipalities Act* of 1867 to establish a library. A council providing a free library service to 1000 people was eligible for a £200 grant toward the purchase of books. A library would 'improve the rising generation' and 'prevent the spread of larrikinism'. Campbelltown Council established a free library in September 1883.[107]

In 1902 the *Campbelltown Herald* complained that the town was old-fashioned and boring: it needed a school of arts with a reading room, a good lending library, games room, musical, dramatic, athletic and debating clubs. This was a reaction to the opening of Minto School of Arts in December 1901. Campbelltown School of Arts opened in the town hall in October 1905 with John Kidd as president and a membership of 40. Open daily, Sundays excepted, from 3 pm to 9.30 pm, it provided members with a reference and lending library, reading room and games room.[108]

In 1887 Alderman Graham proposed the formation of an agricultural society, but no action followed. More than a decade later Fred Sheather, reporter on the *Campbelltown Herald*, arranged a parade of animals for a children's fete. Following a public meeting in December 1898, the Campbelltown Agricultural Society was formed and held its first show in March 1899. In 1901 it acquired 13 acres (5.2 ha) for a showground in Warby and Moore Streets. Payten designed a brick pavilion to display the horticultural exhibits, stalls were built for the stock and an exhibition ring laid out.[109]

Membership of the Campbelltown Agricultural, Horticultural and Industrial Society was not confined to farmers or stud owners. It attracted commercial and professional people from the town. Publicity about the annual show in the city and provincial press advertised the district. With competitions, riding exhibitions, a brass band and sideshows, the show was a great attraction for the local community.[110]

Musical groups, often short-lived, included the Campbelltown Dancing Class (1885), the Campbelltown Minstrel Troup (1886), the Campbelltown Amateur Orchestral Society (1906), the Campbelltown Orchestral and Musical Society (1910) and the Campbelltown Fire Brigade Brass Band (1911). Tableaux depicting a gypsy encampment, a Japanese tearoom and biblical stories were popular at local concerts. Hand-painted invitations were sent to guests for more select occasions, such as the Campbelltown Bachelors and Spinsters Balls. Church social activities included tea meetings, concerts and lectures. St Johns Catholic Church had a debating club which met fortnightly in 1902 to consider topical issues such as 'women's franchise'.[111]

Wirth's Circus came to town in 1907 with a menagerie, vaudeville acts, equestrians, elephants, lions and tigers, wire-balancing acts, Maori war dances and a Japanese contortionist. Playing for one night only, with tickets from 2 shillings each, the circus drew a crowd of 400, one-third of the town's population. A great attraction in 1910 was a boxing match in the town hall between Jimmy Sharman of Narellan and Bull Booth of Lithgow for £10.[112]

Cricket was popular. In 1902–03 the Campbelltown Cricket Club was one of the strongest outside Sydney, and its annual meeting against Goulburn was regarded as the Test match of the south-west. There was also a women's cricket team which played against a team in Camden. The Campbelltown Cricket Club met each Friday night at Hogan's Royal Hotel, while the Campbelltown Bicycle Club met on Wednesday evenings at Hannaford's Federal Hotel in 1906.[113]

A lawn tennis club was proposed in 1886. The larger homes, such as Holly Lea, had their own courts. Fred Moore and Fred Merewether offered trophies for a local tennis competition, but no-one would draw up the list of events: 'like everything else of any good that is mooted in Campbelltown it looks as though it is going to be allowed to drop, simply because there is wanting the one active and unselfish member with sufficient go in him to push it along'.

Prior to World War I, the Campbelltown Austral Tennis Club, with T. McGlynn as secretary, played in Oxley Street behind the Presbyterian church.[114]

Campbelltown's leading sports figure was Rose (Babe) Payten, the only daughter among the six children of James and Sarah Payten of Woodbine.

Rose (Babe) Payten (1880–1951) of Woodbine,
around 1900 PAYTEN COLLECTION

At eighteen in 1898 she played her first major tournament in Sydney and
took the town by storm, even though defeated in the finals.

Miss Payten is a bright, lively little lady . . . tanned and freckled with the sun, with
pretty fair hair, laughing light eyes and very white teeth. She wore an ankle-length
dark blue serge dress, tan shoes, black stockings, a large sailor hat with a Katoomba
ribbon, and a free and unembarrassed manner.[115]

In the first decade of the twentieth century Rose Payten had the rare
distinction of holding the triple crown in State tennis, being simultaneously the New South Wales Lawn Tennis Association's singles,
women's doubles and mixed doubles champion for 1901 to 1904 and
again in 1907. Her victory was even more applauded because she was the
first Australian-born woman to win for several years.[116]

Rose Payten retired from competition tennis at the end of 1907. *Smiths*
Weekly commented that she had revolutionised tennis for women simply
because she had played a man's game, volleying from the net instead of
standing back and waiting for the ball. Rose attributed her success to
being the only girl in a household of athletic brothers. From a child she
rode astride rather than side-saddle, even down the streets of Campbelltown, 'where the Paytens are as much a part of the district as are the
Onslows at Camden'.[117]

A racecourse was built at Studley Park, Narellan, and meetings were
held regularly in the 1890s. Patrons caught the train to Campbelltown,
then the Camden tram to Narellan. Races were held at Menangle Park
from the 1870s. Its location next to the railway attracted Messrs J. J.
Smith, H. Pateson and Dr L. J. Lamrock who acquired 80 acres (32 ha)
and laid down a new track. Two railway sidings were built to bring
spectators, competitors and horses directly to the track. Alfred Rose
Payten was widely known as a handicapper for the Australian Trotting

161

Club. In 1914 he designed, and E. C. Lusted of Campbelltown built, the three grandstands at Menangle Park Racecourse.[118]

Rabbiting, fox and kangaroo hunts were popular. Whether the result of a day's fishing or a country visit to shoot wallabies or parrots, the outdoor leisure of landed families like the Paytens, Roses and Bulls was reported in detail in the local press. An overland hike to the Royal National Park was a popular weekend excursion for many Campbelltown boys.[119]

Five

1914–1945

IN August 1914 European political tensions exploded into open war. Britain declared war on Germany and on 5 August 1914 the Prime Minister of Australia, Joseph Cook, announced that Australia too was at war. Australians responded enthusiastically and an army of 20 000 men, the Australian Imperial Force (AIF), was raised within days. The AIF sailed for the Middle East in November 1914. En route the *Sydney* sank the German cruiser the *Emden* off the Cocos (Keeling) Islands. Five months later, in April 1915, there was a more bloody baptism of fire when Allied and Turkish troops met on an isolated beach in the Dardenelles Straits. The legend of Anzac was born. In Campbelltown the newspaper office sold maps of the Dardenelles so that the Gallipoli campaign could be studied in detail.[1]

In September 1915 the military proposed a camp for 1000 men on the Campbelltown Showground in Moore Street. The project was not received with enthusiasm. The Agricultural Society objected, but agreed to cooperate for suitable compensation. Campbelltown Council's concern was more mundane—the increased use of the sanitation-collection service. The *Cambelltown Herald* chided the town about its attitude; the soldiers would have money to spend; families and friends would discover Campbelltown's scenic beauty and inexpensive living; landowners, professional people and the business community could profit.[2]

Campbelltown had a recruiting association and a Local Lads Committee which arranged farewells for the men who had joined up. After an enthusiastic response in the first year recruitment declined, though in country towns, which lacked the anonymity of cities, recruiting campaigns put greater pressure on young men to enlist. By the first anniversary of Gallipoli, recruiting was becoming difficult in Campbelltown. In July 1916 the local newspaper claimed that of 90 prospective recruits only 8 had enlisted; 18 were medically unfit; 23 had failed to attend their medical examination and nearly half had sent evasive replies. In August 1916 Prime Minister W. M. Hughes announced a referendum on conscrip-

163

tion. Replacements were needed for 23 000 Australian casualties of seven weeks' fighting at the Somme. To the surprise of many, the 'no' vote won narrowly. High losses continued on the Western Front and a second conscription referendum was held in December 1917. Again the 'no' vote won.[3]

Campbelltown unveiled its roll of honour of local recruits on the first anniversary of Anzac in April 1916. Additions were made as men joined up or the casualty lists were received. At the 1911 census Campbelltown municipality had only 868 men of all ages, Ingleburn only 167. The 147 names on the completed honour board represented 17 per cent of the total male population of the municipality, and a much greater percentage of those of military age. At Wedderburn every eligible single man over sixteen enlisted for active service. Campbelltown men who were killed in action or died of wounds included W. Harry Etchells (3rd Battalion, AIF); L. Horniman (55th); Frank Nicol (1st Battalion Australian Machine Gun Corps); W. Eggleton (13th); J. R. Longhurst (36th); Ted Roberts; Basil Williamson (18th Battalion, killed at Gallipoli); R. Cox; F. Mack; S. Vance (29th); R. Underwood; A. Larkin (2nd); J. Orvad (1st Australian Pioneers); W. J. Hagan M. M. (36th); Hilton Nicholls; W. W. Williamson; E. B. Johnson (55th); S. Longhurst (54th); Arthur Hill (33rd); M. Westgarth and D. Nash.[4]

The War Service Committee at Campbelltown supported conscription. Defeat of the referendum increased a sense of frustration and the committee would have ceased meeting but for the town clerk, Fred Sheather, who argued that there were duties which had to be performed by an organisation in the town. After 1917 the committee included women, as repatriation rather than recruitment became its main concern. After the war it organised Anzac Day celebrations and a permanent memorial, the School of Arts. A foundation stone was laid in Queen Street, near Patrick Street, by the governor of New South Wales during centenary celebrations in 1920. The building, on a different site, was opened in 1925.[5]

Two days after war was announced the Red Cross called on councils to start branches. A branch was started at Menangle with Sibella Macarthur Onslow as president and Mary Cummins as secretary on 17 August 1914. It sent flannel shirts, hand-knitted socks, handkerchiefs and eggs to the front. The Campbelltown Red Cross Committee with Miss R. Payten and Miss R. Genty as secretaries and Mrs Sedgwick as treasurer organised entertainments to raise funds to purchase goods. Concerts by the Campbelltown Musical Society, euchre parties and socials in the town hall contributed to the local war effort. A Campbelltown Christmas Gift Committee sent parcels to the front. The women who gathered at Glenalvon in September 1917 packaged parcels containing two tins of tobacco, a pipe, cigarettes, toothbrush and paste, shaving soap and towel, Lifebuoy soap, sardines, camp pie, potted meat, tinned cheese, plum pudding, lead pencils, Indian Root pills (for constipation), a tin of cocoa, hand-knitted socks and a cap.[6]

There were military camps at Liverpool, Casula and Holsworthy. Conditions were primitive and unhealthy. At liverpool in February 1916, 15 000 soldiers rioted. The men marched on Liverpool, ransacked the hotels and hijacked trains to Sydney. Their drunken hooliganism shocked the nation and led to shorter drinking hours. More effective than earlier temperance campaigns, the early closing referendum in June 1916 voted in favour of 6 pm closing for hotels during the war.[7]

German goods and German ancestry came under attack. Chemist Ian W. Tyerman advertised that he no longer stocked German pharmaceuticals and asked his customers not to purchase 4711 eau de cologne, Lysol disinfectants and a range of toothpastes. The *War Precautions Act* of 1914 required aliens to register with the local police and swear loyalty to the British Empire. In 1916 the definition of 'enemy subject' was extended to any Australian-born person whose father or grandfather was a subject of the German Empire. In effect this applied to nearly every Australian of German descent, even those whose families had settled in Australia 70 years earlier. German immigrants and their children were respected leaders of commercial, political and social life in Australia. They now found themselves declared 'enemy subjects', liable to internment without trial on suspicion of disloyalty and dismissed from the public service, the post office and the railway.[8]

Holsworthy internment camp was opened in 1914 and by May 1916 housed 4299 internees, almost all male. Some were German prisoners from New Guinea and the Pacific, but most were German-Australians. Others were held at a camp on Menangle Park Racecourse. Drawn from all social groups, crowded together under primitive conditions, brawls

Packing Christmas parcels for the Front at Glenalvon, 20 September 1917.

and riots were common. So, too, were petitions, for release, alleging that jealousy of neighbours and business associates had led to arrests. The internees organised brass bands, sporting clubs and a German café which made pastry to sell in Liverpool. Of those still interned in early 1919, several fell victim to the influenza epidemic and were buried in pauper graves in Liverpool cemetery.[9]

Though Campbelltown did not have the large German-speaking minorities of South Australia, winemaking and vineyards had attracted German migrants. Several Campbelltown families of German ancestry endured hostility. The Kershlers were related to the leading commercial and farming families. Two Kershlers enlisted in the AIF and Alderman George Kershler, though personally opposed to conscription, was a member of the Campbelltown recruiting committee. At a heated council meeting in January 1919 he referred to comments that had been made about his German ancestry and passionately defended his Australian identity. Kershler was re-elected to council without difficulty. His son was an alderman and mayor during the 1920s and 1930s, and his daughter, Annie Marlow, was mayoress in the 1940s.[10]

Honour boards were erected in most schools and churches. At Campbelltown Public School the roll of honour with 65 names was unveiled in August 1918. Wedderburn school formed its Parents' and Citizens' Association in 1919 to arrange for the war service honour board. St Barnabas Church of England at Ingleburn erected a roll of honour for fifteen soldiers from its parish; Ingleburn Baptist Church recorded the names of seventeen parishoners. G. E. O. Craft was secretary of the Ingleburn Reception Committee which arranged an honour board at the Ingleburn School of Arts and the Soldiers' Memorial Park which was opened in December 1924.[11]

Even before the war ended, there was concern about employment for returned soldiers. The Campbelltown War Service Committee in March 1916 appealed to local employers to take on a returned man: 'nearly all the men on discharge are feeling the effects in greater or lesser degree of their service experiences and for a time at least will need to be treated as indulgently as the circumstances will permit'.[12] Campbelltown had a branch of the Returned Sailors' and Soldiers' Imperial League of Australia (RSSILA), formed in September 1916 to assist returned sailors and soldiers and their families and to commemorate their service. It warned that many were 'shattered in constitution, [their] mental attitude towards the normal conditions of civil life ... entirely changed by their ... experiences'. They would need help before they could be absorbed into the community.[13]

The soldier returning during the war was greeted with much fanfare. Campbelltown station was decorated with bunting, the local volunteer riflemen formed a guard of honour and the only motor car, owned by Fred Moore of Badgally, drove the soldier home. Most soldiers returned in different circumstances. War ended in November 1918. Convoys of ships brought home the troops and with them came Spanish influenza. Soldiers who had survived the trenches died of influenza on their way home. Influenza killed 12 000 Australians in 1919, half the fatalities being in New South Wales. There was no cure, only precautions to minimise risk of infection. Schools, churches and public places were closed and protective gauze masks were worn. Shops were not allowed to hold bargain sales; drinkers could not stay in an hotel bar for more than five minutes. Empty public buildings became hospital wards for the infected and dying.[14]

At Campbelltown school 150 children were enrolled before the emergency was declared. When school reopened in May less than 30 attended, the rest kept home by fearful parents. Campbelltown Council spent £245 on prevention measures and a mortuary was erected for about £30. The infants' school became an emergency hospital for six weeks from March to May 1919. The local Red Cross assisted and the service of eight Voluntary Aid Detachments (VADs) was recognised with certificates at the 1920 Campbelltown centenary, festivities made more significant because of the absence of community gatherings in 1919. There were 21 cases of influenza in Campbelltown, but officially only two deaths—an elderly man and a child. A third victim was the Reverend J. R. Hunter of St Peters who died in July 1919.[15]

Campbelltown's soldier settlement

Many soldiers wanted to farm their own land. Despite their lack of rural experience and capital, State governments agreed to provide land and the federal government would provide low-interest loans and pay an allowance while the men established their farms. Throughout Australia 37 361 returned soldiers took up farms after World War I. By 1929, 71 per cent remained on their farms, but arrears in interest payments and other expenses totalled £33 million. By 1942, when schemes for another generation of soldiers were under consideration, less than half of the soldier settlers were still on their land. Lack of capital, unsuitable land, war injuries, lack of training and the falling value of primary products contributed to their failure.[16]

In the Sydney region small-scale, labour-intensive farms for poultry, pigs, orchards and market gardens were considered appropriate for the soldier settlers. Settlements were established at Bankstown (poultry), Grantham at Seven Hills (poultry), Chipping Norton (poultry, vegetables and fruit), Doonside (poultry) and Campbelltown (poultry).

In October 1917 the Campbelltown War Service Committee examined government plans to purchase Cransley estate for small poultry farms for ex-servicemen. Cransley was 2.5 kilometres east of Campbelltown at the end of Broughton Street. Originally granted to Michael Wholohan, in 1881 it was purchased by John Knight, a builder and alderman on

167

Campbelltown Soldier Settlement, looking north with Cransley Cottage in the centre, 1919. NEW SOUTH WALES GOVERNMENT PRINTER

Campbelltown's first council. Knight built a cottage, sold the land in the mid-1880s but remained as lessee. Thomas Houghton, an engineer, purchased Cransley and 400 acres (160 ha) in 1907 for a dairy farm.

The Campbelltown War Service Committee believed Cransley was unsuitable, overvalued and the proposed 5-acre (2 ha) farms too small. Despite continued opposition from the committee, the government paid £4000 for 373 acres (149 ha) of Cransley in 1918 and subdivided it into 38 soldier blocks. Work started in August 1918 to clear the land and build cottages and poultry runs. Sun-dried tiles were made at the old Kendall mill. The cottages, finished by June 1919, were identical. All had four 12-feet-square (3.6 m) rooms, 12-foot ceilings and no hallway. Doors, skirtings and picture rails were stained with oak varnish; kitchens had dark-green walls; toilets and laundries were outside. Each man received 36 hens, four cockerels and three 500-egg incubators. There were breeding and rearing pens, a brooder house warmed with a hot water system to rear chickens, and land to grow green feed for the birds and vegetables for the families. A resident manager provided the technical knowledge and practical experience, and arranged bulk purchase of poultry feed and cooperative marketing of the eggs.

The soldier settlers at Campbelltown in 1921 were G. L. Atwell, P. Barrett, J. Batholomew, A. Crowe, W. Crowe, J. Casey, T. S. Dwyer, G. Duncombe, D. Dewhurst, A. French, F. Halloran, J. C. Hepher, A. E. Jerrett, G. F. Marsh, W. Mullany, W. Milham, Mrs Moore, D. C. Menzies, F. T. McLean, C. Nicholls, J. Nicholls, G. Parkin, J. B. Porter, J. F. Reed, A. Ross, H. A. Rogers, J. C. Smith, K. K. Stewart, E. J. C. Taylor, W.

Thomson, J. Turner, F. Warner, N. Wilson, A. J. Williams and W. B. West. Most were married men and some, for example, the Hepher and Mullany families, had lived nearby before the war.[17]

The Campbelltown soldiers called their settlement Waminda, an Aboriginal word meaning 'comrade'. Most of Campbelltown referred to it simply as 'the Settlement'. A Waminda Progress Association was formed and a Waminda Poultry and Pigeon Club. The community hall, a gift from the Liverpool Red Cross, came from the Liverpool Military Camp in February 1920. The fibro and galvanised-iron building was assembled by twenty volunteer carpenters in one day. It became the venue for regular Saturday night dances with a band indoors and a beer keg outside.[18]

Initially one of the more successful projects, Waminda produced 176 843 dozen eggs in 1912–22 for a return of £16 344, but the settlers were in debt to the government for about £1300 each. The scheme had calculated that one man working 10 acres (4 ha) with 600–700 laying birds could make a living as a member of a cooperative. But the hens did not lay in winter. The farms were overcapitalised; incubators were expensive and unreliable and needed constant attention to control temperature and turn the eggs. Poultry farming was more scientific than either government or soldiers had appreciated.

In 1924 government assistance was reduced. The managers were dismissed, leaving the settlers to run the cooperative themselves. Lack of capital quickly destroyed the work of earlier years. Lack of professional advice added to their problems. The Waminda store closed and the advantages of bulk purchases were lost. When some of the original settlers left in 1924, their farms were taken up by others who were not war veterans and the earlier sense of identity faded. Of those who battled through the 1920s, few remained at the end of the depression. Some took jobs in the city or Campbelltown and ran poultry as a side interest. The Waminda Progress Association in 1932 asked Campbelltown Council to reduce their rates. By 1934 there were only 7 of the original 38 farmers and by 1942 only 2, Arthur Ross and William P. Mullany, were left.[19]

A sense of history

Touring by private car became more common from the 1920s, opening up the countryside and its historic landscape to urban Australians. Country towns bypassed by the building booms found their old buildings had a curiosity value for suburban tourists coming from streets of red brick-and-tile bungalows. Since the late nineteenth century Campbelltown had been increasingly seen by outsiders as an antiquity. Its attractions, frequently described in the Sydney press, included the old buildings along the main street, three historic churches—St Peters, St Johns, with the quaint Ruse gravestone, and the chapel at Denham Court—the windmill at Mount Gilead and a ghost story. There was the added bonus of being just outside the 30-mile (50 km) limit so travellers could drink at the hotels on Sundays. Campbelltown became a regular destination for the weekend tourist.

When Campbelltown celebrated its centenary in 1920, the celebrations were planned by an informal chamber of commerce chaired by Mayor C. N. Hannaford which included the Reverend I. D. Armitage (Church of England), Dr Mawson, P. C. Marlow (storekeeper), D. Frame (State Nursery), A. G. Taylor, B. Haydon (farmer), J. Vardy (farmer), H. V. Denholm, M. and J. Solomon (grocers), J. H. Richardson, T. Kitching (plumber), R. L. Gamble (storekeeper), H. H. Kitching (agent) with Fred Sheather (council clerk) and G. Klein (schoolmaster). Vardy was the only member of the pioneering free and convict families. The aldermen were Mayor Hannaford, George Kershler, William Piggott, Roy Gamble, V. A. Ducat, P. C. Marlow, J. R. Quilty, H. A. Morgan, B. Longhurst with Sheather as town clerk. Kershler and Sheather were descendants of mid-century immigrants, but the others came from families who had arrived in the 1880s or later. Campbelltown's centenary was arranged by the newest residents of the district.

Centenary festivities included a sports day in September; trotting on the newly fenced showground; a centenary queen competition (won by Edie Kershler); a vice-regal visit; a parade; races for the children, and a ball. The centrepiece was the pageant depicting phases in the history of Campbelltown—a group of Aborigines beside a bark gunyah, explorers, early settlers and rural industries, followed by hundreds of marching schoolchildren. J. P. McGuanne, Irish-born but Campbelltown raised, became its first historian. James Waterworth, coach driver, and James Bocking, storekeeper, were feted as the oldest residents. Neither was born in Campbelltown. Those publicly recognised as founding fathers were the 'Johnny-come-latelies', descendants of mid-century free immigrant families. McGuanne named only three convicts—James Ruse, James Meehan and Thomas Hammond. This sanitised history was not accepted without comment. One writer queried the neglect of those whose ancestors had made the town and district. Where, he asked, were the Rixons, Mrs Chinnocks senior, Mrs Payten, the Sheils or the Tabers, the Warbys, the Cummins, Egglestons, Hurleys or Fitzpatricks?[20]

The centenary of St Peters in 1923 and of Hume and Hovell's expedition in 1924 maintained popular interest in Campbelltown. St Johns celebrated Father Dunne's jubilee with a 'Back to Campbelltown' festival in 1929. Three years later it was the jubilee of local government. M. A. Vardy, assisted by F. Sheather and V. Winton, organised a 'Back to Campbelltown Committee' with the Manchester Unity Independent Order of Oddfellows (MUIOOF) (W. Skeers), the School of Arts (C. Asher), the Agricultural Society (D. J. Chernich), the Parents' and Citizens' Association (J. Malone), the Boy Scouts (Dr W. R. Morris), the Independent Order of Oddfellows (IOOF) (P. Solomon), the tennis club (H. R. Wilkinson) and the hospital auxiliary (H. W. Brown and R. R. Winton). [21]

The Macquarie towns of the Hawkesbury, Camden and Campbelltown inspired Campbelltown-born architect and artist William Hardy Wilson (1881–1955). From 1913 he recorded many buildings, including Macquarie Fields House and Denham Court. Wilson published *The Cow Pasture Road* in 1920 and *Early Colonial Architecture in New South Wales and Tasmania* in 1924, stimulating considerable interest in Australian architectural history. Colonial buildings provided inspiration for his architectural designs and Wilson was a leading architect of the Colonial Revival style.[22]

Town and country

Beyond Chamberlain Street in the north and Bradbury Park in the south stretched open paddocks. At night no lights were visible.

Queen Street was a mixture of commercial and residential buildings. Kidd's Lane was the western extension of Dumaresq Street. It was not an attractive part of town and was usually called Sewer Lane. Kidd's Lane and Milgate Lane were very narrow, with no footpaths and houses built directly onto the street. As late as 1939 there was no properly formed road. Subdivision of Warby and Kershler properties in the north created Iolanthe and King Streets in 1918. In 1919 St Peters subdivided its glebe, creating Reddall and Moore Streets. The Rudd estate, between Chamberlain Street and Leumeah Road, was subdivided into 119 allotments in 1926 creating small blocks for orchards or poultry farms and several commercial and residential sites near Leumeah station. Rudd Road, Kingsclare, Hughes and Thomas Streets and O'Sullivan Road were formed by this subdivision.[23]

In 1924 the *Daily Telegraph* listed Campbelltown's most distinguished residents as C. H. Crammond, managing director of Richardson and Wrench; Dr Morris, dentist; A. G. Southward, an executive with the Government Savings Bank; Andrew A. Lysaght, solicitor, member of parliament for Illawarra and soon to serve as Attorney-General and Minister for Justice; C. J. Passmore and P. E. Payten, lawyers; W. S. Mowle, clerk of the parliaments; W. Farrow of the City Underground Railway scheme; F. Genty of Messrs Fez and Company, wine merchants; and J. G. Vardy of the post office. With strong family links in the district, most were involved in community organisations. C. H. Crammond was an active member of the Campbelltown Presbyterian Church and W. S. Mowle, a parishioner of St James, Minto, was Campbelltown's representative at the synod for the diocese of Sydney.[24]

At Minto and Ingleburn most purchasers were speculators rather than residents. At Menangle Park there were small subdivisions near the trotting track in 1920. Between the soldiers' settlement at Waminda and the George's River the Campbelltown Common was subdivided into 5-acre (2 ha) allotments and called the Kent Farms by Sydney developer Sir Arthur Rickard. For £2 deposit anyone could become a farmer only 1.5

kilometres from Campbelltown railway station. These farmers applied to Campbelltown Council in July 1935 to have their district named Kent Lyn (Kentlyn).[25]

Mawson Park, opposite the courthouse, was eventually named after belated recognition that it was the gateway to the town by road or rail. Dr William Mawson had served the town for 28 years. A pergola and picnic sheds were opened in January 1938. The gardens were planted with roses and dahlias and watered by the fire brigade when it practised. Barkley Haydon retired from the Botanic Gardens in 1939 and became part-time gardener at Mawson Park. Hurley Park was used by the cricket club with swimming and regattas held on the reservoir. The showground in Warby Street became the main venue for sporting activities and in 1940 was handed over to the council, with the Agricultural Society retaining access for its annual show.[26]

Milton Park dominated the landscape between Ingleburn and Macquarie Fields. The old Warby home was purchased by Thomas James Hilder of Yerranderie in February 1909 for £1000. Hilder's family lived at Milton Park while he managed the silver mine at Yerranderie. It was offered for sale in 1933 for £5500. The elegant two-storey house, encircled by verandahs, had a rooftop garden, tennis courts, a private golf course and a newly planted orchard. A model stud and poultry farm covering 44 acres (18 ha) was stocked with 1500 white leghorns, some prize-winners at the Hawkesbury Agricultural College. Close to the railway, equidistant from the racecourses at Warwick Farm and Menangle Park, it was a fine location for a horse stud. Unable to find a purchaser, it was sold four years later to Gallipoli veteran Captain Allen Dickenson Newmarch.[27]

Macquarie Fields estate was owned by the Ross brothers until 1924 when the northern half was sold to the government for a veterinary research station, Hurlstone Agricultural College and Glenfield Park Special School. The southern portion, about 635 acres (254 ha) including Macquarie Fields House, was sold to Sydney solicitor J. C. Kershaw of Kershaw Matthew Glasgow and Lane. Kershaw lived in the city and employed his brother, Frank Kershaw, to manage the dairy farm. Following Kershaw's death his trustees sold the estate in 1944 to the Department of Agriculture to extend the veterinary research station. After more than a century in the Throsby family, Archer Throsby subdivided and sold Glenfield estate. James Freeland Leacock, veteran of both the Boer War and World War I, purchased Glenfield in 1920 for a dairy farm. Leacock had married a descendant of the Broughton family of Appin and remained at Glenfield House until his death in 1974.[28]

Local Amenities

While postwar councils argued about the proportion of rates to be spent in the town or the rural areas, the citizens of Campbelltown complained

172

Above View from St Peters tower, looking west across the Green (Mawson Park), the Federal Hotel and courthouse to the State Nursery, c. 1925.

Below Milton Park, Ingleburn around 1912.

that their town was dark and its streets and parks neglected. Campbelltown Council was stirred into providing electricity and sewerage. Taken for granted by later generations, these conveniences improved health standards and reduced the physical labour on the farm, in shops and in the home.

Electric light had been demonstrated in Sydney in 1863, but the first town to install generating equipment was Tamworth where the streets were lit by electricity in 1888. The City of Sydney did not build a power station until 1904. Campbelltown Council held a referendum among ratepayers in January 1921 to gauge support for electric lighting. With 80 votes in favour and 65 against, the decision to go ahead was not a unanimous one. Council investigated purchasing electricity from the railways or from Port Kembla, but decided to build its own generating plant. In 1923 it borrowed £10 000 from the State Superannuation Board. Sale of electricity was soon a significant proportion of council revenue: in 1927 Campbelltown's income from rates was £2501 and from electricity sales, £2241. By 1941 revenue from electricity in Ingleburn was £5872 while rates produced only £1847.[29]

The power station, a modest building of weatherboard and fibro in Cordeaux Street, was opened by the mayoress, Mrs C. N. Hannaford, on the evening of 23 January 1924. A crowd of 1000 people gathered to look at the illumination of hotels and shops in Queen Street and the mayor's home. The two American diesel-powered generators had less than one hour's blackout in four years, but were soon obsolete and in 1929 Campbelltown was connected to the railway electricity system. A substation was erected in Cordeaux Street and the old powerhouse demolished in 1931. Campbelltown Council embarked on a marketing campaign to encourage residents to 'make electricity your servant'. The council's electrical engineer, Norman Tuck, advised on the use of electric stoves, bath heaters, clothes washers and vacuum cleaners.[30]

Demand for water within Campbelltown, especially on the higher, eastern part of town, had increased since 1888. In 1913 a small pumping station was erected at the old reservoir in Hurley Park. Water from the mains system was pumped from Hurley Park to an elevated iron tank near Waminda Avenue and then distributed to eastern Campbelltown. H. S. Reeve, the local draper, bicycled to the pumping station each morning to start the diesel engine which ran the pump. Each evening he returned to switch off the engines. T. Herbert Bottin later operated the pumps. In 1933 Campbelltown's water supply was connected to the high-level reservoir at Kenny Hill.[31]

Alderman Roy L. Gamble, one of the agitators for electricity, proposed a sewerage system as an unemployment project in 1932. Campbelltown farmers blocked it, fearing pollution of Bow Bowing Creek where they watered stock. At the 1937 municipal election there was active lobbying for sewerage: 16 candidates stood for the 9 seats and 580 votes were cast, compared with only 374 votes in the 1934 election. For the first time a polling booth was set up at Kentlyn, though only six votes were cast there. There was a clear mandate to proceed with sewerage works. Thomas George Armstrong, an alderman, worked for the Metropolitan Water Sewerage and Drainage Board and did much of the surveying. Construction was officially launched in May 1939 by E. S. Spooner, Minister for Works and Local Government. Because of drought, there was insufficient water to operate the system until 1941.[32]

Minto and much of Ingleburn were not connected to water or electricity until the mid-1930s because of the cost. The Ingleburn storage dam, built in 1934 to store water while the canal was closed for maintenance, enabled the water supply to be extended to Ingleburn, parts of Campbelltown and Minto in 1935. Electric light was connected to Minto in January 1937. Water and electricity were only available at Denham Court from World War II when facilities at the new military camp were extended to the neighbouring farmers.[33]

At Ingleburn development was hindered by an inconvenient municipal boundary running down the main street. The northern side of Oxford Road, with the school of arts and billiard room, was in Liverpool municipality, as was Ingleburn railway station. Ingleburn municipality had the southern side of Oxford Road and the public school. Flood-mitigation schemes in Oxford Road were undertaken jointly by Liverpool and Ingleburn Councils. Ingleburn mayors, Chivers and Harper, and town clerk, P. J. Smith, campaigned to increase the municipality's population and rating area by extending the municipality south to Leumeah railway station, absorbing all of Leumeah, East Minto and Minto and north to the Crossroads. After much discussion with Liverpool Council, Ingleburn's boundaries were extended in 1924 to include Glenfield, Macquarie Fields and North Ingleburn, doubling the municipality to 21 square miles (54 km²).[34]

The *Rating (Exemption) Act* of December 1931 reaffirmed that all school lands, whether public or private, all religious institutions and any statutory body representing the Crown were exempt from local government and Water Board charges. A significant portion of Ingleburn municipality had passed from private ownership to the government during the 1920s with the establishment of the veterinary research station (1923), Hurlstone Agricultural College (1926) and Glenfield Special School (1927). East of the railway many landowners could not be traced and their property was resumed for unpaid rates. By the late 1930s Ingleburn ratepayers were considering amalgamation with a neighbouring council.[35]

Ingleburn Council was unable to borrow to install its own electric plant. Residents protested that the cost 'would be a blister that would burn into the bone of the ratepayers for many a year to come'. A cheaper alternative, costing £3000, supplied 120 households in Ingleburn township with low-voltage power from the railway from April 1930. As Ingleburn could not afford to employ an electrical engineer it shared staff with Bankstown and Campbelltown Councils to read meters, replace streetlamps and maintain the system.[36]

After experiencing the convenience of electricity, Ingleburn ratepayers accepted the cost of its extension. Loans were raised in 1936 to extend electricity to 500 consumers at Macquarie Fields, Glenfield and Denham Court using labour funded under unemployment relief schemes. G. R. A. Winton was appointed electrical engineer in 1936 and within ten years had a staff of three. Tennis courts and parks were lit for night sport.[37]

In 1916 Ingleburn Council had purchased land in Ingleburn Road and the following year had built a meeting room with an office. In 1936 the old building was demolished and new chambers were built on the same site—an unemployment relief project. Costing £800 including fittings, the brick building had a meeting room, four offices and a strong room. A war memorial clock on the front of the building was donated by the Ingleburn sub-branch of the RSL.[38]

By the 1930s many Campbelltown residents, including the mayor, J. W. Kershler, worked outside the district. Other aldermen left for business opportunities elsewhere. Roy Gamble, an alderman for ten years, moved to Auburn in 1928. Thomas Devlin, who topped the municipal vote in 1934, left the district in 1939.[39]

Continuity in both Campbelltown and Ingleburn was provided by long-serving town clerks. At Campbelltown Frederick Sheather, town clerk from 1901, retired in 1927, but when his replacement left in 1929 Sheather returned and served until 1944. At Ingleburn there was no salaried clerk until 1931 when Harley Daley was appointed. Daley was town clerk of Ingleburn until 1948, then became clerk of the combined Ingleburn and Campbelltown municipalities. In 1924 as well as the clerk Campbelltown employed an electrical engineer (N. A. Tuck), a health officer (R. C. Adams) and an overseer of works (Charles Asher). By the early 1930s Ingleburn employed a clerk, a part-time general hand and two road men, and staff numbers increased after electricity was connected.

Campbelltown was a law-abiding town that enjoyed a little illegal gambling. Two-up was played at the rear of the bakery in Dumaresq Street or in Hurley Park. Its SP bookies were occasionally raided by the Liverpool or Parramatta police. In May 1928 Sergeant William Loftus retired after 30 years in the police force, the last five as officer in charge at Campbelltown. At his farewell reception, where the town presented him with a wallet of banknotes, Loftus commented that its people were 'of the old stock and there was no larrickinism whatever'. Loftus and his family remained in Campbelltown and he was secretary of the Memorial School of Arts and church warden at St Peters. He died, aged 75, in the late 1930s. Yet the situation it seems was changing. In September 1928 the businesspeople of the town joined together to hire a private nightwatchman to counter a recent spate of robberies.[40]

Fire was an ever-present threat to both town and country. Campbell-

CAMPBELLTOWN LOCAL HISTORY COLLECTION

Frederick Sheather, town clerk of Campbelltown 1901–1944.

Campbelltown Fire Brigade behind Reeve's Emporium, around 1910. *Top row left to right* R. Adams, G. Trives, W. Jones. Front row *left to right* E. Hodges, P. C. Marlow, B. Bugden, C. Bailey, H. Reeve.

CLISSOLD COLLECTION

town Fire Brigade was organised from 1907 to 1947 by H. S. Reeve and a group of volunteers. Ingleburn Council wanted a permanent brigade at Glenfield where the sawmill frequently caught fire. The nearest brigade was at Liverpool. In January 1929 sparks from a goods train started a fire which devastated Leumeah, East Minto, Ingleburn and Minto. Volunteer bush fire brigades were subsequently formed in these settlements. The Wedderburn Bush Fire Brigade was formed in 1939 by the Wedderburn Fruitgrowers' Association following a disastrous summer when almost 80 per cent of the Wedderburn fruit crop was destroyed by fire and storm. Captain of the brigade was J. H. Scobie and members included Alderman R. E. Arundel, C. R. Bostock, C. F. Knight and T. Swann.[41]

Commerce

Business in Campbelltown in 1915 was stagnant. There was little momentum for change because so much of the town was still owned by the old families, often as absentees. During the 1920s the estates of Hurley, Rudd, Kidd, the Fieldhouses and Warby were put up for sale by heirs who did not live in the district. Subdivisions encouraged building. Electricity, water and rail access to the industries at Granville and the offices of Sydney stimulated development and attracted city employees. By the mid-1920s about 100 commuters a day travelled by train to work. Ten new houses were erected in 1925, 25 in the following year when a picture theatre was built, and by the late 1920s new houses averaged 20 per year.[42]

Local journalist Robert Allan urged the council to take a more active role in building roads to the new subdivisions. No one moved to Campbelltown because there were no vacant houses worth renting, a common complaint from the 1880s.[43]

The editor of the *Campbelltown Herald*, Joseph McGlynn, left in 1915 and the paper was published briefly by Walter Jago. The proprietor and editor in 1918 was E. J. (Ted) Lynch, but he moved to Newcastle. The next proprietor in 1919 was F. H. N. West. A second printing plant was owned by Tasman George Carey and in October 1919 Carey sold his presses to the Sidman brothers who established the *Campbelltown News*, the first issue of which appeared on 20 November 1919. Campbelltown could not support two papers and in 1920 Sidman's *News* absorbed the *Herald*. Robert Alfred Sidman had served his apprenticeship on the *Campbelltown Herald* under McGlynn. The office of the *Campbelltown News* was in Patrick Street, Campbelltown, though Sidman lived at Croydon until 1929 when he moved to 'Leura', Condamine Street, Campbelltown. His brother, George V. Sidman, published the Camden newspaper and ultimately the Campbelltown newspaper was printed in Camden.[44]

The telephone exchange opened in August 1913 with a continuous service from July 1914. By mid-1915 there were about 50 subscribers between Menangle and Minto. Some businesspeople connected to the exchange by 1919 included the undertaker (Burnett Parker); monumental mason (F. W. Rose); car hire service (John Miller); Mrs Newbury's private hospital; storekeepers (Bursills, Marlows and Packer); two butchers (Conley and Kitching); a stock and station agent (Morgan); the two banks and the hotels (Mrs Sexton at the Federal, Thomas Meehan at the Royal, Reidy at the Commonwealth and Sellar at the Club).[45]

Town businesses depended on the prosperity of the surrounding rural areas. The larger landowners and businesspeople dealt directly with city merchants and banks while the structure of the dairy industry channelled funds to Camden rather than Campbelltown. Local employment was largely confined to dairy and farmwork, or the railway where there was steady work for track and engine maintenance or transferring goods from the Camden branch line to the main line. There was a sawmill at each railway station and a milk factory at Campbelltown from 1923, but no other local manufacturing or processing. Professional, administrative and commercial careers usually meant working outside the district.[46]

Retail competition increased in the 1920s and 1930s as transport improved and shoppers became more mobile. From the beginning of 1929 Anthony Hordern and Sons offered twice-weekly deliveries, free of charge, to Campbelltown. Most of the big city stores had attractive, comprehensive mail-order catalogues offering anything from clothing to kitchen items and hardware. Salesmen called door to door at the farms. Hawkers in horsedrawn carts or on bicycles sold needles and threads, inkstands and laces and were particularly common during the depression years.

The railway tempted shoppers away from Campbelltown with discounted fares to Parramatta and the city. More and more essential household supplies were packed in 'foreign wrappers'. Out-of-town purchases were always made in cash, but in Campbelltown everyone had monthly accounts at the local store. The local storekeeper provided the credit and service, but lost the customer and the cash.[47]

By the 1930s Campbelltown had its first branch of a shopping chain. Bussell Brothers had twelve stores in the eastern and northern suburbs and five country branches, including Campbelltown. They sold groceries, hardware, china, ironmongery and produce. The Campbelltown branch was managed by Mr Goldspink. Bussell's, 'the Busy Grocers', brought modern marketing to Campbelltown with full-page newspaper advertisements announcing grocery 'specials'. Prices included delivery in Campbelltown daily, twice weekly to the soldiers' settlement and once a week to Appin, Wedderburn, Kent Farms (Kentlyn), Minto, East Minto, Ingleburn and Narellan. Unemployment relief orders were accepted in payment for groceries.[48]

Other grocers and general stores were Bursill's store, started by Samuel

Syd Percival's butcher shop, Ingleburn, around 1900.
CAMPBELLTOWN LOCAL HISTORY COLLECTION

Bursill junior in 1918 and transferred to his son, William, about 1928 Solomon Brothers who purchased Marlow's store in 1919; Reeves Empor ium and Longhurst Brothers, one of the newest businesses in 1937.[49]

Many homes had no electricity until the late 1930s and used iceboxes or kerosene refrigerators. Butchers and bakers had shop displays but much of their business was done out of a cart. The butcher's cart did the rounds with carcasses of meat and the housewife selected the cut she wanted Reginald Tildsley established his Campbelltown butchery in 1922 with a slaughteryard at Narellan. George New and Sons purchased the business of Messrs Tildsley Brothers in the mid-1930s. D. MacDonald and Com pany in the 1930s used the large slaughteryard at Bradbury Park (now the Bradbury swimming pool). At Ingleburn the Percivals had the butche shop. Regular cattle sales were held in the yards near the railway (now the civic centre) by auctioneer A. E. Baldock. A. Romalis was the fishmonger. Poultry for Christmas dinners was cooked in the ovens o Crowe's bakery.[50]

Non-perishable items such as flour and sugar were purchased in large 70-pound (32 kg) bags. With no local transport system, it was easier to have items delivered in bulk than to travel to a store to purchase smalle quantities. Fruit from the home orchard was converted to puddings preserves and jams for longer storage. Convenience foods and take aways were unknown but there were several tearooms, milk bars and cafés offering afternoon teas and snacks in Campbelltown. At Ingleburn in the 1920s Mrs K. M. Seymour had refreshment rooms and in the 1930s Mrs C. J. Collins offered refreshments at her store.[51]

At Minto there were two general shops on the western side of the railway. William J. Harris had a store in a two-storey brick building near the railway crossing in Redfern Road. He stocked groceries, cheese, fruit, sweets, hardware, kerosene and grain. Mrs R. J. (Janey) McInnes ran the other small store from her house in Somerset Street. The postmaster, Mr J. Williams, was next door. Barnsley had a butcher shop at Minto on the eastern side of the railway. Along Campbelltown Road at Denham Court were a few small shops. Best known was a black and white building called the Magpie Inn, a small shop and milk bar on the corner of Zouch Road. Opposite was an afternoon tea stop, the Teapot Inn.[52]

Scotsman Ian Tyerman ran his pharmacy in Campbelltown from 1902 until his death in 1933. Raymond Veness operated his pharmacy from 1931 in Queen Street until he retired. Norman Gilbert, the local dentist, died in 1921 but his practice was continued at The Retreat, Dumaresq Street, by Desmond John Chernich.[53]

The Silver Star Garage of Charles Tripp and Sons was on the south-eastern corner of Queen and Dumaresq Street. Expanding from a black-smith and coachbuilding business under the first Charles Tripp, his sons had a motor garage and sold Neptune petrol, and car and radio batteries. Messrs J. Bryne and Company were the Ford car agents, the only new car dealers in Campbelltown. The Ryder brothers, Ernest and Stanley, had a motor garage and taxi service from 1928 in Queen Street, near Patrick Street. There were no petrol bowsers and fuel was pumped from drums.[54]

Plumber, drainer and tinsmith was Milton J. Triglone whose soldering skills were needed to repair roofing and guttering, water tanks, mending milk cans and buckets. Brunero and Sons took over Stephenson's sawmill between Patrick Street and Milgate Lane in 1924. Domenico Brunero was born near Turin, Italy, in 1862 and migrated to Australia with his wife, Maria, and young family about 1889. A wood-turner by trade, he established a factory at Elderslie, near Camden, where he made wooden handles for hoes, picks, hammers, umbrellas and whips. Horse teams and later trucks brought the timber from Wedderburn, Darke's Forest, Moss Vale and Burragorang. Building timber was railed to Sydney, and firewood, fencing timber and building supplies were sold locally. Domenico Brunero died in 1927 and Maria died in 1934, but the business was continued by two of their sons and managed by their daughter-in-law, Rita Brunero née Tripp.[55]

There were four hotels in Campbelltown during the 1920s and 1930s. At the Sydney end of town were the Club and the Federal—diagonally opposite in Queen Street near the courthouse—and the Royal, near the railway station. In 1917 Thomas Meehan, the licensee, purchased the Royal Hotel and half an acre (0.2 ha) of land from Railway Street to Patrick Street from the Hurley estate for £1700. Nearby Hayes and Howell operated a cordial factory in the old creamery off Patrick Street. At the opposite end of town was the Commonwealth, formerly the Jolly Miller.[56]

Herb Lack, formerly licensee of the Royal Hotel, purchased the freehold and licence of the Federal Hotel in 1928. Lack's Hotel and its dining room became a popular spot to break a journey to the southern highlands. The hotel remained in the Lack family until 1972, managed from 1951 by Lack's daughter, Phyllis, and her husband, Guy Marsden. A new hotel, the Good Intent, was built in 1938 at the southern end of town, the first new hotel for 60 years. It opened in March 1939 with Mr and Mrs Kerr as licensees. The old Commonwealth Hotel was converted to flats.[57]

War brought little stimulus to trade in Campbelltown. Soldiers from Ingleburn Military Camp patronised the hotels but it was easier to go to Liverpool. In 1943 the Bank of New South Wales closed its branch in Campbelltown. Always the smaller bank, for many years it lacked a strongroom which gave its rival, the Commercial Banking Company, a distinct advantage. The Bank of New South Wales fell victim to the politics of war and government control. In 1942 the Minister for war organisation of industry ordered the banks to rationalise. Each town was permitted a Commonwealth Bank (not affected by rationalisation) and one other bank as the first step in a campaign to nationalise the banking industry.[58]

Transport

Increasing numbers of residents at Campbelltown and Ingleburn travelled to the city to work. By the mid-1920s commuter trains to the city left Campbelltown at 5.30 am (arriving 7.07 am), 6.12 am (7.47 am) and 7.20 am (8.45 am). Returning trains left Sydney at 4.15 pm (5.45 pm at Campbelltown), 5.15 pm (6.16 pm), 5.20 pm (6.51 pm) and 5.50 pm (7.28 pm). First-class return fares were 6s 4d weekly, second class 4s 8d. During the depression there were fears that the commuter services would be reduced to one train daily.[59]

Among the regular commuters was John George Vardy of 'Hillcrest'. Vardy started work at the General Post Office in Sydney when he was sixteen in 1894 and was eventually head of the staff department. He held the local record for seasonal rail tickets, purchasing one each season for 43 years until his death in 1937. Another regular traveller was G. A. Kitt of Caversham who was accountant for Newtown Municipal Council.[60]

In 1925 Herbert Miles moved from Manly to Campbelltown and started a motor service to Camden in a seven-seater car. For the same fare as the railway, passengers were offered a more comfortable and faster ride. The road was improved and Miles invested in a 21-seater bus. Competition with government services was prohibited in the 1932 *Transport (Co-ordinated) Act* which put Miles and other small bus services out of business.[61]

By 1939 there were barely a dozen cars in Campbelltown, owned by the clergymen, the mayor, a few storekeepers and farmers. In 1931 a 20-foot (6 m) wide bitumen surface was laid along the Cowpastures Road from the Crossroads at Liverpool to Narellan. The new route was 3 miles (2 km) shorter and 2 feet (60 cm) wider than Campbelltown Road. Campbelltown was no longer a town on the main road and protest meetings with neighbouring Menangle and more distant Picton could not alter the reality.[62]

The railway restricted road entry to Campbelltown. Whether travelling south along the Campbelltown Road or north-east along the Camden Road, travellers had to cross the Great Southern Railway. Gatekeepers, Morgan on the north and Mortimer on the south, regulated the road and train traffic. The gates were always shut at night and travellers had to wake the gatekeeper to cross the tracks. In 1937 the northern gate was replaced with an overbridge and the old gatekeeper's lodge was demolished. Crossings at Minto, Ingleburn and Glenfield were less strictly patrolled. The gates were always shut and travellers had to stop, dismount, open the railway gates, cross the line, close the gates and then continue on their journey.[63]

Dairying and agriculture

By 1939 Campbelltown district was sending 16000 gallons (72800 L) of milk each week to the city. Dairying and its related services was the largest employer.

In 1922 a new milk depot was proposed for Campbelltown railway station. There were about 68 dairies in the district and 45 major dairies were interested in taking shares in a cooperative factory on the western side of town in Badgally Road (then called Broughton Road). Built at a cost of £6000, the milk depot was a branch of the Camden Vale Milk Company and opened in mid-1923. The secretary-manager was G. R. McPherson with A. Lyons as engineer. Farmers delivered their milk to the factory in cans which were scalded and steam-cleaned before return to prevent contamination. A 20-horse power (15 kW) boiler produced steam to pasteurise the milk and sterilise the cans. A 60-horse power (45 kW) oil engine drove a 20-ton compressor for refrigeration and ice-making. Within a year the district was railing 13000 gallons (59150 L) of milk per week to Sydney. In 1924, 220000 gallons (over 1 million L) were delivered within six months. In 1929 the Camden Vale Milk Company amalgamated with the Dairy Farmers Milk Company.

With increased output by the mid-1920s less than half the milk was accepted at the factory. The balance was separated into cream which returned only 7½ pence per gallon, compared with 1 shilling for full milk. The price of milk fell, reaching 7 pence a gallon in 1931. The government created the New South Wales Milk Board in 1932 and new pricing

Milking time at St Andrews dairy, 1935. *Left to right* Jack Thomson, Arthur Collins, Leo Kelly.

arrangements offered hopes for improved returns. Yet in mid-1933 half of Campbelltown's milk was separated for cream and sold to the Menangle Butter Factory and prices were still low. Milk prices were fixed at 8½ pence per gallon in mid-1937.[64]

Most dairy farmers were tenants paying up to £2 per acre for good land. Struggling to cover their rents, they relied on natural grasses and did little to improve grazing or store feed. Milk yield declined in winter. If there were insufficient natural pasture, hand-feeding added a burden at the most unproductive season and depleted farmers cash reserves. Participation in local shows and the Sydney Royal Easter Show helped to improve the quality of stock, but in the bad seasons of the mid-1930s farmers bought feed not stock. Years of low milk prices were followed by severe drought in 1939–40. Dairy farmers were carting water as well as feed by the end of the summer of 1940 and local milk production had fallen 25 per cent. Many could not afford to restock when the seasons improved.[65]

While some Campbelltown landowners leased their estates to tenants, others such as the Fitzpatricks of Glenlee operated their own dairies and employed herdsmen. Some Campbelltown dairies, like Varroville, were owned by city milk distributors. The Smith brothers of Concord leased Varroville from local dairyman, W. H. Staniforth of St Andrews, in 1923 and purchased it in 1929. They operated dairies at Robin Hood Farm and Varroville until 1958, running their own dairy herd and purchasing milk from surrounding farmers. By the late 1920s J. Carroll owned a chain of dairy farms along the Menangle Road totalling 700 acres (280 ha) and held leases over a further 1400 acres (560 ha). Carroll purchased two farms from the Hurley estate, three from the O'Donnell estate and the Sugarloaf farm from Mrs E. S. Sedgwick née Fitzpatrick.[66]

Fruitgrowing at Wedderburn expanded. Orchardists and farmers in the early 1920s included F. J. Coles, H. G. Corderoy, L. E. Edwards, F. Foster, H. Hircock, A. R. Knight, R. Lewis, J. H. Scobie, A. B. and J. H. Spencer, J. Swann and H. Vogt. The local blacksmith who made and repaired tools and transport was T. H. Gibson. Oranges, lemons, mandarins, apples, pears, peaches, plums, grapes, passionfruit, peanuts and a variety of fruits were grown. In 1924 Wedderburn farmers railed almost 15 000 cases of fruit from Campbelltown to city markets. When the fruit season was over, they planted peas and tomatoes for winter crops.

Water supply was a problem. The high ridge had no natural watercourses and rainwater was trapped in tanks and dams or carted from creeks. Prolonged drought was followed by a hurricane which swept fire through the orchards in December 1938. Hail destroyed most of the peach crop in 1941. Fruitfly became a serious problem from the 1930s. Inspectors were appointed to eliminate non-productive orchards. In 1939 the Wedderburn Fruitgrowers' Association was restructured as a Rural Co-operative Society. The old association had operated a bulk-purchasing scheme to reduce expenses for its growers. C. Knight was secretary for nearly 25 years and the last secretary, Tom Swann junior, was grandson of the first president.[67]

Most people had their own vegetable garden and hen house but there were a few Chinese market gardens in Campbelltown and Camden. In 1924 Charlie Low Wah of Camden acquired a motor lorry. He delivered his vegetables to Appin and the Cordeaux Dam on Thursdays, Campbelltown on Fridays, Minto and Ingleburn on Saturdays and the Avon Dam on Tuesdays.[68]

Agricultural and horticultural societies encouraged pride and quality.

The Swann family bottling and canning fruit at Ferndale orchard, Wedderburn. (T. Swann c. 1915)

Minto Horticultural Society held its first show in 1916. The Ingleburn Horicultural Society followed in 1928. The Campbelltown Agricultural Society felt the depression in 1933 and 1934. Declining membership and a significant reduction in the number of cattle at the show (over 100 fewer than in earlier years) reflected hard times in the stud and dairy industries.[69]

The State Nursery at Campbelltown cultivated 3 million seedlings and 100 000 potted plants in 1929–30 at an annual expense of £3000. Trees from the nursery were planted at the military and internment camps at Liverpool and Holsworth, the soldiers' settlement at Campbelltown and in many war memorial avenues of remembrance. The nursery closed without warning in August 1930. Convoys of lorries moved seedlings, potted plants and over 100 established trees to the Botanic Gardens in Sydney, leaving a scar across the western hillside. Most of the permanent staff lived in Campbelltown. David Frame, the superintendent, had been there fourteen years as propagator, foreman and superintendent. George Huckstepp, the head gardener, had given 26 years' service. Barkley Haydon was gardener for 30 years; Cosmos Meredith, for 24 years.

There were no plans for the land. Some suggested Campbelltown Council purchase it for a park and sporting complex but the prospect of spending ratepayers' funds in the midst of the depression was unrealistic. Others proposed that the Agricultural Society buy it for a new showground and subdivide the old ground for housing. The nursery site was on the western side of the railway, away from the commercial centre and it was not attractive for residential use. Searl and Jeans purchased it as a flower nursery for Searl's Florist Shop in Sydney. The Malvern family moved in as caretakers in 1938. Flowers were cut and sent by train to the city each day. Pines, elms and lilacs were planted and once again it was a special point on the western landscape of Campbelltown. A generation later it became an industrial site.[70]

Education

In November 1914 Campbelltown South Provisional School opened with Miss E. Bratt as its first teacher. The school was established due to the efforts of the Scattergood family who were selectors on Crown land south-east of Campbelltown. It became Kentlyn Public School in 1937. Attendance at Wedderburn Provisional School fell and it closed in 1922. It reopened in 1929 but closed again in 1942.

In 1914 St Patricks Primary School on the Old Menangle Road moved to new buildings closer to the church in Cordeaux Street. In 1922 Westview, the boys' preparatory school on St Johns Road, was rebuilt. The two-storey brick college, designed by Austin McKay, was opened at a cost of £5000 in July 1922.[71]

Badgally was sold by the Moore family in 1918. Five years later the

1000-acre (400 ha) estate was purchased by Thomas Joseph Donovan (1843–1929). Sydney-born, Donovan was a banker, a vigneron and a student of law and Shakespearean texts. He made several large gifts to Catholic and educational organisations. At Campbelltown in 1923, with the St Vincent de Paul Society and the Marist Brothers, Donovan established a home for 80 boys as a rural extension of the Westmead Boys' Home. A chapel, St Gregorys, was built using materials recycled from Greenway's 1820 Georgian school which had been demolished to build David Jones' Elizabeth Street, Sydney, store. In 1926 the boys' home became St Gregorys Boarding School and developed as an agricultural secondary school for boys.[72]

In 1927 Georgina Rudd of Campbelltown and Wagga Wagga died. Her Campbelltown estate, Maryfields, was inherited by her niece, Sarah M. Keane. The family desired that the property, once owned by Father Therry, be given to the Franciscan order and Sarah Keane donated it to the Catholic Church in 1929. In May 1935 Dr Sheehan, co-adjutor archbishop of Sydney, laid the foundation stone for a Franciscan novitiate. At its opening in December 1935 an audience, drawn largely from Franciscan parishes at Waverley, Paddington and Woollahra, was entertained by the Westmead Boys' Band. Father Bernard Nolan was the first superior of the Maryfields Novitiate.[73]

At Easter the following year the first annual Via Crucis pilgrimage was held at Maryfields, attracting a crowd variously estimated at between 6000 and 35 000. The success of Via Crucis startled Campbelltown, but it recognised the promotional and financial potential of the ceremony and events were better organised in 1937. While the church arranged for statues from France, the government extended the platform at Rudd's Gate, renaming it Maryfields station. J. G. Vardy donated one of the Stations of the Cross and Miss Keane gave the grotto.[74]

In 1910 there were only five State high schools in New South Wales, though some primary schools were graded as superior public schools and taught a small range of secondary subjects. A high school was opened at Parramatta in 1913 and in 1926 a junior technical school was established at Granville. Five boys and four girls from Campbelltown and one boy from Ingleburn attended high school at Parramatta in 1921. A similar number were enrolled in seventh grade at Campbelltown Public School. Seventh grade, equivalent to the first year of high school but without a foreign language, was offered from 1921 to 1929 at Campbelltown. From 1922 parents and teachers in Campbelltown campaigned for the courthouse, the largest and least-used building in town, to be converted to a high school. They claimed a commercial or intermediate high school in Campbelltown would serve about 235 pupils from the southern regions who travelled daily from Picton, Appin and Campbelltown to city high schools. The Department of Education estimated fewer students would benefit.[75]

At Ingleburn 461 children attended State schools and 30 were educated at private schools in 1933. In Campbelltown, where the choice was greater, 374 children attended public schools and 175 private schools, mostly the Catholic secondary colleges—St Patricks for girls, St Johns for boys and St Gregorys Agricultural School. In the 1920s Mrs Daintrees ran the Campbelltown District Church of England Grammar School for Girls. Some children attended boarding schools or travelled to private schools near the railway such as the King's School, Parramatta, Newington at Stanmore, Sydney Grammar School and the Presbyterian Ladies College, Croydon.[76]

Two young men from Campbelltown and one from Ingleburn were attending university in 1933. No-one from Campbelltown or Ingleburn had attended university in 1921. Ten years later in 1931 Olive Schofield became the first Campbelltown woman to receive a Bachelor of Arts degree from the University of Sydney. She had been educated at the Dominican Convent, Moss Vale. In the same year William Farrow, who had attended Sydney Grammar School, was awarded an engineering degree. George F. K. Naylor of Ingleburn, educated at Parramatta High School, had taken his BA in 1930 and the following year received first-class honours in science and the university medal in geology. In 1940 Stanley Reeve of Campbelltown was studying agriculture at Columbus University, Ohio.[77]

Hurlstone Agricultural School had been established by the government near Ashfield in 1907 to provide a practical education for boys who intended following rural careers. In March 1926 it moved to Glenfield. Built at a cost of almost £40 000 in grounds covering 100 acres (40 ha), the central building was a two-storey block with the principal's residence on the upper floor and students' dining-room and assembly hall on the ground floor. Nearby were four classrooms, science rooms and a manual arts building with carpentry and metalwork facilities. The dormitory block, designed for 72 boys, was already overcrowded with 92 boarders when the school was officially opened. The first principal from 1926 to 1938 was George F. Longmuir. The deputy headmaster, Stanley Cook, was mayor of Ingleburn in 1943.

The school taught a standard curriculum of languages, social and physical sciences with additional practical work in the school stables, dairy and poultry yards, piggery and orchards. Useful skills such as plumbing, blacksmithing and carpentry were taught. The boarding school was supplied with its own vegetables, milk and eggs. Quality stock, including a pure Ayrshire dairy herd, encouraged the boys to participate in agricultural shows. Many students continued their training at Hawkesbury Agricultural College or at the Faculty of Agriculture at the University of Sydney.[78]

The State had concentrated on establishing first a broad network of primary schools, then secondary schools. Education for children with special problems and intellectual or physical disabilities was largely ignored until the 1920s. Glenfield Park Special School opened in 1927 as the first school in the State designed for such children. It was a boarding school and was to be one of a statewide network of similar schools. Only Glenfield was built.[79]

In 1923 the Department of Agriculture established a veterinary research station at Glenfield. Investigation into animal diseases had been undertaken by the department since the late nineteenth century. Approval was given for a separate research facility in 1913 and 112 acres (45 ha) were purchased in 1916 from the Macquarie Fields estate. The station was designed by Dr Sydney Dodd of the University of Sydney in 1919 and was officially opened in November 1923.

Its first director was veterinary pathologist Dr H. R. Seddon (1887–1964) with a staff of nine. Research concentrated on problems of direct economic importance to the cattle, sheep, poultry and pig industries, such as the effect of poisonous plants, infectious diseases, worm and blowfly attack. A library wing and additional research laboratories were added in 1927 and the McGarvie-Smith wing was added in 1930. A further 123 acres (50 ha) were purchased in 1937 to extend research into brucellosis in cattle. The research station pioneered techniques for artificial insemination of cattle, offering its facilities to dairy farmers near Glenfield. In 1944 the station extended again, purchasing the remaining 300 acres (120 ha) of the Macquarie Fields estate, including Macquarie Fields House.

Seddon left to become foundation professor at the Veterinary School at the University of Queensland in 1936 and his successor was W. L. Hindmarsh. J. S. (Stan) Freeman (1894–1970) came to Glenfield as a senior technician in 1923 and was a member of Ingleburn Council from 1937 to 1940, serving as mayor in 1940. Freeman then stood for Liverpool Council where he was an alderman from 1941 to 1945 and mayor in his final year. In August 1945 he was elected as the Labor member for Blacktown, a seat he held until he retired in 1959.[80]

Campbelltown and Ingleburn during the Depression

During the 1920s Australia borrowed extensively from overseas. These debts were to be repaid by selling Australian products, but by the late 1920s its exports were not competitive. In 1929 Australia's recession became part of a worldwide depression when the American stock market collapsed, precipitating an international trade crisis. At its worst more than one-third of Australian wage earners were unemployed, a rate higher than any other Western nation, except Germany. Many remained unemployed until 1940.[81]

Farming communities such as Campbelltown and Ingleburn suffered less dramatically than city and suburban families who depended on work in manufacturing and service industries. For many country people times were tough from the mid-1920s when prices for milk, poultry and orchard products had fallen and the cost of feed had been increased by drought.

For these families the 1930s were more of the same. In 1921 there were 48 men out of work in Campbelltown and 7 in Ingleburn. In 1933, 192 men and 30 women were unemployed in Campbelltown municipality and 155 men and 21 women in Ingleburn.[82]

In June 1930 the mayor of Campbelltown, J. W. Kershler, appealed to ratepayers and businesspeople to assist the unemployed, and a depot was established at the town hall for clothing and other donations. A euchre party and dance in the town hall raised funds to purchase boots and clothing for the children of the district's unemployed in 1932, and another euchre party and dance was organised by the Campbelltown Unemployed Association in December 1935. Proceeds paid for a children's picnic to which all the children in the district were invited to avoid stigmatising children of the unemployed.[83]

The government, through the Unemployed Relief Council, funded relief work. Campbelltown Council wished to use the money on essential community services such as electricity and water-supply extensions, but initially it could only be used for roadworks. Other projects were funded by the Water Board and Main Roads Department. In 1935 mains water was extended to the Kent Farms (Kentlyn) and Leumeah as unemployment relief work. As late as May 1939 the Water Board and Main Roads called up unemployed men for work, employing 12–15 men who passed the medical test at the Campbelltown Police Station.

The seemingly humble road and construction works of these years were an important benefit for Campbelltown and Ingleburn municipalities which lacked permanent maintenance or engineering staff. Unemployed workers at Ingleburn ballasted and gravelled 12 miles (19 km) of roads, formed a further 18 miles (29 km), built three tennis courts and a clubhouse, extended water supplies, built the town hall, landscaped parkland and made a weir on the George's River to form a swimming pool. In Campbelltown gangs of about twenty men were employed on the Woolwash Road, Menangle Road, Appin Road and the Minto water scheme.[84]

Part of the unemployment work in Campbelltown and Camden municipalities was done by tender. Some contractors sacked men after a few hours' work, claiming they were not suitable, and did not pay them for their work. The unemployed were allocated work at the labour exchange in the police station and they dare not refuse as they then lost their entitlements. Unemployment fell after war was declared though in early 1940 Ingleburn Council refused unemployment relief work to local men because they had earlier refused to take up work at Bell in the Blue Mountains.[85]

For most Campbelltown and Ingleburn families food and shelter were available in the lean years. Thanks to their home vegetable garden, orchard, hens and cow they were largely self-sufficient in food and any surplus was swapped with neighbours. There were rabbits to snare and fish in the river, sometimes caught with a safety pin and a cork on a line. The surrounding bush had ample firewood and timber and stone for building. Everyone made do with mended clothes and few boys wore shoes to school anyway.

Cash was the greatest problem. During these years over half the work-force earned less than £2 per week. Money was needed to buy manufac-tured items, shoes, clothes and entertainment. Cash aid was rare, though in New South Wales child endowment payments helped. Unemployment relief provided coupons for groceries. Sometimes storekeepers gave cre-dit. Sometimes payment was made in kind. Williams, the Campbelltown baker, supplied bread to Wedderburn farmers in exchange for firewood for his ovens. Cash was needed for rent and house repayments, but a substantial proportion of local families already owned their own home (46.3 per cent in Campbelltown and 52.5 per cent in Ingleburn) and only a small proportion were still paying off homes in 1933. The rest paid rent, varying from 10 shillings to £1 a week. In Campbelltown in 1933, 886 men had work but 274 (31 per cent) were paid less than £1 a week and 50 per cent less than £2. In Ingleburn the situation was worse. Of 511 men working, 193 (38 per cent) received wages of less than £1 per week and 60 per cent less than £2.[86]

At Ingleburn, and especially Macquarie Fields, vacant land became a refuge for homeless families who built shacks along the George's River. In November 1932 Cannon Hammond bought 12 acres (4.8 ha) near Liverpool and established a housing settlement for unemployed families who had been evicted. About 33 children from Macquarie Fields travelled by train to schools at Glenfield or Ingleburn. The Department of Educa-tion would not establish a school at either Macquarie Fields or Long Point because there was no permanent population: families had only taken refuge in the area until work was available elsewhere.[87]

Leisure and daily life

'Health means Happiness and Ingleburn means Health' claimed a real estate brochure in 1927. Keatings at Ingleburn ran the Resthaven Board-ing House on Campbelltown Road just north of Brooks Road. A single-storey building set in extensive grounds, city visitors came to enjoy fresh country air, horseriding, walks, tennis, croquet and musical evenings around the piano. Community activities in Ingleburn included a Comedy Club and the Ingleburn Brass Band which played outside Collins store one night a week.[88]

Crystal radios with earphones were gradually replaced by larger battery-powered radio sets and listening became a family activity. Charles Tripp of the Silver Star Garage was Campbelltown's pioneer radio buff. Tripp was a member of the Wireless Institute of Australia from 1914, and in the 1920s he installed a loud speaker at his shop on the corner of Queen and Dumaresq Streets. On Friday and Saturday evenings people gathered outside to listen to broadcasts of the fights at the Sydney Stadium or popular serials. He sold large-valve sets with batteries, ear-phones, plug, aerial and earth for about £12. In the 1930s Jack Hepher also ran a radio business.[89]

Silent movies were screened in the Campbelltown Town Hall and the Ingleburn School of Arts. The Macquarie Cinema, on the corner of Queen and Browne Streets, was Campbelltown's first picture palace. Designed by A. W. M. Mowle and owned by Dr Mawson with Mr Molesworth as manager, it opened in 1927. The first film screened was *The Lost World*. Talkies came to Campbelltown in 1931 when Harry Nickless was mana-ger. The cinema seated 400 and a dress circle was added in 1931 to seat another 200. Initially it screened on Wednesday and Saturday nights but later a Saturday matinée was shown. The seats were removable and concerts and dances were held on other nights. A quarter of the Camp-belltown newspaper in the 1930s was regularly filled with movie gossip about Australian and American screen stars.[90]

Dances were held on Thursday nights at the Ingleburn School of Arts and Saturday nights at the Campbelltown Town Hall. Fights behind the hall were not unusual. The local brothel was conveniently located oppo-site the town hall, with a similar establishment at Ingleburn near the railway station. The town hall was also used for rollerskating.[91]

Motor cars brought great changes to the social life of women. One of the first women in Campbelltown to have her own car was Annie Marlow who was a very modern 'Woman of the Day', an energetic worker for charity and an active sportswoman. With her car she could enjoy social activities in both Campbelltown and Sydney. As the first president of the Freemasons Women's Auxiliary, Annie Marlow arranged many social functions, including an annual debutantes' ball in Sydney. Rose Payten also had a car and travelled widely to play golf.[92]

Social events organised by sporting groups and charities were impor-tant occasions in small towns. The newspaper usually devoted a full column to name those who attended and describe the ladies' dresses. Orchestras were hired from Sydney for the larger functions. Jazz was still a novelty in 1928, provoking debate whether it would replace old time dancing in Campbelltown. A social evening at the soldiers' settlement hall might feature, as well as singing and dancing, a potato race, bun-eating competitions, a women's nail-driving competition and men's nee-dle and thread race.

Campbelltown had two Rugby League teams in 1920. The Campbell-town Kangaroos, formed in 1912, and the Campbelltown Originals reg-ularly played against Liverpool, Camden, Smithfield, Cabramatta and Cordeaux Dam. The two teams, the result of a split in 1918 between the older and younger players of the Campbelltown Kangaroos, reunited as the Campbelltown Original Kangaroo Football Club in 1921. A junior team was formed in the mid-1920s. Alfred Duguid, the local shoemaker, was referee and treasurer of the football club for nearly 30 years from 1913. The football field was at the northern end of town in Charlie Nicol's paddock. At one memorable game against Fairfield in the mid-1930s, Campbelltown architect and club supporter Geoff Gore fired a revolver into the air to stop brawling spectators.[93]

At Ingleburn there was a football field but the adjoining tennis courts were more popular. During the 1930s controversy flared over Sunday sport. The council permitted use of the tennis courts on Sunday but forbade football. When the football club ignored the ban it provoked even greater controversy. Two aldermen, the families of several other aldermen and the town clerk were enthusiastic tennis players but none played foobtall.[94]

There were four tennis clubs in Campbelltown in 1924 and tennis was very popular among the congregation of St Peters Church of England where tennis courts were opened to celebrate its centenary in 1923. Campbelltown Bowling and Recreation Club was formed in 1921 and opened its green on the corner of Browne and Howe Streets in 1923 with a membership of 40. The Campbelltown Ladies' Bowling Club was formed in 1927, the fifth women's club in New South Wales. Afternoon dances, with the patrons wearing sandshoes, were held on the bowling greens in the late 1920s. The Campbelltown Waratah Cricket Club raised funds in 1929 for a concrete pitch in Hurley Park. At Minto and Glenfield there were active cricket clubs.[95]

Golf was played in 1905 on Rudd's paddock at Leumeah but it had ceased before World War I. A second club was fomed and land rented from Mr Flitcroft near Menangle Road. The Campbelltown Golf Course, laid out by Mr McMillan of the Moore Park Golf Club, opened in August 1926. Foundation president was J. G. Vardy who retained the position until his death in 1937, with F. W. Drinkwater, the postmaster, as the first secretary. Women were admitted as associate members from 1927. Rose Payten (1880–1951) was captain of the Campbelltown associate members. Playing with her 'old-style hat perched on her head and a cigarette eternally between her lips', she brought to golf the enthusiasm and skill she had earlier shown in championship tennis. She was Campbelltown Golf Associates Champion in 1930, 1931, 1934, 1936, 1938 and 1939. Dr K. O. Jones of Campbelltown was the main instigator for a district association and the Nepean Golf Association was formed in 1932. The following year Campbelltown women initiated a similar group, the Nepean and Illawarra District Associates Golf Association.[96]

The Campbelltown Ladies' Rifle Club was established in 1925 and competed regularly from the late 1920s. It was the only women's club in New South Wales, though other rifle clubs, such as Edgecliff and Mosman, allowed women to compete. Active members were Mrs Marlow, Scattergood, Kershler and Olarenshaw. The men's rifle club met regularly. Both clubs used a miniature shooting range in the showground pavilion for night competitions.[97]

Racing cyclist Joe Williams of Appin was a younger brother of the 1920 winner of the Goulburn to Sydney race. Williams held informal cycle races for the youngsters at Campbelltown in the 1930s—a shilling to enter, winner take all. These were so popular that the Campbelltown District Cycle Club was formed in 1933 by Reg Rutter and Jack Hepher. The Campbelltown club held its first road race, a 6-mile (10 km) event between Campbelltown and Minto, in July 1933. Races were held every weekend, regardless of weather, with the times of each competitor kept scrupulously in the record books. In January 1934 a quarter-mile (400 m) cycle track, unbanked, was cut at the football field on Charlie Nicol's picnic grounds on the Sydney Road. Later the trotting track on the showground was used. Races were held on the cycle track from October to May and road racing during the winter months, when the police permitted it. As cars became more popular, the cyclists were forbidden to race on major highways. In 1939 a road race organised at Campbelltown by the NSW Cyclists' Union attracted over 300 entries.[98]

A branch of the Boy Scouts was formed in Campbelltown in 1922 with F. S. Blades as the first scoutmaster. Geoff Gore designed a scout hut in 1927 and it was built by Jorgensen and Stephenson of Campbelltown on land donated by Sarah Payten in Lindesay Street. As it was one of only three brick buildings owned by the scouting movement in New South Wales, it was opened by the head scout, the governor of New South Wales, Sir Dudley de Chair, in April 1928. Ingleburn Scout Hall was opened the following year.[99]

The Campbelltown Hospital Auxilliary Committee continued to meet during the 1920s when its fund-raising efforts supported the Camden District Hospital, the Hospital for Infants and the Liverpool Ambulance Service. Kyla Private Hospital in Lithgow Street offered surgical, medical and midwifery services under Matron Newbury from 1918, as did Norma Hospital in Warby Street under Nurse Brock and Nurse Wilson, who later moved to Nattai in Lindesay Street. Milby Private Hospital, opened by Dr Mawson in 1925 in Kendall's old flour mill, was managed by Sister

Campbelltown Ladies Rifle Club around 1930. *Back row left to right* P. Loftus, W. Longhurst. *Middle row left to right* Scattergood, A. Marlow, M. Forbes. *Front row left to right* T. Reeve, N. Smith CLISSOLD COLLECTION

194

B. Hausfeld in 1932. It closed in 1941. In 1944 a baby health clinic was started as a memorial to Karl Jones, a popular doctor who died in February 1944. The clinic, under Sister Tomlinson and Mrs Gaul, used temporary premises until the centre was built in 1950. Beverley Park, home of Mr and Mrs J. H. Yates, was donated to the Crippled Children's Association in 1938.[100]

At war again

War was declared on 3 September 1939. Once again a military camp was set up at the Campbelltown Showground. The First Machine Gun Regiment was training there when W. M. (Billy) Hughes visited in October 1939. Menangle Park Racecourse became a training ground for men of the 45th Battalion of the militia and later a base for the air force. Construction work at Ingleburn Military Camp continued around the clock in late 1939 and Ingleburn council was responsible for the installation of electricity. Eshcol Park was taken over to intern the staff of the German embassy.[101]

Recruiting rallies were arranged by the local branch of the RSSILA and, as in the earlier war, funds were raised to send extra comforts to the men on active service. Local women joined the Voluntary Aid Detachments (VADs) of the Red Cross, commanded by Miss Sedgwick in Campbelltown and Mrs Michael King in Ingleburn. Eight Campbelltown VADs— Misses Mayo, Molesworth, Gately, Payten, Cobcroft, Pentland, Steel and Baldcock—served in military hospitals.

Campbelltown's roll of honour recorded the names of 459 volunteers, 21 of whom were killed in action. Corporal John Hurst Edmondson was the first Australian awarded the Victoria Cross in World War II. In April 1941 at Tobruk, Edmondson, though wounded, ensured the success of his platoon's mission and saved the life of his officer. He died from his wounds. Edmondson was a descendant of Harry Angel, a member of Hume and Hovell's expedition in 1824, and had attended Hurlstone Agricultural College. Sergeant Gus Longhurst, another Hurlstone boy, was awarded the Military Medal in 1942 for action in Libya. Ingleburn town clerk, Harley Daley, enlisted in early 1940, as did his assistants, A. L. Birkett and George Kayes, and Alderman W. C. Hosking. Menangle Park village farewelled its first soldier, William Thomas, in mid-1940 with a party. The local member of parliament, Jeff Bate, also enlisted.[102]

Following the Japanese attack on Pearl Harbour in December 1941, national defence became more urgent. Air-raid shelters were built, volunteers joined the National Emergency Service and first aid classes were held in Campbelltown and Ingleburn. In March 1942 the Metropolitan Fire Brigade gave a demonstration in Mawson Park on incendiary bombs and fire-fighting. Petrol, food and clothing were rationed and could be obtained, legally, only with ration coupons. Waste paper, cardboard and old rags were collected by the council for recycling.[103]

War meant the suspension of most sporting activities in Campbelltown because so many of the young men had joined up. There were no formal meetings of the Campbelltown Cycle Club between 1940 and 1946, nor of the Campbelltown Kangaroo Rugby League Club. The annual Agricultural Society Show was not held because the army occupied the showground. Women's sporting activities were also curtailed. The New South Wales Ladies' Golf Union formed a Patriotic and War Fund and urged its members to knit socks and raise funds for the forces. Meetings and competitions were suspended from May 1941 till March 1946. Women still played golf but the rationing of clothing forced changes to the previously stringent dress rules. They were permitted to play golf with bare legs— though only for the duration. Petrol rationing meant fewer cars on the road and the bicycle club hoped that the police would permit them to use the Bulli Pass Road and the Hume Highway for cycle races.[104]

While the younger generation went off to war, the committee of the Campbelltown War Memorial School of Arts had difficulty maintaining its activities. On a committee of seventeen, less than 10 per cent were veterans of the 1914–18 war. Most returned soldiers were members of the Campbelltown sub-branch of the RSSILA which maintained a hut at Ingleburn Military Camp and assisted with recruiting. They had little interest in the literary institute that the town had erected as its war memorial. Campbelltown Council had previously subsidised the rates of the school of arts, but would not continue to do so during the war when its own revenue had fallen because no charge was made for patriotic functions held in the town hall. In 1942 the School of Arts Committee invited the council and the RSL to take over their premises. Ten years later the school of arts became Campbelltown Council Chambers and the RSL occupied the adjoining land.[105]

Six

1945–1988

THE populations of Campbelltown and Ingleburn in 1947 totalled 6995. Over the next 40 years the population increased more than tenfold, reaching 93 250 in 1981 and an estimated 120 000 in 1986. For most of the 1970s Campbelltown was the fastest-growing region in Australia, with new residents arriving at a rate equivalent to 80 new people per day per year.

Change in the immediate postwar years was gradual. Development had been confined before the war by rural estates surrounding the town. In 1945 the Blair Athol estate west of the railway was sold to Crompton Parkinson, a Sydney electrical-goods manufacturer, though the company did not build there for another decade. New homes and factories were postponed for several years after the war because of credit restrictions and a shortage of materials. Army Nissan huts were recycled for homes, churches and meeting halls.

In the early 1950s Campbelltown was still a rural town, many families keeping their own cow and fowls. Weatherboard houses with corrugated-iron roofs were common. So were fuel stoves, burning either wood or coal. Though electricity had been available before the war, economic depression and a reticence to replace trusted old with new-fangled modern had slowed the introduction of electric appliances. After the war Campbelltown Council, which was the local electricity supplier, revived its campaign to sell electrical appliances. In 1958 Campbelltown Council relinquished control of electricity supply to the Nepean River County Council, formed in 1954 and amalgamated as the Prospect County Council in 1980.[1]

There was little social distinction between areas in the town, though the poorest-quality housing was in Broughton Street near the railway and the milk factory. Campbelltown's business centre had been gradually moving northward along Queen Street from Bradbury Park as subdivisions on the northern side of town attracted residents. The council chambers moved from southern Queen Street to the corner of Lithgow Street in 1953 and to the northern end of Queen Street in 1964.

Campbelltown, 1969, looking south with the intersection of Broughton and Lindesay Streets in the foreground. CAMPBELLTOWN LOCAL HISTORY COLLECTION

The rapid increase in population in Campbelltown from the mid-1950s was caused by external, not local, conditions.

Urban Planning—the government as developer

As World War II drew to a close, governments turned their attention to postwar reconstruction. Planning the development of the cities and suburbs was high on the agenda as a method of improving social and economic conditions. In 1945 the New South Wales government amended the *Local Government Act* to ensure that local councils, advised by professional town planners, would prepare planning schemes. For the Sydney metropolitan area the legislation established the Cumberland County Council, an umbrella group with 10 delegates from 40 municipalities and shires within the county of Cumberland. Its task was to prepare within three years a planning scheme for the county of Cumberland, taking into consideration residential needs for a growing population, the location of industry, recreational space, transport routes, water supply and sewerage. The Cumberland County Council completed its task in 1948. After three years of discussion, the plan was formally accepted in 1951.

Campbelltown, with Fairfield, Liverpool, Camden, Wollondilly and Wollongong, was represented on the first Cumberland County Council by C. C. Murray of Ingleburn Council. From 1951, when the scheme was approved, the delegate from Campbelltown and the south-west was F. J. Sedgwick. He resigned in 1956 and was replaced by L. Powell. G. G. Marsden of Campbelltown was a member in 1960 and Clive Tregear sat on the last Cumerland County Council in 1963.

The County of Cumberland Scheme sought to coordinate the physical growth of suburban Sydney and to contain its urban sprawl with an encircling green belt of open space. Within the older areas higher-density development would use land and service utilities more efficiently. New residential and industrial growth would be directed to rural satellite towns beyond the green belt, thus relieving congestion on transport networks and providing work close to homes. Campbelltown was identified as a satellite town and its population target was set at 30 000 people. Already on a major transport route, under the plan Campbelltown's social and recreational facilities would be expanded to attract new industries and new residents. Another feature of the plan was its emphasis on conserving natural and historic landscapes, and a survey of historic buildings in the county of Cumberland was started.

Problems implementing the plan occurred from the beginning. Councils and developers holding land in the green belt objected to the freeze on expansion. Population grew more rapidly than predicted, reaching targets set for the 1970s by the mid-1950s, and creating pressure to release green belt land. Funds were not sufficient to improve road and rail transport quickly. Nor were detailed proposals considered for the satellite towns. Having identified appropriate existing towns like Penrith, Campbelltown, Blacktown and Windsor, no further planning or funding was assigned to them and their futures remained in the hands of local government authorities.[2]

The Cumberland County Council was abolished in 1963 and replaced the following year with the State Planning Authority. There was a change of government in 1965, the Liberal–Country Party replacing Labor after 25 years in opposition. One of the first visits of the new Minister for Local Government and Main Roads, P. H. Morton, in June 1965 was to Campbelltown. The State Planning Authority was anxious to convince the new minister of the importance of its plans for controlled development. The minister met with Campbelltown Council and the local member, R. A. Dunbier. Morton supported a plan for Campbelltown to develop into a city for 40 000 people and approved an assessment of its potential for a much larger city of 250 000.

A new plan for the expansion of metropolitan Sydney, 'The Sydney

Region Outline Plan 1970–2000 AD', was published in 1968. This directed urban growth along three existing transport corridors—westward to Blacktown, Penrith and Katoomba; south-west to Campbelltown, Camden and Appin, and north to Gosford, Wyong and Newcastle. New self-contained regional cities would be established, providing a better quality of life than the existing dormitory suburbs. Industry would be located nearby, relieving the personal and community stress of long journeys to work.

Campbelltown was identified in the Outline Plan as a city of 230 000 people by 2001. With its neighbours Camden and Appin, the three cities would house and employ 500 000 by 2001. In 1970 responsibility for more detailed planning of the three new cities was given to a development committee. Its members represented the State Planning Authority (J. J. Wickham), the Housing Commission (J. M. Bourke), Department of Main Roads (A. F. Schmidt), Metropolitan Water, Sewerage and Drainage Board (E. G. Warrell), Treasury (N. Oakes), Australian Gas Light Company (J. W. W. Butters) and the local councils (R. B. Ferguson, mayor of Camden, and C. W. Tregear, alderman on Campbelltown Council). The committee was supported by a technical team of planners, architects, engineers and geographers. The director of this team was Jim Waugh who had previously been on the engineering and planning staff of Campbelltown Council. Campbelltown Council contributed to the cost of the planning project. The development committee published its proposals in 1973 as 'The New Cities of Campbelltown, Camden and Appin Structure Plan'.

Campbelltown would be the first, and largest, of the three new cities. The plan outlined the physical layout of the new Campbelltown. Residential development would expand east from the railway at Macquarie Fields, Ingleburn, Minto and Campbelltown. Between the railway and a new freeway, land was reserved for industrial uses. West of the freeway on the Central Hills would be one residential area, Badgally. In the south residential development was planned for Menangle Park, with an industrial area and a regional sports centre nearby. Campbelltown would be the region's commercial and administrative centre, a status reinforced by building a major tertiary institution. Corridors of open space along the Central Hills and the George's River would provide an attractive setting for the new city, and freeways and transport interchanges would give quick access to and within the Campbelltown area.[3]

To fulfil its plans for Campbelltown and to ensure that they were not invalidated by speculators, the government, through the State Planning Authority and its successor, the Department of Environment and Planning, purchased extensive tracts of land. Like Canberra, government ownership of broad acres at Campbelltown provided control over land use, layout of streets and services, design of houses and the location of industry.

Land acquisition at Campbelltown was considered by the planning authorities from the early 1960s. Cumberland County Council, the Department of Local Government and Campbelltown Council accepted that since about half the area of any city was used for public purposes, including roads, land should be acquired for these purposes by the planning authority. Land was cheaper at Campbelltown than at Blacktown, the other satellite area, and in 1966 funds were approved for the State Planning Authority to acquire land. Its first purchase was 66 acres (26 ha) at Minto, purchased for $48 000, for industrial use. In 1968, prior to the release of the Sydney Region Outline Plan, the State Planning Authority purchased about 10 000 acres (4000 ha), averaging $1000 per acre, for future industrial use and for education and Housing Commission development. Land acquisition also involved protection of landscape and historic buildings.

Before the new city in the south-west could become a reality, major capital works had to be undertaken by other government authorities. The timing of Campbelltown's growth depended especially on agreement with the Water Board on the need for, and the priority of, a major sewer link to serve the towns along the southern railway. After initial hesitation, the Water Board accepted this project in 1968 and work started in 1970 on a sewer along Smith's Creek, followed by a larger scheme to sewer the Bow Bowing Creek catchment area. 'Cooperation of the Housing Commission was also considered essential to provide a start-up population for the new city. Transport was another relevant factor. Electrification of the line to Campbelltown had been announced in 1965 and by 1970 the Department of Main Roads was constructing the South-Western Freeway from Liverpool to Minto.

In 1965 the New South Wales government created a Department of Decentralisation and Development with John Fuller as minister. This became the Department of Planning and Environment (later called the Department of Environment and Planning) in 1973 and took over the role of the State Planning Authority. In 1974 the *New South Wales Growth Centres (Land Acquisition) Act* and the *Growth Centres (Development Corporations) Act* laid the foundations for new cities in the metropolitan south-west (Campbelltown, Camden and Appin), at Bathurst–Orange, Albury–Wodonga and Gosford–Wyong.

The Sydney South-west Sector Planning and Development Board was established under the Department of Planning and Environment in 1975 to manage the growth centre. It was a logical extension of the development committee which had prepared the report on the area in 1973. The new board was given authority to acquire and develop land in the region, and to manage the environmental and historic building conservation programme. Its chairman was Peter Kacerick, an English town planner who was deputy chief planner at the New South Wales State Planning Authority from 1967. Kacerick was influential in selecting the district's new name, Macarthur, renaming the coordination body the Macarthur Development Board. On the surface Macarthur was an obvious choice as

John Macarthur was one of the best-known Australian historical figures and his home at Camden Park was protected under the heritage plans for the three new cities. Yet Macarthur was not a popular choice in Campbelltown. Campbelltown was the first of the cities to be developed and its residents felt slighted because the new name in its local context was identified only with Camden, Campbelltown's traditional rival since the 1840s. A decade later hackles still rise in Campelltown whenever the name Macarthur is bestowed, for example, on the new railway station.

Most of the land owned by the Macarthur Development Board was zoned for industrial sites and lay on the floodplains of the Bow Bowing Creek. Expensive flood-mitigation schemes, drainage and filling were necessary before it could be released for sale. The board sought to attract factories, so essential for generating local employment, but the late 1970s were years of recession in Australian industry and less land was sold than anticipated. It also owned some commercial and residential land, mostly in Raby and Denham Court, land for open space, government uses and heritage protection.

A key element in the 1973 plan for Campbelltown was a new regional centre, south of the existing business area, which would incorporate retail, administrative, transport and educational facilities. The Macarthur Development Board was responsible for bringing these plans to fruition. By 1985 the Macarthur Regional Centre included the Macarthur railway station, the Macarthur Institute of Higher Education, the Campbelltown College of Technical and Further Education, Macarthur Shopping Square, Campbelltown Motor Registry and Campbelltown Hospital, with plans for new offices for the Macarthur Development Board. A road linking the new centre with the older retail centre was opened in 1987.

In 1972 the new federal Labor government had established the federal Department of Urban and Regional Development. It supported decentralised 'growth centres' and federal funds were allocated to assist their development. Under this programme the Macarthur region received $10.1 million in 1974–75 and $15.7 million in 1975–76, about 20 per cent of available funds. Federal funding was not continued when the Liberal government came to office in 1975. The State government became increasingly unwilling to bear the long-term investment costs incurred by the land acquisition role of the Macarthur Development Board. The Board's functions changed to marketing activities, developing and selling its land to the private sector. Responsibility for the Macarthur Development Board was transferred to the Department of Industrial Development and Decentralisation in June 1981. The board was renamed the Macarthur Development Corporation in 1986 and its activities will be phased out by 1992.[4]

The Housing Commission of New South Wales, established in 1942, directed many new residents to Campbelltown. Some housing commission accommodation had been built along the Sydney Road near the railway line in the early 1950s; however, for most of the 1950s the Housing Commission had little interest in Campbelltown because land was available closer to Sydney. By 1957 its existing stock of land was almost exhausted and the Housing Commission announced plans to acquire 5460 acres (2184 ha) at Minto to build a satellite town of 10 000 houses for 50 000 people, together with schools, playgrounds and churches. Protest meetings were called at Campbelltown. The project was abandoned two months later, not because of the local protests but because the Cumberland County Council considered the project premature and in conflict with its scheme.[5]

For the next decade the Housing Commission's main developments were at Green Valley and Mount Druitt, though a small number of buildings, including units for the aged, were built at Campbelltown. With the release of the Sydney Outline Plan in 1968, the Housing Commission purchased large areas at Campbelltown. Work started on its first major project, homes for 5000 people, at Macquarie Fields in 1972. Conscious of critics who accused the Housing Commission of creating social and economic problems by building vast isolated estates which lacked facilities, the Macquarie Fields project incorporated schools, sporting facilities, a general store and a community information centre. By 1975 the Housing Commission had started building at Claymore, Minto, Kentlyn (Ruse) and Bradbury and had acquired land at Rosemeadow for $2.24 million. Its estates used the Radburn design, pioneered in the United States of America, which separated vehicle and pedestrian traffic. Designing streetscapes, homes and public buildings in new areas challenged the architects from the Housing Commission and the Public Works Department. Townhouses in Housing Commission estates in Campbelltown received awards from the Housing Industry Association while Claymore Public School, built in 1980, has been recognised as an outstanding example of contemporary Australian architecture.[6]

By 1982, 38 000 people, 36.5 per cent of Campbelltown's population, lived in townhouses and cottages built by the Housing Commission. Macquarie Fields by 1987 had 1557 Housing Commission dwellings, Minto 1220, Airds 1250 and Claymore 1102, with less intensive development in Campbelltown (546), Ingleburn (265), Bradbury (256), Leumeah (64), St Andrews (41) and Ruse (5). The Ambarvale estate will be its last major project in Campbelltown (434 dwellings by 1987), though there remains an undeveloped site known as Bow Bowing, near the Ingleburn industrial estate. Constant adverse publicity and the social stigma attached to Housing Commission areas and their residents determined the Housing Commission to adopt a more low-key approach with scattered infill developments in older areas.[7]

The largest land developer in the Macarthur region is Landcom, the Land Commission of New South Wales. Landcom was established by Neville Wran on coming to office in 1976, fulfilling an election promise to imitate a similar federal body established by Whitlam's federal government. Landcom sought to fulfil the Australian dream of owning one's house by supplying low-priced fully serviced land. Created as the land boom of the early 1970s collapsed, Landcom was able to purchase cheaply from developers who had overextended their holdings in outer Sydney. By the end of 1977 Landcom had acquired large blocks at Campbelltown. In the late 1970s and early 1980s Landcom developed areas of Eagle Vale, Ambarvale, Woodbine, St Andrews and Rosemeadow. The purchasers of home sites were mostly young couples buying for their first home. Between 1981 and 1984 Landcom provided half of the residential sites available in Campbelltown.[8]

The private developers

St Elmo House with grounds was leased in December 1946 by Neil and Meryl McLean. They planned to expand the chicken-hatchery business they had established at Lindfield when Neil McLean had returned from the RAAF. Limited by the residential areas of Lindfield, they turned to rural Campbelltown and leased the property with an option to purchase. With the release of the County of Cumberland Planning Scheme, the McLeans recognised the potential for Campbelltown within the scheme. They took up the option to purchase St Elmo in 1949, obtained subdivision approval and closed the chicken hatchery.

St Elmo Estate No. 1, designed by surveyor W. E. Lewis, created Lillian Street, off Broughton Street, and was developed in 1950. It was a quality subdivision offering sealed roads, with kerbs and gutters—a rarity in Campbelltown. On the eastern hill overlooking the town and Leumeah, Lillian Street became Campbelltown's first prestigious address, nicknamed 'Snob's Hill' or 'McLean's Folly'. Here, two-storey brick homes with views cost £6000–10 000 and 53 new houses were built between 1950 and 1953. Early purchasers included Bill Bursill and Harley Daley, the town clerk.

In 1952 the McLeans acquired more land and developed St Elmo No. 2, aiming this estate at the returned serviceman seeking a house and land for his young family. With deposits of £80–120, finance was arranged through the War Service Homes Commission. Architect J. H. Donaldson designed the houses. The McLeans' next development was south of the town. They applied to subdivide Bradbury Park estate into 400 blocks in October 1954. Six St Elmo estates had been put on the market by 1959 when the McLeans sold their interest to Lend Lease and left Campbelltown.[9]

Another group which recognised the potential for development in the satellite city was Reid Murray Developments Pty Ltd under F. R. Wolstenholme as managing director. The group, a retail organisation which had diversified into property development, acquired much of the land west of the railway between Camden Road and St Andrews Road. Development costs would be comparatively low because most land had already been cleared for dairy pasture. Reid Murray Developments proposed to the Cumberland County Council an extensive residential development on the Central Hills, with an industrial estate in the valley near the railway. Surveyors commenced work in 1959 but the project was never completed. The Reid Murray group collapsed when a deficiency of £15.7 million was announced in September 1963. Its land at Campbelltown was sold back to the original owners or purchased by State and local government authorities.

Lend Lease Corporation was created in 1958 as an extension of a Dutch construction partnership, Civil and Civic Contractors, formed in 1950 to undertake work on the Snowy Mountains Hydro-electricity Scheme. Lend Lease was a new concept in the Australian real estate business, offering finance, architectural and engineering design, and construction skill. It grew quickly as a development company for large, high-rise city projects. Its founder, Gerardus Jozef Dusseldorp, was also interested in residential development and the long-term proposals for Campbelltown caught his attention. Dusseldorp attended a meeting of Campbelltown Council to learn the council's attitudes to the development of the new satellite city. In 1959 Lend Lease Corporation purchased part of the St Elmo estate, renamed it Macquarie Heights estate and subdivided into 192 allotments.[10]

More land was purchased south of the town in 1960. Zoned residential by Campbelltown Council in 1963, the Lend Lease subdivision was designed by Sydney architect and town planner George Clarke of Clarke Gazzard and Partners. The estate, called Sherwood Hills, brought a new style of suburban living to Campbelltown. Covenants over the land controlled the quality of buildings; there were no front fences, no overhead power lines; native trees were retained and others planted and all blocks were sewered. Fifty-five acres (22 ha) of parkland was reserved along Fisher's Ghost Creek. Exhibition homes were designed to attract young first-home buyers. Lend Lease had accepted that the immediate future for Campbelltown was a dormitory suburb because there was no local industry. Its attraction for home buyers had to be the promise of a better-quality home in a more pleasant environment for less than it would cost elsewhere.[11]

Blocks were offered for sale in 1965 and the first residents arrived in September. The subdivision was served by a private bus service. In 1968 Campbelltown Council built a nine-lane Olympic swimming pool on land provided by Lend Lease and the Deparment of Education built a primary school, designed by Hely, Bell and Horne who also designed the local shopping centre. Three hundred and fifty homes were built in three years and by 1972 Sherwood Hills was home to 3500. In the economic difficulties of the 1970s, with house and land prices rapidly outstripping the resources of the first-home buyer, Lend Lease experimented with cluster housing (townhouses) at Campbelltown. Locksley Mews, a group of 27 townhouses at Sherwood Hills, won an award for the best-designed housing estate in the State. Sherwood Hills estate later merged into the suburb of Bradbury.[12]

Lend Lease owned land between the Appin and Menangle Roads where the State Planning Authority planned to build the new regional city centre announced in the Sydney Region Outline Plan in 1968. Complicated negotiations, exchanges and rezonings resulted in Lend Lease agreeing to build on its land a new golf course for Campbelltown Council. Around it Lend Lease could develop five villages incorporating a mixture of low- and medium-density housing. Work on the Ambarvale estate started in 1973 and it was opened by the premier in June 1976. On the western side Lend Lease released its executive Glen Alpine estate in 1986. Nearby, Lend Lease built the Macarthur Square regional shopping centre for the Macarthur Development Board.

City centre redevelopment

Campbelltown Chamber of Commerce was formed in January 1949. From the beginning it fought to encourage residents to shop in Campbelltown. Cheap shoppers' rail excursion fares attracted Campbelltown housewives to the larger retail centres in Parramatta or the city. A shopping trip to the city was a regular Friday outing for many women. Most young people worked outside Campbelltown and tended to shop near their place of employment.[13]

From 1951 planning decisions at Campbelltown were affected by its future as a satellite city. One of the earliest changes proposed by the Department of Main Roads was a bypass road around the Queen Street shopping area. In 1954 five alternative routes were proposed, with Main Roads favouring Moore and Oxley Streets where vacant land was available in the subdivision around Beverley Park and the new high school. Campbelltown Chamber of Commerce and Campbelltown Municipal Council opposed the bypass and wanted to retain Queen Street as the main route. The debate continued for several years. One 1957 proposal suggested a bypass west of the railway, joining southern Queen Street at Fisher's Ghost Bridge. Work on the Oxley Street bypass was still in progress 30 years later.[14]

The Commonwealth Bank opened a branch at Campbelltown in 1947, though most residents preferred the service of Miss Huckstepp who ran the local agency for the bank. Another branch of the Commonweath opened at Ingleburn in 1957 and in the same year the Bank of New South Wales returned to Campbelltown after an absence of fourteen years. A branch of the Rural Bank opened in 1961. Campbelltown's first department store, Downe's, opened in Queen Street in 1952, expanding from grocery and hardware lines to furniture and clothing. The large chains of variety stores did not come to Campbelltown until the 1960s. The first was Woolworths which opened in Queen Street in 1962, followed by Nock and Kirby Hardware and Coles, whose 1967 store was the largest in the district.

From 1947 terminating building societies in Campbelltown offered finance for home construction. Ron McDonald became secretary of seven terminating societies in 1966. Building societies grew rapidly in the late 1960s throughout the State. In 1970, 36 Campbelltown terminating building societies joined to form the town's first permanent building society, the Campbelltown City Building Society. Its chairman was Basil Thorburn and the directors were Arch Walker, Bruce McDonald, Mort Clissold, Ross Fitzpatrick and Vince Confeggi, with Ron McDonald as manager. Between 1971 and 1978 the society lent $8.25 million to 539 members. Changes to the operation of building societies in 1978, introducing cash payments of $500 on request, made operations very difficult for small societies like the Campbelltown City Building Society, and in 1979 its members resolved to merge with the larger Illawarra Mutual Building Society.[15]

In 1965, following indications that its long-term population would be 250 000 people, Campbelltown Council and the State Planning Authority prepared a plan for the redevelopment and expansion of the Queen Street business area. Council zoning had restricted commercial development to

---

Don Topman and Pat McGeldrick behind the counter of Bursill's general store, around 1950.

CLISSOLD COLLECTION

the western side of Queen Street between Railway and Allman Streets. Campbelltown Council had acquired houses and land in Coogan Place and Milgate Lane for carparks. East Queen Street was mostly residential, with some commerical uses. The 1965 redevelopment plan ended the mix of residential and business use between the Oxley Streeet bypass and the railway. It proposed low-rise commercial development along Queen Street, with extensive carparking behind both sides of Queen Street, the closure of Queen Street to through traffic and the creation of a pedestrian plaza.

Following the release of the Structure Plan in 1973, attention turned to the smaller commercial centres at the railway stations between Glenfield and Campbelltown. These were considered too limited in area for expansion and new district shopping centres were planned. Glenquarie, to serve Glenfield and Macquarie Fields, was proposed in 1974 on vacant land along Harold Street, but a bridge had to be built across Bunbury Curran Creek to give access from Glenfield. Minto Mall followed some years later.

The Sydney Region Outline Plan in 1968 proposed a regional retail and business centre south of the existing Queen Street business area, to the consternation of existing businesses which feared that a large new centre would fragment the small market. Plans for the regional centre moved slowly. The Macarthur Development Board acquired the land in the 1970s. Macarthur Shopping Square was financed by the State Superannuation Board and developed by Lend Lease. It featured Campbelltown's first multistorey department store, David Jones', a discount store and a number of small boutiques. Isolated from the existing retail area until Kellicar Road was opened in 1987, the centre struggled to attract shoppers.

Meanwhile, new developments in Queen Street sought to retain customers in the existing retail area. Alpha House and the Good Intent Hotel were replaced in July 1984 by Campbelltown Mall, whose major attraction was a huge K-Mart discount store, covering 14 000 square metres, at the time the largest in the southern hemisphere. Between 1985 and 1987 Lend Lease Retail invested $88 million in purchasing Campbelltown Mall and the Macarthur Shopping Square. The northern end of Queen Street changed from 1985. The first major redevelopment at this end of town was the Centre Court, which opened in November 1985 on the site of the Forbes Hotel. It was developed by the Brticevich family, Yugoslav migrants who came to Minto to farm in the 1960s. High-rise offices and shops along Queen Street changed the face of the older business area.[16]

Local government

During World War II, the small rural municipalities of Ingleburn and Nepean applied to amalgamate. Their request was deferred pending a more general investigation into local government in the county of Cumberland after the war. A royal commission in 1946 considered suggestions to amalgamate the 66 councils into larger units. The following year a Legislative Council select committee took further evidence. Its recommendation to create 39 councils became the basis for the *Local Government (Areas) Act* of 1948.[17]

In 1947 Ingleburn, Campbelltown, Camden and Nepean municipalities considered amalgamation. Smaller councils favoured it because they could not afford staff or equipment to provide a level of service expected by ratepayers. Ingleburn wanted to join with Campbelltown and Nepean, accepting that Campbelltown would become the dominant commercial centre as it was on the main road and Ingleburn was not. Camden Council strongly opposed suggestions that it amalgamate with Campbelltown. There was 'no common interest or affinity' between the two areas. Camden considered it was more innovative and did not wish to be burdened with the less progressive Campbelltown. In the north, Liverpool Council suggested it might extend southward and take over Ingleburn and Campbelltown. The Progress Associations at Glenfield, Macquarie Fields and Ingleburn strongly opposed this.

Ingleburn and Campbelltown in 1947 had similar-sized populations (3274 in Ingleburn, 3746 in Campbelltown). Ingleburn covered 20 square miles (52 km^2) and included three villages, Glenfield, Ingleburn and Macquarie Fields, sharing Minto with Campbelltown. Only 4 miles (6.5 km) of road had a tar surface. Campbelltown municipality was almost five times larger (96 square miles [249 km^2] with 50 miles (80 km) of surfaced roads, but only 2 miles (3 km) kerbed and guttered. About half its area was non-ratable Crown land. Good land around Campbelltown, Minto and Menangle Park formed only one-third of the municipality, but contained 97 per cent of ratable land.[18]

Campbelltown and Ingleburn were amalgamated in August 1948 and the first election for the combined council was held in December 1948. There were two wards and both were well contested—27 candidates for Campbelltown ward and 9 for Ingleburn. The sixteen members of the new council were, for the Campbelltown ward, P. Solomon, F. Sedgwick, C. J. Clark, J. G. A. Farnsworth, E. M. Clissold, W. A. Longhurst, P. C. Marlow, E. S. Claydon and H. L. Lea and, for Ingleburn ward, I. A. Hazlett, W. J. Apperley, J. E. Baldwin, D. B. Livingstone, F. G. Goodwin, C. H. Dench and J. R. V. English. The town clerk of the new council was Harley Daley, previously clerk at Ingleburn. The former town clerk of Campbelltown, R. F. Blomfield, became his deputy. Daley was succeeded on his retirement in 1971 by Bruce McDonald who had joined Campbelltown Council in 1956. McDonald was town clerk until June 1976 when he resigned to take up the appointment as general manager of the Macarthur Development Board. Keith Garling became town clerk in 1976.[19]

In 1947 Ingleburn Council had applied to the Registrar General for title to 200 acres (80 ha) on the eastern side of the railway at Macquarie Fields.

It had been subdivided in about 1890 into half-acre (0.2 ha) blocks, the owners could not be traced and no rates had had been paid for 40 years. A further 1100 blocks were resumed in 1954. This acquisition policy gave Campbelltown Council a considerable advantage in later years when it held a stock of land that it was able to sell to government authorities, private enterprise or develop on its own account.[20]

With its future determined as a satellite city from 1949, aldermen on Campbelltown Municipal Council became involved in policy making within various statutory authorities. When Syd Percival was elected one of the first aldermen on Ingleburn Council in 1896, the council's interests did not extend beyond its boundaries. His grandson, H. G. (Greg) Percival, fourth generation of the local family, was elected to Campbelltown Council in 1956. During 30 years on Campbelltown Council, he also served as local government representative on the Sydney Metropolitan Water Board (1967–83), the executives of state and federal local government associations and the New South Wales Planning and Environment Commission (1974–80). He was awarded an OBE in 1976 and became a member of the New South Wales Legislative Council in 1977–78 and again from 1986. Clive Tregear, mayor of Campbelltown from 1964–72, sat on the council of the regional electricity supplier, the Nepean River County Council from 1958, serving as deputy chairman from 1964–71. He was the local government representative on the New South Wales Board of Fire Commissioners from 1969, and a member of the Cumberland County Council in 1963–64 and of the Campbelltown Development Committee (later the Macarthur Development Board) from 1970–75. He was awarded an MBE in 1977.

In June 1953 Campbelltown Council moved its offices to the Memorial School of Arts on the corner of Queen and Lithgow Streets. Council had

Harley Daley, town clerk of Ingleburn 1931–1948, town clerk of Campbelltown 1948–1971.

taken over the building and its library the previous year because the School of Arts was virtually defunct. The RSL continued to occupy a portion of the land. In 1964 multistorey offices were erected on a new site at the northern end of town near the railway and the courthouse. Nearby a civic centre and library were built. The council offices were the first high-rise in the municipality, anticipating the planned growth of the area and the expansion of council responsibilities. These responsibilities were acknowledged when Campbelltown was declared a city in May 1968. By 1979 council required more office space. It had two options—to expand its facilities on its present northern site or to select a new location on the southern perimeter, adjacent to or within the proposed Macarthur Regional Centre. 'Council considered that it had a moral obligation to the Queen Street commercial sector to continue on its site, as an "anchor of confidence", the Civic Centre occupying ... a prominent location on the northern gateway to the commercial area of Campbelltown.' A four-storey building adjacent to the existing offices was opened in 1982, the centenary of local government in Campbelltown.[21]

From the 1960s Campbelltown Council borrowed heavily to finance services and facilities for its rapidly growing population. The community was still too small to provide sufficient rate income to fund these projects and too small to attract private enterprise. Government funding was erratic and could not always be applied to projects that council wanted. Other methods of fund-raising were explored and the council embarked on entrepreneurial activities in commercial and residential developments. Half of the income was used to provide community facilities and the rest reinvested in entrepreneurial projects. This enabled the council to provide services to the new communities more rapidly than would have been possible using rate income alone.

The first project was the annual Fisher's Ghost Festival. In June 1955 the story of Fisher's ghost had been re-enacted, using a sheet over the rump of a cow. In 1956 Campbelltown Council decided to hold a fund-raising parade. No name had been chosen for the festival by June when a Sydney radio station ran an item about Fisher's ghost. A Ghoul League claimed that the ghost appeared at midnight each year on the anniversary of Fisher's murder at the bridge over the creek. An estimated crowd of 1500 Sydneysiders arrived in Campbelltown to wait for the ghost's appearance, convincing council that a Fisher's Ghost Festival could become an attraction. A public holiday was declared for Campbelltown on 19 October 1956 for the first parade led by Campbelltown Camden District Concert Band, formed in 1946. In succeeding years the Fisher's Ghost Festival and the Miss Spirit contest raised funds to build the ambulance station, opened in 1961, and the music shell in Mawson Park, built in 1963.[22]

Council raised funds by selling its land to the Housing Commission and other government bodies. These sales provided funds to build Glenquarie Shopping Centre at Macquarie Fields. The 60 shops, opened in

1975, have provided a steady revenue to council. In Queen Street the council built Milgate Arcade with shops and offices, linking the carpark to the main shopping thoroughfare. Council owned a large tract at Woodbine which it subdivided into 160 prestige residential lots in the late 1970s. In 1981 it built a cinema in Dumaresq Street because it was unable to attract commercial interests to build leisure facilities. The council purchased the Royal Hotel near the railway in 1975 to demolish for road widening. Until the new road became essential in the mid-1980s, council maintained the licence and operated the hotel under a lessee.

The council also embarked on joint developments with other government bodies. With the Department of Education it built halls, libraries and playing fields that were joint school and community facilities for use seven days a week. In partnership with the Housing Commission it built the Claymore Shopping Centre in 1985–86. In 1986 Eagle Vale Neighbourhood Centre opened on the Landcom development, jointly funded by the State government and Campbelltown Council to provide facilities for playgroups, community meetings, youth groups, recreation, education and social activities. The Airds Activity Centre, an indoor sporting facility, was built by the council on Housing Commission land and operated by the RSL youth club.

Suburbia

Until the 1950s there was no suburban Campbelltown. The rural communities had separate identities and promoted their interests through progress associations (Minto District, Menangle Park, Macquarie Fields and Glenfield), the East Minto Agricultural Bureau and the Kentlyn Association.

The first suburban area was Leumeah and from the beginning it had a strong sense of its own identity. It formed a progress association, with Tom Boland as first president, and purchased land in O'Sullivan Road to build a community hall for social and church gatherings. The hall was opened in 1953 and the following year was used by the primary school until its own building was ready. It was renamed the Helen Stewardson Community Hall in recognition of Helen Stewardson who had lived at Leumeah since 1935 and was a correspondent for the Campbelltown newspaper and active patron of many community groups. The Leumeah Progress Association lobbied for a park, which it named Orana Park in 1955, the Aboriginal word for 'welcome' being an appropriate one because there were so many new residents. In 1960 the post office opened as North Campbelltown, but within three months the residents had convinced the authorities to rename it Leumeah Post Office.[23]

With plans for the rapid expansion of Campbelltown underway from the late 1960s, names were sought for the new areas. Suburb, neighbourhood and locality names were chosen and debated during 1975. A list of names that received acceptable public responses was gazetted by the Geographic Names Board in March 1976. Seven suburbs were created. Five were existing villages along the railway—Glenfield, Macquarie Fields, Ingleburn, Minto and Campbelltown, with two new suburbs at Eagle Vale to the west and Ambarvale in the south, both named after nineteenth-century farms. The seven suburbs would become centres for large shopping complexes and high schools.

Neighbourhoods were smaller areas within the suburbs, based around primary schools and local shops. The neighbourhood areas, except Leumeah, were in undeveloped areas. West of the railway from Minto to Campbelltown were Bow Bowing, St Andrews, Raby, Kearns, Eschol Park, Claymore, Woodbine and Blairmont. South of Campbelltown was Bradbury (previously Sherwood Hills estate), Glen Alpine, Rosemeadow and St Helens Park. To the east along the George's River were Minto Heights, Ruse and Airds. The rural areas, retained under scenic protection and open space plans, were designated localities—Long Point, Denham Court, Varroville, Kentlyn, Wedderburn, Gilead and Menangle Park.

A few of the new names recognised local pioneers, such as William Kearns, James Ruse and Thomas Rose (Rosemeadow), but most of the names were existing property and placenames, though not always applied to their original sites. The neighbourhoods of Raby, Eschol Park, Woodbine and Ambarvale are not on the properties of those names, while Airds, once a name covering most of the City of Campbelltown, was confined to one residential area. Selecting names with widespread approval was not easy. Warby was rejected in favour of Minto Heights. Claymore was a compromise following objections that Badgally was not suitable for a Housing Commission development likely to include many single-parent families. Badgally could easily become an insult as 'Bad Girlie' or 'Bad Gully'. Claymore, a double-edged Scottish sword, was the name of a nearby farm and was an acceptable compromise.

The rate of suburbanisation followed a geographic pattern, with the northern suburbs of the City of Campbelltown growing rapidly in the early 1970s, the middle area in the late 1970s, and the southern suburbs in the 1980s. Glenfield and Macquarie Fields almost doubled their population between 1971 and 1976. The Housing Commission developed an area bounded by Victoria, Harold and Cadogan Roads in eastern Macquarie Fields in 1972 and by 1974 had built 1035 dwellings there. In the same period (1970–75) 615 private homes were built. Minto until 1976 was still a village on the railway line. It did not grow significantly until the Housing Commission estate was developed in late 1976. Change at Ingleburn, Leumeah and Bradbury was less spectacular, depending on private developers rather than public housing.

Central Campbelltown had been well built on by subdivisions in the 1950s and early 1960s. The last poultry farm on the Waminda soldier settlement closed in 1960 and the area east of the old town toward the

George's River was redeveloped for residential use. Ambarvale, to the south, and Raby, to the north-west, were developed as private subdivisions of house and land packages with some townhouses in the late 1970s. Land at Eschol Park and Eagle Vale was released by Landcom during the same period, and Claymore was developed by the Housing Commission. The late 1980s will see expansion mainly in the south at Ambarvale, Glen Alpine, Rosemeadow (all three by Lend Lease) and St Helens Park.

The most heavily populated suburbs are Woodbine, Leumeah, Campbelltown, Ruse, Bradbury and Airds. In contrast to these suburbs, land on the outskirts of the city has been designated either scenic or rural to preserve natural landscape around the more densely developed centre. High-density subdivision is prohibited along the George's River at Minto Heights, Kentlyn and Wedderburn, in the south at Gilead and Menangle Park, and in the north-west along the Central Hills in Denham Court and Varroville. The large blocks and scenic surroundings have attracted many expensive homes.[24]

The population of the Macarthur region in 1981 was 224 500, greater than either Canberra or Wollongong. Almost half the region's population lived in Campbelltown. For many, the move to Campbelltown in the 1960s was a 'quality-of-life' decision, a preference to live in a country village yet still be close to the city. The pace was slower; Saturday-morning shopping along Queen Street was a leisurely affair, with frequent stops to chat to friends and acquaintances. Inevitably this sense of community faded as the city grew rapidly in the 1970s and the faces in the street were more often those of strangers.

At the Census in 1976 the population of the City of Campbelltown was 53 700. By the next Census in 1981 it had increased by 70 per cent to 91 525. Estimates in 1983 indicated a population of 105 500, almost double the figure of 1976. Inevitable delays between population growth, local job creation and the provision of community facilities has created strains.

Government housing policies as well as cheaper land and houses in private developments have attracted a young population. From 1966, when the average age of Campbelltown residents was 27.3 years, the population has become rapidly younger. By 1981 it had more young people than the rest of Sydney, with 38 per cent under 15 years of age and 46 per cent under 20, compared with the Sydney averages of 23 per cent (under 15) and 31 per cent (under 20). Most of the young were concentrated in the newly developed suburbs. Middle-aged and older people were rare, with only 18 per cent of Campbelltown's population over 40 years of age (Sydney average, 36 per cent).

Young populations create heavy demands for health, education, leisure and welfare support services. The expense of providing such services was increased by the physical isolation of Claymore and other areas west of the freeway, where there was no direct access to existing facilities in the old villages along the railway line. Over 14 000 people in 1985, about

214

one-fifth of the adult population, received government benefits—unemployment, invalid, supporting parents or old age pensions. At the 1981 census Campbelltown had the highest Sydney average of public housing tenants—27.7 per cent compared with Sydney average of 5 per cent. By 1985 this had climbed to an estimated 33 per cent.[25]

These social imbalances are seen most clearly in the suburbs of Ruse and Airds, east of Campbelltown. Ruse was developed privately in the mid-1970s and in 1976 had a very young population, with 75 per cent under 29 years of age and 86 per cent under 34. Airds, developed at the same time by the Housing Commission, also concentrated a young population with 91 per cent of residents below 34 years of age in 1976. These suburbs were away from the railway and residents had to rely on private bus services or cars to get to shops and the railway station at Campbelltown.

Juvenile crime and family law matters are the most frequent cases before the magistrates at Campbelltown. Lack of privacy in the Housing Commission developments has been cited as a factor causing domestic conflicts to escalate into community problems. Cases of domestic violence and child abuse are increasing; in 1981–82 it had the State's largest number of referrals of children at risk. The high rate of juvenile crime, 132 cases per 1000 juveniles in the population compared with a metropolitan average of 73 per 1000, reflects the age imbalance and poor local employment prospects.[26]

Unlike other districts with rapidly growing populations, Campbelltown did not attract migrant groups from non-English-speaking backgrounds. Because of the lack of secondary industry in the area in the 1950s, few immigrants were attracted. Some Italian and Yugoslavian families settled on 5-acre (2 ha) farms at Ingleburn where land was cheaper than Campbelltown. Most of Campbelltown's new residents were Australian-born from other parts of Sydney. Bradbury residents included many British migrants who learned of the Lend Lease estate in migrant hostels in the 1960s. With 78 per cent Australian-born and 12 per cent British-born, Campbelltown was more homogeneous in ethnic origins that the rest of Sydney (90 per cent compared with 82 per cent). Since 1981 this has altered slightly with small groups of non-British migrants, especially Lebanese and Vietnamese, coming to the area.

The Census of 1971 identified only 62 Aborigines living in the City of Campbelltown. By 1981, 734 Aboriginal and 41 Torres Strait Islanders lived there. Estimates by community workers in the mid-1980s indicate about 3500 local residents who identify themselves as Aboriginal. Most live in Airds, transferred there by the Housing Commission from Nowra and Moree in the mid-1970s. The Tharawal Aboriginal Land Council was created in September 1983 to provide services for Aboriginal people in the Campbelltown area. When the RSL Bowling Club went into receivership in 1985, the lease of the property was transferred to the Tharawal Aboriginal Co-operative Society Ltd. Funded through the Department of

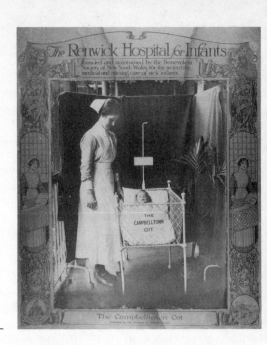

The Campbelltown Cot. Without a local hospital until 1979, Campbelltown citizens sponsored beds in other hospitals.

Aboriginal Affairs, the Tharawal Co-operative Centre provides medical, dental, alcohol and drug counselling services, advice about legal and accommodation difficulties and a child day-care facility. The Tharawal Land Council is developing an Aboriginal arts centre next to the Thirlmere National Park, using converted railway carriages to house a museum, lecture rooms, kitchens and on-site accommodation.[27]

Land for a public hospital at Campbelltown had been reserved on the corner of Stewart and Lithgow Streets in 1907, but, with a small population and lack of funds, the hospital was never built. In 1973 a new hospital site was approved and planning started. By 1977 work had not commenced and protest meetings and street processions demonstrated community concern about the lack of hospital and medical facilities. Stage 1 of the Campbelltown City Hospital was completed in 1979, but it did not offer a full range of medical services. Though statistics from the mid-1970s had shown a concentration of women of child-bearing ages and a higher birth rate than the New South Wales average, stage 2 of Campbelltown Hospital, incorporating maternity facilities, was not opened until 1986. Stage 2 included a children's ward, rehabilitation unit and psychiatric annexe. The first public-hospital-based day surgery unit was established at Campbelltown Hospital. Coordination of health facilities has been the responsiblity of the Macarthur Area Health Board, covering Camden, Campbelltown and Wollondilly, since 1983.

In 1946 the government considered resuming Glenlee estate to build a new mental health hospital. The proposal met strong opposition in Campbelltown and the local member, Jeff Bate, conveyed these feelings to parliament pointing out the historic significance of Glenlee and the Fitzpatrick family's contribution to the district. Furthermore, the 1400-

hectare estate was a working dairy farm and market garden where 32 people earned their living. Debates on the Glenlee Mental Hospital continued until 1950 when the proposal was dropped.[28]

Homes for the aged were opened at Glenfield in 1950. In 1946 Ethel Easton Symonds, widow of Charles Joseph Symonds, gave 21 acres (8.4 ha) at Ingleburn to the Freemasons to build a home for the aged and infirm. Called Easton Park, it became one of the Frank Whiddon Masonic Homes. The first cottage was built in 1950 and by 1956 it provided accommodation for 120 aged men and women. In August 1963 a home for aged White Russians and a monastery were built by the Russian Orthodox community at Kentlyn. White Russians had fled from Russia to China following the revolution in 1917. When the Chinese Communists came to power in 1949 many Russians migrated to Australia in the 1950s, often bringing elderly grandparents with them.[29]

Working in Campbelltown

Work in Campbelltown changed from the 1950s. As the town grew as a residential area, rural industry declined and with it the number and type of jobs available locally. More people had to travel to work, most by the mid-1960s finding jobs in manufacturing in the inner city.[30]

Dairying remained the most prominent rural occupation until the 1960s when farms were sold for residential development. An average dairy farm was 80–120 hectares with 50–75 cows, usually Friesians. Dairying became more mechanised after the war and most farms had milking machines. Campbelltown dairymen had been worried that Dairy Farmers Co-operative planned to close the Campbelltown milk depot. Instead, the plant was modernised in 1950. There were 38 registered suppliers to the factory in 1950, increasing to 41 in 1951. The milk quota system, setting production limits for each farm, was introduced in 1955. Campbelltown was represented on various dairy industry organisations. F. J. (Mate) Sedgwick had been active on the Milk Zone Dairymen's Council before the war, and after the war was the producers' representative on the Milk Board. He served on Campbelltown Council from 1944 to 1959 and was an active member of the Campbelltown Agricultural Society and board of the Camden Hospital. Another long-serving alderman, Arch Walker, a chartered accountant and Campbelltown dairy farmer, joined the board of Dairy Farmers Co-Operative Ltd in 1952, becoming its chairman in 1981. He retired from the board in 1986.[31]

Milk was collected in tankers from the farms by 1966. In 1967 only eighteen local dairies supplied milk to the Campbelltown depot, and the depot was closed. Shortly afterwards it burnt down. In 1968 Dairy Farmers Co-operative opened a new depot in the Campbelltown industrial estate to handle bottled milk. Regional development plans had eroded rural industry in Campbelltown by the late 1960s. Glenroy dairy had been owned by the McClelland family since 1929 when Charles and Minnie McClelland transferred their milk business from Turramurra. Allan McClelland died in 1959; over the next decade dairying became less viable and the family sold Glenroy to the State Planning Authority in 1969.[32]

Milton Park, Ingleburn, was purchased in 1952 by the McGarvie Smith Veterinary Research Institute. John McGarvie Smith (1844–1918) was a metallurgist who became interested in bacteriology. During the 1890s he discovered a vaccine which prevented anthrax in cattle and sheep. One inoculation gave lifetime protection from the disease and the vaccine kept indefinitely so it could be exported throughout the world. McGarvie Smith kept the formula a secret until just before his death when the New South Wales government urged him to confide the formula to two well-known scientists. McGarvie Smith then established a fund for an institute, controlled by a joint board representing the government and the pastoral industry, to manufacture and distribute the vaccine. The McGarvie Smith Institute converted Milton Park to research laboratories and continued its work into dairy cattle husbandry at Ingleburn until 1972. The following year Milton Park was purchased by Campbelltown City Council.[33]

Glenfield Veterinary Research Station expanded its research laboratories after the war with several new facilities for studying poultry diseases in 1963 and noxious and feral animals in 1972. The South-Western Freeway cut through the station's property in the mid-1970s and its surroundings became increasingly urban. In the mid-1980s plans were made to move the research station to Camden Park to join other rural-science research institutions there.

Coal deposits had been found south of Campbelltown in the nineteenth century. The Illawarra coastal coalfields were developed from the 1850s, but the inland fields of the Wollondilly district were not opened until the 1930s. After World War II these mines were expanded. Coal was trucked from Burragorang to Narellan, then taken by the Camden tram to Campbelltown and the main rail network. The Joint Coal Board improved coal-loading facilities at Campbelltown in 1953 and a new siding was built at Glenlee on the main rail line in 1958, replacing the Narellan coal depot because the gradients on the Camden line were too steep to increase the loads. Output from the Burragorang mines increased significantly in the 1960s. The coal was exported via rail facilities at Glenlee and Campbelltown. In 1963 a new coal-loader at Balmain and coal elevators at Campbelltown were built. The value of the exports justified electrification of the rail link from the city to Campbelltown to speed up the freight trains. Work on electrification started in 1965 and was completed in 1968.[34]

With the expansion of the Appin mines and changing economies in the industry during the mid-1970s, coal was increasingly trucked by road to the Port Kembla coal-loader, built in 1964. The coal-loading facilities at Campbelltown were phased out and demolished in 1986. The Glenlee rail siding and coal washery, owned by Clutha Mining, was also phased out because of fears of its environmental impact on the nearby Nepean River. Long-term plans for the south-western coalfields include a rail link from Maldon and Dombarton to Port Kembla.

Sand deposits along the George's River had been mined, often illegally, since the 1930s when trucks were able to reach the sites. The sand was sold for building uses in Sydney. In the 1950s one of the best-known rogues among the sandminers was Bob Simmonds, better known as Simmo. A picnic site and recreation area formed in regenerated bushland along the George's River was named Simmo's Beach in 1986.[35]

Industrial development was an essential element in regional planning. In practice, the government faced considerable difficulties in generating sufficient local jobs for the large number of people who settled at Campbelltown. From 1975 the Macarthur Development Board had limited success in attracting high-employment industries to the district. Some companies were deterred because Campbelltown was outside the metropolitan telephone district.

There was little manufacturing industry in Campbelltown before the 1970s. During the war Gala Sports Wear established a clothing factory in 1942, employing mainly women. Staff turnover was negligible because there were few other local jobs for women, and in 1953 it had a waiting list of potential employees. Other local manufacturers were small family businesses. Two small factories made surgical and tennis gut in Ingleburn in 1947. The Spiroflex Manufacturing Company, founded by Eric Klages in Cambridge Street Ingleburn, exported gut surgical sutures and strings for sporting equipment and musical instruments. It closed in 1986. Thomas Gonsalves started making boat oars and sculls in a large fibro and iron garage in northern Campbelltown in 1947, employing up to five men. After his death in 1956 the factory was taken over by his son-in-law, Brian Favelle, and a former employee, Roger Woollard. They broadened the range of timber products, making packing cases as well as marine supplies. A much larger enterprise was the fireworks factory which Celestino Foti established at Campbelltown in 1954. His family had been making fireworks at Messina in Italy since 1798. Foti moved to larger, and more isloated, premises at Menangle Park in 1956 where he employed as many as 89 people. Later the factory moved to Leppington.[36]

Crompton Parkinson, an electrical-equipment manufacturer, purchased the Blair Athol estate in July 1945, but postwar credit restrictions delayed its plans to move to Campbelltown. Its new factory finally opened in 1957. Nile Industries, manufacturing clothing and table linen, started construction of its factory on the western side of the railway at Campbelltown in July 1959 and opened in April 1960. However, it was not until the late 1960s and the Sydney Region Outline Plan that there was significant interest among manufacturers in moving to Campbelltown. Among the early companies who came to Campbelltown were Harco Steel (1968), Blue Strand Industries (1969), Bullmer's Strongbow Cider and Metroll (1970). In 1970 the government announced that Chrysler would build a car plant at Campbelltown. These plans came to naught, as did plans for a Ford automotive plant. Comalco and Wunderlich Aluminium built a plant at Minto in 1973. Volvo Australia, five years after starting business in Australia, opened a $30 million computerised warehouse for spare parts at Minto in May 1975. Pirelli–Ericsson Cables and Johnson and Johnson opened their Campbelltown plants in 1977, followed by Lever and Kitchen which built a detergent-powder plant in 1979. A proposal by Pilkington ACI in 1987 to build a glass factory at Ingleburn was considered a major boost for local employment prospects.[37]

Most of these companies were relocating from inner-suburban areas. Nile Industries had moved from Ashfield; Crompton Parkinson from Five Dock, attracted by cheaper land in areas not hemmed in by residential suburbs. By the mid-1970s many postwar factories were obsolete. New technologies required different factory layouts and old sites could not always be converted economically to new production methods. In 1987 this was the major reason for investment in factories at Campbelltown. Comalco planned to move operations from Yennora to Minto, and likewise the Otis Elevator Company from Bankstown to Minto, both seeking additional space for new technology. Lever and Kitchen extended its Minto plant, building a $12 million liquid-detergent plant there, to take advantage of technology which could not be installed so effectively on its former site at Balmain.[38]

The increased presence of manufacturing industry at Campbelltown from the mid-1970s was not necessarily an effective stimulus in creating local jobs. Most companies were relocating and their employees often commuted to the new location at Campbelltown. New technologies required fewer staff than the old ones.

In the 1970s and 1980s most people in Campbelltown found work in manufacturing, retailing, the public sector and community services. In 1971, 32.8 per cent of Campbelltown people worked in Campbelltown. A further 13.5 per cent travelled to nearby Liverpool. Sydney was the destination of 10.8 per cent and 7.7 per cent worked in Bankstown. A decade later the statistics were much the same, the only significant variation being an increase in the numbers working at Bankstown, an area which grew rapidly in the 1970s. There were few jobs at Campbelltown for skilled tradespeople, process workers and clerical staff. Female clerical workers formed the largest group of commuters.[39]

Transport networks to travel to work and around Campbelltown were put under stress from the 1960s as the population soared. Upgrading of the railway in the 1960s and 1970s was due less to population growth than to the importance of the coal export trade. The Camden tramway closed in January 1963, replaced with a bus service. Diesel engines replaced steam trains on the Campbelltown route in 1964 and the railway to the city was electrified in 1968, but as commuter pressure on the suburban rail network increased in the 1970s, many Campbelltown residents believed they had a less satisfactory service than in the years of the old

'Milk Pot' steam train. A new railway station, Macarthur, opened in July 1985 to serve Macarthur Shopping Square, Campbelltown Hospital and the tertiary education centres west of the railway. Peak-hour services between Campbelltown and Sydney Central station took 60 to 70 minutes with trains running every half-hour. Work started on the long-planned East Hills to Glenfield railway. Due for completion in late 1987, it will improve access to jobs at Bankstown and shorten the journey to Sydney.

The rapid spread of residential areas in the 1970s was rarely accompanied by adequate transport. Road access to Campbelltown was improved with the opening of the first stage of the South-Western Freeway from the Liverpool Crossroads to Raby Road in 1973, but major traffic problems remained within and between the new areas. Responsibility for road construction within Campbelltown was divided between the local council, the Macarthur Development Board and the Department of Main Roads. Railway crossings provided a major obstacle to traffic flow within the City of Campbelltown. The level crossing at Broughton Street was closed in 1962 and from the late 1970s bridges were planned to replace crossings at the main suburbs. The Gilchrist Drive bridge (East Bridge) near the Macarthur Regional Centre was completed in 1978 and Henderson Road bridge at Ingleburn was opened in 1987.

In the 1981 census 67 per cent of Campbelltown residents depended on private cars to get to work; only 16 per cent used the train. Yet half of the families had access to only one car and 11 per cent had no cars. Private buses operate under the general planning control of the Urban Transit Authority, but services to new areas with small populations concentrate on weekday peak-hour feeder routes to the railway or local schools. Services outside these hours are irregular and the alternative—taxis—are expensive. With few local shops within walking distance because retailing is concentrated at centres accessible by car, car-less mothers with young children and low-income families living in the more distant suburbs are especially isolated.[40]

An expanding community

Amalgamation of the councils of Campbelltown and Ingleburn in 1948 did not automatically merge the communities of the two districts. Ingleburn did not have a newspaper but from 1951 the *Campbelltown News* published a page of Ingleburn news. Ownership of the *Campbelltown News* changed in September 1952 when the Sidman family sold it to Sid Richardson of the *Picton Post*. J. H. Vernon became editor. The newspaper was renamed the *Campbelltown–Ingleburn News* from January 1953 to attract readers in the northern districts. In 1969 Richardson, who also owned the *Camden News*, the *Picton Post* and the *Macarthur Advertiser*, retired and sold his interests to Suburban Publications, a group owned by John Fairfax and

Consolidated Press. Vernon remained as manager and editor until his death in 1974. By the 1980s as many as six local newspapers covered Campbelltown each week—the *Campbelltown District Star*, the *Macarthur Advertiser*, the *Leader*, the *Champion*, the *Crier* and the *Illawarra Mercury*. Other community information was spread through the radio from May 1978 when Campbelltown Community Radio, broadcasting as 2CT, was established. A community-access public broadcasting station, it was the first of its kind in Australia. Staffed by volunteers, it sought revenue by advertising local businesses but financial difficulties forced its closure in 1981.[41]

Before World War II the schoolteacher had been a dominant figure in small communities. This status changed as the number of schools increased from 1950. Campbelltown was classified as country service by the Department of Education. Teachers appointed to Campbelltown schools served for two or three years, then transferred elsewhere. Few were local people or lived permanently in the district. Usually they had just graduated from teachers' college and had neither teaching nor community experience. This reduced their leadership role.[42]

Before the 1950s young people had little contact with Campbelltown after primary school, leaving the district to go to high school and then to work in the city. This changed when Campbelltown High School opened in 1954, initially in Liverpool then moving to new weatherboard buildings in Rudd Road opposite Beverley Park in 1956. Ingleburn High School also started in temporary premises six years later, moving to its own buildings in 1963. Several high schools were built in the 1970s. Population pressures forced innovation to meet school and community needs. James Meehan High School at Macquarie Fields opened as the State's first community high school, sharing recreation facilities and a hall with the surrounding community. Sarah Redfern High School at Minto was also built as a community school, integrating preschool, primary, secondary and special education in one complex with a community library. Campbelltown had ten public high schools by 1986 with three others planned. Despite the expansion of facilities there was a low retention rate among senior students. In 1981 less than 25 per cent of students in the south-western region continued to final-year high school.

New primary schools were built from the 1950s and existing ones were extended or replaced. East Minto Primary School burnt down in 1947 and the new school was built on a more central site in Minto. At Campbelltown the original school building and teacher's residence, built in 1876, were demolished in 1965 to make room for new buildings as student numbers soared. Despite an initially vocal group who believed that women should care for their own children, a preschool kindergarten opened in the Campbelltown Masonic Hall in November 1946. A kindergarten started in Ingleburn the following year. By 1987 Campbelltown Council provided eight day-care centres.[43]

Non-government schools increased, with eight private schools in the

City of Campbelltown by 1986. Catholic education retained its strong local role, opening the John Therry High School at Ambarvale in 1981. It was the first coeducational Catholic school in the district, joining St Patricks College for girls and St Gregorys College for boys, the latter having increased its intake of local day boys from 1963 and broadened its agricultural curriculum. Mount Carmel Catholic High School at St Andrews was opened in 1986. After a century during which the government and the Catholic Church were the most active educators, other religious denominations entered the field in the 1980s. St Peters Anglican Church returned to education, opening its primary school in 1983. Church-based secondary schools were built—Broughton Anglican College in 1986, Berea College (formerly Macarthur Christian College) and the Sherwood Hills Christian College.[44]

Land had been reserved near the Macarthur Regional Centre for tertiary education facilities. A college of technical education was established in 1980 on a campus at Macquarie Fields. The following year Campbelltown College of Technical and Further Education took its first students at the Narellan Road campus near the regional centre in February 1981. The Macarthur Institute of Higher Education was established as an extension of the Milperra College of Advanced Education. Plans for the Campbelltown campus at the regional centre were announced in 1983. While it was built, students were taught in rented premises at the nearby Maryfields monastery. Hopes that the south-west would be the location of Sydney's fourth university were disappointed in 1986 when a decision was made in favour of a new university along the western railway.

Church building boomed in the 1960s. Denominations already in Campbelltown built additional facilities, the Catholic diocese opening new parish churches at Minto, Macquarie Fields and Glenfield in 1962, while religious orders moved into the rural districts. The Patrician Brothers acquired Smeaton at Narellan for a novitiate in 1963; the Carmelite Fathers built a monastery off St Andrew's Road, Varroville, in 1964, and the Irish Poor Clare Sisters moved to Maryfields, opening Bethlehem Monastery in 1968. The earlier Protestant churches were joined by new ones with a Church of Christ congregation in 1963 and the Campbelltown Baptist Church and Seventh Day Adventist Church in 1964. By 1985 the City of Campbelltown had a large and diverse religious community with 8 Catholic churches, 7 Anglican, 7 Baptist, 3 Church of Christ, 3 Uniting, 3 Jehovah's Witness, 2 Salvation Army, 1 Presbyterian, Apostolic, Assembly of God, Baha'i, Russian Orthodox and a Seventh Day Adventist congregation.

In 1953 Campbelltown had five recreation places—the golf course south of town, a football field in the north, the showground, Mawson Park and Hurley Park. By 1986 there were over 1100 sporting teams, many of them junior teams, with facilities both indoor and outdoor for a wide range of sports from swimming, tennis, football and cricket to netball courts, three rollerskating rinks, ten-pin bowling and BMX tracks. The Agricultural

Society moved its annual show to Menangle Park Paceway in 1975. Nearby the National Equestrian Sports Centre was planned. The old Campbelltown Showground became a football field. A new golf course opened in 1979 at Ambarvale, replacing the old site that had become the regional centre. Orana Park grandstand at Leumeah opened in 1985, attracting the Western Suburbs Rugby League Club from Sydney's inner western suburbs to make its home in the new south-west.

While Campbelltown concentrated on the problems of urban expansion in the 1960s and 1970s, Australian military forces were fighting in Vietnam. From 1962 to 1973 Australian troops served alongside American and South Vietnamese forces against Vietcong guerillas and the army of North Vietnam. In 1964 the Australian government introduced conscription for overseas military service. Holsworthy Army Camp was one of the main training centres and many of the soldiers' families lived nearby in Ingleburn. The earliest unit to serve in Vietnam was the Australian Army Training Team in Vietnam (AATTV). One of its members was Warrant Officer Kevin 'Dasher' Wheatley. He had joined the Australian Army in 1956, fought in Malaya and later trained at Holsworthy. In November 1965 Wheatley was one of three Australians on patrol with South Vietnamese Irregulars in Quang Ngai province. He was killed while trying to save a wounded comrade. For his heroism Wheatley was awarded posthumously the Victoria Cross, the first Australian to receive this award for action in Vietnam. In 1968 Campbelltown decided to commemorate Wheatley by naming a new sports centre in his honour. Ten years later the Kevin Wheatley Memorial Oval at Airds was opened as the headquarters of the Campbelltown RSL Youth Club.[45]

The earliest service clubs had appeared in Campbelltown in the 1950s with Legacy (1952), the Country Women's Association (1954) and Apex (1956), the latter becoming involved in the initial Fisher's ghost parades. Rotary was formed at Campbelltown in 1958 with town clerk Harley Daley as president, followed by Lions and Quota (1961) and the VIEW Club in 1964. These organisations usually opened new groups at Ingleburn within a few years. Ingleburn Apex was formed in 1963 and Ingleburn Rotary in 1977. By the 1980s there were more than 400 community organisations, clubs and hobby groups in the City of Campbelltown. The larger clubs provided much needed community facilities for entertainment. The Campbelltown RSL Club opened its new Lithgow Street premises in February 1962, followed by Ingleburn RSL in December 1962 and the Catholic Club in Camden Road in 1968.

Close to the south coast beaches, in the 1950s Thirroul and Austinmer were popular Sunday and weekend outings for Campbelltown residents. Improved transport has increased access to these resorts and opened up nearby riverside and bushland areas for recreation. New reserves along the George's River joined the traditional spots at the Woolwash and Frere's Crossing. Two major city parks are being developed. Koshigaya Park, named after Campbelltown's sister city in Japan, recognises an active programme of student and cultural exchanges between Japan and Campbelltown. City Park will be developed around the regional centre. Further south at Kenny Hill the State premier announced in September 1984 that 500 hectares would be developed as a botanic garden and arboretum for the Bicentenary in 1988. The Mount Annan Botanic Gardens will become a major centre for Australian native plants.

With the eastern backdrop of the George's River bushland and the western horizon marked by the rolling slopes of the Central Hills, Campbelltown has retained the most impressive element of the nineteenth-century country town—its landscape.

Appendix 1

Population of Campbelltown and Ingleburn

Year	Campbelltown		Ingleburn
	Town[1]	*District*[2]	
1821		1 973	
1828		1 691	
1836	775		
1841	446	3 072	
1846	541	1 935	
1856		7 827	
1861	938		
1871	592	1 873	
1881	688		
1891	2 381		
1901[3]	2 152		362
1911	1 825		379
1921	2 345		545
1933	2 835		1 881
1947	3 746		3 274[5]
1951[4]	8 430		
1956	10 440		
1961	18 700		
1966	25 695		
1971	34 235		
1976	53 700		
1981	93 250		
1986	121 297		

Notes
1 Town usually means Parish of St Peter.
2 Police district, extending south occasionally covering Picton but never north (Minto–Glenfields). Figures for the northern areas were aggregated with Liverpool.
3 Figures cover municipalities.
4 Figures cover combined municipalities of Campbelltown and Ingleburn.
5 In 1948 Ingleburn amalgamated with Campbelltown.

Source Compiled from colonial returns and musters, Census of New South Wales and Census of Australia.

Appendix 2

Mayors of Campbelltown and Ingleburn

Date	Municipality of Campbelltown	Municipality of Ingleburn
1882	J. Ahearn	
1883	C. Bull	
1884	A. Munro	
1887	W. B. Caldwell	
1888	W. Cummins	
1889	W. Graham	
1890	J. Bocking	
1891	D. H. Barker	
1892	W. B. Caldwell	
1893	H. E. Vaughan	
1894	N. Doyle	
1895	T. Gamble	
1896	D. H. Barker	S. G. Barff
1899	E. Sedgwick	"
1900	W. Cummins	"
1901	F. Moore	S. J. Percival
1903	"	P. Scanlon
1904	"	W. Piggott
1906	"	P. C. Lucas
1907	"	W. Piggott
1908	"	P. C. Lucas
1909	S. Bursill	"
1912	"	J. H. Whitehouse
1913	"	W. Harris
1914	F. Moore	"
1916	"	O. Black
1919	C. Hannaford	A. J. Harper
1921	"	H. Chivers
1925	R. L. Gamble	"
1926	P. C. Marlow	"
1930	J. W. Kershler	"
1931	"	G. Naylor
1932	"	G. Hopping

Campbelltown

1932	J. W. Kershler	H. J. Maze
1934	"	C. C. Murray
1937	J. Westbury	"
1939	P. C. Marlow	H. H. Bainbridge
1940	"	J. S. Freeman
1942	"	W. C. Hosking
1944	"	S. Cook
1946	P. Solomon	"
1948	"	C. C. Murray

Amalgamated Municipality of Campbelltown

1949	P. Solomon
1951	P. C. Marlow
1953	J. G. Farnsworth
1957	F. J. Sedgwick
1960	H. G. Percival
1962	K. V. Whitten (Mrs)
1963	T. K. Fraser
1965	C. W. Tregear

City of Campbelltown

1968	C. W. Tregear
1973	C. C. Mulholland
1974	R. A. Barton
1976	G. K. Fetterplace
1981	G. Thomas
1983	B. Regan
1984	G. K. Fetterplace
1985	G. Thomas
1986	B. Regan
1987	P. Primrose

Notes

Abbreviations used in notes:

ADB	*Australian Dictionary of Biography* (unless otherwise stated entry is for person mentioned in text)
AONSW	Archives Office of NSW, Sydney
CAHS	Campbelltown and Airds Historical Society, Campbelltown
CLHC	Campbelltown Local History Collection, Campbelltown City Libary
CH	*Campbelltown Herald*
CN	*Campbelltown News*
C–I News	*Campbelltown–Ingleburn News*
HRA	*Historical Records of Australia*
HRNSW	*Historical Records of New South Wales*
JRAHS	*Journal of the Royal Australian Historical Society*
JRSNSW	*Journal of the Royal Society of New South Wales*
LTO	Land Title Office, Sydney
ML	Mitchell Library, Sydney
pers.comm.	personal communication
SG	*Sydney Gazette*
SMH	*Sydney Morning Herald*
T&C	*Australian Town and Country Journal*

Chapter 1 *1788–1820*

1 Evidence of lifestyles and customs before and during this turmoil is scattered, often conflicting and inevitably drawn from European accounts. Spellings have been standardised.
2 A. Capell 'Aboriginal Languages in the South Central Coast, New South Wales: Fresh Discoveries' *Oceania* 41, 1, p. 21; D. K. Eades *The Dharawal and Dhurga Languages of the New South Wales South Coast* Canberra: Australian Institute of Aboriginal Studies 1976.
3 K. Wiley *When the Sky Fell Down* Sydney: Collins 1985, p. 8; R. J. Lampert and V. Megaw 'Life Around Sydney' in P. Stanbury *10,000 Years of Sydney Life* Sydney: Macleay Museum, University of Sydney, 1980, pp. 70–1; NSW

229

Legislative Council, Select Committee on the Conditions of the Aborigines, 1845; Sydney Prehistory Group *In Search of the Cobrakall* Sydney: National Parks and Wildlife Service 1983, p. 29; Cappell *Aboriginal Languages* p. 22.

4 Lampert and Megaw 'Life Around Sydney' p. 70.

5 Sydney Prehistory Group *Cobrakall* p. 29; E. Stockton 'The Search for the First Sydneysiders' in Stanbury *Sydney Life* p. 54; Lampert and Megaw, 'Life Around Sydney' pp. 67ff.

6 R. H. Mathews 'Ethnological Notes on the Aboriginal Tribes of New South Wales and Victoria' *Journal of the Royal Society of NSW (JRSNSW)* vol. 38, 1904, pp. 203ff.; Sydney Prehistory Group *Cobrakall* pp. 30–53.

7 F. Bodkin-Andrews and G. Andrews 'T'haraua' in R. Lawrance *Why Campbelltown?* Campbelltown: Campbelltown City Council 1985; Wiley *Sky Fell Down* pp. 8, 26ff; W. Tench *Sydney's First Four Years* Sydney: Royal Australian Historical Society and Library of Australian History 1979, pp. 36–7.

8 H. Reynolds *The Other Side of the Frontier* Ringwood: Penguin 1984, pp. 6ff; Wiley *Sky Fell Down* p. 72.

9 D. Collins, *An Account of the English Colony in New South Wales* Vol. 1 Sydney: Royal Australian Historical Society and A. H. and A. W. Reed 1975, pp. 26–7, 76; *Historic Records of Australia (HRA)* series 1, vol. 1, pp. 50, 55; Tench *Sydney's First Four Years* pp. 61, 262.

10 Sydney Prehistory Group *Cobrakall*; Reynolds *Frontier* p. 9; *HRA* vol. 5, p. 585.

11 Collins *English Colony in NSW* vol. 1, pp. xxxix, 365–6, 370; *HRA* vol. 1, p. 550.

12 Collins *English Colony in NSW* vol. 1, p. 402; *HRA* vol. 3, pp. 11, 590; vol. 4, p. 74, 229, 344, 581, 591; vol. 5, pp. 585, 589–90; *Sydney Gazette* 10 July 1803.

13 *HRA* vol. 4, pp. 161, 510–11, 576ff; Australian Dictionary of Biography (*ADB*).

14 *Sydney Gazette* 21 September, 26 October 1806, 22 October 1809.

15 *HRA* vol. 3, pp. 590, 791, 801–2; vol. 4, pp. 462–3; vol. 5, pp. 579ff.

16 Alternative spellings include Gogy, Goguey, Koggie; *HRA* vol. 5, pp. 587–8.

17 *Sydney Gazette* 17, 31 March, 7 April 1805; Wiley *Sky Fell Down* p. 144.

18 Wiley *Sky Fell Down* pp. 123–5, 168–70; *Sydney Gazette* 3 September 1809.

19 T. M. Perry *Australia's First Frontier* Melbourne: Melbourne University Press 1963, pp. 23–24; *HRA* vol. 6, pp. 145–6, 641.

20 *HRA* vol. 7, pp. 174–5; J. Waldersee *Catholic Society in New South Wales 1788–1860* Sydney: Sydney University Press 1974, p. 125; ADB.

21 *HRA* vol. 7, pp. 304–13.

22 *HRA* vol. 7, pp. 268, 318, 436.

23 L. Macquarie *Journals of His Tours in New South Wales and Van Diemen's Land 1810–1822* Sydney: Trustees of Public Library of NSW 1956, p. 17.

24 *Sydney Gazette* 15 December 1810; *Historic Records of New South Wales (HRNSW)* vol. 7, p. 498; M. Ellis *Lachlan Macquarie* Penrith: Discovery Press 1972, pp. 229, 232; Macquarie *Journals*.

25 *HRA* vol. 7, p. 387; F. Walker 'The Southern Road', *Journal of the Royal Australian Historical Society, (JRAHS)* vol. 3, pt 8, 1916; *Sydney Gazette* 12 August, 28 October 1815.

26 Subscriptions for a Court House 1813, Archives Office of NSW (AONSW) 4/1728, f.122.

27 Macquarie *Journals* pp. 113–22.

28 Land Title Office (LTO) PA 6878; PA 9723.

29 LTO PA 8253; V. Fowler *A Chronicle of Campbelltown, NSW* Campbelltown: (n.p.) 1980; Mary Wade History Association *Mary Wade to Us* Sydney Mary Wade History Association 1986.

Notes

30 P. G. Harvey 'Eschol Park Estate—A History' typescript nd, Campbelltown Local History Collection (CLHC).
31 ADB; J. T. Bigge *Report into the Colony of NSW*, Adelaide: Libraries Board of South Australia 1966, p. 141; H. Proudfoot *Colonial Buildings, Macarthur Growth Centre* (Sydney): Macarthur Development Board 1977, pp. 30–33.
32 Proudfoot *Colonial Buildings* pp. 22–4; LTO PA 6116.
33. ADB; AONSW 4/1728, p. 345; LTO PA 6462.
34. Proudfoot *Colonial Buildings* pp. 13–15.
35. AONSW 4/3495, pp. 104, 222, 396.
36 M. Sainty and K. Johnson (eds), *Census of NSW, November 1828* Sydney: Library of Australian History 1980.
37 ADB; AONSW 4/1721; Surveyor's Field Books, AONSW 2/4732–5; Fowler *Chronicle; Sydney Gazette* 5 February 1809, 10 September 1814.
38 *Sydney Gazette* 16 July 1829; Waldersee *Catholic Society in NSW* pp. 125ff; HRA vol. 8, p. 609; G. Dow *Samuel Terry, Botany Bay Rothschild* Sydney: Sydney University Press 1974, pp. 129–30; A. Baldwinson, 'Macquarie Field House and its Restoration' *JRAHS* vol 51, pt 3, September 1965; Philip Bradley pers. comm. February 1987; ADB; J. P. McGuanne 'A Century of Campbelltown' *Campbelltown News*, 1920, p. 4 (pagination from copy held CLHC).
39 Mitchell Library (ML) BT Box 24, p. 5150; *Sydney Gazette* 12, 17 February, 23 June 1824; R. H. Webster *Currency Lad: The Story of Hamilton Hume and The Explorers* Avalon: Leisure Magazines 1982, p. 52.
40 Webster *Currency Lad* pp. 82–3.
41 Waldersee *Catholic Society in NSW* p. 135.
42 ADB; HRA vol. 8, p. 26; vol. 10, pp. 182–3; Webster *Currency Lad* pp. 29–30, 38, 41; R. H. Cambage 'Exploration between the Wingecarribee, Shoalhaven and Murrumbidgee Rivers' *JRAHS* vol. 7, pt 5; W. Leah *The Glenfield Story* Glenfield: n.p. 1984, p. 62.
43 Budbury, Bootbarie, Boodberrie; Macquarie *Journals* pp. 6–10; Wiley *Sky Fell Down* p. 168.
44 *Sydney Gazette* 14 May, 18 June 1814; ML A752, f.183ff.
45 *Sydney Gazette* 18 June 1814; Ellis *Macquarie* p. 354.
46 *Sydney Gazette* 4 June 1814.
47 Bitugally, Bootagallie; Ballanyabbie; Yellooming, Yellaman; Macquarie *Journals* p. 117; AONSW 4/1730, f.213, 218, 224, 227; CLHC.
48 *Sydney Gazette* 9 March 1816; Hassall Correspondence, ML MSS 1177/4, f.619ff.
49 HRA vol. 9, p. 54; *Sydney Gazette* 16, 23 March 1816; AONSW 4/1734, f.149.
50 Wentworth Papers 5 April 1816, ML A752, f.183ff; *Sydney Gazette* 23 March 1816.
51 AONSW 4/1735, f.1–29; Ellis *Macquarie* p. 358.
52 AONSW 4/1735, f.50–9; N. Gunson *Australian Reminiscences and Papers of L. E. Threlkeld* Canberra: Australian Institute of Aboriginal Studies 1974, pp. 4, 316.
53 AONSW 4/1735, f.58–60.
54 ML A752, f.205; HRA vol. 9, pp. 141ff, 342ff; Barry Bridges, Aboriginal and White Relations in New South Wales 1788–1855, MA thesis, University of Sydney, 1966, p. 212; Ellis *Macquarie* p. 358.
55 Elizabeth Macarthur junior to Miss Kingdon, 8 March 1817, in S. Macarthur Onslow (ed.) *Some Early Records of the Macarthurs of Camden* Sydney: Rigby 1973, pp. 310–12.
56 Meehan Papers, ML C90.

57 Elizabeth Macarthur senior to Eliza, 4 February 1826, in S. M. Onslow *Macarthurs* pp. 455–6.
58 John Macarthur to Elizabeth Macarthur, n.d. (1824?), ibid. p. 450.
59 Cambage *Exploration*; Webster *Currency Lad* p. 42.
60 Walker 'Southern Road'; Onslow *Macarthurs* p. 449; M. H. Ellis *John Macarthur* Penrith: Discovery Press 1972, pp. 510–53.
61 Cambage *Exploration* p. 261; E. Buscombe (ed.) *The Blomfield Letters* Sydney: Eureka Research 1982, p. 38; Leah *Glenfield Story*.
62 Sainty and Johnson *Census of NSW 1828*, p. 15; 'Ager Cottage, Airds ... the residence of John Scarr, sketched by himself', with letter extract, January 1828, Campbelltown and Airds Historical Society (CAHS) Collection.
63 AONSW Papers on Aborigines 1833–1834, 4/6666.3.
64 NSW Legislative Council, Select Committee on the Conditions of the Aborigines, 1845.
65 J. J. Malony *Early Menangle* Newcastle: n.p. 1929; B. Groom and W. Wickman *Sydney—The 1850s: The Lost Collections* Sydney: Macleay Museum, University of Sydney 1982, p. 23; McGuanne 'Campbelltown' p. 40.
66 W. Ridley *Kamilaroi and other Australian Languages* Sydney: NSW Government Printer 1875; Webster *Currency Lad* p. 30; R. H. Mathews 'The Thurrawal Language' *JRSNSW* vol. 35, 1901, pp. 127ff; ADB.

Chapter 2 *1820–1840*

1   Macquarie *Journals* pp. 141–66.
2   AONSW 4/1744, p. 307; Macquarie's journal quoted in M. H. Ellis 'The Foundation of Campbelltown' *Campbelltown and Airds Historical Society, Journal and Proceedings* 1, 1948.
3   AONSW 4/1746, pp. 106, 110, 113.
4   Ellis 'Campbelltown' pp. 8–9.
5   AONSW 4/1748, p. 275.
6   *St John the Evangelist Parish Campbelltown: 150 Years* Campbelltown: n.p. 1984.
7   St Peters Church of England, Campbelltown, archival collection.
8   AONSW 5/2296; Macquarie *Journals*.
9   J. Jervis 'Notes on the Early History of Campbelltown' *Campbelltown and Airds Historical Society, Journal and Proceedings* 1, 2, pp. 109–10; AONSW 4/6907; AONSW 2/1544.
10 Jervis 'Early History of Campbelltown' pp. 111–12; *Sydney Gazette* 16 September 1826; AONSW 2/2306.
11 AONSW 2/2306; ADB.
12 St Peters newsclippings. Unlikely to be named after Mary Bannister Brown, Reddall's married daughter, as she was still single when the streets were named.
13 D. N. Jeans 'Town Planning in New South Wales 1829–1842' *Australian Planning Institute Journal* October 1965; Governor's Minute No. 58, 7 May 1828, AONSW 4/992; Report of Committee 18 June 1828, Appendix MM, Executive Council Meeting 15 October 1828, AONSW 4/1516, 4/1439.
14 Quoted in Jervis 'Early History of Campbelltown' p. 109; W. A. Bayley *History of Campbelltown* Campbelltown: Campbelltown City Council 1974, p. 28.
15 ML A331, p. 48.

16 AONSW Reel 1135; 2/2306.
17 *Sydney Gazette* 1 June 1830; Fowler *Chronicle* p. 45.
18 Jervis 'Early History of Campbelltown' p. 110; CLHC.
19 *NSW Calendar and General Post Office Directory* 1832, pp. 56–8.
20 AONSW 4/2370.4.
21 AONSW Maps 1951, 1954, 1967; 2/1537.2.
22 AONSW Map 50.
23 C. Turney *Pioneers of Australian Education* vol. 1, Sydney: Sydney University Press 1969, p. 10; ADB.
24 St Peters archives, Campbelltown; AONSW 4/1774.
25 Reddall to colonial secretary 12 February 1822 (transcribed by Downing), St Peters archives, Campbelltown.
26 AONSW 4/1774.
27 AONSW 4/1774; NSW Colonial Returns.
28 NSW Colonial Returns; ADB.
29 Legislative Council Archives LA015.
30 Legislative Council Archives LA007; NSW Colonial Returns; *Census of NSW* 1841.
31 ML MSS 1810/67, f.40ff; *St John the Evangelist*; J. Kerr and S. Broadbent *Gothick Taste in the Colony of New South Wales* Sydney: David Ell Press and Elizabeth Bay House Trust 1980, pp. 58–9.
32 NSW Colonial Returns; Census of NSW 1841.
33 ML BT 25, p. 5395; AONSW 4/1774.
34 AONSW 4/6671; ML MSS 2482; ML BT 24, p. 5150.
35 *Sydney Gazette* 30 December 1824; 11 March 1826.
36 *Sydney Gazette* 16 September 1826; 25 August 1829; 2 February, 21 August 1830; *Grist Mills* 1, 5, August 1983.
37 Legislative Council Archives LA 011.
38 AONSW 4/2202.1; 4/2370.4; J. Backhouse, *A Narrative of a Visit to the Australian Colonies* London: Hamilton Adams 1843, p. 418.
39 E. Grainger *The Remarkable Reverend Clarke* Melbourne: Oxford University Press 1982, p. 85; *Australian* 5 August 1829; ADB.
40 AONSW 4/2290.4.
41 *NSW Government Gazette* 17 June 1835.
42 Buscombe *Blomfield Letters* pp. 36–7.
43 Perry *First Frontier* pp. 24–5; *Census of NSW* 1828; NSW Colonial Returns; AONSW 4/7257.
44 NSW Colonial Returns; 4/7257; D. N. Jeans *An Historical Geography of New South Wales* Sydney: Reed Education 1972, p. 230.
45 Quoted in J. Ritchie *The Evidence to the Bigge Reports* vol. 2, Melbourne: Heinemann 1971, pp. 55–6.
46 Quoted, ibid. pp. 57–8.
47 AONSW 4/2202.1.
48 LTO PA 8829; *Census of NSW* 1828; J. Israel pers. comm. March 1987.
49 AONSW 4/2329.5.
50 ADB vol. 1; M. Herman *The Early Australian Architects and Their Work* Sydney: Angus and Robertson 1973, pp. 173–5; NSW Calendar 1832; Buscombe *Blomfield Letters*.
51 *Census of NSW* 1828; ADB.
52 LTO PA 6623.
53 ML BT Box 25, p. 5652; NSW Calendar 1832; LTO Book 65, no. 271; C. Lucas

'Glenlee, Menangle NSW' in P. Freeman, E. Martin and J. Dean *Building Conservation in Australia* Canberra: RAIA Education Division 1985.
54 ibid.
55 Harvey 'Eschol Park'; O. Harvard, 'Mrs Felton Mathew's Journal' *JRAHS* vol. 29, pt 2, 1943.
56 ADB: LTO PA 478; *Sydney Gazette* 16 May 1818; McGuanne 'Campbelltown' p. 31; AONSW 4/7267.
57 *HRA* vol. 18, pp. 44–6; AONSW 2/1558.1; 4/3570.
58 *Sydney Gazette* 8 September 1838; *HRA* vol. 22, pp. 449–52; *Australian* 27 June 1840; NSW Colonial Returns 1840.
59 AONSW 4/1249.
60 *Census of NSW* 1828; *Sydney Gazette* 1 December 1825, 12 December 1826; AONSW 4/1843, 4/7267.
61 AONSW 4/7267; *Census of NSW* 1828; ADB.
62 P. Robinson *The Hatch and Brood of Time* Melbourne: Oxford University Press: 1985, p. 232. There were two colonial-born men called George Fieldhouse in Campbelltown in the 1820s. The shoemaker was the son of Fieldhouse of the NSW Corps. The other, father of William and Edwin Fieldhouse, was the son of a convict blacksmith; AONSW 4/7267.
63 AONSW 4/7267.
64 AONSW 4/2370.4; Buscombe *Blomfield Letters* pp. 77–8.
65 *Census of NSW* 1828.
66 NSW Colonial Returns 1830, 1833; *Sydney Gazette* 3 June 1830.
67 *Sydney Gazette* 28 January 1830; *Australian* 15 July 1836; CLHC.
68 ML MSS 1810/55, pp. 185, 293; *Australian* 16 September 1836, 13 January 1837.
69 *Sydney Gazette* 7 April 1821, 18 January 1822.
70 AONSW 4/1814, p. 187; ML A331, p. 294.
71 ML A331, pp. 125–31, 294; AONSW 9/2684, p. 67.
72 AONSW 9/2684.
73 ML Ac 41.
74 *Australian* 16 September 1836; *Sydney Herald* 24 May 1838.
75 A. Harris *Settlers and Convicts* Melbourne: Melbourne University Press 1953, pp. 14–20.
76 J. Tucker *Ralph Rashleigh* Sydney: Pacific Books 1972, pp. 115–46.
77 Buscombe *Blomfield Letters* pp. 47–8, 71–2; *Census of NSW* 1841.
78 *Census of NSW* 1841.
79 *Australian* 3 June, 15 July, 6, 9, 13 September 1836; J. W. C. Cumes *Their Chastity was not too Rigid: Leisure Times in Early Australia* Melbourne: Longman Cheshire/Reed 1979, pp. 124, 127.
80 Backhouse, *Narrative* p. 420; Buscombe *Blomfield Letters* p. 38.
81 *Sydney Gazette* 26 May 1827; Waldersee *Catholic Society in* NSW p. 127; ML MSS 1810/67, p. 107.
82 C. A. Liston, New South Wales under Governor Brisbane, PhD thesis, University of Sydney 1981, pp. 134, 174; NSW Colonial Returns.
83 C. Bateson *The Convict Ships 1787–1868* Sydney: A. H. and A. W. Reed 1974, pp. 340–1, 382; AONSW 4/3495, p. 63; AONSW 4/1865, p. 50.
84 D. R. Hainsworth *The Sydney Traders* Melbourne: Melbourne University Press 1981, p. 183; Ellis *Macquarie* pp. 258, 266–7; AONSW 4/1740, p. 232; 7/2691; *Sydney Gazette* 1 July 1820; Harvey 'Eschol Park'.
85 ADB; ML Af 68; A. McMartin *Public Servants and Patronage* Sydney: Sydney University Press 1983, p. 82.

86   AONSW 4/1865; AONSW 4/1865, p. 50; CLHC; *Sydney Gazette* 23 December 1824.
87   AONSW 5/2296; I. G. Thomas 'Frederick George James Fisher' *CAHS Journal* 1, 2, 1949.
88   C. H. Currey *Sir Francis Forbes* Sydney: Angus and Robertson 1968, p. 461; AONSW 5/2296.
89   *Sydney Gazette* 5 February 1827; ML Af 68.
90   Fisher Family Papers, CLHC.
91   T. L. Robinson, Account of Fisher's death, ML Af 68; *Sydney Gazette* 5 February 1827; *Rex vs Worrell and others* AONSW 5/2296; Gurner's trial transcript, ML A1493; V. Fowler *The Legend of Fisher's Ghost* Campbelltown: Ruse Publishing 1981; Fisher Family Papers, CLHC; Currey *Forbes* pp. 460–2; Thomas 'Fisher'.
92   *Sydney Gazette* 8, 17 March 1827.
93   CLHC.
94   CLHC; *NSW Government Gazette* 4 February, 5 August 1835; *Hill's Life in New South Wales* 7 September 1832.
95   *Hill's Life in New South Wales* 14, 21 September 1832; *Tegg's Monthly Magazine* vol. 1, March 1836; ADB.
96   ML Af 68.
97   *Census of NSW* 1828; ML A5421/1.
98   *Grist Mills* 3, 4; *Sydney Mail* 7 April 1937.
99   ibid.; R. M. Martin *History of British Colonies* vol. 4, London: Cochrane and McCrone, pp. 303–4; *L'Ami de la Maison* 20, 27 March 1856; G. Dutton *The Literature of Australia* Ringwood: Penguin 1972.
100 ML A1493; ML Af 68; AONSW 5/2296.

Chapter 3 *1840–1880*

1   *Census of NSW* 1841, 1856, 1861, 1871, 1881.
2   Waldersee *Catholic Society in NSW* p. 256.
3   C. Smee and J. Provis, *Pioneer Register* vol. 1 Sydney: 1788–1820 Association 1981; McGuanne 'Campbelltown' p. 11; LTO PA 1727; CH 15 February 1899.
4   J. F. Campbell *Squatting on Crown Lands in New South Wales* Sydney: Royal Australian Historical Society and Angus and Robertson 1968.
5   SMH 2 May 1846: T. A. Coghlan *Labour and Industry in Australia* vol. 2, Melbourne: Macmillan 1969, p. 831.
6   ML A281.
7   SMH 5 May 1858; Coghlan *Labour and Industry* vol. 2, p. 835.
8   *Sydney Mail* 14 March 1863.
9   SMH 30 October 1863.
10 M. E. Robinson *The NSW Wheat Frontier 1852-1911* Canberra: Australian National University 1976, pp. 162–8; K. Gibbs (ed.) *The Adventurous Memoirs of a Gold Diggeress* n. p. 1985, pp. 10, 12, 15; Diary, Payten Collection (privately held).
11 *Empire* 25 August 1855; T & C 19 August 1871; AONSW 4/7269.
12 AONSW 4/7268; SMH 28 August 1845; LTO DP 77280; McGuanne 'Campbelltown' p. 47.
13 AONSW 4/7269; T & C 19 August 1871.
14 T & C 30 August 1873, 16 March 1878; *Grist Mills* 2, 1, February 1984.
15 AONSW 4/7257.

16 AONSW 4/7258; Select Committee on the Present State of the Colony, NSW Legislative Assembly, *Votes and Proceedings* 1865–66, vol. 3; Statistical Registers 1861, 1870; T & C 30 August 1873.
17 AONSW 4/508; SMH 12 November 1863; *Sydney Mail* 6 February 1864.
18 Gibbs, *Gold Diggeress* pp. 8–23.
19 T & C 19 August 1871.
20 *Grist Mills* 2, 1; Diary, Payten Collection (privately held); T & C 19 August 1871.
21 T & C 16 March 1878; Scrapbook, Payten Collection (privately held).
22 *Grist Mills* 2, 2; CLHC.
23 S. J. Butlin *Foundations of the Australian Monetary System 1788–1851* Sydney: Sydney University Press 1968, p. 323; *HRA* vol. 21, p. 199.
24 ADB; Dow *Samuel Terry*.
25 ML MSS 1810/55, p. 445.
26 AONSW 2/8786.
27 SMH 19 June, 7 August 1844; ML Map M2 811.11362/1839/1.
28 AONSW 2/8957; McGuanne 'Campbelltown' p. 48.
29 ibid. pp. 5, 45, 49; W. F. Morrison *The Aldine Centennial History of NSW* vol. 2, Campbelltown edn, Sydney: Aldine 1888; Australia Post Historical Office, Campbelltown Post Office, SMH 16 September 1846.
30 McGuanne 'Campbelltown' pp. 47, 49.
31 State Rail Authority Archive Plan 6349/5—'Working Plans for the Liverpool/ Campbelltown Line'; AONSW 4/7269.
32 Statistical Register 1861; AONSW 4/7268.
33 SMH 12 November 1863.
34 ADB; Morrison *Aldine Centennial History*.
35 AONSW 2/9173.
36 AONSW 2/9634; *Grist Mills* 3, 3.
37 D. Paterson, pers. comm. February 1986.
38 McGuanne 'Campbelltown' p 54.
39 *Cumberland Mercury* 13 April 1878; Lucas 'Glenlee'.
40 T & C 16 March 1878.
41 ibid.
42 SMH 21 September 1842, 16 January 1843.
43 SMH 4, 20, 22 October 1845.
44 ML A331; SMH 7 March 1848.
45 ML A2226; ML A331.
46 *Empire* 10 June 1856; McGuanne 'Campbelltown' p. 40; T. Holm, E. McBarron, F. Seers and A. Walker *Campbelltown 1930–1940 Dumaresq Street and Environs* Campbelltown: Campbelltown City Council 1985, p. 5.
47 AONSW 2/9767.
48 *NSW Government Gazette* 14 December 1849.
49 AONSW 2/648.
50 NSW Legislative Assembly, *Votes and Proceedings* 1865–6.
51 *Cumberland Mercury* 25 May 1878.
52 *HRA* vol. 22, p. 238ff.
53 AONSW 4/2682.
54 AONSW 4/2682.
55 SMH 6, 11 September 1843.
56 SMH 19 September, 2 October 1843.
57 *HRA* vol. 23, p. 288; SMH 13 December 1843.

Notes

58 *HRA* vol. 23, pp. 660, 706–8.
59 F. A. Larcombe *The Origin of Local Government in New South Wales* Sydney: Sydney University Press 1973, pp. 199ff.
60 ibid. pp. 247ff.
61 AONSW 4/2682; SMH 30 March 1843; ADB.
62 SMH 18 August 1842, 16 November 1844; *HRA* vol. 22, p. 505; *NSW Government Gazette* 26 December 1843.
63 *Cumberland Mercury* 9 November 1878.
64 E. J. Minchin 'White of Ryde' *Ryde Recorder* December 1971; *Cumberland Mercury* 11 October 1878.
65 *NSW Government Gazette* 26 December 1843; AONSW 2/584.
66 SMH 5 June 1843; *Cumberland Mercury* 3 August 1878.
67 AONSW 2/584; F. Crowley *A Documentary History of Australia* vol. 2, Melbourne: Nelson 1980, p. 434.
68 A. M. Nixon *100 Australian Bushrangers 1789–1901* Adelaide: Rigby 1982; SMH 27 March 1863.
69 *Sydney Mail* 21 April 1866; T & C 5 April 1902.
70 Australia Post Historical Office, Campbelltown Post Office; ML A5421/1; Legislative Council Archives LA073, LA074.
71 SMH 16 June 1846; Larcombe *Local Government in NSW* p. 77; *NSW Government Gazette* 23 January 1855; NSW Legislative Assembly, *Votes and Proceedings* 1862, vol. 5.
72 *NSW Parliamentary Record 1824–1956* Sydney: NSW Government Printer 1957.
73 SMH 16 January, 20 February 1843.
74 SMH 22, 27 June, 4 July 1843.
75 SMH 25 June 1859; Waldersee *Catholic Society in NSW* pp. 247–8, 252.
76 *Australian Men of Mark* Sydney: Maxwell 1888; *Campbelltown News* (CN) 12 February 1932.
77 ADB
78 SMH 23 December 1845; McGuanne 'Campbelltown' pp. 20–1; C. N. Connolly *Biographical Register of the New South Wales Parliament 1856–1901* Canberra: Australian National University Press 1983.
79 ADB; Payten Collection (privately held); J. S. Hassall *In Old Australia* Brisbane: R. S. Hews 1902, pp. 41–4; P. Yeend *King's School Register 1831–1981* Sydney: Council of the King's School 1982.
80 ADB; AONSW 2/8969; A. Dowling, 'Rev. George Fairfowl Macarthur, and St Mark's Collegiate School, Macquarie Fields', *JRAHS*, vol. 10, pt 3, 1924.
81 McGuanne 'Campbelltown' p. 21.
82 AONSW 1/738.
83 AONSW 1/940; 1/963.
84 AONSW 1/963; Legislative Council Archives LA073; Society of Australian Genealogists Archives.
85 AONSW 1/869; 1/963; 5/15248.4.
86 AONSW 1/809.
87 AONSW 1/869, 1/963; J. Burns-Wood *Campbelltown Public School 1876–1976* Campbelltown, n.p. 1976.
88 A. R. Jones in C-I *News* 5 December 1967.
89 AONSW 5/17560.3.
90 AONSW 5/15248.4.
91 D. N. Jeans and E. Koffman 'Religious Adherence and Population Mobility

in 19th Century New South Wales' *Australian Geographical Studies* vol. 10, 1972; *Census of NSW* 1841, 1856.

92 Campbelltown Botanical Collecting Society *Annual Reports 1879–1881* ML; St Peters Archives; M. M. H. Thompson *William Woolls* Sydney: Hale and Iremonger 1986.

93 LTO Book 10, no. 34.

94 *Freeman's Journal* 3 August 1863; McGuanne 'Campbelltown' p. 27 blamed the desecration on Plymouth Brethren among the railway workmen.

95 ADB; *Freeman's Journal* 15 April 1854; Waldersee *Catholic Society in NSW* pp. 198–9, 203–4.

96 CN 7 June 1940 quoting *Sydney Herald* 26 July 1842.

97 E. G. Clancy 'Rural Methodism in New South Wales 1836–1902' in J. S. Udy and E. G. Clancy *Dig or Die* Sydney: World Methodist Historical Society (Aust'asia) 198, p. 97; J. Colwell *The Illustrated History of Methodism* Sydney: William Brooks 1904; SMH 12 October 1846; AONSW Map 2034.

98 McGuanne 'Campbelltown' p. 38; *Sydney Mail* 6 December 1862.

99 ML Map M2 811.11362/[1844]/1.

100 Larcombe *Local Government in NSW* p. 256.

101 *Cumberland Mercury* 15 June 1878; T & C 16 March 1878.

102 *Cumberland Mercury* 24 August 1878; *Australian Handbook and Almanac* 1879.

103 S. Mossman and T. Banister *Australia Visited and Revisited* Sydney: Ure Smith and National Trust of Australia (NSW) 1974, p. 268.

104 SMH 16 January 1843.

105 LTO PA 5241; Dow *Samuel Terry*; P. Cox and C. Lucas *Australian Colonial Architecture* Melbourne: Lansdowne 1978, p. 121.

106 *Sydney Gazette* 24 November 1838; LTO PA 6462; *Sydney Mail* 16 May 1863; McGuanne 'Campbelltown' p. 11; ADB.

107 LTO PA 8380.

108 ML Subdivision Box: *The Holy Bible*, Numbers 12, v., 23–4; Harvey 'Eschol Park'. The original and correct spelling of the estate is 'Eshcol'. In recent years the version 'Eschol' has become common and is the name of the modern suburb of Campbelltown. ADB, entries for Castella, Jenkins and Plunkett.

109 Gibbs, *Gold Diggeress* pp. 7ff; ADB; LTO Book 65, no. 271.

110 G. Rude *Protest and Punishment* Melbourne: Oxford University Press 1978, pp. 104–5; AONSW 4/4008; 4/4508 (there were two men named James Fitzpatrick on the *Mangles* in 1822. Fitzpatrick of Glenlee is not listed in 1828 census); LTO PA 12604, PA 12607, Book 16, no. 90, Book 20, no. 900, Book 363, no. 533.

111 SMH 14 May 1859.

112 T & C 19 August 1871, 31 March 1877, 6 April 1878, 19 April 1879; J. F. Morris, 'Mount Gilead Estate and Windmill, Campbelltown', *JRAHS* vol. 27, 1941; M. H. Ellis *The Beef Shorthorn in Australia* Sydney: n.p. 1932, pp. 155–6.

113 Tom Stootman, Glen Lorne—A measured survey. Unpublished thesis. Master of Built Environment University of NSW, 1982; T & C 6 April 1878.

114 AONSW 2/7955; LTO PA 12643.

115 Malony, *Menangle* pp. 16, 18–19.

116 ML MSS 1810/56, p. 91; SMH 16 September 1846, 26 August 1847; J. Waldersee 'Pre Famine Irish Emigration to Australia', *Journal of the Australian Catholic Historical Society*, vol. 4, 1973; McGuanne 'Campbelltown' p. 23.

117 Percival Collection, CLHC.

118 AONSW 2/9025.

Notes

119 AONSW 2/9337; Fowler *Chronicle*.
120 ML MSS 1810/56; Gibbs *Gold Diggeress* pp. 11–12.
121 AONSW 2/8968; 2/8993; 2/9835.
122 *Illawarra Mercury* 21 March 1879; LTO Book 289, no. 20.
123 SMH 19 May 1842, 3, 12 September 1845, 2, 9 May 1846; *Cumberland Mercury* 29 June 1878; McGuanne 'Campbelltown' pp. 12, 16; LTO Book 20, no. 262.
124 *Cumberland Mercury* 27 April, 29 June, 10 August, 16 November, 7 December 1878.
125 SMH 30 December 1843; *Cumberland Mercury* 20 July 1878; T & C 4 January 1879.
126 *Sydney Mail* 21 May 1870; *Cumberland Mercury* 30 November 1878.

Chapter 4 *1880–1914*

1 *Census of NSW* 1881, 1891, 1911.
2 *Illawarra Mercury* 21 March 1879.
3 AONSW 4/840.1; *NSW Government Gazette* 22 April 1879.
4 AONSW 4/840.1.
5 *Cumberland Times* 4 August 1879, in AONSW 4/840.1.
6 ibid.
7 AONSW 4/840.1; *NSW Government Gazette* 21 March, 2 July, 17 August 1881.
8 T & C 12 April 1905; CH 19 January 1910.
9 F. A. Larcombe *The Stabilization of Local Government in New South Wales 1858–1906* Sydney: Sydney University Press 1976, p. 159.
10 Winton family papers and cuttings, courtesy of Mrs J. Burrell.
11 T & C 12 April 1905.
12 CH 17 February 1904, 19 January 1910.
13 CH 3 February 1897, in AONSW 5/16865A, 17 February 1904.
14 CH 19 September 1906; W. W. Clarke *Official Municipal Year Book and Shires Directory of New South Wales* Sydney: John Sands 1907.
15 *Sydney Mail* 16 November 1889; SMH 21 January 1889; T & C 12 April 1905.
16 SMH 12 October 1888, 21 January 1889.
17 CH 14 February 1880, 15 March 1911; T & C 12 April 1905.
18 CH 14 February 1880; F. J. J. Henry *The Water Supply and Sewerage of Sydney* Sydney: n. p. 1939; ADB; McGuanne 'Campbelltown p. 41.
19 NSW Legislative Council 1890, vol. 1; NSW Statistical Register 1901; T & C 12 April 1905; *Sydney Mail* 5 January 1889.
20 *Sydney Mail* 11 March 1903.
21 Henry *Water Supply* pp. 74–7.
22 I. Dunn and R. Merchant *Pansy the Camden Tram* Burwood: NSW Rail Transport Museum 1982; T & C 20 May 1882.
23 *Census of NSW* 1891, AONSW reel 2536.
24 M. Cannon *Life in the Cities* Melbourne: Nelson 1975, p. 65; 'Glenwood Estate', CLHC; L. Muir 'The Establishment of the Illawarra and Bankstown Lines' RAHS Conference Proceedings 1983.
25 CH 17 February 1904, 19 September 1906, 27 October 1909; T & C 12 April 1905.
26 CH 14 February 1880, 17 December 1902.
27 Crowley *Documentary History of Australia* vol. 3, pp. 264–5; K. T. H. Farrer *A Settlement Amply Supplied* Carlton: Melbourne University Press 1980, pp. 215–21.

28 NSW Legislative Council 1891–92, vol. 2; Clarke *Municipal Year Book*; NSW Statistical Register 1901.
29 *Sydney Mail* 26 August 1893; CH 19 December 1906; *NSW Post Office Directory* Sydney: Wise's Directories 1907.
30 T & C 12 April 1905; CN 1 March 1911.
31 G. E. Fussell *The Farmer's Tools* London: Orbis 1981, pp. 139ff; J. Birmingham, I. Jack, D. Jeans *Australian Pioneer Technology* Richmond: Heinemann Educational Australia 1979, p. 31.
32 E. McBarron 'St Peters Biographia Card Index'; *Census of NSW* 1891.
33 ML Map M3 811.114/1908/1; *Sydney Mail* 4 May 1901.
34 NSW Statistical Register 1901.
35 AONSW 5/15248.4; 5/16355.2; NSW Statistical Register 1901.
36 *Grist Mills* 1, 3 and 4; CN 5 September 1930.
37 *Sydney Mail* 26 August 1893.
38 *Sydney Mail* 15 June 1895.
39 Morrison *Aldine Centennial History*.
40 CH 7 September 1881; LTO PA 12170; CLHC.
41 CLHC.
42 CH 26 January 1910, 10 December 1937.
43 CLHC; T & C 12 April 1905.
44 T & C 12 April 1905.
45 Gore Family Albums, (privately held).
46 T & C 9 February 1884; Morrison *Aldine Centennial History*.
47 Harvey 'Eschol Park'; AONSW 4/1202.
48 Derived from 1884 Rate Book analysis by P. Down, CAHS.
49 Managers' half-yearly report, Westpac Archives; LTO Book 760, no. 715; CH 28 February 1906.
50 Z. Denholm 'James Tyson, Employer' in A. Birch and D. Macmillan (eds) *Wealth and Progress* Sydney: Angus and Robertson 1967; C. Sheil *Doneley, Tyson and Sheil: Some Historical Aspects of Three of Australia's Oldest Families* Sydney: n.p. 1980.
51 1884 Rate Books, CLHC; ML Subdivision Boxes; Lands Department Map C1.2287; *Census of NSW* 1891.
52 CH 14 February 1880; Farrer *Settlement* p. 24; *Grist Mills* 3, 5; *Grist Mills* 1, 4.
53 Various tenders in AONSW school files.
54 CH 19 January 1898.
55 *Sands Sydney, suburban and country commercial Directory* 1901; *Wise's Post Office Directory* 1908.
56 ibid.
57 AONSW 5/15248.4; Burns-Wood *Campbelltown Public School*; L. Whan and A. West *Glenfield Public School 1882–1982: A History* Glenfield; n.p. 1982.
58 *St John the Evangelist*; *Census of NSW* 1891; *Census of Australia* 1901.
59 CH 19 January 1898, 17 December 1902; T & C 12 April 1905; *Census of Australia* 1901; *Grist Mills* 3, 5.
60 CH 14 February 1880, 23 November 1910; J. Jervis *A History of the Berrima District 1798–1973* Sydney: Library of Australian History and Berrima County Council 1978, p. 116.
61 CH 14 February 1880.
62 AONSW 2/9983; R. B. Walker *The Newspaper Press in New South Wales 1803–1920* Sydney: Sydney University Press 1976, pp. 176, 179.
63 CH 23 November 1910; S. Hertog *The Township of Yerranderie* The Oaks: The Oaks Historical Society 1986; AONSW 2/10323.

Notes

64 Walker *Newspaper Press* pp. 190–1; SMH 11, 12, 15 December 1884.
65 Walker *Newspaper Press* p. 230; SMH 28 November 1882; C. N. Connolly *Biographical Register of the New South Wales Parliament 1856–1901* Canberra: Australian National University Press 1983.
66 Connolly *Biographical Register*; H. Radi, P. Spearritt and E. Hinton *Biographical Register of the New South Wales Parliament 1901–1970* Canberra: Australian National University Press 1979; CH 17 February 1904.
67 Connolly *Biographical Register*.
68 ibid.
69 Radi et al. *Biographical Register*; C. A. Hughes and B. D. Graham *Voting for the NSW Legislative Assembly 1890–1964* Canberra: Department of Political Science, Australian National University 1975.
70 ADB; Fowler *Chronicle*; Connolly *Biographical Register*.
71 ML A5407.
72 LTO DP 192596.
73 ML A5407/3; CLHC.
74 AONSW 5/17560.3; 5/16864A.
75 *NSW Government Gazette* 10 March 1879; AONSW 5/16865A; CN January 1954.
76 CH 23 November 1910; *Wise's Post Office Directory* 1908; D. Dolon *Sydney's Colonial Craftsmen* Sydney: Australiana Society and Historic Houses Trust of NSW 1982; W. Gemmell *And So We Graft From Six to Six: The Brickmakers of New South Wales* Sydney: Angus & Robertson 1986, pp. 18–20.
77 LTO PA 6428; PA 8829; DP 56428; DP 58829.
78 *Census of NSW* 1891, AONSW reel 2519; LTO PA 5663; *Liverpool Herald* 11 June 1898 in AONSW 5/16355.2.
79 AONSW 5/16355.2.
80 *NSW Government Gazette* 22 October 1895.
81 *Biz (Fairfield)* 17 October 1946.
82 Morrison *Aldine Centennial History*; Connolly *Biographical Register*; CLHC.
83 *Biz* 17 October 1946; *Grist Mills* 1, 4; CLHC.
84 CH 9 February 1898; Anon, *Fifty Years of Barnabites, Past and Present* Ingleburn: n.p. 1976; W. A. Bayley *History of Campbelltown* Campbelltown: Campbelltown City Council 1976, pp. 124–6; CLHC.
85 T & C 14 June 1911.
86 *Census of NSW* 1891, AONSW reel 2536; LTO DP 65732.
87 LTO PA 15732; Radi et al. *Biographical Register*.
88 ADB; Morrison *Aldine Centennial History*; LTO PA 5241; LTO vol. 618, f.6; ML Subdivision Boxes.
89 F. A. Larcombe *Change and Challenge: A History of the Municipality of Canterbury* Canterbury: Canterbury Municipal Council 1979, pp. 172–3; L. Muir, A Wild and Godless Place—Canterbury 1788–1895, MA thesis, Department of Geography, University of Sydney 1984; CLHC.
90 *Census of NSW* 1891; LTO vol. 680, f. 32; ML Subdivision Boxes.
91 Muir, Canterbury.
92 Whan and West *Glenfield Public School*; CLHC; Bayley *Campbelltown* p. 126.
93 NSW Legislative Assembly *Votes and Proceedings* 1896, vol. 3; Leah *Glenfield* P. 82.
94 LTO PA 6116; ML Subdivision Boxes; G. F. Macdonald *Historic Denham Court* n.p. n.d.; ADB; CLHC.
95 C. O. Etchells, pers. comm. June 1986; Public Works *Annual Reports*.
96 *Grist Mills* 3, 5.

97 L. Horden *Children of One Family* Sydney: Retford Press 1985, p. 164ff; *Census of NSW* 1891.
98 *Sydney Mail* 4 May 1901; *Census of NSW* 1891; 'George's River Regional Open Space Study' Brisbane: Environment Science and Services Consultants Pty Ltd 1977.
99 CH 17 August, 28 September, 12 October 1898, 10 February 1909; CN 30 March 1923; *Grist Mills* 3, 2; *Census of NSW* 1891; G. Percival, pers. comm. October 1986; ADB.
100 Campbelltown Council Minutes 1885–8; SMH 2 October 1886; T & C 31 August 1889; CH 19, 26 January 1898; R. Sutton, pers. comm. November 1986; CLHC.
101 CH 24 January, 15 August 1900, 30 January, 29 May 1901; CN 10 December 1937.
102 CH 2 October 1907.
103 T & C 12 April 1905; ADB.
104 CH 2 October 1907.
105 NSW Legislative Assembly, *Votes and Proceedings* 1896, vol. 3.
106 AONSW School files for Campbelltown area.
107 CH 14 February 1880; Campbelltown Council Minutes 17 August 1882, 4 January 1883.
108 CH 8 January, 6 August 1902, 18 October 1905, 28 February, 19 December 1906.
109 *Grist Mills* 1, 5; CH 14 December 1898, 22 March 1899; T & C 12 April 1905; Campbelltown Council Minutes 17 February 1887.
110 CH 24 June 1903, 28 February 1906.
111 Gore Family Album (privately held).
112 CH 21, 28 August 1907, 19, 26 January 1910.
113 Gore Family Album (privately held).
114 Gore Family Album (privately held); LTO DP 7479.
115 *Sydney Week by Week* 19 May 1898.
116 *Daily Telegraph* 7 May 1900.
117 *Smith's Weekly* 15 January 1938.
118 *Sydney Stock and Station Journal* 27 March 1908; T & C 10 June 1914.
119 Diary, Payten Collection (privately held); Gore Family Album (privately held); CH 21 May 1902.

Chapter 5 *1914–1945*

1 CH 25 September 1915.
2 ibid.
3 War Service Committee Minutes, CLHC; F. K. Crowley *Modern Australia in Documents* vol. 1, Melbourne: Wren 1973, pp. 266–7.
4 CN 25 January, 6 September 1919; Campbelltown RSL; Oke Etchells, pers. comm. June 1986; Commonwealth War Graves Commission.
5 CH 25 September 1915; War Service Committee Minutes, CLHC; *Daily Telegraph* 2 December 1920.
6 CH 25 September 1915, 8 June 1918; M. McKernan *The Australian People and the Great War* Sydney: Collins 1980, pp. 67–72.
7 ibid. pp. 86–7; C. Johnson *Looking Back at Liverpool: An Oral History* Liverpool: Liverpool City Council 1986, p. 6.
8 CH 25 September 1915; McKernan *Australian People* pp. 150ff.

Notes

9   CH 8 June 1918; Johnson *Liverpool* pp. 12ff.
10 CH 25 January, 11 October 1919.
11 CN 24 December 1924; Burns-Wood *Campbelltown Public School*.
12 War Service Committee Minutes, CLHC.
13 Crowley *Modern Australia* vol. 1, pp. 263–4.
14 McKernan *Australian People* p. 209; CH 15 June 1918.
15 CN 11 October 1919; *Sydney Mail* 8 December 1920; Burns-Wood *Campbelltown Public School*; CLHC.
16 J. Ritchie *Australia As Once We Were* Melbourne: Heinemann 1975, pp. 197–206; K. Fry 'Soldier Settlement and the Australian Agrarian Myth after the First World War' *Labour History* no. 48, May 1985.
17 War Service Committee Minutes, CLHC; NSW Parliamentary Papers (joint volumes) 1922, session 2, vol. 1, 'Progress Report of Select Committee of Soldier Settlements'; Department of Lands *Annual Report* 1922; McBarron, CLHC; LTO PA 8379.
18 CN 20 February 1920; Council tenders, CLHC.
19 E. McBarron 'Soldier Settlement' CLHC; J. H. Bell, A Provincial Urban Community in Close Proximity to the Metropolis of Sydney, MA thesis, University of Sydney, 1954, pp. 37ff.
20 *Daily Telegraph* 2 December 1920; CN 20 August, 10 December 1920.
21 CN 12 February 1932.
22 W. Hardy Wilson *The Cow Pasture Road* Sydney: Art in Australia 1920; Cox & Lucas *Colonial Architecture* p. 91.
23 ML Subdivision Maps; Holm et al. *Campbelltown*; CN 25 January 1919, 3 September 1926, 15 December 1939; SMH 8 December 1925.
24 *Daily Telegraph* 18 January 1924; CN 9 April 1925, 22 February 1929.
25 Campbelltown Municipal Council, Register of Transfers of Ratable Land; ML Subdivision Boxes; CN 19 November 1920, 29 October 1926, 12 July 1935.
26 CN 22 February 1929, 14 January 1938, 15 December 1939; *Grist Mills* 2, 2 and 3, 1.
27 CLHC.
28 Edie Ball, née Kershaw, pers. comm. March 1987; Leah *Glenfield*.
29 CN 25 January 1919, 2 September 1921, 9 February 1923, 14 September 1928; Ingleburn Council newsclippings, CLHC; M. Cannon *Life in the Cities* Melbourne: Nelson 1975, pp. 109–10.
30 CN 25 January, 8 February 1924; *Evening News* 21 December 1927; Campbelltown Municipal Council newsclippings, CLHC.
31 Henry *Water Supply* p. 123; Holm et al. *Campbelltown*.
32 CN 6, 13 May 1932, 18 January 1935, 10 December 1937, 12 May 1939.
33 CN 25 January 1929, 14 August 1931, 30 June 1935, 5 February 1937; Henry *Water Supply* pp. 125ff; Beryl Bain, pers. comm. March 1987.
34 *Biz* 17 October 1946; CLHC.
35 F. A. Larcombe *The Advancement of Local Government in New South Wales 1906 to the Present* Sydney: Sydney University Press 1978, p. 90; *Biz* 17 October 1946.
36 CN 10 August 1928, 9 August 1929, 25 April 1930, 21 August 1936; *Biz* 17 October 1946.
37 Campbelltown Municipal Council newsclippings, CLHC.
38 *Sun* 25 October 1936; SMH 26 October 1936; *Biz* 29 October 1936.
39 CN 13 May 1932.
40 CN 14 September 1928; Marlow Scrapbook, CLHC; Holm et al. *Campbelltown*.

41 CN 25 January 1929, 27 June 1930, 5 May 1939; Manager's half-yearly report, April 1939, Westpac archives.
42 Manager's half-yearly report, March 1924, September 1926, September 1927, Westpac archives.
43 CH 9 May 1914.
44 CN 5 August 1927, 22 February 1929; C–I *News* 13 July 1954.
45 CN 25 January 1919.
46 *Census of Australia* 1921, 1933.
47 CN 22 February 1929, 14 December 1937.
48 CN 28 July 1939.
49 Holm et al. *Campbelltown*.
50 CN 16 June 1922; Holm et al. *Campbelltown*.
51 *Sand's Directory* 1926, 1932; Holm et al. *Campbelltown*.
52 *Grist Mills* 1, 6 and 2, 3; Beryl Bain, pers. comm. March 1987.
53 Holm et al. *Campbelltown*.
54 ibid.; *Grist Mills* 3, 5.
55 *Grist Mills* 3, 2.
56 Holm, et al. *Campbelltown*; LTO Book 1108, no. 262; *Grist Mills* 3, 5.
57 CN 14 December 1928, 29 January 1929, 14 December 1937, 24 March, 8 December 1939.
58 Manager's half-yearly report, September 1940, Westpac archives; Bank rationalisation, March 1942, Westpac archives; CN 24 September 1943.
59 CN 31 June 1924, 5 September 1930.
60 ibid. 10 December 1937, 9 February 1940.
61 ibid. 13 November 1925, 28 October 1932.
62 ibid. 9 January 1931.
63 ibid. 27 August 1937.
64 ibid. 7 July 1922, 12 October 1928; Manager's half-yearly reports, 1922–31, Westpac archives.
65 Manager's half-yearly reports, 1932–42, Westpac archives.
66 CN 28 July 1922, 26 April, 10 May 1929; *Grist Mills* 2, 2 and 3; LTO vol. 1079, f.61.
67 Manager's half-yearly reports, 1930–42, Westpac archives; *Sand's Directory* 1921; CN 20 February 1920, 30 March 1923, 28 July, 15 December 1939; *Evening News* 27 November 1920.
68 CN 13 June 1924
69 CN 23 September 1921, 26 April 1929, 2 August 1935.
70 CN 5 September 1930; CLHC.
71 CN 4 August 1922.
72 ADB; CN 4 December 1936; CLHC.
73 CN 19 July 1929; 20 December 1935; Marlow Scrapbook, CLHC.
74 CN 10 May, 28 June, 13, 20 December 1935, 3 January, 17 April 1936, 12 March, 10 December 1937
75 CN 22 October 1926; Marlow Scrapbook, CLHC; Burns-Wood *Campbelltown Public School*.
76 *Census of Australia* 1921, 1933; CN 25 September 1925; *Sand's Directory* 1926
77 Marlow Scrapbook CLHC; *Census of Australia* 1921, 1933.
78 *Sydney Mail* 14 April 1926.
79 J. Burnswoods and J. Fletcher *Sydney and the Bush* Sydney: NSW Department of Education 1980, p. 198.
80 *Australian Veterinary Journal* vol. 49, October 1973; *Agricultural Gazette of NSW*

October 1973; CLHC; CN 6 January 1935; *Biz* 17 October 1946; Radi et al. *Biographical Register.*

81   W. Lowenstein *Weevils in the Flour* Fitzroy: Scribe 1981, p. 16.

82   *Census of Australia* 1921, 1933.

83   CN 27 June 1930, 6 May 1932, 6 December 1935; Campbelltown Municipal Council Newsclipping Album, CLHC.

84   CN 27 June, 5 September 1930, 23 November 1934, 18 January 1935, 18 October 1935, 5, 12 May 1939; Ingleburn Council Newsclipping Album, CLHC; *Biz* 17 October 1946.

85   CN 5 January 1940; Johnson *Liverpool* p. 79.

86   Lowenstein *Weevils* pp. 4, 13; Holm et al. *Campbelltown; Census of Australia* 1933.

87   AONSW 5/16684.3; Johnson *Liverpool* pp. 84ff.

88   Beryl Bain, pers. comm. March 1987.

89   Holm et al. *Campbelltown;* CN 12 June 1925.

90   *Grist Mills* 1, 1–3; CN 28 July 1922.

91   Holm et al *Campbelltown;* CN 28 July 1922, 18 October 1935, 28 July 1939.

92   *Daily Telegraph* 18 July 1928; CN 27 June 1930.

93   *Rugby League Week* 3 July 1976; CN 20 August 1920.

94   *Sun* 14 June 1934; *Smith's Weekly* 11 August 1934.

95   *Daily Telegraph* 18 January 1924; CN 22 February 1929; Marlow Scrapbook, CLHC.

96   CN 3 September 1926, 10 December 1937; *Smith's Weekly* 15 January 1938; Holm et al. *Campbelltown;* Family Scrapbook, Payten Collection (privately held); M. Downes *Golden Jubilee, Nepean Illawarra District Associates Golf Association 1933–1983* n.p.

97   Marlow Scrapbook, CLHC; CN 15 June 1918.

98   CN 4, 18 August 1939; Cycle Club Minute Books, CLHC.

99   CN 1 September 1922, 26 April 1929, 14 January 1930; Cycle Club Minute Books, CLHC.

100   CH 8 June 1918; CN 13 June 1924, 6 May 1932; 4 November 1938, 28 July 1944, 22 June 1945, 23 July 1948, 31 October 1950; SMH 8 December 1925; Campbelltown Municipal Council Newsclipping Album, CLHC.

101   CN 27 October, 1, 8 December 1939; *Biz* 17 October 1946; Proudfoot, *Colonial Buildings* p. 20.

102   CN 9 February, 14, 21 June, 5 July 1940, 10 July, 28 August 1942, 24 December 1947; *Biz* 17 October 1946; Marlow Scrapbook, CHLC; Bayley *Campbelltown* p. 135; J. Kesby, J. Harper and L. Kiddey *A Biography of John Hurst Edmondson V. C.* (roneo), n.d.

103   Campbelltown Municipal Council Newsclipping Album, CLHC; C–I *News* 22 June 1971.

104   Downes *Golden Jubilee;* Cycle Club Minute Books, CLHC.

105   CN 5 July 1940; Bayley *Campbelltown* p. 163.

Chapter 6 *1945–1988*

1   Bell, Provincial Urban Community, pp. 174, 188ff.

2   D. Winston *Sydney's Great Experiment: The Progress of the Cumberland County Plan* Sydney: Angus and Robertson 1957, p. 81.

3 State Planning Authority *The New Cities of Campbelltown, Camden and Appin Structure Plan* Sydney: SPA 1973.
4 P. Scott 'Growth Centres' in P. Scott (ed.) *Australian Cities and Public Policy* Melbourne: Georgian House 1978.
5 C–I *News* 2, 9 April, 21 May 1957, 11 June 1957; H. W. Faulkner 'Campbelltown: A Case Study of Planned Urban Expansion' in R. Cardew, J. Langdale and D. Rich (eds) *Why Cities Change* Sydney: Geographical Society of NSW and George Allen and Unwin 1982.
6 Macarthur Development Board *The District Gazette Macarthur 1980–1981*; L. Paroissien and M. Griggs *Old Continent, New Building* Sydney: David Ell Press and Design Arts Committee of the Australia Council 1983, p. 53.
7 NSW Housing Commission *Annual Reports* 1956–1980; Macarthur Development Board *District Gazette 1980–81*; SMH 23 July 1987.
8 P. Spearritt *Sydney Since the Twenties* Sydney: Hale and Iremonger 1978, pp. 107–8.
9 C–I *News*, 19 October 1954, 30 April 1968; Bell, Provincial Urban Community, pp. 144–5, 194ff.
10 Mary Murphy *Challenges of Change: The Lend Lease Story* Sydney: Lend Lease Corporation 1984, pp. 35, 88.
11 ibid. pp. 120–1.
12 *Real Estate Journal* November 1968; Murphy *Lend Lease* pp. 121, 141 153.
13 Bell, Provincial Urban Community, p. 173.
14 C–I *News* 22 June, 13 July, 3 August 1954, 12 March 1957.
15 W. M. Mercer, The Geography of Campbelltown as a Service Centre, B Litt thesis, University of New England, 1970; *Campbelltown District Star* 13 April 1978; *Dairy Farmers News* May 1986.
16 *Macarthur Advertiser* 1 October 1986; SMH 23 July 1987.
17 F. A. Larcombe *The Development of Local Government in N.S.W.* Melbourne: Cheshire 1961, p. 74.
18 Report of Select Committee on Local Government (Areas) Bill, NSW Parliamentary Papers 1947–48 (second session), vol. 1; CN 16 August 1946.
19 CN 10 December 1948.
20 Report of Select Committee on Local Government (Areas) Bill, 1947–48; CN 13 March 1956.
21 C–I *News* 23 June 1953.
22 C–I *News* 21 June 1955, 1 May, 12 June 1956.
23 C–I *News* 13 January 1953, 1 November 1955; S. Vernon, pers. comm. February 1987
24 Campbelltown City Council, Population Report 1976–83.
25 M. Smith 'Human Services' Working Paper no. 5 *Macarthur Regional Environment Study* Campbelltown: Department of Environment and Planning 1986, pp. 10–14; Macarthur Advertiser, *Campbelltown in Review*, 1985; Campbelltown City Council, 1981 Census Summary, 1983; Campbelltown City Council, Population Report 1976–83.
26 *Campbelltown in Review*, 1985
27 *Macarthur Advertiser* 1 October 1986; Smith 'Human Services' p. 42.
28 CN 14, 28 June 1946, 4 October 1949.
29 E. Russell 'The history of the Frank Whiddon Masonic Homes of NSW' *NSW Freemason* February 1979, October 1982; G. Sherington *Australia's Immigrants 1788–1978* Sydney: George Allen and Unwin 1980, pp. 146, 148.
30 H. W. Faulkner *Spatial and Social Consequences of Sydney's Metropolitan Expan-*

Notes

31 *sion: The Macarthur Experience 1945-1977* Duntroon: Department of Geography, Royal Military College 1979, p. 13.
31 *Dairy Farmers News* May 1986; CN 1 June 1945.
32 NSW Milk Board *Annual Reports*; CN 20 July 1945; R. Lawrence 'Why Campbelltown?' interview transcripts, CLHC; V. Fowler, *Crier* 7 April 1982.
33 A. Jose and H. Carter *The Australian Encyclopaedia* vol. 2 Sydney: Angus and Robertson 1927.
34 C–I *News* 20 January 1959; Bell, Provincial Urban Community, p. 160.
35 *Macarthur Advertiser* 20 May 1986.
36 Bell, Provincial Urban Community, p. 160; CN 22 June 1945; *Grist Mills* 3, 3; *Macarthur Advertiser* 4 March 1987.
37 CN 4 January 1946; C–I *News* 7, 14 June 1955, 12 April 1960.
38 SMH 23 July 1987.
39 Department of Environment and Planning 'Other Major Planning Issues' Working Paper no. 6 *Macarthur Regional Environmental Study* Campbelltown: Department of Environment and Planning 1986, pp. 128–9; NSW Planning and Environment Commission *Work Places and Work Trips 1971* Sydney: n.p. 1976.
40 H. W. Faulkner 'Journey Pattern Adjustments on Sydney's Metropolitan Fringe: An Exploratory Study', *Australian Geographer* 15, 1, May 1981; *Macarthur Regional Environmental Study* Working Paper no. 6, pp. 126–7.
41 *District Gazette 1980–81*.
42 Bell, Provincial Urban Community, p. 232.
43 CN 22, 29 November 1946, 22 February, 24 May 1949, 3 November 1953; Select Committee on Local Government 1947–48; Bell, Provincial Urban Community, p. 232.
44 *Macarthur Advertiser* 25 March 1986.
45 *Sun* 2 May 1968; C–I *News* 19 September 1978; *Macarthur Advertiser* 5 August 1987.

Index

Aborigines, 1–7, 15, 17–27, 62, 215–6
Acres, Thomas, 11, 29
Adams, R. C., 176, *177*
agriculture, 10ff, 41–7, 72–7, 106–10, 127–30, 135, 167–9, 183–6
Ah John Sue, 146
Ahearn, John, 120, 151, 227
Airds, 8, 10, 11, 12, 28, 58, 203, 213, 214, 215
Airey, Walter Thomas, 117, 118, 120
Aitken, Esther, 98
Alkin, Rev. Thomas V., 101–2, 150
Allan, Robert, 178
Allen family, 133
Allison family, 100
Allman, Francis, 33, 34, 40, 90
Alpha House, 131, 134, 208
Ambarvale, 134, 203, 204, 206, 213, 214
Andrews, Sarah and Ann, 52
Angel, Henry, 18, 69, 195
Antill, Capt, 8, 88
Apperley, W. J., 209
Appin, 10, 36, 58, 89
Appin massacre, 23
Armitage, Rev. J. D., 170
Armstrong, John, 36
Armstrong, Thomas George, 175
Arundel, R. E., 178
Ashcroft family, 69
Ashcroft, Amelia, 151
Ashcroft, Elizabeth *nee* Tebbutt, 151

Ashcroft, James, 151
Ashcroft, John, 151
Asher, C., 170, 176
Atkins, Richard, 7, 8, 12
Atkinson, Joseph, 120
Atwell, G. L., 168
Austin Park, 103
Avery, Thomas, 50, 52
Axam, Charles, 129, 134
Axam, F., 158

Badgally, 132, 134, 186, 213
Bagge, C. H. O., 147
Bagge, Kate Ohlfsen, 142
Bailey, C., *177*
Bainbridge, H. H., 228
Baldcock, A. E., 180
Baldcock, Miss, 195
Baldwin, J. E., 209
Baldwin, W., 152
Bamfield, 117
Bamford, Edward, 123
Bamford, Mrs E., 119
banks, 53, 83, 131, 134, 136, 182, 206
Barber, George, 18, 70
Barff, Samuel George, 149, 227
Barker, D. H., 118, 137, 227
Barker, Frank, 74
Barnes, Richard, 12
Barnsley, 181
Barrallier, Francis, 5, 6
Barrett, P., 168
Barton, R. A., 228
Basden, Richard, 92
Bate, Jeff, 195, 216
Batholomew, J., 168
Bayles, 28

Bean, James, 40
Beats, Philip, 44
Beck, Charles, 37, 80, 94
Beecham, 96
Bell, Dr William, 112
Berry, W. W., 137
Beverley Park, 195
Bird's Eye Corner, 5, 11, 14 110
Birkett, A. L., 195
Bitugally, 19–22
Black, O., 227
Blackburn, Elizabeth, 119
Blackwell, Richard, 88
Blades, F. S., 194
Blain family, 100
Blair Athol, 132, 197
Blairmont, 213
Blake, Isadore, 112
Bland, 28
Blomfield, Christiana *nee* Brooks, 51, 102
Blomfield, R. F., 209
Blomfield, Richard Henry, 91, 102, 106, 154
Blomfield, Susan *nee* Gibson 154
Blomfield, Thomas V., 25, ? 87–8, 102
Bocking family, *85*
Bocking, James, 74, 81–2, 85–6, 91, 99, 103, 116, 11 120, 122, 123, 137, 139, 14 170, 227
Bocking, May, 142
Boer War, 158
Boland, Tom, 212
Bolden, Anna M. *nee* Raymond, 106

Bolger family, 100
Bollard, William, 18
Boon, Nathaniel, 11, 52, 111
Bosci, 150
Bossawa, Claude, 18
Bostock, C. R., 178
botany, 101–2
Bottin, T. H., 174
Bourke, Keihone, 142
Bourke, M., 158
Bourke, Robert, 33
Bow Bowing, 203, 213
Bowman, William, 94
Boyd, Rev. David, 96
Boyd, Thomas, 18
Bradbury, 203, 206, 213, 214, 215
Bradbury Park, 29–30, 32, 74, 103–5, 204
Bradbury, William, 29, 32–3, 52, 61, 104
Brady, Daniel, 33, 37
Braill, 147
Bratt, Miss E., 186
Bray, Gilbert, 137
Bray, John, 70, 86, 92, 94, 113, 117, 119
Bray, Mary, 82
Bray, Thomas, 70
Brennan Patrick, 34
Brennan, Peter, 33
bridges, 53, 72, 84–7
Bridges, J. W., 52
Bridle, William, 69, 70
Broinowski, Felix, 156
Broinowski, Gracius Joseph, 156
Broinowski, Jane, 156
Broinowski, Leopold, 156
Broinowski, Lieutenant, 158
Brooker, William, 11, 12, 37, 60
Brooks, Christiana, 45
Brooks, Richard, 9, 12, 33, 45, 59
Brooksbank, Ann, 119
Brooksbank, Mary Ann, 73, 112
Brooksbank, Robert, 73, 76, 117
Broughton, Bishop W., 34
Broughton, Elizabeth nee Kennedy, 14, 17
Broughton, William, 11, 14, 70
Brown, George, 99, 117, 118, 121, 136, 139
Brown, H. W., 170

Brown, Mary nee Kidd, 144
Brown, Thomas, 149
Browne, William, 31
Brticevich family, 208
Brunero, Domenico, 181
Brunero, Maria, 181
Brunero, Rita nee Tripp, 181
Bruton, John, 150
Buckland, Jonathan, 88–9
Budbury, 19–21, 23, 25
Bugden, B., 177
building societies, 207
Bull Cave, 4
Bull, Catherine nee Rowley, 145
Bull, Charles, 116, 118, 120, 139, 145, 227
Bull, Fanny nee Chippendall, 145
Bull, Harriet nee Horden, 155
Bull, James, 11
Bull, Mary nee Morris, 145
Bull, Nathaniel George, 155
Bull, William, 145
Bullock, George, 139
Bundle, 24, 25
Bunker, Eber, 8
Burcher, Charles, 132
Burgess, G. W., 148
Burgess, William, 152
Burke, James, 29
Burke, Robert, 94
Burke, Thomas, 11
Burn, Thomas, 51
Burragorang, 27
Burrows, 62
Bursill, 117
Bursill, Hannah, 119
Bursill, Samuel, 103, 180, 227
Bursill, William, 50, 80, 84, 89, 180, 204
bushrangers, 39–41, 54, 92–3
Bussell Brothers, 179
Byrne, Charles, 33, 57, 78
Byrne, Elizabeth, 78
Byrne, Hugh, 38
Byrne, J., 181
Byrne, Jane nee Warby, 78
Byrne, Michael, 33, 52, 78, 94, 113
Byrne, Sarah, 11
Byrne, Sylvester, 79
Byrne, William, 33, 37, 51–2
Byrnes, Andrew, 7
Byrnes, Thomas, 87

Caldwell, Mary nee Percival, 81

Caldwell, William B., 81, 118, 137, 139, 227
Caley, George, 6, 14
Camden, 83, 85, 86, 88, 91, 125, 131, 202, 209
Camden Park, 24, 26, 37
Camden tram, 126, 220
Campbell, Neil, 51
Campbellfield, 10, 12, 57, 106, 113, 119, 128, 146, 157
Campbelltown, 28, 31, 33, 68, 88–9, 104, 106, 115, 131, 136–9, 169, 211, 213, 214
Campbelltown Agricultural Society, 159, 172, 186
Campbelltown Botanical Society, 101–2
Campbelltown centenary, 167, 170
Campbelltown Chamber of Commerce, 206
Campbelltown City Building Society, 207
Campbelltown Co-Operative Creamery, 129, 137, 139
Campbelltown Common, 147, 159, 171
Campbelltown Community Radio, 222
Campbelltown Council, 118, 120–3, 175, 209–10
Campbelltown Road Trust, 86–7
Campbelltown Unemployed Association, 190
Campbelltown Water Trust, 93–4, 121
Campion, R., 83, 117
Cannabayagal, 23
Cannon, Mary nee Bradbury, 104
Carey, Tasman George, 178
Carolan, A. D., 98
Carroll, J., 184
Cartwright, Rev. Robert, 29
Casey, Archibald, 112
Casey, J., 168
Cataract Dam, 125–6
Caversham, 182
Chaffe, John, 107
Chamberlaine, James, 8
Chaperon, Elizabeth, 146
Chauvel, Arthur B. J., 99, 109
Cheeke, Judge Alfred, 106–7, 113
Chernich, Desmond John, 170, 181
Chinnocks, 117, 170

Chinnocks, Ellen, 139
Chinnocks, George, *138*, 139
Chippendall, John, 57
Chippendall, Thomas, 70, 87,
  91, 99, 104
Chisholm, Caroline, 111
Chisholm, James, 26
Chisholm, James jr, 45, 77,
  88, 90, 118
Chivers, H., 175, 227
Christiansen, M., 153
Christmas, George Beresford,
  50, 86, 109
churches, 34–8, 101–3, 223
churches, Anglican, 29, 31,
  35–7, 45, 102, 111, 147,
  150, 166, *colour section*
  Baptist, 150, *151*, 166
  Congregational, 81, 86, 103
  Presbyterian, 38, 98–9,
    102–3, 153, 156
  Roman Catholic, 29, 37–8,
    102, 141, *colour section*
  Wesleyan, 103, 150
cinema, 178, 192, 212
Clari Montes (Claremont), 32,
  132
Clark, C. J., 209
Clark, Nanno, 100
Clarke, George, 205
Clarke, Miss, 142
Clarke, Samuel, 82
Clarkson, Thomas, 12, 46, 60
Claydon, E. S., 209
Claymore, 203, 213, 214
Cleary, Patrick, 146
Clifton, Patrick, 136
Clissold, E. M. (Mort), 207,
  209
Clissold, Frederick, 132
clothing, 56–7
coal, 83, 91, 218–19
Cobb, James, 81, 86, 92, 103
Cobcroft, Miss, 195
Coddington, James, 61
Coghill, John, 38
Coles, F. J., 185
Coles, Mrs A. L., 136
Collins, Arthur, *184*
Collins, Mrs C. J., 181
Collins, William J., 139, 148,
  149, 150
Colls, Thomas, 96
commerce, 77–84, 136–9,
  178–82, 206–8
commuters, 72, 127, 131, 178,
  182, 220–1
Condamine, Thomas de la, 31

Confeggi, Vince, 207
Conley, 179
Connelly, Misses, 153
Conroy, 133
convicts, 7, 17, 30, 39, 48–9,
  51, 59, 68, 111
Cook, J., 138
Cook, Stanley, 188, 228
Cooper, Daniel, 29, 33, 60, 61
Cooper, Elizabeth, 136
Cordeaux, Ann *nee* Moore, 45
Cordeaux, William, 22, 31,
  45, 51
Corderoy, H. G., 185
cordial factory, 129, 137, 182
Cotter, James, 38
council chambers and town
  hall, *120* 121, 131, 136, 197,
  210–11, *colour section*
country estates, 106–10
courthouse, 30, 33, 34, 92,
  123, 124, 132, 137, 145, 187
Cowpastures, 5, 7, 15
Cowper, Charles, 71
Cowper, Thomas, 33
Cox, R., 164
Craft, George, 37, 150, 166
Craft, Henry John, 139
Craft, William, 139
Crammond, C. H., 171
Crammond, D., 138
Cransley, 167–8
Crisp, Amos, 70
Croghan, Michael, 136
Crompton Parkinson, 197,
  219, 220
Crowe, 180
Crowe, A., 168
Crowe, W., 168
Cummins family, 133, 170
Cummins, Mary, 164
Cummins, William, 118, 227
Cunningham, Thomas, 132
Czarlinski, Paul, 155

daily life, 55–9, 110–4, 158–
  62, 191–5
Daintress, Mrs, 188
dairying, 46, 109, 127–9, 132,
  144, 183–4, 217
Daley, Harley, 176, 195, 204,
  209, *210*, 224
Davies, Elizabeth, 146
Davies, John, 132, 145
Davies, Miss, *140*
Day, Aphrasia *nee* Raymond,
  106
Dench, C. H., 209

Denfield, 57, 129
Denham Court, 7, 8, 9, 12,
  13, 24, 25, 45, 51, 102, 106,
  153–4, 213, 214
Denholm, H. V., 170
depression (1840s), 77–9
depression (1929–35), 189–9
Devlin, Thomas, 176
Dewhurst, D., 168
Dharawal, *see* Aborigines
Dight, John, 50, 57, 70
Dight, Wilfred B., 139
Ditchfield, 28
Donaldson, J. H., 204
Donnelly, Margaret, 119
Donovan, Thomas Joseph,
  187
Downes, Frederick W. A.,
  145
Dowse, Isaac, 51
Dowse, John, 81
Doyle Brothers, 139
Doyle, 133
Doyle, Henty and Co, 82
Doyle, John, 79, 86, 137
Doyle, Nicholas, 118, 227
Drinkwater, F. W., 193
Driver, Charlotte, 8
drought, 19, 44, 47, 75, 93,
  125, 175, 184
Duall, 11, 17, 18, 21, 23
Ducat, V. A., 170
Duguid, Alfred, 192
Dumaresq, Edward, 31
Dumaresq, Henry, 31, 57
Dumaresq, William, 29, 31
Dunbier, R. A., 199
Duncan, N., 152
Duncombe, G., 168
Dunne, Father, 170
Dusseldorp, G. J., 205
Dwyer, Patrick, 99
Dwyer, T. S., 168

Eagle Vale, 12, 46, 60, 107–8
  204, 213, 214
Eaglemount, 129
Eccleston, John, 70, 117
Eckersley, 129–30, 154–5
Edmondson, John Hurst, 19
Edrop estate, 129
Edrop, Adah *nee* Harrax, 110
Edrop, Edward John, 110
Edrop, James, 27, 110
education, 28, 29, 35–8, 96–
  101, 140–2, 186–9, 222–3;
  see also schools
Edwards, L. E., 185

Index

Edwards, W. J., 125
Eggleston family, 170
Eggleston, John, 52
Eggleton, W., 164
Egypt Farm, 134
electricity, 174–6, 197
Emily Cottage, 79, 86
English, J. R. V., 209
Englorie, 133
Epping Forest, 39, 57
Eschol Park, 213, 214
Eshcol Park (Eschol after
  1975), 83, 107–8, 129, 134,
  136, 195
Etchells, Arthur Herbert, 157
Etchells, Ellen, 155
Etchells, Frank, 154–5
Etchells, Harry, 154–5
Etchells, Mrs E., 119
Etchells, W. H., 164
Euglorie Park, 133
Evans, George R., 97
exploration, 5–6, 14–19

Farley, John, 27, 32, 57, 65–6
Farnsworth, J. G. A., 209,
  228
Farrow, William, 171, 188
Favelle, Brian, 219
Fennell, Patrick, 53, 57
Ferguson, Elizabeth, 119
Ferndale, 185
Fetterplace, G. K., 228
Fieldhouse Brothers, 62, 82,
  104
Fieldhouse, Ann nee Bray,
  135
Fieldhouse, Edwin Hallet, 79,
  91, 99, 116, 117, 119, 129,
  135
Fieldhouse, George, 37, 50,
  79, 135
Fieldhouse, William, 79, 119,
  135
fire brigade, 123, 177
fire station, 120, 121, 131, 136
Fisher's ghost, 64–7
Fisher's Ghost Festival, 211,
  colour section
Fisher, Frederick, 29, 59–67
Fisher, R. Henry, 63–4
Fisher, Samuel, 64
Fitzgerald, Richard, 94
Fitzpatrick family, 170, 184
Fitzpatrick, Elizabeth nee
  Cummins, 109
Fitzpatrick, Elizabeth Susan,
  109

Fitzpatrick, James, 18, 70,
  108–9, 117
Fitzpatrick, James Glenlee,
  109, 133
Fitzpatrick, Mary Ann, 109
Fitzpatrick, Mary Ann nee
  Atkins, 108
Fitzpatrick, Ross, 207
FitzStubbs, R., 148
flour mills, 49–50, 74
food, 1–2, 56–7, 111
Forbes, Charles, 88
Forbes, M., 194
Forrest, Rev. Robert, 36,
  96–7
Foster, F., 185
Foti, Celestino, 219
Fowler Brothers, 82
Fowler, 139
Fowler, Daniel, 79, 99, 117,
  119
Fowler, Eliza nee Warby, 108
Fowler, George, 80
Fowler, Mary nee Bursill, 79
Fowler, Nathaniel, 58
Fowler, William, 77, 80, 84–
  6, 91, 93, 99, 107–8, 113
Frame, David, 170, 186
Francis, Ann, 119
Frank Whiddon Masonic
  Homes, 217
Franklin, John, 33
Fraser, T. K., 228
Freeman, 159
Freeman, J. S., 189, 228
French, A., 168
Frere's Crossing, 154
Frere, Charles L., 155
Frere, Gustav, 155
fruitgrowing, 129, 185
Funnell, James, 101, 119

Galloway, J. J., 34
Gamble, Roy L., 170, 174,
  176, 227
Gamble, Thomas, 123, 137,
  139, 227
Gandangara, see Aborigines
Gandid, Jules, 155
gaol, 30, 40–1, 91–2
Garland, 88
Garling, Keith, 209
Garrett, Thomas, 142, 144
Gately, Miss, 195
Gaul, Mrs, 195
Gee, William, 121, 139
Genty, Eugene, 129
Genty, F., 171

Genty, Miss R., 164
Gibson, T. H., 185
Giddy, Mary, 119
Gilbert, Norman, 139, 181
Gilchrist, A., 99
Gilchrist, Rev. Hugh R., 38,
  103
Gilchrist, William, 81
Gilead, 213, 214
Glen Alpine, 35, 36, 132, 206,
  213, 214
Glen Lora, 129
Glen Lorne, 110, 134
Glenalvon, 34, 57, 78, 83,
  116, 135, 164
Glenfield, 8, 9, 13, 18, 21, 57,
  109, 115, 139, 153, 172, 213,
  217
Glenfield veterinary research
  station, 189, 218
Glenlee, 46, 83, 108–9, 133,
  184, 216–7, 218, colour
  section
Glenquarie, 208, 211–12
Glenroy, 217–18
Glenwood, 150, 152
Gogy, 6, 19–23
Gonsalves, Thomas, 219
Gooch, Robert, 46
Goodair, Ruth, 16
Goodwin, F. G., 209
Goold, Father James, 38, 102,
  111
Gordon, Miss, 97
Gordon, Rev. Henry, 96
Gore, A. J., 83, 134
Gore, Geoff, 192, 194
Gorus, Elizabeth, 134
Gorus, John Tangelder, 108,
  119, 120, 123, 134
Graham family, 52, 119, 137
Graham, George, 50
Graham, James, 79, 85, 89, 94,
  113
Graham, John, 79
Graham, William, 79, 117,
  118, 120, 139
Graham, William jr, 123, 227
Grant, James, 98
Grant, John, 87
Greenhill, Catherine, 119
Greenwood, Elizabeth, 156
Grodno, 130
Guthrie, Edward, 86, 117

Hagan, W. J., 164
Halloran, F., 168
Hammond, Ann nee Byrne, 32

Hammond, Thomas, 29, 30,
 32, 33, 52, 96, 170
Hannaford, C. N., 170, 227
Hardie, William, 130
Harper, A. J., 175, 227
Harpur, Thomas, 5
Harrax, James, 11, 110
Harrington Park, 113
Harris, Alexander, 55
Harris, William J., 149, 181,
 227
Hassall, James, 88
Hassall, Rev. Thomas, 33
Hassall, Samuel, 20
Haydon, Barkley, 170, 172,
 186
Hayes and Howell, 181
Hazlett, I. A., 209
Helm, C., 119
Hennessy, David, 50
Hepher, J. C., 168
Hepher, Jack, 192, 194
Hewitt, Elizabeth *nee* Tyson,
 136
Hewitt, Stephen, 136
Hickey Brothers, 136
Hickey, J., 138
Hickey, Mrs, *82*
Hilder, Thomas James, 172
Hill, Arthur, 164
Hill, Thomas, 150
Hillcrest, 132, 182
Himmelhoch, Isaac, 130, 155
Hinde, 117
Hinde, Mary H., 119
Hindmarsh, W. L., 189
Hinsch family, 153
Hircock, H., 185
Hobbs, Thomas, 92
Hoddle, Robert, 30
Hodges, E., *177*
Hodgkins, Paradine, 152
Hodkin, H., 147
Hogan, T. F., 137
Holden, George K., 40
Holdsworth, P. R., 143, 147
Holland, Rev. Edward, 99, 103
Hollingshead, Charles, 50
Holly Lea, 132, 146, *colour
 section*
Holman, R., 158
Holsworthy, 129–30, 165, 224
Honory, Peter, 7
Hope, Dr R. C., 89, 112
Hopping, G., 227
Horniman, L., 164
horse racing, 57–8, 106–7,
 113, 161

Hosking, John, 70, 78, 88
Hosking, Martha Foxlow, 78,
 106, 151
Hosking, W. C., 195, 228
hospitals and health care, 112,
 158–9, 194–5, 216
hotels and inns, 32–3, 51–2,
 58, 78–9, 179
hotels, Brewer's Arms, 52
 Club, 137, 181
 Coach and Horses Inn, 79,
 84
 Commonwealth, 62, 137,
 182
 Crown and Anchor Inn, 52
 Crown Inn, 52
 Cumberland, 104, 137
 Federal, 123, 181, 182
 Forbes, 33, 52, 79, 137, 208
 Good Intent, 182, 208
 Harrow Inn, 52
 Horse and Jockey Inn, 60
 Joiner's Arms, 78–9
 Jolly Miller Inn, 62, 79, 84,
 132, 136, 137
 King's Arms, 52
 Plough Inn, *colour section*
 Railway, 79, *80*, 137
 Royal, 127, 134, 137, 181,
 212
 Royal Oak Inn, 32, 52
 Rudd's inn, 84
 Sportsman's Arms, 113,
 135, 137
 St Patrick's Inn, 52, 132, 137
 Three Brothers Inn, 52, 111,
 145, *colour section*
 Traveller's Rest, 52
 Wheelwright's Arms, 52
Houghton, Thomas, 139, 168
houses, 56–7, 111–12
Housing Commission, 201,
 202–3, 213, 214, 215
Hovell, Esther *nee* Arndell, 17
Hovell, William Hilton, 14,
 17, 70, 85, 108
Howe, Edward, 70, 86, 90
Howe, Ephraim, 108
Howe, Mary, 108
Howe, Thomas, 88, 90
Howe, William, 14, 30, 31, 35,
 37, 40, 42–3, 46, 88–90, 108
Howe, William jr, 70, 86, 88,
 90, 92
Howell, J. S., 88
Huckstepp, 117
Huckstepp, Charles, 81
Huckstepp, George, 158, 186

Huckstepp, Miss, 206
Hume, Andrew, 10, 11, 16,
 20
Hume, Edward, 84
Hume, Elizabeth *nee* Dight,
 16, 18
Hume, Hamilton, 16–18, 22,
 108
Hume, James, 103
Hume, Rawdon, 88
Hume, William, 84
Humphries, John, 100
Humphries, Thomas, 52
Hunt, John Charles, 145
Hunter, Rev. J. R., 167
Huon, A. A., 70
Huon, Paul, 50, 89
Hurley estate, 185
Hurley family, 134, 170
Hurley Park, 172
Hurley, John, 37, 48, *52–4*,
 57, 70, 78, 81, 86, 88, 94–5,
 99, 104, 108, 111, 117, 119
Hurley, Mary *nee* Byrne, 53
Hurley, Patrick B., 116
Hurley, Sarah, 135
Hurley, William, 83
Hurlstone Agricultural
 College, 172, 188, 195
Hurst, J., 129
Hyman, Miss, *140*

immigrants, 215
 Chinese, 68, 136, 185
 English, 68, 111
 European, 68, 77, 115, 155,
 156
 Irish, 7, 16, 56, 58, 68, 95,
 110–11
 Scottish, 68
Inch, Jane Ann, 107
Inch, Joseph, 107
industries, 49–51, 77–84,
 136–9, 148, 219–20
influenza, 166–7
Ingleburn, 115, 130, 139, 146,
 148–51, 166, 175–6, 182,
 187, 195, 203, 213
Ingleburn Council, 148–50,
 189, 208–10
Ingleburn Horticultural
 Society, 186
Ingleburn House, 44, 148, *14*
Ingleburn Progress
 Association, 148
Inglis, 146
Innes, Archibald Clunes, 30
Ireland, John, 55

Jackson, John (Bush), 20, 21
Jago, Walter, 178
James, Thomas, 79
Jamieson, William T., 87–8
Jamison, A. L., 148
Jenkins, Jemima *nee* Pitt, 37, 46
Jenkins, John, 70
Jenkins, Louisa *nee* Plunkett, 107
Jenkins, Robert, 59
Jenkins, Robert Pitt, 70, 88, 107
Jenner, Samuel M., 137
Jerrett, A. E., 168
Johnson, E. B., 164
Johnston, Ann, 44
Johnston, Sarah Ann, 148
Johnstone, David, 88
Johnstone, G. R., 91
Joll, George, 36
Jones, Dr Karl O., 193, 195
Jones, J. jr, 139
Jones, W., 177
Jorgensen and Stephenson, 194
Jug, The, 146

Kacerick, Peter, 201
Kavanagh, Alexander Bede, 139, 149, 150
Kayes, George, 195
Keane, Sarah M., 187
Kearns, 213
Kearns, William, 19, 39, 57, 213
Keating family, 100, 191
Keighran, John, 70, 71, 74, 78, 84, 113
Keighran, Patrick, 11
Keighran, Thomas, 70
Kelly, Leo, 184
Kelly, Thomas, 86
Kelso, Charles, G., 155
Kelso, Edmond G., 155
Kendall, Laurence, 74, 85, 86, 94, 103
Kennedy, James, 112
Kennedy, John, 11, 17, 22, 23
Kennedy, Mary *nee* Ruse, 44, 148
Kennedy, Sophia, 119
Kenny, Dr W. R., 37, 89, 111, 112
Kenny, H. M., 125
Kenny, James jr, 33
Kenny, Rev. M, 103
Kentlyn, 147, 171–2, 203, 213, 214, 217

Kerr, Mr & Mrs, 182
Kershaw, Frank, 172
Kershaw, J. C., 172
Kershler family, 166
Kershler, Edie, 170
Kershler, Elizabeth, 77
Kershler, George, 139, 166, 170
Kershler, J. W., 176, 190, 227–8
Kershler, Mrs, 193
Kershler, Peter, 77
Kidd, Fred, *144*
Kidd, John, 81–2, 98, 99, 116, 118, 128, 129, 132, 143, *144–5*, 146, 159
Kidd, Sophia *nee* Collier, *144*
Kilbride, 133
Kilduff, William, 139
King, Honoria *nee* Raymond, 106
King, Mrs Michael, 195
Kirby, Mathew, 51
Kitching, 179
Kitching, H. H., 170
Kitching, T., 170
Kitt, G. A., 182
Klages, Eric, 219
Klein, G., 170
Knight, A. R., 185
Knight, C., 185
Knight, C. F., 178
Knight, John, 120, 157, 167
Knock family, 100
Knock, E., 119

Lachlan Vale, 11, 14
Lack, 117
Lack, Herb, 182
Lack, Robert, 50
land grants, 7–8, 11
Landcom, 203–4, 214
Larkin, 117
Larkin, A., 164
Larkin, Edward, 73, 75
Larkin, Mary, 119
Larkin, Samuel, 134
Latter, Thomas P., 149, 150
law and order, 39–41, 215
Lawson, Mary, 44
Laycock, A., 148
Laycock, Elias P., 148
Lea, H. L., 209
Leacock, James Freeland, 172
Leary, Catherine *nee* Keighran, 95
Leary, Joseph, 71, 95–6, 99, 118, 139

Lebinski, Casimir, 155
Lees, W. Oswald, 136
leisure, 113–14, 191–4, 223–5
Lend Lease Corporation, 204–5, 208, 214
Lennox, Agnes, 117
Leppington, 22, 31, 45, 76
Leslie, 103
Leumeah, *15*, *43*, 115, 203, 212, 214
Lewin, J. W., 5, 9, 110
Lewis, R., 185
Lewis, W. E., 204
library, 159
Lindesay, Patrick, 30
Linklater, Charles, 148
Lithgow, William, 31
Livingstone, D. B., 209
Livingstone, James, 149
Lloyd, Arthur Fisher, 158
local government, 87–9, 90–1, 116–24, 208–12, 227–8
Lodge Federation, 146
Loftus, P., *194*
Loftus, William, 176
Lomas, Edward, 98
Loney, Jessie *nee* Kidd, *144*
Long Point, 191, 213
Long, J. jr, 122
Longhurst Brothers, 180
Longhurst, B., 170
Longhurst, Gus, 195
Longhurst, J. R., 164
Longhurst, S., 164
Longhurst, W., *194*
Longhurst, W. A., 209
Longmuir, George F., 188
Lovely, Samuel, 50
Low Wah, Charlie, 185
Lowe, Robert, 20, 38, 88
Lubeck, Arthur, 148
Lucas, Percy Charles, 150, 227
Lusted, E. C., 162
Lusted, Edward, 92
Lusted, George, 121, 134, 139
Lusted, Mrs E., 119
Lusted, Sarah, 140
Lynch, Ann, 119
Lynch, E. J., 178
Lynch, James, 139
Lynch, Monsignor J. T., 101
Lyons family, 100
Lyons, A., 183
Lyons, Jeremiah, 119
Lysaght, A. A., 171

Mabbott, G., 138

253

Mac, *see also* Mc
MacAlister, L, 88
Macarthur Development
Board, 201–2, 208, 219
Macarthur Development
Corporation, 202
Macarthur Onslow, S., 164
Macarthur Regional Centre,
202, 208, *colour section*
Macarthur, Elizabeth, 24
Macarthur, Elizabeth *nee*
Veale, 19, 20
Macarthur, James, 71, 84, 88
Macarthur, John, 5, 7, 24, 25
Macarthur, Rev. George
Fairfowl, *96*, 97
Macarthur, William, 17, 19,
84, 87–8
MacDonald, D., 180
Mack, F., 164
Macleay, George, 88
Macquarie Fields, 7, 9, 16, 28,
35, 78, 97, 106, 115, 151–3,
172, 189, 191, 203, 213
Macquarie Fields House, *96*,
148, 151, *colour section*
Macquarie Heights estate,
205
Macquarie, Lachlan, 8–11,
21, 23, 28
Magee, Mrs, 139
magistrates, 9, 38–41, 90–4
Malone, J., 170
Malvern family, 186
Mannix, William, 49–50
Manns, Henry, 92–3
Mansfield, G. A., 100, 110,
134
manufacturing, 219
Marleford, 134
Marlow, Annie *nee* Kershler,
139, *140*, 166, 192, 193, *194*
Marlow, C. J., 139
Marlow, P. C., 120, 158, 170,
177, 209, 227, 228
Marsden, G. G., 182, 199
Marsden, Phyllis *nee* Lack, 182
Marsden, Sydney, 121
Marsh, G. F., 168
Martin, Alexander, 88
Maryfields, 58, 187, 223
Masterman, James, 51
Mathews, R. H., 27
Matthei family, 156
Matthews, Charles Edward,
120
Mawson Park, 92, 113, 157,
172, *173*

Mawson, Dr William, 170,
172, 192, 195
Mayne, A. Maude *nee*
Macdonald, 154
Mayne, John Colburn, 154
Mayo, Miss, 195
Maze, H. J., 228
Mc, *see also* Mac
McAlister, Matthew, 26, 84
McCarthy, Honora, 137
McClelland, Allan, 218
McClelland, Charles, 218
McClelland, Minnie, 218
McCourt, William, 145
McCudden, Henry, 43–4
McDonald, Alexander, 103
McDonald, Bruce, 207, 209
McDonald, Ron, 207
McEnnally, William, 37
McEwen, Alice, 140
McEwen, James, 141
McEwen, John, 130
McGarvie-Smith Institute,
189, 218
McGeldrick, Pat, *207*
McGlynn, James, 123
McGlynn, Joseph, 143, 178
McGlynn, T., 160
McGuanne, J. P., 170
McGuanne, Kate, 140, *141*
McGuanne, Patrick, 141
McIlveen, 150
McInnes, Malcolm, 149
McInnes, R. J. (Janey), 181
McKee, Rev. William, 103
McLean, Donald, 88–9
McLean, F. T., 168
McLean, Neil and Meryl, 204
McLeod, John, 148
McMahon, Patrick, 111, 151
McPherson, G. R., 183
McSullea, E., 82, 116
Meehan, James, 7–11, 16, 17,
24, 28, 58, 60, 170
Meehan, Mary, 16
Meehan, Mary Ann *nee*
Trees, 16
Meehan, Thomas, 16, 37, 48,
179, 181
Meehan's Castle, 16
Menangle, 5, 6, 84, 115
Menangle Ford, 53, 84–5, 89,
93
Menangle Park, 9, 72, 126,
161, 171, 213, 214, 219
Menangle Park racecourse,
165, 195, 224
Menzies, D. C., 168

Meredith family, 100
Meredith, C., 119
Meredith, Cosmos, 186
Merewether, F. L. M., 132,
160
Merewether, H. J. M., 134
Merewether, Wilhelmina *nee*
Gore, 134
Merritt, Susan Maria, 119
Meyer, 136
Miles, Herbert, 182
Miles, Robert, 44
Milgate Arcade, 212
Milgate, Spencer S., 82–3,
108
Milham, W., 168
military bases, Holsworthy,
130, 155, 224
Ingleburn, 182, 195
military forces, volunteers,
137, 157–8
milk depot, 183, 217
Miller, John, 179
Mills, Henry, 98
Milton Park, 148, 172, *173*,
218
Minto, 8–14, 42, 58, 100, 11
115, 139, 146–8, 201, 203,
213
Minto Heights, 213, 214
Minto Horticultural Society,
186
Mitchell, Surveyor General,
18, 53
Molesworth, 192
Molesworth, Miss, 195
Molle's Mains, 49
Monk, Emma, 119
Moore, Alexander, 130
Moore, Benjamin, 133
Moore, Edward Lumas, 69,
117, 134
Moore, Edwin, 153
Moore, Fred, 123, 160, 166,
227
Moore, James, 36
Moore, John, 133
Moore, Joshua John, 88
Moore, Miss, 142
Moore, Mrs, 168
Moore, Mrs E. L., 132
Moore, Patrick, 7
Moore, S., 139
Moore, Samuel, 88
Moore, Sarah *nee* Warby, 13
Moore, Thomas, 88
Moore, Thomas and Rachel,
8

Moore, William Lyttlemore, 157
Morgan, H. A., 170, 179
Morris, Charles, 55, 71, 79, 84, 85
Morris, Dr W. R., 170, 171
Mossberry, 11
Mount Annan Botanic Gardens, 225
Mount Arden, 9
Mount Gilead, 11, 47–8, 50, 109–10, 113, 129, 133–4
Mowatt, William, 108–9
Mowle, A. W. M., 192
Mowle, W. S., 171
Muckle, George, 50, 81, 87–8
Mulholland, Patrick, 37
Mulholland, William, 70
Mullany, William, 168, 169
Mullholland, C. C., 228
Mumford, James, 11
Munn, Abedmego, 44
Munro, Alexander, 76, 86, 118, 120, 227
Munro, Alexander jr, 122
Munro, William, 86
Murphy, Hugh, 74, 80
Murphy, Patrick, 44
Murray, C. C., 199, 228
Murray, Darby, 38, 69, 70
Murray, Martha *nee* Dwyer, 69
musical groups, 160
Myerson, Edward H., 143

Narellan, 14, 23, 27, 36, 50, 91, 94, 108
Narelling, 17, 18
Nash, D., 164
Nat Bull's Tanks, 155
Naylor, G., 227
Naylor, George F.K., 188
Neale, 28, 148
Neil, John, 33
New, George, 180
Newbury, Matron, 179, 194
Newling and Walker, 137, 138
Newman, Eliza, 98
Newman, Gerald, 141
Newman, Lieutenant, 158
Newman, Patrick, 98, 101, 140, 159
Newmarch, Allen D., 172
newspapers, 137, 142–3, 178, 221–2
Nichol, John, 130
Nicholls, C., 168

Nicholls, Hilton, 164
Nicholls, J., 168
Nickless, Harry, 192
Nicol, Charlie, 139, 192, 194
Nicol, Frank, 164
Nihill, P., 37
Nile Industries, 219
Niver, Mary, 58
Noble, Thomas, 22
Nolan, Father Bernard, 187
Noonan, David, 44
Noonan, Patrick, 44
North, Ann, 119
North, Charles, 139
Northampton Dale, 111
Norton, James, 60, 61
Nutt, Elizabeth, 97

O'Brien, Dennis, 37
O'Donnell estate, 185
O'Donnell, James Francis, 133
O'Donnell, Mary Ann *nee* Fitzpatrick, 133
O'Neil, Eliza, 119
O'Shanessy, Michael, 137
Oadham, James, 12
Oatway, Charles, 157
Oddfellows Lodge, 122
Olarenshaw, Mrs, 193
Oliver, H., 142
Olsen, Nicholas, 152
Onslow, George, 81
Oran Park, 134
Orana Park, 212, 224
orchards, 129, 185
Orielton Park, 113
Orr, William, 74
Orvad, J., 164
Oxley, John, 30
Oxley, John Norton, 75, 86, 95

Packer, 179
Palmer, Dr, 112
Park, Alfred Leath, 132
Parker, Burnett, 179
Parkholme, 132, *colour section*
Parkin, G., 168
parliamentary representation, 54, 94–6, 143–6
Passmore, Charles J., 139, 171
Patrick, John, 33, 48, 52
Patrick, William Nunn, 132
Payten, Alfred Rose, 121, 139, 158, 159, 161–2
Payten, James, 73, 75, 76, 96, 116

Payten, Nathaniel, 46
Payten, P. E., 171
Payten, Rose (Babe), *160–1*, 164, 192, 193
Payten, Sarah, 195
Payten, Sarah *nee* Rose, 76, 170, 194
Pendergast, Margaret, 119
Pendergrass, John, 70
Pendergrast, J., 81, 100
Pentland, Miss, 195
Percival, H. G. (Greg), 210, 228
Percival, John, 111
Percival, Mary Ann, 156
Percival, S. J. (Syd), 149, 150, *180*, 210, 227
Phelphs, Joseph, 11, 28
Phillips, William E. H., 152
Pidcock, William, 148, 149
Piggott family, 100
Piggott, William, 170, 227
Pockley H. R., 129
Point Farm, 153
police, 40, 62, 124, 137, 176
population, 58–9, 68, 104, 115, 164, 197, 214, 226
Porter, J. B., 168
Porter, Robert, 147–8
post office, 16, 55, 80, 93, 181, 212
post office, Campbelltown 131, 136, 145
poultry, 167–9
Powell, L., 199
Power, Arthur, 136
Presswell, Rev. P., 150
Primrose, P., 228
Pritchard, William, 87–8
progress associations, 209, 212

Quelch, Henry, 152
Quilty, J. R., 170
Quondong, 142

Raby, 213, 214
railway, 69–73, 79, 81, 126–7, 218
railway stations,
  Campbellfields, 72, 146
  Campbelltown, 26, *128*, 129
  Glenfield, 72, 153
  Glenlee, 126
  Ingleburn, 44, 72, 127, 148, *149*
  Leumeah, 127, 146
  Macarthur, 202, 221

Macquarie Fields, 72, 127, 146, 148, 152
Menangle, 126
Menangle North, 127
Minto, 72, 146
Raith, 134
Randle, William, 71
Ray, 117
Ray, Eliza *nee* Jackson, 111
Ray, John, 93
Ray, Sarah, 11
Ray, William, 11, 69, 111
Ray, William jr, 111
Raymond, Elizabeth S., 106
Raymond, James, 106
Raymond, James jr, 106
Rea, Edward, 151
Rea, Thaddeus Bourke, 151
Reach, Elsie, 119
Reddall, Amelia, 110
Reddall, Clara, 110
Reddall, Eliza, 110
Reddall, Isabella, 97,110
Reddall, John, 33,110
Reddall, Luke, 69,110
Reddall, Misses, 110, 117, 119
Reddall, Thomas, 15, 28–9, 35–6, 62, 110
Reddall, Thomas jr, 110
Redfern and Alexander, 70
Redfern, Sarah *nee* Wills, 12
Redfern, William, 9, 10, 12, 29, 146
Reed, J. F., 168
Reeve, H. S., 174, *177–8*
Reeve, Stanley, 188
Reeve, Tasma, *194*
Reeve, Thomas Henry, 83, 123, 139
Regan, B., 228
Reid Murray Developments, 204–5
Reidy, 179
Rennett, Charles, 33
Reverce, Alexander, 155
Reynolds, Thomas, 8
Richardson, J. H., 170
Richardson, Sid, 221
Richmond Villa, 34, 57, 78, 135
Rider, John C., 147
Riley, Robert, 36
Riversford, 72, 93
Rixon, 62, 117, 170
Rixon, Thomas, 73
Rixon, William, 50
roads and streets, 10, 30–4, 53–4, 84–7, 104, 117, 121,

123, 149–50, 171, 183, 201, 206, 221
roads, Cowpastures Road, 9, 15, 89
Old Coach Road, 154
Queen Street, 62, *80*, 104, 111, 123, *131*, *136–9*, 171, 207–8
Roberts, Ted, 164
Robin Hood farm, 184
Robin Hood Inn, 52, 79
Robinson, Thomas L., 36, 65
Rochaix, J. P., 155
Roche, Father John Paul, 100, 102
Rogers, H. A., 168
Romalis, A., 180
Rose, Alfred, 76, 96
Rose, C. Henry J., 86, 96, 109
Rose, F.W., 179
Rose, Reuben, 96
Rose, Sarah *nee* Pye, 47
Rose, Thomas, 37, 47–8, 50, 59, 109, 213
Rosemeadow, 203, 204, 213, 214
Ross, Alexander, 153
Ross, Arthur, 168, 169
Ross, James, 152
Ross, John, 152
Ross, Robert, 152
Ross, William, 152
Rourke, Cornelius, 21
Rowley, John, 27
Rowley, Thomas, 18
Rudd, Georgina, 187
Rudd, Isaac, 70
Rudd, James, 70
Rudd, Thomas, 11, 58
Rudd's Gate, 187
Ruse, 203, 213, 214, 215
Ruse, James, 38, 44, 170, 213
Ruse, Mary, 44, 148
Rush, Rachel, 107
Russian Orthodox community, 217
Rutherford, Miss, 142
Rutter, Reg, 194
Ryan, J. F., 130
Ryder, Ernest, 181
Ryder, Stanley, 181

Sabar, 84
Sadlier, Richard, 88
Saggart Field, 100, 140, 146
Salter, Thomas, 129
Saunders, W., 124
Saywell, Thomas, 152

Scanlon family, 100
Scanlon, J., 118
Scanlon, Patrick, 146, 227
Scarr, George, 141
Scarr, John, 25, 48, 70, 89, *colour section*
Scattergood family, 186
Scattergood, Mrs, 193, *194*
Schofield, Olive, 188
school of arts, Campbelltown, 124, 159, 164, 196
Ingleburn 148, 150, 166
Minto 147, 159
schools, high schools, 222–3; non-government, 37–8, 102, 141–2, 186–8, 222–3; special, Glenfield Park, 172, 188
schools, *see also* education schools, Campbelltown, 130, 140, *141*, 166, 167, 187, 222
Campbelltown South, 186
East Minto, 140, 147, 222
Glenfield, 140, 153
Ingleburn, 140, 148
Kentlyn, 186
Minto, 140, 147
Wedderburn, 140, 156, 166, 186
Scobie, J. H., 178, 185
Scott, Joseph, 52
Scouler, Dr Arthur, 94, 112
Scrivener, Charles A., 91, 146
Scrivener, Charles R., 158
Seddon, Dr H. R., 189
Seddon, Joseph Pickles, 129, 137
Sedgwick, Edward, 227
Sedgwick, Elizabeth *nee* Fitzpatrick, 133, 164, 185
Sedgwick, F. J. (Mate), 199, 209, 217, 228
Sedgwick, Miss, 195
Sellar, 179
service clubs, 224
sewerage, 123, 174–5, 201
Sexton, 179
Seymour, Mrs K. M., 181
Shadforth, Henry, 88
Sharman, Jimmy, 160
Sharp, Thomas, 151
Sharp, William, 148, 151
Shaw, J., 153
Sheahan, 84
Sheather, Frederick, 122, 159, 164, 170, 176, *177*

Sheil family, 170
Sheil, Mary *nee* Bradbury, 104
Sherack family, 100
Sherack, Joseph, 77, 137
Sherack, Marie, 77
Sherwood Hills, 205–6, 213
shops and stores, 31, 51, *62*,
    79, *80–1*, 136–9, 178–82,
    206–8, *colour section*
shops and stores, Bursill's,
    179, *207*
  Downes', 206
  Marlow's, 180
  McIlveen's, *149*
  Reeve's, 137, *138*, 180
showground, 159, 172
Sidman, George V., 178, 221
Sidman, Robert A., 178
Simmonds, Bob, 219
Simons, Mary Ann, 111
Simons, Thomas, 111
Simpson, W. R., 139
Sims, Samuel, 74
Skeers, W., 170
Smeaton, 36, 109, 133, 223
Smith brothers, 184
Smith, Henry Arkell, 91, 99
Smith, J. C., 168
Smith, L. W., 158
Smith, N., *194*
Smith, P. J., 175
Smith, Thomas, 18
soldier settlement, *167–9*
Soldiers Flat, 44
Solomon Brothers, 180
Solomon, Lewis, 52
Solomon, M & J, 170
Solomon, P., 170, 209, 228
Sons of Temperance Friendly
    Society, 112–13, 121
Southward, A. G., 171
Spellman, Miss, 142
Spence, John, 119, 121
Spencer, A. B., 185
Spencer, J. H., 185
Spooner, A., 158
sport, 113, 158, 160–1, 192–4
Spring Hill, 49
squatting, 69, 84, 134, 135
St Andrews, 8, 9, 45–6, 128,
    203, 204, 213
St Andrews dairy, *184*
St Elmo, *133, colour section*
St Elmo Estate, 204, 205
St Helens Park, 134, 213, 214,
    colour section
Stack, R. F., 121, 125
Stack, Rev. William, 101

Staniforth, W. H., 184
Stanley, Charles, 113, 135,
    136
Stanley, Emma *nee*
    Fieldhouse, 113, 135
State Nursery,
    Campbelltown, 126, 130,
    139, 186
State Planning Authority,
    199–201
Steel, Amy, 140
Steel, Miss, 195
Steel, Rev. Robert, 157
Stewardson, Helen, 212
Stewart, Col. William, 30
Stewart, George, 40
Stewart, K. K., 168
Stewart, Robert, 40, 117
street lighting, 123, 150
Stubbs, William, 152
Sturt, Charles, 18, 30
Sugarloaf, 122, 129
Sutton, Cecil G. B., 147
Suttor, Frederick A., 150
Swann family, *185*
Swann, Agnes *nee* Scobie,
    156, 157
Swann, Joseph, 139, 157, 185
Swann, Mrs Joseph, *156*
Swann, Tom, 157, 178
Swann, Tom jr, 185
Sweeny, Johanna, 119
Sweetman, Georgiana, 51
Sykes, W., 11, 23
Symonds, Charles Joseph,
    217
Symonds, Ethel Easton, 217

Taber family, 119, 133, 170
Taber, George, 37, 85
Tasker, John, 37
Taylor, A. G., 170
Taylor, E. J. C., 168
Taylor, Edward, 50
telephone, 178–9
temperance hall, 86, 112–13,
    121, *colour section*
Tharawal Aboriginal Land
    Council, 215–16
Therry, Father J. J., 29, 37,
    58, 70
Thomas, G., 228
Thomas, William, 195
Thompson family, 100
Thompson, Andrew, 8, 9
Thompson, Mrs, 139
Thomson, Jack, *184*
Thomson, W., 169

Thorburn, Basil, 207
Thorn, Charles, 150
Thornwaite, 146
Throsby, Archer Broughton,
    153
Throsby, Charles, 8, 9, 13,
    17, 18, 21, 25, 70
Throsby, Charles jr, 109
Tildsley, Reginald, 180
Tooth, John, 50
Topman, Don, *207*
town growth, 33, 103–4, 134,
    171–2, 197–208
town planning, 31–2, 34,
    103–4, 171, 197–208
Townson, Robert, 9, 10, 13
transport, 53–5, 69–72, 84,
    127, 182–3, 220–1
Tregear, Clive W., 199, 200,
    210, 228
Triglone, Milton J., 181
Tripp, 117, 138
Tripp, Charles, 139, 181, 191
Tripp, Thomas, 139
Trives, G., *177*
Trott, Wyndham Albert, 155
Tuck, Norman, 174, 176
Tucker, James, 55–7
Turner, J., 169
Tyerman, Ian W., 139, 165,
    181
Tyson, Isabella *nee* Coulson,
    68, 135
Tyson, James, 70, 135–6
Tyson, William, 11, 22, 70,
    135

Underwood, R., 164
Uther, Reuben, 11, 47

Vance, S., 164
Vardy family, 119
Vardy, Emily, 141
Vardy, John, 33, 58, 70, 78,
    79, 84, 87, 113, 117
Vardy, John George, 171,
    182, 187, 193
Vardy, Joseph, 158, 170
Vardy, M. A., 170
Vardy, Michael J., 133
Varroville, 9, 10, 13, 18, 106–
    7, 129, 150, 184, 213, 214
Vaughan, Henry Edward,
    118, 132, 227
Vaughan, John, 61
Veness, Raymond, 181
Vernon, J. H., 221
Via Crucis, 187

Vidler, John, 103
vine growing, 77, 129–30
Vogt, H., 185

Wade, Sarah, 111
Wait, John, 18
Walker, Arch, 207, 217
Wallace, Hugh, 152
Wallace, William, 152
Wallis, Captain James, 21–3
Walsh, J. P., 150
Waminda, 169, 213
Warby family, 170
Warby, Benjamin, 37, 94, 103
Warby, David, 148
Warby, Elizabeth, 133
Warby, Ephraim, 133
Warby, James, 70
Warby, John, 5, 9–11, 14, 20, 21, 35, 43, 62, 69, 74, 84
Warby, Joseph, 87, 133
Warby, Sarah nee Bentley, 15, 35, 74
Ward, John, 148
Ward, Joseph, 9, 39–40, 57
Ward, Mary Ann, 39
Warner, F., 169
water supply, 32, 47–9, 93–4, 121, 124–6, 174–5, 185, 190
Waterworth, James, 86, 93, 127, 170
Watt, Hugh, 57
Waugh, Jim, 200
Weavers, George, 51
Webb, Jonathan, 34
Webb, William, 142–3, 157
Wedderburn, 139, 156–7, 164, 178, 185, 213, 214
Weir, Charlotte, 8
Welsh, John, 33
West, F. H. N., 178
West, W. B., 169

Westbury, J., 228
Westgarth, George Charles, 134
Westgarth, Lucy nee Mansfield, 134
Westgarth, M., 164
Weston, W., 130
Westview, 141, 186
wheat, see agriculture
Wheatley, Kevin, 224
White, George, 91
Whitehead, Emma, 139
Whitehouse, family, 147
Whitehouse, Joseph, 149, 227
Whitten, Mrs K. V., 228
Wholohan, Michael, 167
Wiggins, Miss, 140
Wild, John, 88, 134
Wild, Joseph, 18
Wilkinson, H. R., 170
Wilkinson, Margaret, 119
Wilkinson, Miss, 140
Williams, 191
Williams, A. J., 169
Williams, J., 181, 193
Williamson, Basil, 164
Williamson, J., 149
Williamson, W. W., 164
Willis, Miss, 140
Wilshire, 150
Wilson family, 100, 138
Wilson, Dr John, 123
Wilson, James, 80, 139
Wilson, N., 169
Wilson, William Hardy, 171
windmills, 47–8, 73
Winton, G. R. A., 176
Winton, Mary Anna nee Larkin, 122
Winton, R. R., 170
Winton, Thomas Jenner, 121, 122
Winton, V., 170

Winton, William, 122
Wolstenholme, F. R., 204
women, 8, 58, 111, 118–9, 130, 161, 164, 192, 193, 19 206
Woodbine, 73, 76, 204, 212, 213, 214, colour section
Wood, Rev G. N., 98, 102
Woodhouse family, 119
Woodhouse, Agnes nee Ne 134
Woodhouse, E., 70
Woodhouse, Edmund Bingham, 110, 123, 133–
Woodhouse, Edmund Hun 99, 109–10
Woodhouse, Ellen, 70
Woodhouse, George M., 1(110
Woodhouse, Gertrude nee Bingham, 109, 134
Woodhouse, Marshall D., 1
Woodhouse, Sculdham, 11
Woolbridge, Robert, 94
Woollard, Roger, 219
Woollock, Richard, 50
work, 49–53, 76, 90, 124–3(217–22
World War I, 163–7
World War II, 195–6
Worner, Anna, 77
Worner, Frederick, 77
Worner, Leah, 77
Worrall, W. George, 61
Wroblewski, Charles, 155
Wroblewski, J., 155

Yates, Mr & Mrs J. H., 195
Yellooming, 20–22
Young, Alfred J., 152

Zouch, Henry, 154
Zouch, Maria nee Brooks, 1